THE STATE AN

THE STATE
AND CIVIL SOCIETY

Studies in Hegel's Political Philosophy

edited by
Z. A. Pelczynski

FELLOW OF PEMBROKE COLLEGE, OXFORD

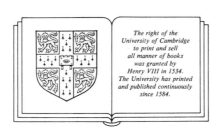

The right of the
University of Cambridge
to print and sell
all manner of books
was granted by
Henry VIII in 1534.
The University has printed
and published continuously
since 1584.

CAMBRIDGE UNIVERSITY PRESS

Cambridge

London   New York   New Rochelle
Melbourne   Sydney

Published by the Press Syndicate of the University of Cambridge
The Pitt Building, Trumpington Street, Cambridge CB2 1RP
32 East 57th Street, New York, NY 10022, USA
296 Beaconsfield Parade, Middle Park, Melbourne 3206, Australia

First published 1984

Printed in Great Britain by the
University Press, Cambridge

Library of Congress catalogue card number: 84-3144

British Library Cataloguing in Publication Data
The State and civil society.
1. Hegel, Georg Wilhelm Friedrich—Political science
I. Pelczynski, Z. A.
320.5'092'4   JC233.H46

ISBN 0 521 24793 4 hardcovers
ISBN 0 521 28969 6 paperback.

CONTENTS

PREFACE

The present volume is in some respects a sequel to *Hegel's Political Philosophy: Problems and Perspectives*, first published by the Cambridge University Press in 1971 as a volume of essays commemorating the 200th anniversary of Hegel's birth. However, what links the essays in this volume is not an occasion but a common theme. The focus of the volume is the distinction, fundamental to Hegel's political philosophy, between the state and civil society. The distinction has been disputed, though on completely different grounds, by marxism and liberalism. Marxism is heavily indebted to the concept of civil society but it denies the Hegelian conception of the state as a political *community* (the young Marx first dealt with the matter in *On the Jewish Question*) and regards the state as an apparatus of coercion and class exploitation superimposed on society. Liberalism, on the other hand, treats the state and civil society as synonymous — a legal and institutional framework for the pursuit of individual interests.

The exploration of the Hegelian distinction, then, throws into relief a fundamental difference between the three great traditions of political theorizing. At the same time it raises a number of questions about the relation of Marx to Hegel and about the validity of the marxist critique of Hegel; directly or indirectly nine of the essays in this volume are concerned with these questions. Since Hegel's distinction has roots in the tradition of classical political philosophy which goes back to Plato, four other essays consider Hegel's relation to the thought of his predecessors. The remaining essays are mainly concerned with the relevance of the Hegelian distinction to contemporary issues in political theory and to some practical problems of the modern capitalist welfare state. As in *Hegel's Political Philosophy* the essays represent a wide spectrum of approaches and attitudes to Hegel, from sympathetic to highly critical, but substantially agree on the importance of Hegel's political and social thought.

None of the essays has been previously published in English, and all but three have been specially written for this volume. The three, which originally appeared in print in other languages and have been translated for this collection, are: Klaus Hartmann, 'Ideen zu einem neuen systematischen Verständnis der Hegelschen Rechtsphilosophie', *Perspektiven der Philosophie*, II (1976); Karl-Heinz Ilting, 'Hegels Begriff des Staats und die Kritik des jungen Marx', *Rivista di filosofia* nos. 7–8–9 (October 1977); Gabris Kortian, 'Remarques sur le rapport entre subjectivité et societé civil', *Dialogue* IX, 2 (1970). Thanks are due to the editors of the three periodicals for permission to translate and publish the articles in English.

Finally, I wish to thank Mrs Carole Charlton and Mrs Susan Ousley for typing the bulk of the collection, and also warmly thank my wife Denise for her help with the final stages of editorial work.

Oxford, April 1984   Z. A. Pelczynski

ABBREVIATIONS

The works of Hegel and some other authors cited in the text of the Introduction and the subsequent essays are abbreviated as follows:

GP	*Vorlesungen über die Geschichte der Philosophie*
HP, LHPh	*Lectures on the History of Philosophy*
LPhWH	*Lectures on the Philosophy of World History*
PhH	*Philosophy of History*
PhR	*Philosophy of Right*
PS	*Phenomenology of Spirit*
PW	*Political Writings*
Pol	Aristotle's *Politics*
Rep	Plato's *Republic*

Introduction
The significance of Hegel's separation of the state and civil society

Z. A. PELCZYNSKI

The distinction between the state and civil society was first made by Hegel in print in his *Philosophy of Right* published in 1821.* Within the philosophical mode of exposition which he adopted in his work, civil society (*bürgerliche Gesellschaft*) represented a 'stage' in the dialectical development from the family to the state which contradicted the kind of ethical life found in the human micro-community in order to be itself contradicted and overcome (i.e. cancelled and preserved, *aufgehoben*) by the macro-community of the politically independent, sovereign nation. While social life typical of civil society was radically different from the ethical world of the family and, Hegel believed, equally different from the public life of the state, it formed a necessary element (or 'moment' in Hegel's terminology) within the totality of rationally structured modern political community.

The conceptual separation of the state and civil society is one of the most original features of Hegel's political and social philosophy although a highly problematic one. The distinction has been both praised and attacked and its significance assessed in diverse ways; even within the present volume a number of contrasting interpretations and evaluations can be found. But in discussing the implications of the distinction far more is at stake than simply matters of Hegelian scholarship. The term 'bürgerliche Gesellschaft', which also means 'bourgeois society', was taken over from Hegel by Marx and became a fundamental concept of Marx's social theory, indeed in a way *the* foundation of the theory. Of course before it became suitable for his purposes Marx had to subject it to thorough criticism and modification, which went chiefly into three directions. First, Marx questioned the philosophical context of the concept, the validity of the Hegelian form of the dialectic, and its mystifying treatment of real human, social, historical facts and processes as elements in the development of a metaphysical entity, the Spirit or the Idea.

* This is the date on the title page of the original text, and the one normally attributed. There is evidence, however, that the book was published in 1820, the year given in Hegel's preface.

Second, while retaining the state/civil society distinction, Marx rejected the view that the state was an all-inclusive political community with a distinct ethical character, and denied it primacy in social and historical life. He reversed the Hegelian relation of the two and made civil (or rather bourgeois) society the ground of political life and the source of political change. Third, Marx decomposed the Hegelian civil society, which was a highly complex, structured concept, and reduced civil society virtually to the economic sphere of labour, production and exchange.

In his two essays in this volume K.-H. Ilting tackles the first of Marxian criticisms of Hegel's concepts of the state and civil society. He argues that in fundamental respects they are simply misplaced. Hegel's references to 'the Spirit' or 'the Idea' do not, *pace* Marx, totally vitiate or invalidate his socio-political philosophy though they certainly greatly obscure it and often successfully disguise his theoretical intentions. There are other factors which would have made a more rewarding target of criticism. These range from the desire for political accommodation or political influence in Prussia to the enormous difficulty of reducing concrete social and cultural phenomena with a historical locus to abstract philosophical categories according to the requirements of a timeless dialectical logic. It is factors such as these that, in Ilting's opinion, vitiate though not wholly invalidate Hegel's philosophical analysis of the modern state and society, an analysis which still has many merits. In my second essay I also examine Marx's criticisms of Hegel's ideas on the state and civil society, especially as they bear on Marx's concept of the nation and his theory of nationality. I argue that Hegel's systematic exclusion of national characteristics from civil society found its way so to speak automatically into Marx's social theory and made the theoretical problems of it insensitive to nationalism.

The selective Marxian appropriation of 'civil society' and the state/civil society distinction has added a large element of contestability to the two concepts. It has forced writers sympathetic to Hegel to question Marxian interpretations, while writers who are marxist or sympathetic to Marx's standpoint have felt it necessary to repeat his criticisms in order to distance themselves from Hegel. The aura of contestability around the state/civil distinction is still further enhanced by divisions within the marxist camp itself. Many marxists – and this is particularly true of most eastern (i.e. communist) marxists and those marxists in the west who seek to minimize the Hegelian heritage of marxism – treat civil society as a merely historical concept which has no particular relevance to the understanding of contemporary capitalism. However, some marxist or neo-marxist writers have not only revived the concept as a valuable tool of analysis, but have also restored to it much of its broad, Hegelian meaning as a cultural, social and even semi-political category in opposition to the narrowly economic interpretation of Marx and the more orthodox marxists. An outstanding example earlier in the twentieth century was Antonio Gramsci whose attempt to work out a non-leninist revolutionary strategy relied crucially on the concept of civil society.[1] Gramsci argued that in Italy (and Western Europe generally) the working class under communist leadership had a better chance of gaining hegemony within civil society than within the national/political arena and having achieved it could make it the springboard for the conquest of political power in the state.

A renaissance of the concept of civil society and the problems associated with it has occurred also among the group of writers called the Frankfurt School or the Critical Theory School. As Seyla Benhabib, a scholar sympathetic to the School, argues in her essay in this collection, Hegel had a clearer insight into the complexity of the socio-cultural phenomena accompanying and fostering the development of modern industrial society than Marx and most of his followers have had. In particular Hegel had a rather subtle conception of the relation between normative, social and economic structures and did not reduce the legitimation function of legal norms to a simple ideological justification of bourgeois property relations. While aspects of Hegel's analysis, on both systemic and political level, seem to her unacceptable, she argues that contemporary radical social theory must today turn to Hegel rather than to Marx for inspiration in constructing an adequate theoretical framework for understanding modern exchange relations. However, Garbis Kortian, another contributor to this collection sympathetic to the Critical School, gives a rather more critical assessment of Hegel's theory of civil society and its applicability to the problem of modern capitalism, although he too believes that, in re-examining the problem of subjectivity, the Critical School must proceed by re-assessing Hegelian ideas on the subject since marxism has little to offer in this respect.

The fact that Hegel's distinction between the state and civil society heavily influenced the thought of Karl Marx and stimulated his theoretical activity, and that it has proved a source of inspiration for some of Marx's followers, including contemporary neo-marxist thinkers, requires further discussion. One may wonder whether the distinction would have proved so influential or persistent had it not reflected a fundamental change in modern European consciousness, which followed an equally fundamental change in modern European society. Manfred Riedel, in his pioneering, scholarly and perceptive essay on the history of the concept of civil society first published in 1962, argued that such a connection did exist and that Hegel's separation of the state and civil society, which was an abrupt break with tradition, corresponded to a revolutionary historical change.

What Hegel, with the term civil society, raised to the consciousness of his time was nothing less than the result of the modern revolution, the rise of a depoliticized society through the centralization of politics in the princely or the revolutionary state, and the shift of its point of gravity to the economy, a change which this society experienced simultaneously in the Industrial Revolution and which found an expression in 'political' or 'national economy'. It was in this process within the European society that its 'political' and 'civil' conditions were first separated, conditions which before then, in the classical world of the old politics, meant one and the same thing – 'communitas civilis sive politica', as Thomas Aquinas or 'civil or political society', as John Locke put it.[2]

Riedel shows that the phrase *koinonia politike* (political union or association), which Aristotle first used, was afterwards normally translated as *societas civilis* and became, together with its synonyms *civitas* and *res publica*, a general term for an independent political entity or the state. Thomas Aquinas, Bodin, Hobbes, Spinoza, Locke and Kant – not to mention a host of lesser writers – used 'political' and 'civil' as synonymous. Hegel's alteration of the traditional usage was, in Riedel's view, the boldest innovation in the language of political philosophy since Bodin introduced the concept of sovereignty and Rousseau the idea of the general will.

Riedel's point that classical political theory did not distinguish between 'state' and 'society' is well taken. But, as he points out himself, the theory always recognized some sections of the population – identified at different times with slaves, serfs, artisans, domestic servants and hired labourers, and of course, always women and children – who were not members of the *res publica* or *societas civilis*, although they resided within its territory and were subjects of its government. 'There is no polis for slaves' as Aristotle said (*Pol.* III, 9, 1280a 32); for him they could only be members of the household (*oikos*). Later writers talked of 'domestic society', to which servants and other non-citizens belonged. Hegel's 'discovery' of civil society may therefore have come through the realization that in his own time such non-political existence was the fate of the majority of citizens who had to earn their living through labour, production and exchange, and therefore belonged, for much of their lives, to a sort of national 'domestic society' or state-wide 'household'. An early glimpse of this occurs in his earliest political work, the unpublished pamphlet on the constitution of the German Empire.

With the change in manners and way of life each individual was more preoccupied with his own necessities and his own private affairs. By far the greater number of free men, i.e. the strictly bourgeois class, must have had to look exclusively to their own necessities and their own living. As states became larger, those people who must have had to concern themselves exclusively with their own affairs formed a class of their own. There was an increase in the mass of things needed by the free man and the noble, who had to maintain themselves in their social position respectively by industry or by the work for the state.[3]

We can see the young Hegel clearly recognizing the rise of a largely economic sphere of 'private affairs', especially typical of the bourgeoisie, which he goes on to contrast with the sphere of public affairs, managed in the modern state by the monarch, the Estates and the civil service. Hegel is unable to conceptualize the historical process at this stage. Only some twenty years later, in the *Philosophy of Right*, was Hegel able to do so by calling the private sphere '*bürgerliche Gesellschaft*' and the public sphere '*der Staat*' or, as he sometimes puts it, 'the strictly political state' (*PhR*, §§267, 273, 276) as if to emphasize even more strongly the conceptual contrast between the 'civil' and the 'political'.

There is no need to chronicle the evolution of Hegel's political theory during those twenty years. It was described in detail by Shlomo Avineri in chs. 5 and 7 of his *Hegel's Theory of the Modern State* (Cambridge, 1972) and more briefly by Raymond Plant in ch. 5 of his *Hegel* (London, 1973). The most important influence was Hegel's study of Adam Smith and other British political economists during the stay in Jena, reinforced by the reading of the British press and parliamentary reports. Their mark is most clearly visible in the second, 1805–6, series of his Jena University lectures on the philosophy of spirit (sometimes called *Jenaer Realphilosophie* II). There Hegel tries hard to theorize, but although he describes the effects of industrial society on human powers in vivid terms reminiscent of Marx, he is not yet able to produce a systematic theory of civil society, still less to integrate it into a more comprehensive social and political philosophy.

At the same time, and equally unsuccessfully, Hegel wrestles with the concept of the state. In the pamphlet on the constitution of the German Empire, Hegel defined the state rather conventionally as a multitude united for common defence or a people (nation, *Volk*) subject to a supreme public authority (state power, *Staatsgewalt*).[4] During the Jena period Hegel rejects this viewpoint in favour of a Platonic concept of the state as an ethical substance rather than a multitude of individuals. It is an organic ethical community in which a special class of rulers is charged with the task of maintaining independence and integrity of the ethical whole and the health of its spiritual life (the key concepts here are *Volksgeist* and *Sittlichkeit*).[5] The moral consequence of this concept is the absolute primacy of community ends over the private ends of its individual members; any predominance of the latter over the former marks the decay and eventually the death of the body politic. As G. Kortian shows in his essay, in Jena Hegel still regarded subjectivity and particularity (twin elements of individualism in his view) as enemies of ethical and political life; he had not yet recognized civil society as an arena where individualism found legitimate scope and could express itself safely without harming the community.

Neither at Jena nor during the subsequential period of his life which he spent in Bamberg and Nuremberg did Hegel resolve the conceptual and theoretical problems of the state and society, which preoccupied him in the early years of the nineteenth century. Partially he laid them aside to devote himself to more purely philosophical and systematic concerns. The crowning achievement of his Jena period was of course the *Phenomenology of Spirit* published in 1807, which Judith N. Shklar has rightly called 'an elegy for Hellas'.[6] The work clearly reflects Hegel's nostalgia and admiration for the ethos of the Greek polis, which for several years of his youth he regarded as an unsurpassed form of communal life. Yet it is tempered by a realization that the ideal could not be achieved in the modern world; the heroic attempt to establish a democratic political community on the basis of a revolutionary *Sittlichkeit*, quite alien to the moral, intellectual and political tradition of modern European civilization, ended in Hegel's view in a gigantic fiasco. The brilliant treatment of the Jacobin republic in the chapter on 'Absolute Freedom and Terror', particularly well discussed in Charles Taylor's writings,[7] cannot disguise the fact that Hegel in the *Phenomenology of Spirit* is unable to provide an analysis of the ethical, political and social consciousness of modern Europe to match his sympathetic analysis of the vanished world of the Greek polis. He makes few references to contemporary political reality and his ideas about modern politics and society are fragmentary and negative.

One should, however, mention here another celebrated chapter of the *Phenomenology of Spirit*, that on the master and slave (or master and servant, as it should perhaps be translated). The chapter has given rise to a sizeable volume of interpretative and critical literature and through Alexandre Kojève's work has strongly influenced contemporary neo-marxism. The essay by J. M. Bernstein in this volume brings out the significance of the chapter for the understanding of Hegel's conception of community while polemizing with a materialist critique of the master–slave dialectic. According to Bernstein Hegel has shown in the *Phenomenology* that human self-consciousness is impossible without reciprocal recognition by the members of a community. The kind of reciprocity and recognition characteristic of a community, however, is radically different from the exchange and end–means relationship typical of the social interaction which Hegel was later to call civil society. Thus the master–slave dialectic of the *Phenomenology* is as important as the analysis of the Athenian polis for the understanding of Hegel's views on the nature of political community and its distinction from civil society.

It was ten years after the *Phenomenology of Spirit* that Hegel's ideas about the state took on a clear and definite shape. His main philosophical preoccupation during his stay in Bavaria – between Jena and Heidelberg – was the writing of the *Science of Logic* (published in Nuremberg, 1812–16), a work far removed from the realm of political philosophy though not wholly irrelevant to it. It was the dialectical method and the basic categories of analysis formulated there that Hegel was to apply later to the sphere of ethics, law, politics and society. We find the first systematic treatment of this sphere in the section on 'Objective Spirit' in the third volume of the *Encyclopaedia of the Philosophical Sciences* (Heidelberg, 1817), dealing with the philosophy of spirit (or mind). The first outline of the *Philosophy of Right*, published a few years later in Berlin, is clearly visible in the Heidelberg *Encyclopaedia*. *Recht* (right or law) is subdivided into 'abstract right', 'morality' and 'ethical life', but there is no further division into subsections and the relevant paragraphs are few and short. §434 deals with the family, §§436 and 437 with civil society, and §§438–41 with the state, but 'civil society' does not occur in the text, and even the word 'state' occurs only in the context of international relations. But something else happened in Heidelberg. The copy of the *Encyclopaedia* from which Hegel lectured at Heidelberg University has been preserved, and it contains marginal notes written by him at the time of the lectures and dated end of February/beginning of March 1818. The phrase *bürgerliche Gesellschaft* occurs in these notes for the first time. We can thus pinpoint with considerable accuracy the time when Hegel made a conscious and explicit distinction between civil society and the state, and began using the former term systematically.[8]

The *Philosophy of Right* may best be described as a philosophical reconstruction of modern ethical life (*Sittlichkeit*) – the totality of ideas, practices, sentiments and relations which not only prevail in fact, but are regarded by the modern man as valid in some normative sense. It is not just an account of its main features, as Hegel perceived them about 1820; nor is it a historical account of how ethical life had come into existence. Both these elements, however, play an important role. Hegel had studied ethical life and observed its contemporary forms for some thirty years before he felt able to construct a detailed theory in which ethical ideas, sentiments, practices and relations were expressed in philosophical concepts and systematically related to each other. A vast quantity of empirical and historical raw material, transformed into concepts and compressed into theory, had gone into the making of his *chef d'oeuvre*.

Although the *Philosophy of Right* is concerned with modern ethical life, it contains many references to the remote past, including Greek and Roman antiquity. This is not at all puzzling. In the *Phenomenology of Spirit* Hegel sought to demonstrate that modern European culture was a product of a long historical evolution, traceable as far back as ancient Greece. Each major stage in the evolution – Roman Empire, Christianity and secular Enlightenment – contributed some important ideas, points of view and philosophical concepts, which became part of what one might call the collective consciousness of modern Europe. Ethical life was part and parcel of that consciousness – its practical as opposed to its theoretical part – the part that concerned men's conduct and relations with each other rather than his place in history and the universe. Hegel of course believed that in the last resort practical and theoretical matters were inseparable and constituted different manifestations of the same *Geist* – a point forcefully argued by Charles Taylor in *Hegel*, his major study of the thinker.

The explanation and justification of Hegel's philosophical method is contained in the *Science of Logic*, to which he refers the reader in the Preface to the *Philosophy of Right*. In general terms the method involves demonstrating the inherent rationality, necessity and truth of various elements of ethical life by placing them in a scheme of dialectical logical development, which begins with the concept of individual will abstracted from all ethical, social and historical context and ends with the state.

... the truth about Right, Ethics, and the state is as old as its public recognition and formulation in the law of the land, in the morality of everyday life, and in religion. What more does this truth require – since the thinking mind is not content to possess it in this ready fashion? It requires to be grasped in thought as well; the content which is already rational in principle must win the *form* of rationality and so appear well-founded to untrammelled thinking (*PhR*, p. 3).

Right, ethics (or ethical life) and the state are clearly the key concepts of the *Philosophy of Right*, and they are logically related to each other. By Right (*Recht*, which is normally translated as law) Hegel means the whole sphere of norms of various kinds, rationally grounded, by which men determine their conduct in the world. Ethical life (*Sittlichkeit* or social ethics) includes the actual conduct of men guided by those norms, and is the result of a social process of character-training and habit-forming fostered by institutions but also (in the modern world) of critical reflection and intellectual grasp. The latter aspect of the process Hegel calls *Bildung* (education) and describes as follows:

education is the absolute transition from an ethical substantiality which is immediate and natural to the one which is intellectual and so both infinitely subjective and lofty enough to have attained universality of form (*PhR*, 187R).

This process of education results in distinguishing within ethical life two subordinate normative spheres, that of 'abstract right' (rules governing the rights of person and property based on reciprocity) and of 'morality' (disinterested, conscientious conduct). The state in the sense in which Hegel frequently uses it in the *Philosophy of Right* (e.g. as 'the actuality of the ethical Idea', *PhR*, §257) is a politically organized, independent ethical community – a people or a nation permeated by the normative order of *Recht* and manifesting *Sittlichkeit* in their actions and relations.

The originality of Hegel's political philosophy, compared with that of other modern thinkers, consists in grounding it not in some universal characteristics of human nature or in the idea of fundamental human rights, but in ethical life or *Sittlichkeit*, and seeing political life as a concrete manifestation of *Sittlichkeit* in the public realm. It is *Sittlichkeit*, together with other cultural factors and historical traditions which Hegel stresses particularly in the lectures on the philosophy of history and calls 'the spirit of the people' (*Volksgeist*), which binds the population of a state spiritually, and forms it into an ethical community. Hegel derived the idea of *Sittlichkeit* from the ethos of the ancient Greek polis. In this he was heavily influenced by Plato's *Republic*, a work of which he had the highest opinion and which, as he says in the Preface to the *Philosophy of Right* (p. 10), 'is in essence nothing but an interpretation of Greek ethical life'. M. J. Inwood's essay in this volume critically analyses Hegel's views on Plato and Greek *Sittlichkeit*, and points out difficulties in the concept itself. My own essay on 'Political community and individual freedom in Hegel' argues that Hegel attempted to remedy what he took to be the fundamental inadequacy of Plato's (and ancient Greek civilization's) conception of ethical and political community by deriving the necessity of the state and its organic, highly differentiated modern structure from the structure of the individual will. In this way he also hoped to meet the challenge of Rousseau's conception of individual freedom characteristic of modern civilization. To put it differently, according to Hegel the destiny and capacity of the individual human being to be free is actualized in the modern state as a rationally organized, politically sovereign, ethical community.

In the *Philosophy of Right* Hegel subdivides the sphere of ethical life into family, civil society and the state. They are 'moments' of 'the ethical order', and 'are the ethical powers which regulate the life of individuals' (*PhR*, §145). The norms of the ethical order are actualized in a different way in the actions and relations of individuals who belong to the three types of ethical order. In the family, as in the Greek polis, the individuality of its members is submerged in a transcendent unity. Ethical duties are determined by one's place in the family, which ultimately depends on the natural factors of sex and birth. Love, altruism and concern for the whole are the dominant features of ethical disposition in the family community. In civil society this type of 'substantial', 'immediate' or 'natural' ethical unity disintegrates. Men are primarily concerned with the satisfaction of their private, individual needs, which they do by working, producing and exchanging the product of their labour in the market. This creates bonds of a new kind. While individuals behave selfishly and instrumentally towards each other they cannot help satisfying other men's needs, furthering their interests and entering into various social relations with them. Men are 'socialized' into playing socially useful roles for which they are not merely rewarded with money but also with respect and recognition. Their self-interest becomes enlightened ('educated' in another sense of the word *Bildung*) and they become self-conscious and respectable members of society. Ethical life, therefore, reasserts itself in civil society albeit in a different form than in the family and the state, and civil society comes to resemble community or the state.

> In the course of the actual attainment of selfish ends . . . there is formed a system of complete interdependence, wherein the livelihood, happiness and legal status of one man is interwoven with the livelihood, happiness and rights of all. On this system, individual happiness, etc., depend, and only in this connected system are they actualized and secured. This system may be prima facie regarded as the external state, the state based on need, the state as the Understanding envisages it (*PhR*, §183).

The economic exchanges in civil society take place within a framework of rules, which define the rights of individuals, their person and property. The acquisition and exchange of property, as well as its loss through the operation of market forces, therefore forms a major part of Hegel's analysis of civil society. Alan Ryan's essay in the volume distinguishes Hegel's concept of property from that of other modern political theorists, and examines what happens to Hegel's rather original justification of it when the individual finds himself faced with the ethical claims of the state. As already mentioned, the interaction of exchange relations, the norms of abstract right and positive law and state authority is the subject of Seyla Benhabib's essay.

Although the ultimate bases of civil society are human needs and the activities and relations involved in their satisfaction (which give rise to social classes or 'estates', and associations of producers or 'corporations'), Hegel includes in the concept of civil society also public authorities (courts of law, welfare and regulatory agencies), which normally are thought to be organs of the state. The reason is that in his view such public or civil authorities are just as much concerned with 'the livelihood, happiness and rights of all' as are the individual members of civil society. Private activities form the bulk of activities in civil society. Public authorities, however, intervene in the operation of the market in order to ensure the safety of person and property and to guarantee every person's right to livelihood and welfare, the *raison d'être* of civil society (cf. *PhR*, §230). Obviously, Hegel does not have the same faith in the beneficial results of the unregulated market economy as the classical British political economists and their contemporary followers have, and while his solutions to the problems of poverty, unemployment, market fluctuations and so on resemble Keynsian economics they have been often questioned on practical and theoretical grounds.

The historical context of Hegel's concept of civil society raises the question how far it can help us to understand contemporary social reality. Hegel formulated the concept when capitalism was in its infancy in Germany and even England, which served Hegel as the main source of knowledge of modern industrial society, was still at a relatively early stage of capitalist development. How well do Hegel's theoretical structures and specific practical solutions apply to the problems raised by industrialization in the stage of advanced capitalism? This is discussed in Raymond Plant's essay 'Hegel on identity and legitimation'. He sees tensions within the conceptual framework of Hegel's civil society, which seem to anticipate the contemporary phenomenon called 'the legitimation crisis'. The contemporary expansion of state activity poses in his view a threat to the relative autonomy of the civil and the political spheres, which is the essence of Hegel's social philosophy. A. S. Walton argues in his essay, however, that Hegel's theory of civil society is sufficiently well grounded in empirical economic reality and a philosophical theory of human powers and capacities to suggest a way out of the dilemmas besetting modern industrial society.

When Hegel passes on from civil society to the state in the *Philosophy of Right* he has in mind the state as a political entity or 'the strictly political state and its constitution' (*PhR*, §163). This is to be distinguished from the wide sense of the state as an ethical community ('the actuality of the ethical Idea') of which the family, civil society and 'the political state' itself are specialized 'moments', 'powers' or spheres of activity.[9] The difference between civil society and the state in this narrow, political sense lies in the ultimate ends of their activities, not their character. The activities in the civil sphere are aimed at particular interests or private rights of individuals and groups; those of the political sphere – at the general interests of the whole community. The private ends of civil society and the public ends of the state can be realized by private and by public means. In both cases there is a mixture of spontaneous individual and group actions and planned, organized, authoritative actions of people exercising public functions. In civil society market exchanges and the work of the courts and 'the police' are examples of the two categories of activities. In the political sphere patriotism or as Hegel also calls it 'the political sentiment' (*PhR*, §268), motivating citizens at large, belongs to the spontaneous, private category; so does public opinion, defined by Hegel as citizens' 'private judgments, opinions, and recommendations on the affairs of state' (*PhR*, §316). The authoritative, public actions are those of the monarch, his cabinet, the higher civil service, the members of the Assembly of Estates (the representative body) and the citizens who have voting rights. The supreme ethical duty of all who participate in the work of the sovereign authority of the state (*Staatsgewalt*), whatever their specific position in the constitution, is to promote the common good of the community (*das Allgemeine*). Ethical life reaches its highest form in the political sphere as an explicit, self-conscious, deliberate identification of citizens and office-holders with the welfare of the ethical community. The essay by Merold Westphal examines in detail the nature of ethical life in the state and compares it with that of the family; both are sharply contrasted, as ethical communities, with civil society.

Having distinguished civil society and the state as two distinct spheres of ethical life, with characteristic attitudes, forms of activity and institutional structures, Hegel is most concerned to show the linkages or 'mediations' which exist between them in reality and to argue that they have rational justification. The specialization of labour gives rise to social groups (estates or classes), which foster ethical characteristics in their members (cp. *PhR*, §207). The process goes even further in the corporation, which provides an organized opportunity for 'conscious effort for a common end' (§254) and so is, after the family, 'the second ethical root of the state, the one planted in civil society' (§255). Estates and corporations are therefore essential elements of Hegel's idea of representation; it is predominantly as members of estates or deputies of corporations, and not as isolated citizens, that people enter the political arena in Hegel's conception of the modern state. Such a representative system also ensures that the political state and its universal interests are not wholly divorced from the concerns of civil society. The Hegelian idea of the modern state as 'a state of estates' (*Ständestaat*) not only runs counter to modern ideas on political participation, but seem to militate against the originality of his distinction between civil society and the state. Klaus Hartmann in his essay criticizes Hegel for sacrificing the categorial purity of the state and society for the apparent reasons of pragmatism and questionable requirements of the dialectic. He shows how Hegel's categories of civil society and the state can be reformulated to provide a conceptual framework which fits the modern democratic welfare state very well – far better than the framework constructed by Hegel in the *Philosophy of Right*. It is in this manner, rather than through a Marxian or quasi-Marxian critique of the state concept and the simplification of the civil society concept that Hegel's theory can be rescued from the negative influence of the time and place in which it originated.

The preface to the *Philosophy of Right* has a conservative ring to it, but the well-known phrase about philosophy coming on the scene too late to give practical instruction (*PhR*, p. 12) is misleading. Action does not take place in a mental void, and one's theoretical perception of political and social facts shapes it in a decisive way. By constructing a conceptual framework of ethical, social and political reality Hegel was seeking to influence the development of his native Germany in the direction of greater freedom within the civil sphere and greater participation in the political arena. A good example of Hegel's interest in praxis is his article on the English Reform Bill, which M. J. Petry analyses in detail in his essay. He points out that there was no basic inconsistency between philosophical analysis and political propaganda; the leading ideas of the article are those of the *Philosophy of Right*. At the same time the article gives us a fascinating insight into the sources of Hegel's knowledge of contemporary social structure and social conflicts, which in that particular case included the British radical press.

But the *Philosophy of Right* — and Hegel's philosophy in general — has had a more fundamental relation to praxis than that of simple political propaganda of institutions and policies. As Raymond Plant and Charles Taylor have shown,[10] in different but complementary ways, Hegel's deepest concern was the coherence of all of European man's experience — intellectual, religious, moral, social and political — which had been undermined by the ideas of the Enlightenment and the forces released by the French Revolution and the industrial revolution typified by Britain. His philosophy was the result of a search for community in the culture and society of the modern world. Until the modern Europeans had gained a systematic, philosophical grasp of their place in history and the universe, including the man-made ethical universe, they could not — Hegel believed — reconcile and unify the various tendencies straining the fabric of their civilization. His philosophy was meant to provide such a grasp. Since many of the tendencies he was worried about have become even stronger since Hegel's death it is obvious that he has failed in his self-appointed task. But to have made us aware of the problem and given us tools with which we might grapple with it is by no means an achievement without worth.[11]

From self-consciousness to community: act and recognition in the master–slave relationship

J. M. BERNSTEIN

> Because I am a person...my only realization is in the Being of other Persons, and I am an actual person for myself exclusively in the Being of others.

Marxists discussing Hegel run the risk of throwing away the baby with the bath water. In their eagerness to condemn his idealism and to defend a materialist point of view they are apt to lose sight both of the validity of some of Hegel's insights and of their importance for their own philosophical anthropology. What this means is that in the battle between idealism and materialism one need not necessarily choose one or the other side. And much of the battle has been spurious in any case.

The position I take up in this essay can be called Left Hegelian. As a philosophical program Left Hegelianism represents the attempt to reconstruct Hegel's critique of modernity whilst abjuring those moments and principles which in its view ground his worrying 'reconciliations'. Even a minimal philosophical sense of austerity would recommend our abjuring the moment of recognition and appropriation, the presuppositions of Schelling's philosophy of identity, and the immanent teleology of the absolute concept. The goal of this radical surgery is a dialectical theory which remains at the interface of philosophy and history, forming a perpetual tympanic membrane between them.

The moment of ideality is the philosophical moment *par excellence*, the moment of reflexivity, reconstruction and critique; in fine, all that is constitutive of human transcendence over the environment. The moment of materiality is the recognition of determination and causality, of process and flux in history. A lapse into either pole falsifies human experience. Idealism, whether immediate or mediate, institutes an escape from history either by means of a permanent insight, accomplished through intellectual intuition or transcendental reflection, say, into what is forever outside history; or through a premature closure of the historical process itself, which in its turn presupposes, in the form of an absolute teleology, a resting place outside history. Materialism, in opposition, occludes the possibility of transcendence, and thus of any concrete manifestation of human freedom.

Even to begin its project Left Hegelianism must confront the founding principle of modern philosophy: self-consciousness. Focusing on the analysis of Master and Slave in the *Phenomenology of Spirit*, we shall essay a partial reconstruction of Hegel's theory of self-consciousness by means of a colloquy with its materialist critics. The materialist critique claims Hegel's theory to be idealist. In answering this critique our goal is to pose Hegel's theory between the idealist and materialist extremes.

I

Why is it, according to Hegel, that in order for me to be a self-conscious agent capable of subjugating my natural instincts for the sake of my creative and rational purposes, my awareness of myself must be mediated through my knowledge of another subject who knows me as a subject? Why in order to be a self-conscious agent must I first be recognized by another self-conscious agent whom I recognize as possessing self-consciousness? The correct Hegelian response to this question is that unless I were so recognized my sense of myself as a self-conscious agent would be nothing more than an unjustified assertion, an inner certainty, and hence would lack the objective validity and publicity we normally require for all epistemic and evaluative claims. Without the recognition of another self-consciousness, my sense of myself as a self-consciousness would lack content since nothing outside my inner awareness would correspond to it. Moreover, the recognition by the other of me would be invalid if I did not recognize him as a self-conscious agent; for if he were not himself free from natural inclinations and impulses then his recognition of me would not count as recognition, just as coerced confessions from prisoners are not truly confessions. Hence Hegel's requirement that successful recognition interactions must be mutual.

The primitive condition in which Hegel imagines this search for recognition taking place naturally generates a situation in which mutual recognition *cannot* be achieved. Both myself and the other desire recognition of our independence from the natural inclinations which govern our animal being. Taken collectively these inclinations are equivalent to the drive for self-preservation. In a primitive situation the only way I can demonstrate my independence from my animal being is show that it is nothing to me; I must risk my life in the eyes of the other. But since the other must be a self-consciousness for me before his recognition can be of worth, then he too must risk his life. But it is not adequate for each of us to simply risk our life with the other watching, for each of us could reasonably conclude from such demonstrations that the one risking his life was doing it strictly to impress the other, thus admitting that the onlooker was the sole arbiter of independence and hence only he truly possessed self-consciousness. Consequently, the only way in which each of us could assert our independence from our animal nature and be an adequate beholder of the other's independence from his animal nature would be by engaging in a struggle to the death for pure prestige.

It is at this point, at the beginning of the battle for pure prestige, that the materialist raises what he believes to be a decisive objection to the Hegelian account. If I am to engage in a struggle with the other, then I must be able to pick out and identify among the objects outside me the other as another *human* subject. By what criteria am I to make this identification? The materialist claims that given the Hegelian conception of subjectivity there can be no such criteria.[1]

The concept of the other is defined in the way in which I (as self-consciousness) define myself: the other is another me, i.e., he too is defined by his capacity to abstract from and channel his instinctual, natural side. This comes down, in the last analysis, to his ability to overcome the imperatives and pressures of his body. If, therefore, the other is identical with the pure universal power of repressing his body then, at least to that extent, he turns out to be a disembodied subject.

In making this charge against Hegel the materialist commits three major errors of interpretation. First, and most evidently, he introduces self-consciousness in its full-blown form *before* it in fact arises. Self-consciousness, as the capacity to channel instinctual drives through non-instinctually given goals and intentions is what is learned by the slave in his obedient service to the master. If we could be self-conscious agents in a strong sense prior to going through the educative process represented by the master/slave dialectic, then the master/slave dialectic would not be necessary. It is Hegel's contention, as we shall see more fully later, that prior to the master/slave dialectic we can only possess a 'sense' of ourselves as free and autonomous agents, but this sense lacks structure and reality without the complex intentional structure that the experience of servitude provides. Moreover, even after the experience of servitude men are not recognized as self-conscious agents; rather the experience of servitude begins the process whereby autonomy is achieved, but that achievement is the work of the whole of history and is not complete yet. This is obviously so for the slave who is a slave because he fears death more than he desires recognition. But it is also true for the master. The master is not a full self-conscious agent in that his ability to repress his instincts can take only one very limited form, namely repressing his drive for self-preservation in battle. But this is something substantially less than being able to channel his instinctual drives for the sake of a complex order of non-instinctually given goals and intentions.

The materialist's second error of interpretation arises because he illicitly abstracts Hegel's account of self-consciousness from what precedes and what follows it, forgetting that the structure of Hegel's argument is presuppositional (sense-certainty, for example, presupposes perception) and cumulative (sense-certainty is equally a component of perception). Now between the discussion of consciousness, by which Hegel intends, as we shall see, Kant's 'transcendental unity of apperception', in Chapter III and the risk of life in Chapter IV Hegel presents us with a discussion of 'life', that is, the biological or organic aspect of the material world. The transition between consciousness and self-consciousness is made by means of the phenomenon of life. Consciousness presupposes life for its existence, and the phenomenon of life anticipates, is the first form of the peculiar kind of self-referentiality which Hegel denominates 'infinitude', whose truth is self-consciousness. Not only are consciousness and self-consciousness implicated in a radical sense in the life processes of nature, but one of the truths that come to light in the life-and-death struggle is precisely that life is necessary to the existence of self-consciousness, 'indeed that self-consciousness is itself necessarily life'.[2] Although implicit at the outset of the life-and-death struggle, the necessity of life to self-consciousness becomes explicit in the course of the struggle. And this is not an incidental point in Hegel's analysis, it is the pivot on which it turns. If two putative self-consciousnesses do engage in a life-and-death struggle, the problem arises as to how this struggle could possibly come to an end. If neither combatant were willing to submit, if both prized their unrecognized and therefore unactual existences as self-consciousnesses more than their individual lives, then that battle could only end with the death of one of them. But such a result would leave the survivor still unrecognized and thus his autonomy still unactualized. A battle to the death for the purpose of recognition is a self-defeating project. 'This trial by death, however, does away with the truth which was supposed to issue from it, and so, too, with the certainty [i.e., my inner sense of myself as a self-consciousness – JMB] of self generally. For just as life is the *natural* setting of consciousness ... so death is the natural negation without independence, which thus remains without the required significance of recognition' (*PS*, 114). *Both* the future master *and* the future slave must recognize the fact that to battle to *death* is to commit themselves to a natural, non-spiritual standard of independence from nature. In other words, lack of fear of death is a necessary but not sufficient condition for autonomy from nature. The slave demonstrates his knowledge of this fact by preferring to stay alive as a slave, and hence as unrecognized, rather than dying in the attempt to gain recognition. But the master must recognize this fact as well, otherwise he would have no reason for letting his future slave remain alive after he has submitted. What the master recognizes is that the death of the other will not give him recognition; he can only receive recognition from a living being. Those who survive the struggle, Hegel says, 'put an end to their consciousness in its alien setting of natural existence, that is to say, they put an end to themselves, and are done away with as *extremes* wanting to be *for themselves,* or to have an existence of their own' (*PS,* ibid.). What Hegel means by this is that those who survive the struggle realize that in order to be self-consciousnesses they will have to set themselves in some kind of *intentional* relation with others; they will have to accept that their consciousness of themselves is mediated, in one way or another, by how others regard them. This is the first, crucial step whereby human beings are transformed from natural beings who regard natural life and death as their constituting parameters into spiritual beings whose possibilities for self-understanding are constituted by, in part, progressive or regressive relations with others, by spiritual forms of life and death. The slave, in becoming a slave rather than a dead man, accepts spiritual death, the reduction to thinghood, over natural death, just as the master accepts spiritual victory in recognition over natural victory in the death of the other.[3] 'In this experience', Hegel says, 'self-consciousness learns that life is as essential to it as pure self-consciousness' (*PS,* 115). Man can only *be* a *pure* (*sic*) self-consciousness if he recognizes that life, bodily existence, is essential to it. It is, then, simply false to argue, as the materialist does, that Hegel defines self-consciousness in abstraction from our bodily existence. The recognition of the essentiality of life to self-consciousness is the core of Hegel's argument.

The materialist could attempt to rebut my defense of Hegel in the following way: he could argue that although the recognition of the essentiality of life to self-consciousness is indeed the upshot of the battle for recognition, if he is right about how Hegel *first* defines self-consciousness, then the battle could never have taken place to begin with. In a sense I have already answered this objection in pointing out how Hegel introduces the phenomena of life prior to the battle for recognition. But put this answer aside. The materialist is still mistaken, and this is his third and worst error of interpretation, for he misunderstands or overlooks one of the defining features of Hegel's method, and in so doing misunderstands the actual significance of the account Hegel offers. Central to Hegel's procedure is a movement whereby features of a situation start out as immediate, implicit or unconscious and become explicit, conscious or mediated. This is part at least of what Hegel means by his technical terms 'in itself' and 'for itself'. The *an sich* is always undeveloped and self-identical; because self-identical it is self-contained and not dependent on anything outside itself. The *für sich* involves a developmental process of externalization whereby the self-containedness of the other is overcome and it becomes for another, and in that sense dependent on another.

We have already seen how as a result of the battle for recognition the surviving parties stop being purely for themselves (and so in themselves) and realize that they can only be for themselves by being for another, for this is precisely what the acceptance of a spiritual existence implies. But this is only part of the story. In the middle of his account of the battle for recognition Hegel has the following sentence: 'The individual who has not risked his life may well be recognized as a *person*, but he has not attained to the truth of this recognition as an independent self-consciousness' (*PS*, 114). I cannot remember any of Hegel's many commentators calling attention to this passage, yet without it Hegel's analysis is open to the following interpretation and refutation.[4] The point of Hegel's analysis, it is argued, is to demonstrate the origins of human self-consciousness in inter-subjectivity. As a result of the battle for recognition men first enter into intentional relations with one another and thus become spiritual beings. But if this is so, then Hegel must be trying to *explain* the transition between nature and society, between natural existence and spiritual existence by means of the battle for recognition. But this is impossible, as Rousseau long ago pointed out. If we could explain the transition between natural existence and spiritual existence, that is, if we could explain how men stop taking a natural attitude toward one another and start taking an intentional stance, then there would be no distinction between the natural and the spiritual. The spiritual or social would be a result of some natural process and hence continuous with it. We may be able to analyze what is involved in taking an intentional stance toward another, but if intentional relations are primitives which define self-consciousness then they cannot be explained by anything else, for to explain them in this sense is to reduce them to some other phenomena.

One need not abandon an anthropological reading of Hegel in order to refute this reading. Its refutation is already implicit in the above-quoted passage. Hegel nowhere attempts to explain how men first enter into intentional relations; his analysis is rather an attempt to explain how certain primitive kinds of intentional relations, by means of the battle for recognition, generate full human self-consciousness. Now one may wonder how it is possible for us to recognize each other as persons but for this recognition not to be at the level of truth; how we can be persons in ourselves but not for ourselves? To probe this question is to probe, in part, Hegel's methodology generally, the legitimacy of his methodological categories.[5] Now as a matter of fact we have within analytic philosophy a *model* of an intentional relation very similar to Hegel's which is normally *an sich* and only rarely *für sich*.

I am thinking, of course, of Grice's account of meaning, where an agent's meaning something by doing or uttering something is defined in terms of the intentions of the agent. Grice defines non-natural (spiritual) meaning in the following terms:

'U meant something by uttering x' is true if, for some audience A, U uttered x intending

(1) A to produce a particular response r.

(2) A to think (recognize) that U intends (1).

(3) A to fulfil (1) on the basis of his fulfilment of (2).[6]

For an Hegelian condition (2) is central since it is what demonstrates the necessity of reciprocity (mutual recognition) for spiritual meaning: U must intend that A recognize that U intends that A produce r. Any third order intentions of *this* kind – not all third order intentions define a situation of reciprocity – will give us a situation of mutual recognition. Without the existence of such intentions we have no reason to believe that the partners to a verbal interaction are *communicating*. As Dennet has rightly pointed out,

> The transaction in Fortran (a computer language) between man and machine are often viewed as cases of man communicating with machine, but such transactions are pale copies of human verbal communication precisely because the Gricean conditions for non-natural meaning have been by-passed. There is no room for them to apply. Achieving one's ends in transmitting a bit of Fortran to the machine does not hinge on getting the machine to recognize one's intentions.[7]

If the Gricean account fails to give an accurate picture of language, which is certainly the case, or if it blurs the fact that normally we detect intentions by means of conventions, that conventions are normally epistematically prior to intentions, nonetheless it would be hard for us to give up this account altogether for it does permit us, as above, to distinguish spiritual from blatantly non-spiritual forms of interaction.

Any case of interaction fulfilling the Gricean conditions for meaning will be a case of mutual recognition and hence a spiritual interaction. Cases of this kind define if anything does what it is for one *person* to recognize another as a person and for him to be so recognized himself. Yet as has been recently pointed out,[8] the Gricean conditions are almost never *für sich*; people rarely consciously frame these elaborate intentions when they communicate with one another, and prior to Grice's pointing them out it is doubtful if anyone ever noticed their existence at all. Moreover, if people are not aware of these intentions in speaking, then it is difficult to see how the verbal actions they supposedly underlie can be intentional at all, for an intentional action is one is which we consciously do an action under the appropriate description. The only way in which Grice's position can be salvaged is if we consider these intentions as normally unconscious or preconscious preconditions of verbal communication; they are *an sich* but not *für sich*.

If this is correct then Hegel's claim that the partners to the battle for recognition may, prior to the battle, have been recognized as persons but failed to attain to the truth of this recognition is coherent. Prior to the battle for recognition men have to be credited with at least the capacity for symbolic (linguistic or gestural) communication with one another. This much is phenomenologically assumed as far back as sense-certainty. To the extent to which non-natural meanings are communicated men are set in some form of intentional relation. But this mutual recognition is tacit, implicit or unconscious; nothing in these men's activity *shows* they are spiritual creatures except the fact that they do manage to communicate with one another. It is still possible for these beings to be driven by their instinctual needs, and further for none of them to be either willing or need consciously and overtly recognize any other of them as a spiritual being. In fine, these men are spiritual beings only *an sich*, where *an sich* means now 'implicitly' or 'potentially'. Their potential for being spiritual beings lies in the fact that their implicit recognition of one another in symbolic interaction has the potential of being altered into full self-consciousness. The continuity between the Gricean condition for non-natural meaning and the logic of recognition in the battle for recognition is, at any rate, obvious.

F does x intending
    (1) A to recognize x as desirable (or F as a self-consciousness).
    (2) A to recognize that F intends (1).
    (3) A to fulfil (1) *only* on the basis of the fulfilment of (2).

All that separates this from the Gricean conditions for non-natural meaning is that F must here *consciously* intend at least (1) and (2);[9] unless this were the case there could be no battle for *recognition*. The implicit conditions for mutual recognition in symbolic interaction become explicit in the battle for recognition; thus the battle for recognition is a necessary condition for the development of spiritual existence.

The materialist's charge that Hegelian subjects could not enter into a battle for recognition because they could not identify one another as subjects is wholly unfounded. Hegelian subjects do not enter into the battle for recognition as self-consciousnesses, they only become self-consciousnesses, as a result of the battle and the ensuing master/slave dialectic; Hegelian subjects are embodied selves, and the central lesson of the battle for recognition is that life is essential to self-consciousness; finally, the point of the Hegelian account is not to show how spiritual existence develops *ex nihilo* but, rather, to demonstrate how the capacity for self-consciousness develops out of a more primitive kind of intentional relation.

II

How, then, does Hegel ground self-consciousness in recognition? The survivors of the battle for recognition realize that life is essential to self-consciousness; mastery over nature, without and within, cannot be achieved if you are dead. Each survivor must recognize this for himself and recognize the other's recognition of this fact; unless there was a recognition of the other's recognition of the necessity of life the conditions for the battle ending would never arise. As mentioned earlier, the form in which the

recognition of the necessity of life to self-consciousness is made is not uniform. In part it involves a recognition of the fact that the *risk* of life for the
sake of recognition is self-defeating since you cannot have self-consciousness
without life. In part it also involves the insight that even if the risk is
worthwhile, a combat *victory* is not worthwhile since dead men cannot offer
recognition. Since these two insights are what the recognition of the necessity
of life to self-consciousness amounts to, then each survivor must implicitly
possess both insights and recognize the other's recognition of them. Each
combatant is dependent on the other in this; all that distinguishes different
combatants is the weighting given the two clauses of the recognition. Those
who weigh the first clause higher will be masters. Since the experience of
mastery only stabilizes, gives intersubjective form to, the master's victory
over the blind, unmediated, drive for self-preservation and his weighting of
the second clause of the recognition of the necessity of life to self-consciousness over the first, it is non-dynamic. If we are to gain an understanding of
the nature of self-consciousness, then it is the experience of slavery that we
must examine.

Hegel's account of self-consciousness is going to turn on the theoretical
interconnection between what look to be two heterogeneous phenomena: (i)
mastery over nature both within and without; and (ii) the mediation of
individual self-understanding through the understanding that the other has
of one. The master/slave dialectic is one of dependence. The men who
entered the battle for recognition sought recognition of themselves as
independent self-consciousnesses. The recognition they were to receive from
the other was to signal their independence from nature. As a result of the
battle the master is dependent on the slave for recognition (even if he also
receives recognition from other masters, for his *status* as a master is dependent
on his having a slave who recognizes him as such). The recognition the master
receives from the slave is inadequate, however, because the slave in accepting
slavery renounced his claim to be an independent self-consciousness. His
recognition of the master is like the coerced confession of a prisoner. The
situation is one which lacks reciprocity: 'for recognition proper the moment
is lacking, that what the lord does to other he also does to himself [but he
does not – JMB], and what the bondsman does to himself he should also do
to the other [but he does not – JMB]. The outcome is a recognition that is
one-sided and unequal' (*PS*, 116). Self-consciousness is not *given*; if
self-consciousness is going to be achieved it will have to be as the *result* of
a *process*.

How is the intersubjective relation between master and slave going to be
made into a dynamic process? What is required for it to be a process which
allows for the continual overcoming of nature within (set desires and
propensities) and without? Hegel puts forward two ineliminable conditions

for the achievement of self-consciousness: fear of death and service (work) for another.

Let us look first at what Hegel has to say concerning fear of death.

For this consciousness has been fearful, not of this or that particular thing or just at odd moments, but its whole being has been seized with dread. In that experience, it has been quite unmanned, has trembled in every fibre of its being, and everything solid and stable has been shaken to its foundation. But this pure universal movement, the absolute melting-away of everything stable, is the simple, essential nature of self-consciousness, absolute negativity, pure being-for-self, which consequently is *implicit* in this consciousness. This moment of pure being-for-self is also explicit for the bondsman, for in the lord it exists for him as his object (*PS*, 117).

How are we to overcome the attitude which takes any givens, within ourselves or external nature, as givens that cannot be altered? Hegel's answer is that the fear of death makes everything stable and solid appear not to be so. In situations of dire emergency, when our life is at stake, we are willing to forgo any of our settled habits and actions; and similarly, we know that whole civilizations will suddenly in circumstances of war find, for example, certain technological achievements possible which under less threatening circumstances appeared impossible, to be incompatible with the laws of nature, say. That nothing is given, or that nothing is obviously given (even the laws of nature are *discovered* only through effort and regimented activity), is essential to the nature of self-consciousness since it is essential to the possibility of mastering nature within and without.

Marshalling a more naturalistic vocabulary, the materialist urges a similar point in claiming that in actual combat-situations with other humans we must always be prepared to give up settled propensities and habits. The inadequacies of this hypothesis as an explanation of the genesis of self-consciousness will be detailed below, in Section III. For present purposes, however, it is sufficient to note one major difference between the Hegelian and materialist accounts. For the materialist the fear of death generated by the presence of the other is specific, occurring just at the odd moments of actual combat. For Hegel this fear is *structured, stabilized, and given objective form* in the person and presence of the master. With the institution (noun and verb) of slavery the slave becomes *fixed* in his dependence on the master for his life. Only the master's desire for recognition, and later his greed or mercy or insecurity, require him to let his slaves survive. The master/slave relation is the (phenomenologically) first fully social form of human dependence; the character of this dependence marks this relation as a socialization of the fear of death. Once established, however, this social relation may take on social, economic, religious and political forms; it may exist between individual persons, groups of persons, classes or nations. The formation of human self-consciousness and the entrance of man into sociality are one and the same process according to Hegel. Hence it is only with its socialization that the fear of death can become efficacious in shaping attitudes and activities. A simple line of thought leads directly from the socialization of the fear of death to history as the story of human self-creation and self-making.

The socialization of the fear of death is equivalent to the socialization of the repression of desire. The risk of life in the battle for recognition tokens a dismissal of the *drive* for self-preservation; this moment, however, is gratuitous and unprecedented. It marks the transition point between the world of needs and drives on the one hand, and the world of desire on the other. The natural world is splintered with the *desire* for recognition; need becomes desire, in a systematically inexplicable way, when the object of consciousness itself possesses the capacity for spiritual autonomy. Initially, then, it is the desire for recognition which is repressed; but through the 'standing' fear of death represented by the presence of the master, by the institution of the master/slave dialectic, each and every desire of the slave becomes subject to the possibility of repression. Since no desires are allowed to escape the dynamic of social evaluation (social accreditation or repression), and further, since desires in their reflexivity are, in part, constitutive of the being of persons and their self-understanding, it follows that the master/slave dialectic as an abiding form of self-understanding and social interaction creates the context wherein and whereby it becomes plausible to regard men as historical creatures, as products of earlier social configurations with their dynamic of social evaluation who can reshape themselves by reshaping their given social context. Central in all this is the idea that as beings possessed of self-consciousness our self-understanding, who and what we *think* we are, is partially constitutive of our being as persons. Hegel's social placing of the (possibility of the) reflexivity of desire, and so of the will, explains how self-understanding can enter into, be a component of, our being as social creatures. We cannot step outside history because human desires, desires which, after all, determine what we do and what we seek, are always the products of some form of reflective evaluation. We become persons by first learning the social script which figures our desires, and later coming to recognize that as scripted and figured our desires are alterable, parts of a social process and dynamic where acceptance, denial, negotiation and elimination have their place. Alterity is written into the structure of our wills because our desires always initially come from elsewhere, and later are subject to the play of recognition and non-recognition for their implementation.

Significantly, this social dynamic of evaluation does not take place in an idealistic vacuum with nothing but fear, dependence, desire, and reflective self-evaluation as its elements. The stabilization of the repression of desire prepares the way for the social appropriation and transformation of nature by stabilizing, giving social form to, the dissolution of nature as given. When I repress my desire for 'this' object I am also, ipso facto, repressing it as the *given* object of my desire. The givenness of things is determined by my desiring them as such, naturally; but if all my immediate desires are subject to repression, then nothing is given to me as such.

This is not just the socialization of the repression of desire which the master/slave relationship generates. It also brings about intelligent activity or *work*. Hegel states that the experience of slavery is not only 'the dissolution of everything stable merely in principle; in (the slave's) service he actually brings this about. Through his service he rids himself of his attachment to natural existence in every single detail; and gets rid of it by working on it (*PS*, 117). The experience of slavery is the transformation of random and chaotic activity into specifically human work; work is the socialization of the human capacity for intelligent activity. But without the discipline of servitude activity could not be transformed into work. What makes work is its being done for another. It requires the repression of given desires, and the substitution of the desires of another. It is initially in this substitution that the sociality of desire becomes established, thus allowing human work to begin. This is one point where Kojève's analysis cannot be bettered.

The slave who works for the master represses his instincts in relation to an idea, a concept. And that is precisely what makes his activity a specifically *human* activity. By acting, he negates, he transforms the given nature, his nature; and he does so in relation to an idea, to what does not exist in the biological sense of the word, in relation to the idea of a master – i.e., to an essentially social, human, historical notion.[10]

For the materialist intelligent activity is mute; it appears as nothing but quick-wittedness, the ability to out-think the other under pressure. There is nothing distinctively human about this. Desire unrepressed and activity which is not work leave the object as given and unsocialized; desire will lead me to devour the object, and intelligence (wit) may help me in acquiring the object ('I'll need a stick to knock the apple off the tree if I am to eat it.'), but the situation is without structure or stability (the repression of my desire for the apple is only momentary). 'Work, on the other hand, is desire held in check, fleetingness staved off; in other words, work forms and shapes things' (*PS*, 118). Through the structured repression of desire and service for another the self's desires and acts are socialized; through the slave's formative activity nature is transformed in accordance with human needs, desires and ideas. The experience of slavery is the beginning of the overcoming of nature within and without. Man has entered into the domain of the spiritual.

III

The 'spiritual' understanding of self-consciousness exhibited by Hegel's phenomenological account of its genesis marks it out as social and practical in character in a manner which departs radically from the dominant tradition of analysis in modern philosophy. This tradition is idealist; yet Hegel's critique can proleptically include the materialist counter-argument within its purview by revealing its premise to be one with the dominant tradition. Extracting this premise thus becomes the first step in limning the essential features of Hegel's critique.

That for Hegel the materialist analysis of self-consciousness contains an idealist premise should in a way be surprising since the materialist's primary error is to reduce interaction from an intentional to a causal relation, which, significantly, entails the reduction of reasons to simple means–ends rationality. Typically, the materialist will want to claim that 'the Hegelian risk of life is only an extreme expression of that material struggle between men; for to the extent to which there is nothing I can safely rely upon in my struggle with the other, I may have to put at stake my whole life.'[11] The 'material' moment in this is given by the ultimate *cause* of the battle: scarce resources. But for the materialist the 'other' too is nothing but a cause, namely, the cause of our having to forgo established habits and propensities. For the materialist there are no intentional or internal relations between human subjects; each is but an *occasion* for the other to act in a particular manner. Further, since what the other threatens is my means for satisfying my ends, then the transcendence of my bodily drives, of my natural habits of action, can only token the possibility of novel means towards attaining established ends. Values, ends, remain determined by the pressures of my bodily wants, and reason remains instrumental.

Hegel's reply to this aspect of the materialist's argument lies in his alternative diagnosis of the origins of battle: the desire to have my penumbral sense of myself as not determined by the vicissitudes of my body recognized and publicly confirmed. In phenomenological terms, that is, in terms of a minimal genetic account which comprehends the phenomenon in question in terms of its essential possibility as a component of a philosophically perspicuous self-representation, the original battle (the battle itself is, of course, a phenomenological tool of analysis) must be for pure prestige. Radical scarcity is not only not a precondition for the development of human self-consciousness, it makes the origins of self-consciousness (phenomenologically) incomprehensible since: (a) in such a situation the other would always be justified in believing that I was fighting simply in order to preserve my life, and consequently that I was wholly dominated by the drive for self-preservation; and (b) the only possible conclusion to such a battle would be the death of one of the competitors since under conditions of radical scarcity having a slave to work for me would disadvantage me with respect to other competitors who had only their own well-being to consider. Reason (a) looks decisive; no matter how *intelligent* my behaviour in a battle for scarce resources may be, if the other, justifiably, believes that I am battling solely for the purpose of preserving my life then he has no grounds for regarding me as a spiritual being as opposed to, say, a very clever animal; which is to say, he would be justified in regarding my responses to him as simply very complex instinctual responses (ones he does not quite understand) and not reasoned actions. Crudely put, unless condition (3) of my reformulation of the Gricean conditions for meaning into a logic of recognition were fulfilled recognition would not take place. If the other always responded to what I did because he was hungry (too), then I would have no way of knowing if he was also responding *at all* in recognition of my original intention. In fine, unless condition (3) is operative, then condition (2) cannot be operative; but we have already seen that condition (2) defines mutual recognition and hence human (spiritual) intersubjectivity.

How does the materialist elide recognition of this intention structure? Simply by supposing the contestant in the struggle to be *already* immersed in the world of praxis.[12] This gives to these men *all* the capacities that the Hegelian analysis attempts to account for. If men in the primitive condition already possess the capacity for intelligent behaviour, then all the materialist's story can show is the conditions under which they *extend* these capacities; there is no room in his account for qualitative change. More importantly, the possession of self-consciousness is itself a *premise* of his theory; and it is this premise which he shares with the idealist. Persons are constituted as self-conscious agents outside of and independently of their entanglement with other human beings. Any series of events incapable of anticipation could provide sufficient conditions for the materialist's primitives to realize their need to repress their natural habits; and this means that intercourse with other human beings is not a necessary condition for these beings to develop self-consciousness. The materialist is a methodological solipsist; like the idealist he situates human beings in a private space all their own, independently of one another.

The dialectic of master and slave represents a fracturing of the asocial space of self-consciousness presupposed by idealist philosophy. Whatever the difference between their two systems, Kant and Descartes shared the belief that persons were characterized by two unique but separate capacities: self-consciousness and freedom of the will.[13] The Cartesian and Kantian 'I think' (= the transcendental unity of apperception in Kant) represents the capacity of the thinking self to separate and identify itself (in Kant: to identify the self's contribution to the cognitive situation); to distinguish the self that thinks from what it is the self thinks about: the given. In Descartes the self is discovered as foundational by means of a reiterated abstraction (the doubt) from the contents of consciousness. Kant argues that the 'I think' must be capable of accompanying all our representations because it is only in virtue of the rules and standards of judgment that persons being to the cognitive situation that representations represent, that intuitions can have any cognitive significance whatsoever. Self-consciousness for Descartes and Kant is the cognition of the difference between the self and all that it thinks about. Similarly for both, freedom is represented by the difference between the self and what acts on the self; to be free is to be free from the coercion of causal chains. On analogy with the transcendental unity of apperception Kant offers us the categorical imperative as a universal rule which we bring to the practical situation that allows us to judge the ethical validity of our proposed actions. Practical self-consciousness, like theoretical self-consciousness, is the difference between the self that acts and the given.

Without going into the details of their arguments, three difficulties are evident in this scheme. (1) Reason and rationality always stand opposed to the given; hence the given represents a permanent source of irrationality in the system.[14] (2) Although freedom and theoretical self-consciousness are both essential predicates of the self, they are presented as heterogeneous capacities, non-reducible to one another and without any evident internal connection with one another. They are analogous to one another in structure and function, but somehow different. Neither Descartes nor Kant defend this heterogeneity or attempt to overcome it; the best Kant can do is offer the fact that both capacities are rooted in the 'spontaneity' of the mind. (3) Because freedom and theoretical self-consciousness are presented as heterogeneous, the problem arises as to whether practical reason is prior or posterior to theoretical reason. Whatever the validity of the particular arguments Descartes and Kant put forward for their respective theories, Hegel thought that these three systematic points indicated the limits of their position, its structural inadequacies, and that a phenomenological analysis could overcome these inadequacies.

What I have here denominated theoretical self-consciousness is called by Hegel 'consciousness' in the *Phenomenology*; the contention of chapter IV (A) is that consciousness (the object of analysis in Ch. IV) presupposes self-consciousness, and self-consciousness presupposes recognition. From what has already been said, we can easily perceive why the first half of this argument must be correct. If consciousness means not only the possession of norms and standards for judging and acting, but awareness of the existence of these standards, an ability to identify them and distinguish them from the objects they inform, then I must be able to identify those components of practical and theoretical experience which are given. What Hegel shows is that we come by knowledge of the given only through a particular kind of *experience*.[15] In the case of practical self-consciousness it is the experience of fear and the consequent need to repress our given desires, needs and propensities. Through this experience we learn that the reasons for acting are not given naturally, but may be created and evaluated. Further experience, discussed in Chapter V, will teach us that we can in acting disregard both the desires of the self and of the other, that there are standards of reasonableness which are superior to any self, whose validity does not depend on what any self thinks or believes. Kant's categorical imperative would be one such reason. Similarly, theoretical self-consciousness discovers its given through, again, the fear of death, which dissolves all givens, the repression of desires and the activity of work. Work creates objects in accordance with ideas not naturally given. It is only the resistance of the natural world to human projects which, when developed in science, indicates to us the nature and extent of the naturally given, what is alterable and inalterable in the world.

All this is by-the-way, for it leaves the three systematic problems untouched. If we direct our attention to problem (2) first, we shall see how answers to problems (1) and (3) fall out as a consequence. Both Descartes and Kant fail properly to identify the ingredients of self-consciousness. The Cartesian *cogito* appears unmediated; yet it is mediated by at least the reiterated abstraction from the given which is formalized in the Cartesian method of doubt. The Cartesian method of doubt, however, is itself left untheorized; how can a thinking self doubt the validity of what is given to consciousness? How can it, in the first instance, begin the business of doubting? Only the practical experience of the fear of death, Hegel answers, is capable of shocking us out of complacency, of dissolving the given and giving us a distance between ourselves and objects of experience. Doubt in the first instance must be practical; only through the practical negation of the given through work can we require the capacity to abstractly negate the given through doubt. More succinctly, the reflexive/reflective character of doubting shows it to be a form of self-consciousness. According to Hegel, scepticism, the first form of self-consciousness possessing the capacity for metaphysical doubt, is phenomenologically grounded on the anterior experiences of slavery and stoicism, and its possibility is conditioned by them. The Cartesian narrative of crisis in the *Discourse* gives the method of doubt physiological plausibility, not theoretical validity. Radical doubt will arrive on the *terra firma* of the *cogito*, self-consciousness, but only because, as Hegel shows in Chapter IV, doubting is a founded mode of self-consciousness.

We have already questioned Kantian apperception. But what of Kantian self-ascription, the awareness of the self as possessing a unique mental history? This is mediated; my knowledge of myself as carving a unique path through space and time is dependent on my knowledge of a spatio-temporal order which possesses many possible routes through it, of which mine is but one. Knowledge of the inner is hence dependent on knowledge of the outer. Against this Hegel asks the obvious question: why should we conceive of this kind of self-awareness as uniquely human? What makes this self-consciousness human self-consciousness at all? Could not (do not) animals other than man possess this kind of self-awareness? Could not a computerized robot possess self-awareness of this kind? What is wrong, then, with Kantian self-consciousness is that although a necessary condition for human self-consciousness, on its own it fails to justify its claim of being a *differentia* between persons and non-persons.

Hegel develops an analysis of properly human self-consciousness by proceeding along the route Kant had already established. First he demonstrates what extra awareness is required to be aware of living things as opposed to an array of individuals distributed through space and time, and then proceeds to a consideration of human interaction. Human self-consciousness will extend the Kantian dependency of the inner on the outer to the domain of intersubjectivity. However, before this move can be made, or rather, in order to make this move Hegel argues that the *mode* of interaction between self and other must be altered. Modes of cognition are internally related to the kinds of objects with which they deal, and conversely different kinds of objects call for different kinds of cognitive treatment. Hegel argues that 'self-consciousness is desire in general' (*PS*, 105), that is, self-consciousness appropriates its other not through intuition or judgment alone but through desire as well.

The transition from judgment to desire is central to Hegel's argument; it is also extremely difficult to justify. The best I can do here is offer a line of argument which seems to me capable of being developed to establish Hegel's conclusion.[16]

Against Kant it has already been argued that self-ascription, while a necessary condition for human self-consciousness, is not the unique prerogative of human beings. Self-ascription falls short of self-consciousness in that it does not reveal the self, what kind of being the self is. Part of the reason for this is that the point of objective consciousness is to reveal the object of consciousness and not the subject of consciousness. Sensing, perceiving, understanding are modes of cognition in which reflexivity plays no essential role. It is not relevant to the contemplation of the external world what kind of being does that contemplating; in contemplating the world we lose ourselves in the object. Objective consciousness is first and foremost a kind of self-consciousness. What brings the self back to itself is the awareness of an absence; the self turns back on itself only when it finds the object unsatisfying, when it desires but does not possess. Desire is what first reveals and shows the difference between subject and object; in desiring, needing or wanting an object, the subject becomes aware that he is separate from the object. Without the experience of desire there would be no *need* (reason) for the subject to be aware of himself as other than the world. Further, for desire to be truly revelatory of the subject of desire, desire must be focused on an appropriate object, and the only object which could reveal the self to itself would be another human subject. In desiring lesser things all that is revealed to the self is what he shares with those things; in desiring fruit I am an organic being; in desiring animals I am an animal. Only in desiring another's desire, that is, in desiring recognition by the other do I become a self-consciousness. Finally, in desiring I am moved to act since only through action in relation to the object can desire be satisfied. The action appropriate to the desire for recognition is, we have seen, the risk of life. It is in desiring and acting to gain recognition that men achieve self-consciousness.

The desire for recognition generates the battle for recognition which is terminated in the dialectic of master and slave. It is the experience of the slave which produces freedom and self-consciousness. Freedom and self-consciousness share the component figure of mastery over nature within and without. Mastery over nature without is freedom producing only because the objects of the slave's formative activity are mediated by the master's desire for them. By overcoming nature without, by building the world in accordance with his ideas, by objectifying himself in the products of his work the slave overcomes his servitude to the master.

This negative middle term or the formative activity is at the same time the individuality or pure being-for-self of consciousness which now in the work outside it, acquires an element of permanence. It is in this way, therefore, that consciousness, *qua* worker, comes to see in the independent being (of the object) its own independence (*PS*, 118).

The independence of the products of his activity represent to the slave his independence from the master. Why? Because what makes the slave slavish is his dependence; recognition and, at first, the objects of production are for another (the master). But the other is trapped by these for they make him dependent; and they make him dependent because they are *givens*. Negating action, except for battle, is no part of the master's repertoire. Only work produces independent things and men; hence it is that it is only 'qua worker' that the slave is independent. As the slave frees himself from nature without he also frees himself from nature within. The recognition of standards and norms, like the categorical imperative, are the products of the slave; he is able to repress and channel his desires in accordance with ideas and norms that have no natural basis. But it is just an awareness of oneself as having this capacity that defines self-consciousness as pure being-for-self; freedom from nature within and without.

According to this schema there is no such thing as pure theoretical self-consciousness. Freedom and self-consciousness are not two different things, but different ways of talking about the same thing. Theoretical self-consciousness is simply an abstraction from practical self-consciousness. Reason is grounded in work, in the overcoming of nature and hence in the production of freedom. It is no accident that Descartes and Kant offered freedom and self-consciousness as the *differentia* between persons and non-persons, for they are component elements of the same phenomenon, grounded in the same unitary experience.

Once we recognize the primacy of the practical for Hegel, we can understand what Hegel intends by claiming that self-consciousness is the removal of the given. He does not intend by this a material idealism, the devolving of all things into ideas; nor does he intend that we produce the matter of experience — wood, stone, water, gold, etc. — *simpliciter*. Only for theoretical self-consciousness is the matter of experience a given incapable of elimination and hence a perpetual surd in the system. The problem of the thing-in-itself is a problem for theoretical reason, and thus it is that Hegel interprets Kantian consciousness as theoretical and not practical. Pure being-for-self is a practical not a theoretical concept. To remove the given is to socialize the world. We overcome nature within and without by producing a world — objects and institutions — which coheres with human desires and ideals and respects human autonomy.

IV

I now come to the interconnection of self-consciousness, community and politics. Despite his displacement of self-consciousness from the individual to the social, and from the theoretical or representational to the practical, Hegel nonetheless remains a modern philosopher in making self-consciousness foundational. This becomes singularly evident in his account of the 'unhappy consciousness', who installs, in reaction to the failed bids for individual autonomy represented by stoicism and scepticism, as a component of self-consciousness the recognition of our lack of individual completeness (*PS*, 126–38). The unhappy consciousness recognizes the dependency of the self on the 'other', but not of course the true nature of that other. As a consequence of his projection of the other into the 'beyond', he suffers a continual diremption of his self from his true self: the other who would provide recognition without domination. For Hegel the unhappy consciousness is the figure of history, the allegorical form in which history is experienced as a series of displacements in which self-consciousness fails to recognize itself in another self-consciousness but recognizes still its being in otherness.[17] All history is, at least, a variation on the lack of reciprocity: 'for recognition proper the moment is lacking, that what the lord does to the other he also should do to himself, and what the bondsman does to himself he should also do to the other'.

In the section on the unhappy consciousness this failure manifests itself as a gap between the intended significance of our acts and the actual import of their performance. When forced to recognize the existence of this gap Kant conjured up the postulates of pure practical reason, and with them an infinite beyond, in order to bridge the space which threatened the autonomy of practical reason. With his prosaic capacity to detect the social figure in the theoretical carpet, Hegel tends to designate this gap as a contingent product of the conditions of action in the modern world: 'Because the whole of an action, in which only a fragment belongs to each actor, is split into so many pieces, the whole work is also a resultant of so many single actions. The work is not done as a deed [Tat], but as a planned result. The consciousness of the deed as a whole is not present to any of the actors.'[18] Now it has been traditionally argued that the complete and full dissolution of the gap between self and other, finite and infinite, intention and action occurs in Hegel *only* through the medium of philosophical reflection. Because of the fragmented nature of the modern social world the Hegelian philosopher is the only agent whose actions can be complete within themselves, 'whose deeds *Totalität* can be self-consciously achieved; that is, the Hegelian *ergon* is the total articulation of all the deeds and all the speeches of others'.[19]

The textual case for a claim of this sort which sees Hegel displacing social action by philosophical reflection is beyond dispute. What I want to argue here, however briefly, is that on the basis of even our minimal sketch of his conception of self-consciousness the only plausible domain of Hegelian praxis must be, *pace* Hegel, a reformed political community.

Part of the argument for philosophy as the only true bearer of self-consciousness is derived from Hegel's perception of the impossibility of praxis proper in the modern social and political world. This much was evidenced above. Against it one need only posit the Marxian analysis of the contradictions of capital production, for it tokens the radical historical contingency, and hence the surpassability of the economic forms responsible for the functional isolation of individuals as economic agents.

Another limb of the Hegelian argument concerns the sublation of *poiesis*, of making as opposed to action or conduct, as the dominant form of praxis. Pre-Hegelian subjects could secure their objective identities only in products other than and alien to themselves. However, it is argued, 'if Hegel is right, the necessity of making the *poetic* production of *otherness* the route to the actualization of subjects disappears when, in the language of the *Phenomenology*, self-consciousness comes to know itself as really at work in the whole series of self-externalizations it has brought about hitherto'.[20] It is assumed here that, as the *Phenomenology* insists, with out knowledge of history as a process of self-externalizations these objects are no longer necessary to self-consciousness. As a consequence, only the recollection (the work of the *Phenomenology*) and the articulation (the work of the *Encyclopedia*) of the deeds and speeches of others remains.

Now a similar conception of praxis is found in Hannah Arendt's dissociation of 'action' from 'labour' (the cyclical perpetuation of the means of biological existence) and 'work' (the creative transformation of nature into durable artefacts). Action involves the public disclosure of oneself in deeds and speeches; what is thus disclosed is not the 'inner self', but 'who' one is simply in virtue of those sayings and doings. The proper arena of action is a political community, and the only result of action is the 'recognition' of who we are.[21] In this sense Arendtian action takes up the idea of Hegelian intersubjective self-constitution without domination. One might say, then, that the Arendtian conception represents a direct political analogue of Hegelian philosophical action. Yet, because Arendtian action is primarily political it would appear to provide a model of praxis sharing certain formal features with Hegel's but capable of overcoming what might be regarded as the over-intellectualization of praxis in Hegel.

In fact, neither Arendt's nor Hegel's own ultimate conception of praxis accords with the understanding of self-consciousness present in Chapter IV of the *Phenomenology*. Against Hegel's philosophical conception of praxis it can be contended that it returns self-consciousness to *knowing* or *representing* as its dominant form, which it was the goal of his critique to sublate. The proper riposte to Hegelian philosophy as true praxis comes from the final paragraph of his discussion of the master/slave dialectic where he returns to the problem of the place of the fear of death in his schema. 'If consciousness fashions the thing without initial absolute fear, it is only an empty self-centred attitude; for its form or negativity is not negativity per se, and therefore its formative activity cannot give it a consciousness of itself as essential being' (*PS*, 119). What is at issue here is the *meaning* of work, for to engage in formative activity and reflective self-evaluation by themselves is inadequate if one does these things without a proper understanding of their significance. In the same way as the original risk of life attempts to instantiate a mode of action transcending the contours of biological existence, so equally must all subsequent *work* be directed toward spiritual goals which give value *to* life. Only those values can properly reflect consciousness 'as essential being'. Hence Hegel's conception of 'absolute fear' comes to signify the risk involved in true work, or, to say the same thing in the traditional vocabulary of political theory, acts of human significance require *courage*. On this point Arendt concurs with Hegel: 'Courage liberates men from their worry about life for the freedom of the world. Courage is indispensable because in politics not life but the world is at stake.'[22]

Work, then, is more than a means of satisfying desire or earning a living; it is the way in which man socializes nature, creating a second nature that conforms to human needs, ideas and ideals. Work which does not denaturalize the world, be it the world of first nature or of second nature, work which merely replaces a given nature with another set of givens must fail in its essential task; it remains a 'self-will, a freedom which is still enmeshed in servitude' (PS, 119). Since Hegelian and properly post-Hegelian philosophy is a recollective enterprise, then it must fail to satisfy the criterion of risk, and hence cannot be true work; it is reproductive rather than productive.

Against this Hegelian critique of Hegel stands the traditional reading of Hegel which claims that his philosophy stands at the end of history, that it is no longer the search for wisdom which Hegel represents, but wisdom itself. Behind this claim lies the thesis that history can come to an end when the desire for recognition is fully satisfied, 'when each shall be recognized in his reality and in his human dignity by *all* the others'.[23] And this thesis accords nicely with at least some aspects of the master/slave dialectic and the dialectic of the unhappy consciousness. It is, clearly, the end-of-history thesis which supports the end-of-poetic-production thesis. Now I have been arguing that self-consciousness is irredeemably productive in character, and hence that there can be no end to history: the logic of the dialectic of recognition is only one aspect of the logic of self-consciousness, and that latter logic has an ineliminable productive element. A first foray against the end-of-history thesis would note that universal recognition does not now exist. But this would still leave the in principle claim standing.[24] Where the end-of-history thesis goes wrong is in conflating part for whole: what the recognition of self in otherness allows is the end to the production of necessarily false or inadequate others. The emphasis here is on 'necessarily'. The negation of what is necessarily inadequate as other does not entail the production of what is necessarily adequate. Mutual recognition and its reflection in Hegelian philosophy represent at most a necessary but not sufficient condition for true praxis. How then is true praxis possible now?

We have seen that the goal of Hegelian praxis can not be contemplation since contemplation is, in the requisite sense, unproductive. Further, nothing less than the actual recognition of self in otherness will suffice to ground the possibility of praxis. Given, then, that without reciprocity the sociality of self-consciousness is repressed, and without productivity the practical nature of self-consciousness is unrecognized, we can state the issue thus: how can there be both reciprocity and productivity? Intuitively, it would appear that productivity involves the positing of false or inadequate others, while reciprocity, once achieved, lacks the contradictory quality which issues in the kind of negating action which is self-conscious production. In order to untie the antinomy of reciprocity and productivity two points need to be established.

Firstly, Hegelian as opposed to Arendtian work includes institutions, laws, codes, customs and values. These artefacts are the ultimate shapers of the psyche; and it is the continual production of them, based on the continual human need for human communities to reconstitute themselves, which is underwritten by Hegel's account of self-consciousness. Whatever institutional form our reciprocal recognitions of one another take in that forum, that form is nonetheless an artefact subject to the 'natural laws' of institutional maturation and decay, and hence is in continual need of *innovative* reproduction. Since work, in Hegel's terms, is instrumental in making us who we are, the place of productivity can never be surpassed.

In making self-consciousness both spiritual and productive Hegel intends that it produce both means to ends and new ends. However, and this is our second point, if reciprocity is a necessary end, then it would appear that we can only be productive in establishing adequate means to this end; and this would undermine the claim that we are, as such, spiritually productive creatures, that as persons we possess the capacity to produce new ideals and values. According to this thesis, once reciprocity has been discovered there are no new ends, ideals or values, to be produced. Such a view rests on an error.

It was Aristotle who gave us the idea of praxis as activity having its rationally desired end in itself. According to tradition, this led him to posit contemplation, pure thinking as the highest good, and to relegate ordinary ethical thinking to the region of instrumental, means–ends rationality. In ethical thinking, so the story goes, we possess, as given, either an end-in-view or a general principle of conduct. Ethical thinking itself involves either discovering the necessary and/or sufficient means to that end, or deliberating on whether a particular case falls under a prescribed rule. If such an account were correct, then ethical thinking would be non-spiritually productive in Hegel's sense, and further, would fail to match the Aristotelian paradigm of praxis. Without detailing the complex conceptual and textual issues at stake here, it is nonetheless important to note that Aristotle did not deny that the end of action, the goal of action could itself be an object of ethical deliberation.[25] Very roughly, he argued that practical reasoning could be either ordinary means–ends reasoning *or* constituent–ends reasoning. By this latter he intended the idea that an end, *eudaimonia*, say, could be both necessary *and* incomplete in character such that only through deliberation could one adjudicate what was to count as satisfying or fulfilling that end, that is, what the actual ingredients in that end were to be. Because some end is given or necessary does not entail that we know or have before us the various elements which constitute its satisfaction, and thus that all we need to do is find some way of bringing it about that those things become present. To the degree to which an end is necessary it is beyond deliberation; to the degree to which an end is incomplete or unspecified its constituents remain unknown, undiscovered or unproduced.

It is with this latter model of constituent–ends reasoning that I think we can overcome the antinomy of reciprocity and productivity, and thereby derive a conception of praxis which fulfils the formal criteria Hegel stipulates, but which is nonetheless applicable to worldly actions. Let us begin from the reciprocity side of the problem. For Hegel reciprocity cannot be permanently embedded in laws and institutions which remain outside the *direct* control of the collectivity they are meant to constitute *as* a collectivity with a unique identity. These artefacts inevitably come to represent external constraints upon conduct rather than conditions *überhaupt* of conduct, that is, they become self-externalizations which we are unable to see ourselves 'in', and hence unable to recognize as our 'essential being'. This, of course, is nothing but the familiar complaint against *gesellschaftlich* social relations, where social identity is established mediately through occupation, achievement and the like, and not through direct recognition by one's others. At *some* fundamental level, then, reciprocity requires community, that is, a forum of social interaction in which social identity is formed through direct reciprocal recognitions.[26]

If reciprocity is a necessary condition for praxis, and if reciprocity is impossible without community, then nothing less than activity towards community is sufficient to make praxis possible. Yet, it was the evident lack of the existence of community which first turned Hegel's attention toward philosophy as the dominant form of praxis, and later led to the peculiar turns of argument in the *Philosophy of Right* concerning the relations between state and civil society. It is this very same lack of community which gives to Arendt's model of political action an undeniably utopian flavour. Indeed, her reification of the unrecoverable model of the Greek *polis* is made even more utopian by her insistent exclusion of work, of all things which might be said to belong to the social world (civil society), from the domain of politics. For her politics relates strictly to social identity and, apparently, to nothing else.[27] Both Arendt and Hegel give us what might be termed 'the empty space of praxis', that is, a formal model of praxis which lacks the possibility of application. The empty character of Hegelian praxis is marked by the (now) unproductive status of Hegelian philosophical reflection; and the empty space of Arendtian praxis is marked by its backward looking utopianism. This is not to deny that in *its* time Hegelian philosophy might have been praxial, nor that Arendt's distinctions between action and work, and politics and society do not demarcate the ancient Greek space of praxis. All that I am denying is that they represent recoverable models of praxis for us now.

Our Hegelianism, however, shows us the way out of the dilemma, for we can detect the social figures in their theoretical carpets, namely, again, the lack of an existing community sufficient to the needs of praxis. But we also possess a theoretical figure, that of constituent–ends reasoning which shows us why that present lack need not be a decisive obstacle to true praxis. Community, we have argued, is a necessary end, because a necessary condition, of praxial action. But striving to achieve community involves more than mere means-ends rationality. We can achieve community *now* only by *now* deliberating on what social forms, laws, institutions and values will be the constituents of that community. In those collective deliberations, however, we are *already* forming a new collective will, shaping new social identities, and bringing forth new values and institutional relations, if, and only if, we undertake our deliberations seriously, that is, if in our deliberations we have the courage to risk our present social identities and regard our newly formed forum as the arena in which our new social identity is to be forged. This model of political community is not utopian because it does not depend upon the collapse of existing social and political relations for its instauration; rather, it begins, can only begin now (as perhaps the example of the women's movement illustrates) with the establishment of new spaces for intersubjective self-constitution.

V

Modern philosophy's foundational enterprise depends upon securing self-consciousness as the ground of knowledge and right action. The master/slave dialectic undermines that foundational enterprise by reinscribing the place of self-consciousness. Master and slave are more than social roles, they are functioning features of self-consciousness itself. Mastery and slavery can be components of self-consciousness because self-consciousness is neither an individual capacity nor a social role, but rather the primary mode in which individual persons function as social beings. In Hegelian terms the only possible ground for knowing and right action is 'spirit', history and community. Spirit, however, awkwardly and problematically, manifests itself in a variety of ways, that is, we form and become ourselves in a diversity of mediums: politics, philosophy, religion, science, art and literature.[28] Recognition of this diversity explains the impetus behind this essay: to circumscribe the nature of spirit, and, however tentatively, designate its present medium.

We began, then, with the materialist's charge that Hegel's account of self-consciousness fails because it relies upon the idealistic conception of man as a disintered knower and agent. I have argued that Hegelian selves are embodied selves whose central relation to the world is practical. Against the tide of recent commentaries, I have argued for an anthropological reading of Hegel, one which makes him not the last perpetrator of a cosmic onto-theology, but the first systematic philosopher of human praxis. Now one could argue that either Descartes or Kant have a prior claim to this title;[29] but there is a further distinction between them and Hegel. By grounding freedom and self-consciousness, the *differentia* between persons and non-persons, in recognition and community Hegel adumbrates an answer to the self-destructive versions of free-willing and the mastery of nature which were precipitated by the Cartesian and Kantian philosophies. The major metaphysical trope shared by all three thinkers is the ungrounded free act of reflection/negation: Cartesian doubt and the *cogito*; Kant's *Spontaneität* as the ground of the 'I think' and the autonomy of practical reason; and the Hegelian risk of life, the unprecedented denial of the drive for self-preservation. Because Descartes and Kant never leave, escape from, the unbounded domain of subjectivity and its spontaneity they are ultimately unable to constrain the pretensions of the will. Hegel escapes the either/or of intellectual intuition (pure, speculative reason) or infinite willing (pure practical reason) by sublating spontaneity in sociality. Community and history provide the only possible ground for knowing, and present an inevitable constraint on the demonic ambitions of the will.

However, merely *theoretically* to note the existence of spirit in this way is insufficient; or, rather, to make this argument now is to forget the historicity of spirit and the diversity of its modes of manifestation. The dual distinguishing features of spirit, sociality (reciprocity) and practice, are no longer obviously present in philosophy or theory. For *us* reciprocity requires the establishment of community; and the only kind of community which we can conceive of as being fully practical is a political community. Hence we can now be truly self-conscious agents only by participating in the formation of such a community.

If true, this thesis concerning the location of spirit in political community has a strange corollary. No domain of human experience for Hegel is *a priori* or ontologically autonomous. Each is but a possible place for the manifestation of spirit. In any particular epoch the *kind* of validity a social action may have is determined by the place of spirit at that time, and hence by the forms of legitimacy appropriate to that social domain. Philosophy requires truth as much as art requires beauty. But, I have argued, the time of philosophy is over. What then of this writing, these words? I am spirit's servant. If my words work, if they possess courage, then they bring not truth but friendship.

Hegel, Plato and Greek 'Sittlichkeit'

M. J. INWOOD

Like many of his contemporaries, Hegel enormously admired the ancient Greeks. Their art, philosophy, religion and mode of life were, he felt, in a way unsurpassed and they occupied a large part of his attention and writings. The Greeks were the ethical people (*das sittliche Volk*) *par excellence*.[1] In contrast to earlier societies, Greek society was a humanized society, in which natural forces were felt to have been tamed and subdued. Their gods, for example, were of a human form; their sculpture portrayed human and not animal figures.[2] The world of the Greeks was familiar and friendly to its inhabitants. The chaos of nature was held at bay by social norms and institutions which were recognizably the product of men and in which men felt at home. In contrast to later peoples, then, the Greeks had not yet come to regard their social norms and institutions as alien and oppressive or to distance themselves from them. They acted out their appointed roles without question. Such, according to Hegel, was the character of Greek society when it was at its height, and it is this which is meant by the expression 'Greek *Sittlichkeit*'.

In this rather idealized picture of them,[3] the Greeks simply read off their duties (and their rights) from their social institutions. 'In an *ethical* community, it is easy to say what man must do, what are the duties he has to fulfil in order to be virtuous: he has simply to follow the well-known and explicit rules of his own situation' (*PhR*, §150R). If one's duty was, according to such rules, to repay a debt or to ensure the burial of one's brother, one simply did it, without asking: 'Why should I do it? Even if it is normally regarded as the right thing to do, is it really the right thing to do?' Hegel distinguishes this attitude from that of faith or trust: 'The subject is thus directly linked to the ethical order by a relation which is more like identity than even the relation of faith or trust. Faith and trust emerge along with reflection; they presuppose the power of forming ideas and making distinctions. For example, it is one thing to be a pagan, a different thing to believe in a pagan religion (*PhR*, §147R).[4] Faith or trust is one sort of response to the question: 'Why should I obey these laws? Why should I accept this religion?' Rational argument is another type of response to it. But the man who is simply a pagan does not raise the reflective question 'Why should I accept this?' and does not therefore adopt the stance of faith. Similarly the ethical Greek does not reflect upon his society and his activities to the point of asking why he should follow the laws and customs or accept the religion of his society.

This naive, pre-reflective faith goes together with an undeveloped awareness of oneself as an individual. To ask: 'Why should I follow the laws and customs?' presupposes a distinction between oneself and one's society, just as the parallel epistemological question 'Why should I accept this religion?' presupposes a distinction between oneself and that religion. But '[this ethical substance and its laws and powers] are not something alien to the subject. On the contrary, his spirit bears witness to them as to its own essence, the essence in which he has a feeling of his own selfhood, and in which he lives as in his own element which is not distinguished from himself' (PhR, §147). The Greek does not and cannot draw a sufficiently sharp distinction between himself and others to enable him to ask: 'Why should I do what they do or believe what they believe?' Such differences as there are between what different individuals do are explicable in terms of their socially assigned role and class, whether they are, for example, men or women, parents or children, warriors or craftsmen, not in terms of the deliberate adoption of a mode of behaviour or life. Men share the same norms, institutions, gods and cultic activities, and cannot raise the questions why they do so or whether they should do so.

Hegel sometimes speaks as if a society, or the laws and institutions which constitute it, is a substance and the members of it only its accidents (PhR, §156 and Addition). He also refers to it as mind or spirit (Geist) (ibid.). This expresses, in part, the dependence of the individual on his society and the way in which its laws and customs constitute his subjective mentality. In any society many of a man's desires and cognitive states are possible only because he inhabits a society of a particular sort, the desire, for example, to pay by cheque. And in the special case of an ethical society, men cannot question the norms of their society. It expresses also the fact that social institutions are nevertheless the product of human minds and purposeful behaviour, and depend on them for their existence. Finally it suggests, more controversially, that social norms and institutions are mind-like in their coherence and tensions, and in the way they develop.

The harmony of Greek life is, however, marred by three features. Firstly, different aspects of Sittlichkeit are in potential conflict with one another. Antigone, for example, who wishes to bury her rebellious brother is acting in accordance with the norms of the family. King Creon, who opposes this, adheres to the norms of public, civil life.[5] The parties do not question the laws and customs of their society as a whole, but each identifies himself with one aspect of them to the exclusion of the other. It is unclear how important Hegel thought such conflicts were in actual Greek society, since his examples are largely drawn from Greek tragedy rather than Greek life. In any case, within drama the conflicts are resolved, and the performance of dramas portraying them might assist their containment and resolution in real life.

Secondly, some men, notably Socrates, began to look into themselves for the right way to behave and not to social norms and institutions. They distanced themselves from accepted values and insisted that any particular course of action should meet their own approval before they embarked on it. 'The tendency to look deeper into oneself and to know and determine from within oneself what is right and good appears in ages when what is recognized as right and good in contemporary manners cannot satisfy the will of better men' (*PhR*, §138R). The tendency to question accepted values and to decide for oneself is accompanied by a heightened self-awareness: 'This is the beginning of a self-knowing and so of a genuine freedom' (*PhR*, §279R).[6]

Finally, individual Greeks began in the late fifth and the fourth centuries B.C. to serve their own interests, disregarding the larger interests of their society and the accepted values of their time.

These three types of case are distinct, but connected. Presumably Greeks, like other men, had always pursued their own interests, but, Hegel might argue, they had done so within the accepted rules, and had appealed to generally accepted values in order to justify their demands. Again, although Socrates wants to work out for himself what he ought to do, this does not necessarily mean that he acts in a self-interested way. In Plato's dialogue, the *Crito*, Socrates decides, on rational grounds, to obey the laws of Athens against his immediate interests. What is important about Socrates is that he reflects on the rules, asks why they should be as they are and why we should follow them. His particular answers to these questions are less significant than that he raised them at all.

Nevertheless Hegel regards these three features as connected. Value-conflicts of the first type might eventually give rise to a questioning of the norms as a whole. Again, the view that one should 'know and determine from within oneself what is right and good' easily degenerates in less scrupulous men than Socrates into the view that one can do what one likes. What most men like is what serves their own ambitions and desires. The testing of external constraints by internal constraints leads to the dissolution of all constraints. Thus the growth of purely self-interested conduct goes hand in hand with the emergence of reflective moral autonomy.

It is at this point that Plato, Socrates' pupil and the source of most of our knowledge of Socrates' doctrines,[7] enters the scene. Hegel controversially draws a sharp distinction between the ethical views of Socrates and Plato.

Socrates was a self-conscious individualist, whose moral questioning introduced an alien and disruptive element into Greek life. Plato attempted to
meet this challenge by proposing to extrude moral questioning, as well as
self-interested conduct, from Greek society and restore the harmony of Greek
Sittlichkeit. Socrates constituted, as much as raised, the problem which Plato
was trying to solve, and the fate of Greek society depended on whether or
not some solution could be produced.

Plato's *Republic* is overtly concerned with the questions: 'What is it for
a man to be just?' and 'why should he be just?'. To answer these questions
we should first try to see what it is for a state to be just. For the justice of
a state will be analogous to the justice of a man, and yet, since a state is larger
than a man, it will be easier to see what its justice consists in. The just state
is introduced only to enable us to see more clearly what a just man is like
(*Rep.*, 368 C ff.),[8] Plato answers that an ideally just state is one which is ruled
by a class of trained philosophers, assisted by a class of warriors (*Rep.*, 413E
ff.); neither of these classes is to own property or engage in trade,
manufacturing or agriculture (*Rep.*, 416 D ff.). These tasks are assigned to
a subordinate class of workers (ibid.). None of these three classes is to
encroach on the tasks of any other; each class is to do only its own job (*Rep.*,
434 B ff.). Nor is anyone to be a member of a class for which he is not
naturally equipped (*Rep.*, 415 A ff.). Men are to be assigned to the appropriate
class by the philosopher-rulers (ibid.). The state is just if and only if it consists
of three such classes, each of which does its job and keeps to its position in
the hierarchy (*Rep.*, 434 C 5ff.). Similarly a man's soul consists of three
elements, a rational element, a spirited element and an appetitive element.
These correspond respectively to the philosophers, the warriors and the
workers. A man is just if and only if these three elements are ordered in the
correct manner, that is, if the rational element, assisted by the spirited, is
dominant over the appetitive element (*Rep.*, 443 C 6ff.).[9]

Hegel, reasonably enough, did not accept that Plato's only motive for
introducing the just state was to clarify our vision of justice in a man. He
did so, rather, because he saw that 'justice in its reality and truth is only in
the state', that 'the just man exists only as an ethical member of the state'.[10]
This, of course, would not explain why Plato discussed the just state, as
opposed to states which are in varying degrees unjust. Hegel, for reasons
which will emerge later, tends to see Plato as giving an account of the Greek
state as such rather than of some special sort of Greek state.[11] And neither
Plato nor Hegel seems to believe that a man can be just only if he belongs
to a just state. But why should Hegel (or Plato) believe that a man cannot
be just unless he is a member of some state or other? Hegel becomes obscure
at this point, but he perhaps has three reasons for this doctrine. Firstly, unless
there is a state with laws or, at least, customs, there is no way in which a

man can decide what he ought to do.[12] So a man's being just, his acting rightly rather than wrongly, presupposes his membership of a state. Secondly, a man who was not and never had been a member of any society would as a matter of fact be more like a wild animal than a man.[13] Finally, a man needs to express his purposes in external things and to make them conform to, mirror himself.[14]

Hegel distinguishes Plato's enterprise from two other sorts of venture (GP, II, 106; HP, II, 90). Plato is not constructing or advocating a single supreme moral principle which would tell us the right thing to do in any situation – Hegel himself does not believe this to be possible[15] – nor is he concerned with natural right. Natural-right theorists set out, according to Hegel, from the fiction of a state of nature, in which men have a certain basic character, desires, purposes, and dispositions, and certain basic rights and duties; right obtains in the state of nature. On this postulate they base several conclusions. First, the nature and origins of society and the state are to be explained in terms of the character of men in the state of nature. Second, societies and states are to be assessed in the light of the ethical standard supplied by the state of nature. Third, men still are at bottom as they were in the state of nature; their natural rights and duties, and their natural desires and dispositions persist beneath the accretions with which social life has overlaid them. Moreover, men's natural features are their fundamental features, their essence. Their social aspects are mere refinements. Finally, society and the state are a means for the ultimate end, the individual person. The point of the state is to satisfy the desires and serve the purpose of the individuals who make it up (GP, II, 107f; HP, II 92f.).

Hegel challenges each of these theses. Explanations of society in terms of the state of nature tend to be vacuous, simply attributing to the state of nature whatever features are required, generally social features in disguise, to explain society.[16] Hegel does not compare them with explaining why opium sends you to sleep by referring to its *virtus dormitiva*, but he does compare them with the tendency to explain human capacities by supposing them to be innate ideas (GP, II, 107; HP, II, 92). Secondly, the state of nature cannot supply an ethical standard, since it is not an ethical state; it is an animal state, a war of all against all. Men have no rights and duties in the state of nature. They therefore do not have natural rights which a society might or might not respect. Social life overcomes, reverses nature; it is not a smooth continuation out of it. Thirdly, while there may be psychological states and dispositions of a man which are independent of, and can be described without reference to, his social relationships, these do not constitute the essence of a person. It is rather the socialized man who is the essential man. 'The universal makes him what he is in truth' (GP, II, 108; HP, II, 93). It follows that even if men did have rights and duties in the state of nature, these natural rights and duties would not be authoritative in the social state. Finally, society and the state are not a means for the individual. Those desires and purposes of the individual which are independent of his social state are not important enough to serve as the ultimate end, while the important desires and purposes are social products and therefore not such that society could have been devised as a means for their satisfaction.

Plato, on Hegel's view, 'takes the substantial, the universal [i.e. society or social norms and institutions] as basic. The individual has the universal as his aim, custom and spirit; he acts, wills...for the state. The state is his second nature, his usage and custom' (ibid.). The members of his society are permeated by the social forms. Their desires and purposes are supplied by their society. They follow without question the norms and customs of their society. And they act for the state, they aim at the well-being of their society. Moreover, Plato regards his state as a sort of organism: 'The ethical substance constitutes the spirit, life and essence of individuality and is the foundation. It systematizes itself in a living organic whole; it differentiates itself essentially into its members. The activity of these members is the producing of the whole' (ibid.). The parts of this whole cannot be separated from one another and still remain what they were, nor can we explain the origins and workings of the whole by giving separate and independent accounts of the parts.[17] Plato is, of course, giving an account of a particular sort of society, and from the fact that the natural right theory is inapplicable to it, it does not follow that it is not applicable to any society. But Hegel seems to have held both that the theory is false in general and that it is especially and glaringly inappropriate in the case of the Greek state described by Plato.

Much of Hegel's account is problematic. For example, the fact that a man could not have certain desires, e.g. the desire for a vote, unless he were a member of some society or, even, unless he were a member of some specific type of society does indeed imply that a society cannot have been formed in order to satisfy those desires. But it does not follow that societies cannot be assessed in terms of their ability to satisfy them. A society might be criticized because it fails to satisfy the desires which another society can, or because it generates desires which it is unable to satisfy. It would be implausible too to suppose that a society cannot be criticized if it fails to fulfil the pre-social needs of its members, their desire for food, drink and so on, even if this is not the sole purpose of a society, and even if a society is not to be seen as an instrument or as a means for their satisfaction.

Again it is not clear that Plato is as much at odds with the natural-right doctrines as Hegel represents him to be. For example, the requirements that citizens are to obey the rules unquestioningly and are to act for the state are not incompatible with the view that the point of society and the state is to further the interests of its individual members. It might be argued that a society whose members act only in the interests of the whole society and not for their own self-interest will as a matter of fact serve the interests of its members better than one whose members act in a directly self-interested way. Plato presumably does hold something of this sort (e.g. *Rep.*, 420 B 2f.).

Moreover, Plato does, in a passage which Hegel ignores, attempt to explain why men came together to form a simple community by reference to their pre-social desires and needs, e.g. for food and shelter. These needs persist and are satisfied even within the more elaborate society which he derives from this and the community to which they directly give rise persists in effect as the sphere of the class of workers. The fully developed state is derived from the primitive community by a series of intelligible steps. The growth of the primitive city, and the consequent rise of luxury, disease and warfare generates new problems and needs whose solution requires the tripartition of the state (*Rep.*, 369 B ff.). Since Hegel does not deal with this passage, it is hard to say how it would affect his claim that Plato is not concerned with natural right, but it looks as if the claim would need some modification.

The same is true of another of Hegel's claims, namely that Plato gives no proper philosophical construction of his state, that, for example, he does not 'deduce' the division into classes within his society: 'It appears as outer necessity because such needs are found; it is not developed out of the idea of spirit itself' (*GP*, II, 116; *HP*, II, 100f.). Plato does indeed presuppose that men have certain physical needs, but he does not merely assume that they have needs which only a class of warriors and of philosopher-rulers can satisfy. Rather these needs are generated by the autonomous development of a primitive community concerned initially only with physical needs (*Rep.*, 369 B ff.). This criticism too would require some elaboration, if not modification, in the light of this passage.

An important feature of Hegel's account of Plato is that he does not accept what he represents as the orthodox view, that Plato was proposing an unrealizable ideal. 'Plato's *Republic*, which passes proverbially as an empty ideal, is in essence nothing but an interpretation of the nature of Greek ethical life' (*PhR*, Preface, Knox p. 10). 'In his *Republic*, Plato displays the substance of ethical life in its ideal beauty and truth' (*PhR*, §185 R). This accords with Hegel's view of philosophy in general, particularly with the memorable pronouncements that what is rational is actual and what is actual is rational, and that 'when philosophy paints its grey in grey, then has a shape of life grown old' (*PhR*, Preface, Knox pp. 10 and 13). But it is not easy to see what these doctrines mean or why Hegel accepted them.

In four respects Plato differs from proponents of ideals. In the first place, some ideals, like those of monks or Quakers, are realizable only within a segment of a larger social whole and could not be realized throughout a viable society. Secondly, such ideals are prone to restrict the number of men who can live up to them by attaching too much weight to trivial ordinances. Thirdly, ideals are often inspired by the view that any determinate, forceful activity is likely to involve wrong doing, and see inactivity as the only solution. Finally, some 'idealists' regard any determinate state of affairs as faulty, and therefore perpetually attempt to overthrow the *status quo* with no clear idea of what to put in its place. Plato and his state do not suffer from any of these defects (*GP*, II, 109f.; *HP*, II, 94f.).

Again, there is perhaps a single ideal constitution which every people should progress towards. But this constitution will not suit every people as they now are. It would be absurd to attempt to impose the Prussian constitution on the ancient Greeks or on the Iroquois Indians, since such a constitution would be out of accord with their customs (*Sitten*). There is, then, too, a particular constitution which is ideally suited to a given people at a given stage of its development. This will be in harmony with, or perhaps a little bit in advance of, the customs of that people. Different constitutions will be appropriate for different peoples. Peoples sometimes outgrow their constitutions, and then change must occur; the possibilities are peaceful reform, violent upheaval, foreign domination, and stagnation. Hegel speaks of a constitution as a people's consciousness, its self-knowledge or its concept of itself. Its customs, perhaps, are that people's reality or what it is conscious of. We might compare its customs to its actual linguistic practice and its constitution to a formal grammar of its language, together with, of course, authorities who enforce conformity to that grammar. Plato's state, then, is not the ideal state *simpliciter*, but the appropriate state for his people in their circumstances (*GP*, IIIff.; *HP*, II, 96ff.).

Hegel sometimes speaks as if Plato were merely giving a brief, generalized description of actual Greek society, analysing, but not prescribing. 'Plato does not preach morals, he shows how the ethical moves vitally within itself, displays its functions, its viscera' (*GP*, II, 115; *HP*, II, 100). Part of the point here is that one cannot strictly preach the ethical without thereby betraying it. A community of ethical men, unquestioningly obedient to their social norms, would have no need of preaching. If Plato's state were realized, its members would not be striving to bring about some further ideal. Unlike monks, they would be simply maintaining their on-going society by their activities. But it does not follow from this that Plato himself is not preaching or, at least, prescribing. For Plato himself is not a member of his state nor is he a naive ethical man. He is a man who is choosing between morality and the ethical life, and advocating the establishment or, as Hegel might prefer to say, the maintenance of a purely ethical society rather than one in which men make moral decisions on their own behalf or the *status quo* with all its Socratic impurities.[18]

Nevertheless, Hegel insists, 'the true ideal is not what ought to be actual; it is actual' (*GP*, II, 110; *HP*, II, 95). Plato's state is actual. What he seems to mean by this is that the fundamental structure of existing Greek society remained unchanged in Plato's ideal. Such alterations as are introduced are minor reforms of the surface features of Greek life, reforms which will eliminate destructive tensions and conflict (*GP*, II, 110f.; *HP*, II, 95f.). It would not be too great an over-simplification to suggest that in Hegel's eyes Plato's state is related to existing Greek states as a healthy fully-developed oak tree is related to an underdeveloped, stunted or deformed one. Plato himself thinks of his state as the paradigm of a state, as a proper, healthy state as opposed to diseased or deformed ones. But he is more concerned than Hegel implies to stress the contrast between his just state and other, more or less unjust states. Hegel tends to underplay this feature of Plato's thought, in the light of his belief that at bottom the *Republic* is an exercise in description rather than prescription.

Hegel felt not only that this was the nature of Plato's enterprise, but that this was the only philosophically respectable enterprise open to him, or, indeed, to any political philosopher. 'No one can overleap his time. Its spirit is also his spirit. The point is to know this spirit in its content' (*GP*, III; *HP*, II, 98). Hegel's official view seems to be that history successively instantiates the categories of logic. A society at a given stage of history corresponds to a given phase of logic. For example, Greek society corresponds, roughly, to the category of substance. Similarly the history of philosophy reproduces the structure of logic, and the philosophers of a given period will be at approximately the same stage of logic as their society. It is this logical, categorial structure of a society which is rational and which is not open to ordinary, piecemeal criticism. But even if this were so, it is not clear why a philosopher must have reached only that stage of logic which informs his society, why, for example, Plato could not have proposed and argued for in a Hegelian manner a quite different, 'higher' type of society corresponding to a later phase of logic. At a less metaphysical level, Hegel perhaps felt that no one can coherently describe or imagine a society which is radically different from any with which he is acquainted, let alone argue convincingly in favour of it. If you attempt to cast in doubt or reject all the values and institutions that your fellow-citizens currently accept, then you do not share with them any premises from which you could argue with them. Nor do you have any non-arbitrary premises at all, for there is no other source of reliable moral and political guidance than these shared values and institutions.

It does not follow, however, that a philosopher must simply describe, still less accept, these values and institutions as they stand. For the values and institutions of a society are unlikely to be wholly coherent and they are often seriously discordant with one another. This, according to Hegel, was true of Greek society in Plato's time. Plato's state is designed to suppress and exclude an element of Greek life which was in conflict with Greek *Sittlichkeit*. This element was 'the subjective self-will of individuals, morals; individuals do not act out of respect, reverence for the state, the fatherland, but from their own conviction, according to a moral reflection they grasp a decision from themselves and determine themselves in accordance with it – the modern principle of subjective freedom' (*GP*, II, 114; *HP*, II, 98).[19] Hegel tends to equate this with acting in one's own interests. Though it may lead to this, it should no more be identified with it than acting unreflectively according to the norms of one's society should be equated with acting in the interests of one's society.[20] Nevertheless this principle, on Hegel's view, led to the corruption of Greek states and life. The Greek constitution, laws and customs were unable to accommodate it and eventually the customs had to succumb. Hegel does not intend this to be a tautology, that, because Greek life in its purity lacked this principle, the emergence of the principle ended Greek life in its purity. He means, rather, that because Greek society was unable to withstand, that is either to accommodate or to suppress, this principle and the self-seeking and ambition to which it gave rise, it declined to the point where it could be dominated and supplanted by the Macedonian and Roman empires. Plato's state, he argues, was intended to suppress this principle, and Hegel's discussion of the details of the *Republic* is guided by this thought.

Plato's account of the state displays, according to Hegel's, its inner systematization or articulation. The state is an ethical organism and, like any living organism, it is internally differentiated into organs with distinct functions (*GP*, II, 115f.; *HP*, II, 100). These organs are not independent of or separable from one another and, in some sense or other, they result from the self-differentiation of the organism, much as an apparently homogeneous seed differentiates itself into a plant with different organs.[21] These organs are the three classes, each with its own function. The rulers are concerned with legislation and the overseeing of the whole society. For this reason Hegel identifies them as the universal (*allgemeines*) element in the state; they are concerned with the universal. He regularly describes society as a whole and its objective norms and institutions as universal, in part because they are common to several individuals (*GP*, II, 116; *HP*, II, 100f.). The lowest class, concerned with the provision for physical needs, are identified as the individual (*einzelnes*) element, because they care for what is individual, needs (ibid.). Needs are regarded as individual not because men do not have the same needs. All men need food and drink, and it is these shared needs, not idiosyncratic ones, which the workers satisfy. Rather it is because a man's hunger or thirst is independent of the presence and behaviour of other men, whereas his voting habits, for example, are not. The needs provided for by the workers are pre-social needs. Again, the workers are individual, because, unlike the rulers, each concentrates on some specific task and is not concerned with society as a whole. The idea that the rulers are concerned with the state as a whole, while the workers are concerned only with what is individual is not incompatible with the view that in Plato's state everyone is absorbed in and works for the universal. Each instrumentalist in an orchestra should follow unquestioningly his particular score and the instructions of the conductor, and work for the benefit of the performance as a whole. But the conductor is concerned with and oversees the whole performance in a way that the individual performers do not.[22]

Plato proposes to maintain his state by education, by imbuing individuals with the appropriate norms so that they become customary, a sort of second nature (*GP*, II, 121f.; *HP*, II, 106f.). The rulers both undertake this education and have earlier undergone it. Hegel stresses here Plato's banning of poets, which was proposed in part because their ideas of god were unworthy. Since this measure is not presented by Hegel as primarily intended to suppress subjective freedom, it presents a problem for his view that Plato is not proposing an unrealized ideal. For poetry was an integral part of Greek life and was not excluded from Greek societies. Hegel wants to imply that whereas the poets were once appropriate to Greek *Sittlichkeit*, they no longer were by Plato's time. By then they were taken as an authoritative source of 'universal maxims', as the 'basis of the truth of the ethical'. Earlier they had not been taken in this way and were therefore harmless, but the time had now come for them to be reduced to something 'past, merely historical' (*GP*, II, 122; *HP*, II, 107f.). Plato's exclusion of them is seen, then, simply as a logical next step in the development of Greek society. But some of Plato's arguments, for example those based on the degraded picture of the gods presented by the poets (*Rep.*, 377 C ff.), would clearly warrant the banning of poetry at any earlier time and not simply in Plato's own time. Plato is not merely bringing Greek society up to date, but is proposing, in this respect, a radical reform of it.

Three measures in particular are, on Hegel's view, intended to suppress subjective freedom (*GP*, II, 124 ff.; *HP*, II, 109 ff.). The suppression of such freedom is what Hegel objects to in Plato's state, but it is not entirely clear what he means by it. Apart from the confusion between acting according to one's conscience and acting self-interestedly, it is uncertain whether he meant that Plato sought to render men psychologically incapable of making up their own minds or whether he meant that Plato would prevent men from doing what they would like to do.

The first measure, that men cannot choose the class to which they are to belong, but are assigned to the appropriate class by the rulers, is taken by

Hegel as a straightforward infringement of liberty (*GP*, II, 12f.; *HP*, II, 109f.). It prevents men from doing what they want. Hegel believes on the contrary that a man should be allowed a free choice of occupation or, at least, should be permitted to follow his inclinations.

Hegel's account of the second, the banning of private property, is more complicated (*GP*, II, 125f.; *HP*, II, 110f.). He does not object to it on the ground that it prevents men from doing what they want to do, namely to acquire property. Plato, as he concedes, wanted to exclude property because it was a source of conflict, but more important for Hegel is that private property elevates the individual to independent status and therefore promotes Socratic individualism. The point is not simply that I need physical objects to act upon and to mould, that is to express my freedom. For I do not need to own an object in order to act upon it. Rather, it is that if I own a thing, the relation of ownership between myself and the thing does not obtain in virtue of any special feature of myself or of the thing, apart from the historical fact that I legitimately acquired this thing. By contrast, if I am given something just because I need it and just for so long as I need it (or, indeed, because I deserve it and just for so long as I deserve it), then my relation to the thing is contingent upon special, and perhaps transitory, features of myself and of the thing. Private property abstracts from the particular qualities of individuals in a way that assignment according to need or desert does not. 'In property individuality, the individual consciousness, becomes absolute, or the person is regarded as the being-in-itself without any content ... Everyone is so valid, and I am valid only because all are, or I am valid only as universal; but the content of this universality is fixed individuality' (ibid.).[23] Property thus leads to or accompanies the view that an individual is important as such, apart from any particular feature which he has or the role which he occupies.

A philosopher, Hegel suggests, might well object to private property for two reasons (ibid.). He could in general baulk at the apparent irrationality of a relationship which holds between two things, regardless of the specific features of these things. In particular he might dislike the independent status conferred on individuals, independently of their characteristics and social roles. Hegel replies with the familiar point that if the workers are unable to acquire property, then they will have no incentive to work. This reply would not be to the point if Plato intends also to render them incapable of wanting to pursue their own interests. Only if the workers are already individualists will they require some special incentive apart from the established norms and the welfare of their society. One difficult sentence in Hegel may be intended to meet this objection: 'My capacity for property lies rather in the fact that I am a person' (*GP*, II, 126).[24] The point of this may be that it is the rise of individualism, of 'personhood', which produces the desire for property, rather than the other way about, so that the elimination of property will not abolish individualism, but rather come into conflict with it.

Finally, Plato abolishes marriage (GP, II, 126f.; HP, II, 111f.). It is perhaps odd that Hegel should interpret this as a measure devised to stabilize Greek *Sittlichkeit*, since elsewhere he regards the family as one of the pillars of ethical life.[25] There are two distinct strands in Hegel's thought here. Firstly, the family is seen as a source of individualism in much the same way as property is. A man and his wife are related to each other solely in virtue of their past personal histories and personal affection and not because of any special features which they have. Similarly a person is attached to a particular family and is valued by its other members for himself, just as that individual and not as any particular sort of individual. Secondly, a family is an 'independent whole', an 'extended personality', which may come into conflict both with other families and with the state. This happens in the *Antigone*, where the ethical requirements of the family are at odds with those of the state.[26] Such a situation does not necessarily give rise to individualism, but the conflicts which result from it may, in any case, be damaging, and Hegel does suggest that it is in part through such conflicts of values that men learn to question law and custom and to make conscious decisions whether or not to obey.[27]

By these measures, then, Plato intended to eliminate subjective freedom from Greek life. On Hegel's view, it was neither possible nor desirable that he should succeed, but it is far from clear why this is so. One obstacle to clarity is perhaps Hegel's belief that Plato was not an impractical idealist. For any attempt to show that Plato's state would not work tends to undermine this belief. An example of unclarity is Hegel's attempt to distinguish between Plato's time and modern times. Plato's state, he stresses, is a purely Greek ideal, suitable only for the Greeks at that stage of their history. It is fruitless to ask whether such a state is desirable or possible today, because 'in modern states there is freedom of conscience; each individual can demand to follow his own interests' (GP, II, 114; HP, II, 99). But whether this means that we are now psychologically capable of making up our own minds or that modern states permit us to act on the conclusions we reach, the argument is uncompelling. Modern states are as capable as ancient ones of forbidding or preventing us from acting as we wish, and even of indoctrinating us so that we become incapable of thinking for ourselves. Hegel may simply mean that independent thinking is now more widespread than it was in ancient Greece, and that it is buttressed by Christianity, but apart from this he gives no reason for supposing that Plato's state would have been any more or any less practicable in antiquity than it is today.[28]

Hegel is generally thought of as a practitioner of internal, rather than external, criticism, and he certainly saw himself in this light. He does not test a theory or attitude by applying to it standards or doctrines which its advocates could consistently refuse to accept, but only those which are involved in the theory or attitude itself. All arguments should be *ad hominem*.[29]

It is not easy, however, to find such arguments here. Hegel's basic criticism of Plato is this: 'The true idea is that each moment fully realizes itself, embodies itself and becomes independent, and yet in its independence is sublated for the spirit' (*GP*, II, 127f.; *HP*, II, 113). Everything must have a place, but a place subordinate to the whole, in the properly ordered society: the family, classes, property, the state. In particular, subjective freedom must somehow be combined with an objective order of norms and institutions. Plato's state is onesided, limited. It excludes subjective freedom, individuality, without qualification. The true social order must not straightforwardly exclude and contrast with anything, any more than the true philosophy can exclude any significant philosophical viewpoint, but must include and embrace it in a subordinate position and a modified form.

This approach blurs the distinction between the question whether Plato's state is possible or durable and the question whether it is desirable. Hegel, of course, deliberately refrains from making this distinction. He argues, in effect, that if an ideal is unrealizable then it is undesirable (*GP*, II, 109f.; *HP*, II, 94f.). This corresponds to his apparent equivocation over the question as to whether Plato is describing or prescribing a type of society. Indeed, since Hegel will not assess the desirability of societies in terms of their effects on the individual members of them, it is hard to see how else he could do so except by reference to their internal coherence, and this is intimately connected with their viability. One reply to this criticism is that Plato's state is not as exclusive as Hegel claims. Property is not forbidden entirely, but only to the two upper classes (Rep., 420 A 2f.; 543 A ff.). More importantly, it is quite unclear why Plato could not consistently reject the philosophical approach which underlies the criticism.

Hegel does in fact claim that Plato's state involves a vicious circle. He argues not simply that Plato has failed to accommodate subjective freedom, leaving Plato the option of asking why he should, but that the circle can be broken only by allowing some scope to freedom. 'Public state life depends on customs and customs depend on institutions. Customs cannot be independent of institutions, nor can institutions be directed at customs solely through educational arrangements, religion. Institutions must be seen as the primary thing, by which custom comes about, the way in which institutions are subjective. Plato himself gives us to understand how much contradiction he expects to find' (*GP*, II, 123; *HP*, II, 108f.). Hegel here indicates two problems. First, there is the problem of how Plato's state is to be set up initially. To produce the appropriate customs and attitudes, we need first to set up the institutions which will produce them. But for this to be possible we need people who already have these customs and attitudes, both to man the institutions and, more generally, to acquiesce in their establishment. Plato himself offered no more realistic solution to this problem than to hope that one day an established ruler might also happen to be a philosopher (*Rep.*, 471 C ff.). He believed that there was a problem about setting up his state, but not about maintaining it once it was set up.

Hegel, however, runs this problem into a problem about the maintenance of Plato's state once it is set up. He does this for two reasons. Firstly, he is reluctant to regard Plato as an innovator, who is proposing to found a society. There should, therefore, be no difficulty about its foundation. Secondly, he wants to say that the circle can be broken by accommodating and making use of subjective freedom, the free choices of individuals, within the on-going society. If it were only the foundation of the state that presented problems, he could argue at most that freedom should be exploited in the initiation of the state, but not that it should continue to have a place within it. According to Hegel, the individual should freely insert himself into the objective structure of his society in order to satisfy his needs. '[The individual] sets out from the subjectivity of free self-will, aligns himself with the whole, chooses a class for himself, makes himself an ethical entity' (*GP*, II, 123f.; *HP*, II, 109). Society should be such that 'if I further my ends, I further the ends of the universal, and this in turn furthers my end' (*PhR*, §184 A). But Hegel gives no reason for supposing that Plato's state would have to be like this in order to survive. Even if individuals needed to be offered incentives initially in order to be enticed into accepting it, this does not entail that those individuals or their descendants could not eventually be got to accept it for other reasons. Hegel would need to appeal to empirical facts rather than philosophy to show that Plato's state could not have eliminated the subjective freedom to which Greek society eventually succumbed.

The main reason for Hegel's failure to criticize Plato's state effectively was perhaps his reluctance to concede that Plato was an innovator, proposing an ideal which was not put into practice. Unable to resist the temptation to regard Plato as describing Greek society rather than recommending its reform, he does not clearly distinguish the question whether and why Greek society in fact broke down from the question whether and why Plato's state would have broken down, had it been implemented. Having said that the growth of subjective freedom was the downfall of Greece, he does not seriously confront the question whether the growth of subjective freedom could have been suppressed. In this way Hegel runs together his criticism of Plato with his *post mortem* on Greek society.

Political community and individual freedom in Hegel's philosophy of state

Z. A. PELCZYNSKI

To the best of my knowledge Hegel never once uses the expression 'political community'. He is, in fact, very sparing with the term 'community' (*Gemeinwesen*) itself. It occurs, e.g., in paragraph 150 of the *Philosophy of Right*: 'In an *ethical* community, it is easy to say what man must do, what are the duties he has to fulfil in order to be virtuous; he has simply to follow the well-known and explicit rules of his own situation.' Although the *idea* of community is crucial to his political thought, he is very casual and eclectic about the terms in which to express it. In different contexts he calls it 'substance', 'organism', 'organic whole', 'totality' and 'the universal', *das Allgemeine*.

When Hegel has in mind specifically political community he calls it *der Staat* (the state). His definition of the state is therefore highly stipulative, and quite removed from the conventional meaning of this term. 'The state' for Hegel means any ethical community which is politically organized and sovereign, subject to a supreme public authority and independent from other such communities. Ancient oriental empires, Greek city states, the Roman republic and the modern nation-states are all 'states' in his sense. A few paragraphs after the reference to 'ethical community' in the *Philosophy of Right*, there is a good example of his usage: 'When a father inquired about the best method of educating his son in ethical conduct, a Pythagorean replied: "Make him a citizen of a state with good laws"' (§153). Here, as in innumerable places, Hegel refers to the polis, which was an ethical and political community, simply as 'the state'.

Hegel seems to have been extremely unselfconscious about his esoteric use of the term 'state', so different from the one common in his time and even more today. Only in one place in the *Philosophy of Right* (§267) does he feel the need to distinguish the all-embracing sense of the state as a sovereign ethical community from what he there refers to as 'the strictly political state and its constitution'. 'The strictly political state' is a system of public organs, powers or authorities through which an independent nation, a sovereign community, governs itself.[1] I can think of only one place in the whole corpus of Hegel's writings where the distinction between the esoteric and the common sense of 'the state' is clearly made, and where he offers something that might be taken as a mild apology for his peculiar usage of the term. The place is *Reason in History*, a name sometimes given to the *Introduction* to the *Lectures on the Philosophy of World History*[2]. I would like to quote Hegel's remarks in full.

> The spiritual individual, the nation – in so far as it is internally differentiated so as to form an organic whole – is what we call the state. This term is ambiguous, however, for the state and the laws of the state, as distinct from religion, science, and art, usually have purely political associations. But in this context, the word 'state' is used in a more comprehensive sense, just as we use the word 'realm' to describe spiritual phenomena. A nation should therefore be regarded as a spiritual individual, and it is not primarily its external side that will be emphasised here, but rather what we have previously called the spirit of the nation ... in short, those spiritual powers which live within the nation and rule over it (*LPhWH*, 96).

This is Hegel's clearest admission that the state and its laws 'usually have purely political associations', but that he chooses nevertheless to define it much more widely, to include not just the ethical life of a nation (as he does in the *Philosophy of Right*) but all 'those spiritual powers which live within the nation and rule over it'. Hegel goes on to list these 'spiritual powers' a few pages further on in *Reason in History*:

> A nation's religion, its laws, its ethical life, the state of its knowledge, its other particular aptitudes and the industry by which it satisfies its needs, its entire destiny, and the relations with its neighbours in war and peace – all these are extremely closely connected (*LPhWH*, 101–2).

These two remarks in *Reason in History* are worth quoting in full also for another reason. They draw our attention to an important but to my knowledge never before noticed ambiguity in Hegel's idea of community. In the *Philosophy of Right* it is the narrower concept of ethical life (*Sittlichkeit*), derived from Plato and Aristotle, and Greek experience generally, which underlies his theory of political community. An independent nation is a political community when its members share certain ethical ideals and are united by a generally accepted system of social morality prescribing their duties, roles or functions in society. In other writings it is the wider concept of national spirit (*Volksgeist*) which is the foundation of community life. Derived from Montesquieu, as Hegel generously acknowledges in many places,[3] it is not only a wider but a more modern idea. It corresponds in most respects to our contemporary concept of culture. The state from this viewpoint is a political community because it is a cultural community, because its constitution is grounded in a national culture, because its political institutions are deeply interwoven and interdependent with all the other aspects of culture, and similarly express the genius, character or 'principle' of national culture.[4] While Montesquieu is justly credited with the discovery of the idea of political culture, and Tocqueville with its brilliant use in *Democracy in America*, it seems to me that Hegel too deserves some recognition for the development and application of Montesquieu's insight.[5]

Hegel's primary source of inspiration and model of political community, however, is to be found in Plato and not Montesquieu. Hegel respected Aristotle as a metaphysician and in several ways was deeply influenced by him, but he thought poorly of his practical philosophy. In Hegel's *Lectures on the History of Philosophy* (the Haldane-Simson translation in three volumes published 1892–6)[6] Hegel gives Plato's *Republic* twenty-six pages of print, compared with less than four that he gives to Aristotle's *Politics*. He regarded Aristotle's main political work as a common-sense but pedantic and largely empirical treatise, while the *Republic* seemed to him a work of true genius and a most profound theory expressing the essence of Greek society and culture (*PhR*, Preface). The fundamental presupposition of the *Republic* and ancient Greek political life generally (Hegel argues) was the absolute priority of the community over the individual. Hegel refers to it usually as the 'substantiality' of the polis or 'the substantial character of ethical life' in Greece. The ancient Greek thought of himself as a political animal by nature. He saw himself as a son of his city, a member of an ongoing and historical community and not as an independent individual, facing other similar individuals in an atomistic state of nature or some rather loosely structured society which they had voluntarily established. A Greek citizen was so wholly immersed in the politics and ethos of his city that he cared little for himself. He guided his actions not by his self-interest or some private conception of happiness and virtue, but by the traditional ideals of his city which he accepted without questioning.[7] One could say that he had no individuality in the full sense of the word; he was merely an instrument, a member of an organism, which acted through him in pursuit of its own universal ends.

We are accustomed to take our start from the fiction of a condition of nature, which is truly no condition of mind, of rational will, but of animals among themselves: wherefore Hobbes has justly remarked that the true state of nature is a war of every man against his neighbour ... The fiction of a state of nature starts from the individuality of the person, his free will, and his relation to other persons according to this free will. What has been called natural law is law in and for the individual, and the condition of society and the state has been looked upon as the means of the individual person, who is the fundamental end. Plato, in direct contrast with this lays as his foundation the substantial, the universal, and he does this in such a way that the individual as such has this very universal as his end, and the subject has his will, activity, life and enjoyment in the state, so that it becomes his second nature, his habits and his customs. This ethical substance which constitutes the spirit, life and being of individuality, and which is its foundation, systematizes itself into a living, organic whole, and at the same time it differentiates itself into its members, whose activity, brings the whole into existence (*LHPh*, II, 92–3).

The basis of Plato's *Republic* was the ideal of justice, defined as keeping one's proper place in the city or fulfilling the traditional duties of one's station in life; it was the honouring of the established social morality of the city, its ethical life or *Sittlichkeit*. This, in general, was the true Greek ethical ideal, but in the *Republic* according to Hegel it was given an unusually oppressive interpretation. Plato was conscious of elements of self-interest and critical reflexion, which he feared had undermined the existence of the polis, and he sought to counter them through restrictions on marriage, property, the choice of career and other rights, and the despotic power of the guardians. The fact that he was prepared to go to such length, Hegel argues, revealed a fundamental defect of Greek ethical life – its indifference to 'subjectivity' or 'subjective freedom'. It needed centuries of cultural and social development, above all the rise of Christianity, for the ideal of subjective freedom to become recognized and accepted, at least in the Western world.

The thinker in Hegel's opinion who expressed the ideal most clearly in the context of modern secular life and society was Jean-Jacques Rousseau. Rousseau's political thought is therefore the antithesis of Plato's, so to say the opposite pole of the community–individuality relationship. On Hegel's rather extreme interpretation Rousseau asserts the absolute primacy of the individual over the community. The individual, his conscience and his will, however arbitrary, are the foundation of society and the state. Traditions, customs, established institutions and laws have no validity whatever unless men have accepted them voluntarily. The essence of human liberty consists precisely in this voluntary acceptance. In the *Lectures on the History of Philosophy* Hegel sets up the antithesis of Plato and Rousseau with great clarity.

The lack of subjectivity is really the defect of the Greek ethical idea... Plato has not recognized knowledge, wishes, and resolutions of the individual, nor his self-reliance, and has not succeeded in combining them with his idea; but justice demands its rights for this just as much as it requires the higher elucidation of the same, and its harmony with the universal. The opposite to Plato's principle is the principle of the conscious free will of individuals which in later times was more especially by Rousseau raised to prominence: the necessity of the arbitrary choice of the individual, as individual, the outward expression of the individual (*LHPh*, II, 114, 115).

Later in the *Lectures*, in a short section which does little justice to Hegel's considered estimate of Rousseau's significance in the history of political philosophy, Hegel quotes the famous words of *Du contrat social* with complete approval (if somewhat incorrectly): 'liberty is the distinguishing feature of man. To renounce one's liberty is to renounce one's manhood' (*LHPh*, III, 401). And a page later he writes:

The principle of freedom emerged in Rousseau, and gave man, who apprehends himself as infinite this infinite strength. This provides the transition to the Kantian philosophy, which theoretically considered made the principle its foundation (*LHPh*, III, 402).

Rousseau rejected the validity of all established morality, religion, customs and institutions. Nothing external to the individual could claim any authority. His personal conscience was the supreme judge of morality. Only that to which the individual gave his free consent was binding on his will. The will of each individual, unrestricted and unguided by anything except his own deeply felt conception of virtue or the common good, was the foundation of law and political association. There was nothing to ensure that the General Will *de facto* differed from the will of all or the will of the majority. Rousseau confused the truth that there could be no freedom without the consent of one's mind and will with the very different proposition that such consent constituted freedom. Without an external, objective, rational principle to guide our will it becomes arbitrary and amoral. By systematically rejecting all established order as the source of such principles Rousseau ended with no ethical leg to stand on. The logical consequence of Rousseau's approach when followed in practice was the dissolution of all society, community and state. In a long passage in the *Philosophy of Right* Hegel attributes the excesses of the French Revolution to Rousseau's ideas on will, consent and freedom, and to 'the reduction of the union of individuals in the state to a contract and therefore to something based on their arbitrary will':

... when these abstract conclusions came into power, they afforded for the first time in human history the prodigious spectacle of the overthrow of the constitution of a great actual state and its complete reconstruction *ab initio* on the basis of pure thought alone, after the destruction of all existing and given material. The will of its refounders was to give it what they alleged was a purely rational basis, but it was only abstractions that were being used; the Idea [the true concept of community] was lacking; and the experiment ended in the maximum of frightfulness and terror (*PhR*, §258).

The same idea of course Hegel had expressed thirteen years earlier in the brilliant chapter on 'Absolute Freedom and Terror' in the *Phenomenology of Spirit* (1807).

Hegel's own political philosophy may be seen as his reply to Rousseau's conception of individual freedom or (to put it another way) as an attempt to do justice both to Plato's and to Rousseau's insights into the human condition. *The Philosophy of Right* is the most fully-developed and the most theoretical statement of Hegel's own position and offers us what he believes is a theory of political community adequate to the modern world. Despite its schematic form and extremely difficult and obscure terminology there is unfortunately no better single place in which to explore Hegel's ideas on political community.

Hegel tries to come to terms with the truth of Rousseau's – and Kant's – moral position – the concept of an autonomous subject whose essential freedom consists in not being forced to accept anything as valid unless his conscience, will and reason have given consent to it – in three major but distinct ways. The first concerns the construction of his theory of political community as we find it in the *Philosophy of Right*. There, in the long introduction, Hegel starts with the concept of the individual will (as Rousseau required that one should) and not with the Platonic 'substantial' ethical, legal and political order. He believes, and indeed argues, that such normative order (*Recht*, 'law' or 'right' as he generally calls it) must be proved to be in some deep philosophical sense the creation of the individual will, the outcome of its immanent development towards full freedom, if it is to have legitimacy in the modern world. In this philosophical endeavour he may have learned something from Hobbes – beside Rousseau the only modern political philosopher Hegel takes seriously[8] – who in his 'rational generation of the commonwealth' in *The Leviathan* also starts from the abstract individual and deduces the necessity and authority of the state from the will of the multitude of such individuals.

The second major way in which Hegel seeks to meet the challenge of Rousseau is by developing, within the framework of his theory of political community, a theory of 'civil society' as its distinct but necessary aspect ('moment' in the Hegelian jargon). In the city-states of ancient Greece and in republican Rome, Hegel believes, citizens enjoyed freedom only in so far as they participated in the political life of their community and through their actions – in peace or war – sustained its existence and furthered its welfare. The unhampered pursuit of private, selfish interests, although it made an appearance at the end of the Hellenic era and was institutionalized in civil law in the era of the Roman empire, was not conceived as freedom by the ancients. It is a peculiarly modern idea of freedom – civil or *bourgeois* rather than political or citizen freedom – and it creates a new form of interdependence among men. Instead of men aiming consciously at the common good, they now aim at their own good, the acquisition of property or the furtherance of individuality. But, without realizing it, they indirectly satisfy the needs or promote the interests of other men and establish new kinds of social bonds.

The Greeks were still unacquainted with the abstract right of our modern states, that isolates the individual, allows of his acting as such, and yet, as an invisible spirit, holds all its parts together. This is done in such a way, however, that in no one is there properly speaking either the consciousness of, or the activity for the whole; but because the individual is really held to be a person, and all his concern is the protection of his individuality, he works for the whole without knowing how. It is a divided activity in which each has only his part, just as in a factory no one makes a whole but only a part, and does not possess skill in other departments, because only a few are employed in fitting the different parts together. It is free [i.e. republican] nations alone that have the consciousness of and activity for the whole; in modern times the individual is only free for himself as such, and enjoys citizen freedom alone – in the sense of that of a *bourgeois* and not a *citoyen*. We do not possess two separate words to mark this distinction. The freedom of citizens in this signification is the dispensing with universality, the principle of isolation; but it is a necessary moment unknown to ancient states (*LHPh*, II, 209).

In the *Philosophy of Right* Hegel uses the term 'civil society' to describe this particular dimension of the modern state as a political community – the 'civil' sphere in which individuals seek to satisfy each others' needs through work, production and exchange; in which there is a thorough-going division of labour and a system of social classes; and in which law courts, corporate bodies and public regulatory and welfare authorities ('the police') promote security of property, livelihood and other rights. This system of inter-dependence, says Hegel, 'may be *prima facie* regarded as the external state, the state based on need, the state as the Understanding envisages it' (*PhR*, §183), but only *prima facie*.

   The state in the *proper* sense of the word – as a sovereign political unit, which is also an ethical and cultural community – implies more than 'a system of needs', civil rights and social welfare. It implies an institutional public forum in which matters concerning the community as a whole are debated and decided upon, and the decisions carried out by the government. In this public or political arena the needs of civil society and of the national community are appraised and evaluated, and the unity of private interests and community values is realized in a conscious and organized manner.

The state is the actuality of concrete freedom. But concrete freedom consists in this, that personal individuality and its particular interests not only achieve their complete development and gain explicit recognition for their right (as they do in the sphere of the family and civil society) but, for one thing, they also pass over of their own accord into the interest of the universal, and, for another thing, they know and will the universal; they even recognize it as their own substantive mind; they take it as their end and aim and are active in its pursuit. The result is that the universal does not prevail or achieve completion except along with particular interests and through the co-operation of particular knowing and willing; and individuals likewise do not live as private persons for their own ends alone, but in the very act of willing these they will the universal in the light of the universal, and their activity is consciously aimed at none but the universal end. The principle of modern states has prodigious strength and depth because it allows the principle of subjectivity to progress to its culmination in the extreme of self-subsistent personal particularity, and yet at the same time brings it back to the substantive unity and so maintains this unity in the principle of subjectivity itself (*PhR*, §260).

We are not concerned with the details of Hegel's conception of 'the political state and its constitution', the political organization of the modern national community. After the breath-taking conceptualization of the modern state in §260, Hegel's description of its political organization comes rather as an anti-climax. The supreme public authority consists of hereditary monarchy, an executive of ministers and higher civil servants responsible to the king, a representative body based on estates and corporations, and a system of public opinion or (as he puts it) 'public communication' (§319). Through this political mechanism and the mechanism of civil society the 'abstract' freedom of the individual, conceived by Rousseau in complete isolation from all ethical, social and political context, is made 'concrete'. The individual finds a scope both for his personal interests and subjective choices and for the disinterested service to the ethical ideals and public interests of the community. He is (as Hegel is fond of expressing it) a *bourgeois* by virtue of belonging to the civil realm but a *citoyen* because of his membership of the political realm.

The third major way in which Hegel responds to Rousseau's challenge is by developing in the *Philosophy of Right* a theory of freedom, which is more adequate than Rousseau's own ideas. I use the term theory deliberately, because it is not just a single alternative concept of freedom, say 'positive' freedom, which Hegel offers us instead, but a whole series of separate but related concepts linked together in a systematic way.

At the heart of Rousseau's political philosophy lies the well-known conundrum which Hegel, in the *Lectures on the History of Philosophy*, quotes in full in German and the original French.

The problem is to find a form of association which will defend and protect with the whole common force the person and goods of each associate, and in which each, while uniting himself with all, may still obey himself alone, and remain as free as before.[9]

Hegel denies that Rousseau has succeeded in solving the conundrum. Man cannot 'remain as free as before' after entering the political community. He must either restrict his freedom or transform its nature. Starting from a will that is only potentially free, he must develop it to its full capacity – to make it actually free, in the community. He will then not be 'as free as before', but *more* free; he will have achieved a higher, more adequate and more satisfying type of freedom – true, real or actual freedom. Many of Rousseau's interpreters have seen him as moving in the same general direction as Hegel. As a result of the social contract man no longer 'obeys himself alone' but the 'general will', which is both his own higher will, and the will of the community of like-minded citizens, and is articulated and expressed through the mechanism of direct popular legislation in a republican state. But if this is Rousseau's solution, Hegel rejects it as unsatisfactory; he denies that Rousseau can logically arrive at a conception of a general will which genuinely transcends particular wills.

The merit of Rousseau's contribution to the research for a rational basis of the state is that by adducing the will as the principle of the state, he is adducing a principle which has thought both for its form and content, a principle indeed which is thinking itself... Unfortunately, however, as Fichte did later, he takes the will only in an indeterminate form as the individual will, and he regards the universal will not as the absolutely rational element in the will but only as a 'general' will which proceeds out of the individual will as out of conscious will (*PhR*, §258).

In other words Rousseau's general will remains an artificial construct, the will of all or majority will, instead of becoming the living ethos of a political community which Hegel argues is 'the absolutely rational element in the will'.

In his solution of the problem of liberty in the *Philosophy of Right* Hegel enlists the help of his speculative philosophical method. He treats freedom as a concept which develops dialectically, as a result of contradictions inherent in its own nature and so unfolds new features at different stages of development until the process is completed and 'the idea of freedom' – the full actualization of the concept – is reached in the structure of the rational modern state. The movement is from an 'abstract' concept of freedom, linked to a single individual will, to a 'concrete freedom' actualized in a political community as a rational system of wills. In this essay I shall not follow Hegel's footsteps faithfully, i.e. dialectically. Apart from the enormous difficulty and obscurity of the dialectic method I believe that it does not really work in the *Philosophy of Right*. Hegel does not succeed in proving the *necessity* of transition from one stage to another, and his attempt to do so produces many tortured and implausible arguments. I shall nevertheless follow Hegel's stages of development, restating and simplifying them somewhat, and hoping in this way to throw sufficient light on his solution of the individuality-community problem.

Hegel's conception of freedom might perhaps be called 'contextual', though this is a term which to my knowledge has not been applied to his or any other idea of freedom. I mean by this that Hegel conceives freedom always in a social context or more accurately in the context of human interaction. The structure of such interaction constitutes the context of freedom in which it becomes something concrete and definite, an actuality rather than a mere idea. In pursuing Hegel's line of inquiry it is possible to distinguish four major kinds of freedom and four corresponding contexts or models of human interaction. These are: natural, ethical, civil and political, and I propose to look at them in this order.

Natural freedom

The foundation of the Hegelian theory of freedom rests on his concept of the will. Will is not a separate faculty, distinct from reason; thought and will are simply two aspects or modes of reason: 'the will is . . . a special way of thinking, thinking translating itself into existence, thinking as the urge to give itself existence' (PhR, §4 A). In choosing, deciding and acting a man thinks, reflects and uses concepts; he manifests or expresses his rationality, which is his essential characteristic. The way a man views himself, the image he has of himself or, more adequately, the conception he has of himself as a human being determines what kind of will he has and therefore what kind of interaction with other men is possible for him. Freedom is therefore bound up with self-consciousness and true freedom presupposes true self-consciousness.

The self-consciousness which purifies its object, content, and aim, and raises them to the universality effects this as thinking getting its own way in the will. Here is the point at which it becomes clear that it is only as thinking intelligence that the will is genuinely a will and free. The slave does not know his essence, his infinity, his freedom; he does not know himself as human in essence; and he lacks this knowledge of himself because he does not think himself. This self-consciousness which apprehends itself through thinking as essentially human, and thereby frees itself from the contingent and the false, is the principle of right, morality, and all ethical life (PhR, §21R).

The will itself, at its most basic, is a complex idea; in the simplest act of willing Hegel distinguishes three elements or 'moments'. According to Hegel's theory of 'subjective spirit' foreshadowed in impulse and sentiment, which largely determine our conduct in childhood. At the level of development at which will and thought can be clearly distinguished from desire and feeling an act of will contains according to Hegel: (1.) 'the element of pure indeterminacy or that pure reflection of the ego into itself which involves the dissipation of every restriction and every content' (PhR, §5). This is the element of withdrawal from, or rejection of, all external determinators, an assertion of the will's independence vis-à-vis the external world.

When the will's self-determination consists in this alone, or when representative thinking regards this side by itself as freedom and clings to it, then we have negative freedom or freedom as the Understanding conceives it (*PhR*, §5).

(2.) The second moment, 'the particularization of the ego', consists in the ego giving itself 'differentiation, determination and positing a determinacy as a content and object' (§6). This content may be something natural – a need or desire – or something rational – some thought or principle of action. The determination or focussing of the ego on something definite or particular, the self-identification of the ego with it, constitutes the second, 'positive' element involved in willing, the second partial but essential aspect of the will.

(3.) 'The will is the unity of both these moments . . . It is the self-determination of the ego, which means that at one and the same time the ego posits itself as its own negative, i.e. as restricted and determinate, and yet remains by itself, i.e. in its self-identity and universality' (i.e. as a source of all determinations). 'This is the freedom of the will and it constitutes the concept or substantiality of the will, its weight so to speak, just as weight constitutes the substantiality of a body' (§7). Differently put, an act of will implies an agent capable of rejecting all courses of action except the one that he really chooses to follow.

When a man is so self-determined but the only content of his will – the only source of his determinations – are his impulses, appetites and desires he has what Hegel calls an 'immediate or natural will' (§11). Such a will does not act according to its rational nature although it is capable of utilitarian rationality; Hegel admits that impulses can be compared and evaluated in the light of experience and selected on grounds of satisfaction or happiness (§20). The indeterminacy of the will in the absence of a truly rational criterion of choice constitutes 'arbitrariness' (*Willkür*). Such indeterminate, arbitrary will has sometimes been considered a paradigm of free will, but this is a serious mistake in Hegel's view.

The choice which I have is grounded in the universality of the will, in the fact that I can make this or that mine. This thing that is mine is particular in content and therefore not adequate to me and so is separate from me; it is only potentially mine, while I am the potentiality of linking myself to it. Choice, therefore, is grounded in the indeterminacy of the ego and the determinacy of a content. Thus the will, on account of this content, is not free, although it has an infinite aspect in virtue of its form. No single content is adequate to it and in no single content is it really at grips with itself. Arbitrariness implies that the content is made mine not by the nature of my will but by chance. Thus I am dependent on this content, and this is the contradiction lying in arbitrariness. The man in the street thinks he is free if it is open to him to act as he pleases, but his very arbitrariness implies that he is not free. When I will what is rational, then I am acting not as a particular individual but in accordance with the concept of ethics in general. In an ethical action, what I vindicate is not myself but the thing (*PhR*, §15A).

In other words, true freedom is ethical freedom and can only be reached in an ethical community. Because the arbitrary wills of men do not coincide when they act capriciously, an orderly, structured society of natural men is impossible. It can only be conceived as an abstraction, 'a state of nature', in which impulse and violence reign unchecked, a Hobbesian state of 'war of all against all' in which life is 'nasty, brutish and short' and from which man should seek to escape by all means. Hegel regards 'natural freedom' as the freedom peculiar to such a state of nature; it is the only freedom which independent, egocentric and impulse-driven individuals can possibly have when they find themselves in a shared physical space. However, arbitrary choice has a place in a rational normative order, as Hegel admits in his account of civil society; in fact it is one of its fundamental constituents.

Ethical freedom

In order to have a minimum kind of stable interaction possible it is necessary that all men should recognize certain rules or principles of action, and follow them in practice. The minimum amount of rules that a rational agent will recognize and accept as rational, will obviously be those which safeguard his life, limb and possessions, and which guarantee to him an area of activity free from the invasion and interference of others. Within this area each man can do what he pleases and can exercise his natural, immediate or arbitrary will to the fullest extent compatible with an equal opportunity of everybody else in society to do the same. The system of such rational rules, based on reciprocity and a necessary minimum of restriction, Hegel calls 'abstract right'. It is really the natural law of the seventeenth and eighteenth centuries, which was based on the revival of Roman law; in his discussions of the Roman empire Hegel makes it clear that the idea of law as defining and protecting private rights of individuals was discovered precisely in that epoch of world history.[10]

Hegel's analysis of abstract right and its component elements of personality (capacity for rights), property, contract and wrongdoing in the *Philosophy of Right* add much to our understanding of his conception of freedom. Hegel bases the system of personal rights on man's appropriation of natural objects and the recognition of possessions as rightful property by other men. By appropriating things man rises above nature and asserts his independence as a free agent: 'a person is a unit of freedom aware of its sheer independence' (*PhR*, §35A). However, the principles of abstract right are 'actualized' in the positive legal system of civil society and thus become a part of the broader normative order of *Sittlichkeit*. They need not be discussed separately.[11]

The same applies to the sphere of morality which in Hegel's view forms another element of ethical life. By morality Hegel means conduct determined by one's conscience, noble intentions or subjective judgment of what is absolutely good. Abstract right (and the positive law based upon it) is indifferent to motives and merely requires external conformity to objective rules of conduct. The

question about the self-determination and motive of the will...now enters...in connection with morality. Since man wishes to be judged in accordance with his own self-determined choices, he is free in this relation to himself whatever the external situation may impose upon him...Man's worth is estimated by reference to his inward action and hence the standpoint of morality is that of freedom aware of itself (*PhR*, §106A).

As we have already seen this is the conception of freedom Hegel ascribes to Rousseau and Kant and criticizes as inadequate – false in theory and disastrous in practice. However, as an element of *Sittlichkeit* it has an essential place in modern social and political life. It is a necessary corrective to all normative structures based on positive law, conventional morality and traditional institutions.

Sittlichkeit is the real context in which men achieve freedom or self deter-mination. It is a structure of human interaction based on established laws and institutions which have survived the test of experience but also theoretical scrutiny. It is the actual, social mechanism through which men are shaped into ethical agents – creatures *in practice* acting according to laws, recognizing and fulfilling obligations, sometimes sharing aims and purposes with other men, and pursuing them through their joint endeavours. When Hegel speaks of ethical life as a 'substance' and men as its 'accidents' he wishes to draw our attention to the thoroughgoing way in which ethical life moulds man's nature or 'socializes' individuals.[12] *Sittlichkeit* comprises the existing nor-mative world, the historical world of human relations and ideals, and is so to speak the soil in which abstract right and morality grow. Without it the other two are meaningful only as hypothetical conditions or abstract models of human interaction.

The right and the moral cannot exist independently; they must have the ethical as their support and foundation, for the right lacks the moment of subjectivity, while morality in turn possesses that moment alone, and consequently both the right and the moral lack actuality by themselves (*PhR*, §141A).

In concrete historical terms the right and the moral are simply 'moments' or aspects of *Sittlichkeit*, which develop within the matrix of man's traditional social life in the course of world history, in the modern era, and enrich the primitive, simple, undifferentiated customary ethics with new and important elements: self-interest and conscience or, in Hegelian terminology, 'particularity' and 'subjectivity'. In terms of European culture *Sittlichkeit* is the ethical existence of the modern European man when he has become aware of his individuality, asserted its rights in theory and practice, and at the same time has accepted the necessity of an objectively existing ethical order in which his individuality is realized.

Looked at from another angle ethical life is the sum total of the determinants of the will – the ethical norms, rules or principles of actions which provide the substance of human decisions in so far as they are the acts of concrete thinking, choosing and willing agents. The key normative idea of *Sittlichkeit* is *duty* (*Pflicht*).

In *Sittlichkeit* the agent is faced with clusters of duties arising out of his concrete social position, e.g. as husband or father, employer or employee, teacher or student, member of an estate, profession or corporation, a voter, a parliamentary representative or a civil servant. These duties are not abstract or general as Kantian categorical imperatives are; they are contextual, particularized, tied to our special social roles, dependent on the sphere of activity in which we are engaged. The more complex, articulated and developed a structure society or community forms, the wider is the range of roles available to its individual members, but also the more elaborate the system of duties which ethically bind them. In other words duties are the content of laws, institutions, organizations and communities which together make up the structure of an ethical community. And in so far as they have been internalized as habits and dispositions, they are the content of volitions (cp. *PhR*, §150R).

Hegel defines the freedom peculiar to *Sittlichkeit* ('ethical freedom') in terms of duty. This is paradoxical only if we accept the Hobbesian view that duties bind us and restrict our freedom of movement. But for Hegel there is no paradox.

The bond of duty can appear as a restriction only on indeterminate subjectivity or abstract freedom, and on the impulses either of the natural will or of the moral will which determines its indeterminate good arbitrarily. The truth is, however, that in duty the individual finds his liberation; first, liberation from dependence on mere natural impulse and from the depression which as a particular subject he cannot escape in his moral reflections on what ought to be and what might be; secondly, liberation from the indeterminate subjectivity which, never reaching reality or the objective determinacy of action, remains self-enclosed and devoid of actuality. In duty the individual acquires his substantive freedom (*PhR*, §149).

In the Addition to this paragraph he concludes:

Thus duty is not a restriction on freedom, but only on freedom in the abstract, i.e. on unfreedom. Duty is the attainment of our essence, the winning of *positive* freedom.

This conception of freedom as the conscientious acceptance and fulfilment of one's ethical obligations (in Bradley's famous phrase 'my station and its duties') may at first sight appear somewhat unattractive. Even if Hegel's perfect freedom was not simply the obedience to the Prussian state that it has sometimes been alleged to be, this kind of 'substantial' or 'positive' freedom appears compatible with all sorts of situations in which there is very little liberty as it is generally understood by liberals or democrats. A traditional patriarchial society, a feudal monarchy or a modern collectivist, highly regulated state would all seem happily to fit Hegel's conception of an ethical order. But to think that would be to ignore the peculiar modern dimensions of *Sittlichkeit* represented by abstract right and morality, which have just been mentioned. To count as true *Sittlichkeit* the ethical order in our own epoch must be shot through with personal rights and spheres of autonomy, and be acceptable to individual conscience. It must (in other words) incorporate the principles of particularity and subjectivity (cp. *PhR*, §260 quoted above).

   Hegel develops this point at great length in the *Philosophy of Right* in the sections of ethical life dealing with civil society and the state, but a word must be said about his concept of family which is, in fact, the basic form of ethical life. The family (i.e. the modern family) also has a subjective dimension — for example, in the free choice of partners in marriage or the decision to beget children. It may also satisfy particular needs and desires of individuals for companionship, affection, emotional security and sexual gratification; to some extent it still has an economic function. Yet the dominant elements even in the modern family are 'universality' and 'objectivity'. It is a community which, despite love and affection, often faces its members as something burdensome, something which essentially restricts their arbitrary will. It requires of everybody frequent acts of self-sacrifice and the submersion of particularity in a common life. It is also, for the children at least, a necessity they cannot easily escape. The family is the only community in the modern world where *Sittlichkeit* in its primordial sense operates in a more or less pure form through precept, habit, unconscious imitation and other devices; these shape the individual's natural will and teach him the elements of ethical life — the recognition and acceptance of multifarious duties and moral discipline over desires and appetites, a discipline which is external to start with, but gradually becomes internalized as self-discipline.

   In one sense *Sittlichkeit* pervades all aspects of social life, all relations, institutions, organizations and communities; it is so to speak their ethical substratum. But in the modern world it takes on the shape of two distinct ethical *systems* – complex and interdependent ('organic') social wholes – the civil and the political order. In the latter, as in the family, the universal and the substantial elements predominate.*

Civil freedom

By contrast with the family and the political community the elements of particularity and subjectivity (self-interest and personal choice) come to the fore in, and are the dominant characteristics of, civil society. In civil society men interact with the minimum of ethical or legal constraints. In §206 of the *Philosophy of Right* Hegel observes that in modern society, in the choice of a career or trade (and therefore class or estate membership), 'the essential and final and determining factors are subjective opinions and the individual arbitrary will, which win in this sphere their right, their merit and their dignity'. In Plato's *Republic* and in the ancient world generally (as Hegel points out in *PhR*, §206R) one's social status was largely determined by the accident of birth or by the fiat of a despotic authority, free choice of one's role in society was not recognized or secured by appropriate law and institutions as it is in the modern civil society.

... when subjective particularity is upheld by the objective order in conformity with it and is at the same time allowed its rights, then it becomes the animating principle of the entire civil society, of the development alike of mental activity, merit, and dignity. The recognition and the right that what is brought about by reason of necessity in civil society and the state shall at the same time be effected by the mediation of the arbitrary will is the more precise definition of what is primarily meant by freedom in common parlance (*PhR*, §206R).

'Freedom in common parlance', or what one might call 'civil freedom' in the context of civil society, implies for Hegel the presence of various civil and economic rights, the right of association, the right to a trial by jury, the right to promote group interests through corporations, and the right to public assistance and protection against misfortune or the vagaries of the market. Many of them represent the enactment and institutionalization of the sphere of abstract right – the realm of legal prohibitions which make it possible for men to act without getting into each others' way. In §230 he seems to anticipate the rise of the so-called social or welfare state rights because he argues that 'the right actually present in the particular requires... that the securing of every single person's livelihood and welfare be treated and

---

* This is argued fully in M. Westphal's essay, where Hegel's concept of the family is also discussed in some detail.

actualized as a right, i.e. that particular welfare as such be treated'. 'The police' in his special sense of the word and the corporation are concerned with the security of such social rights.

If we consider the question of duties, we can see that civil society with its complex and increasingly articulated structure provides individuals with a host of new social roles and ethical duties. They are not left to custom or convention alone. They are formulated in clear and unambiguous laws. Positive law, when rationally reformed, ensures that our actual social obligations do not contradict the principles of abstract right and morality, e.g. do not involve slavery, serfdom, arbitrary restrictions on property, compulsory religious attendance or membership of a religious sect. As a self-conscious ethical agent the modern man accepts his obligations gladly and performs them willingly. But he does nevertheless make a sacrifice of a part of his individuality in so doing. Modern community, so to speak, compensates the individual for this sacrifice by furthering his self-interest, by protecting his private rights and welfare, by caring for him as an individual. And this care is extended to him equally and universally as a man, irrespective of religion or nationality, as his basic human right (cf. *PhR*, §209R).

Political freedom

The culminating point of the development of individual will towards freedom in the *Philosophy of Right* is the political realm, the sphere of the supreme public authority or 'the strictly political state'. It would seem to follow that 'political freedom' — the ethical freedom corresponding to this sphere of interaction — is the highest form of human freedom. We find, however, that 'political freedom' is an elusive concept in the *Philosophy of Right* and Hegel has rather more to say about it in his minor political works, especially those which he wrote before he took up residence in Berlin. The most likely explanation is that the completion of the *Philosophy of Right* coincided with the onset of reaction in Prussia, after a period of considerable liberalism, and it is more than likely that prudence (or political expediency) tempered Hegel's theoretical zeal in this area of his political philosophy.★ In fact the clearest acknowledgement of the importance of public freedom occurs in the *Philosophy of Right* not in the section on the constitution of the state, but in the context of Hegel's discussion of the corporation, which is an institution of civil society. The primary work of the corporation is to achieve security and other sectional benefits for its members, to promote group interests, but it incidentally fosters various ethical characteristics in its members — a sense of honesty, group pride, a sense of belonging and the consciousness of a common end for which they are united. 'As family was

★ This point is argued at length in K.-H. Ilting's first essay.

the first, so the Corporation is the second ethical root of the state, the one planted in civil society' (*PhR*, §225).

Under modern political conditions, the citizens have only a restricted share in the public business of the state, yet it is essential to provide men – ethical entities – with work of a public character over and above their private business. This work of a public character, which the modern state does not always provide, is found in the Corporation...It is in the Corporation that unconscious compulsion first changes into a known and ethical mode of life (*PhR*, §255A).

In the strictly political section of the *Philosophy of Right* we get only a vague idea what political freedom means and why it is the culminating moment in the development of the will to complete self-determination. Although Hegel purports to offer a dialectical argument, it is clear that for pragmatic reasons he does not think that the opportunity to exercise political freedom need be as wide as the scope to enjoy civil freedom, and makes political freedom a universal right of all citizens only in a very attenuated form. Effectively political participation is a privilege of an elite.

There are a number of reasons why Hegel nevertheless thinks the state to be vitally important for freedom and why it is in the state, a *politically* organized and governed community, that human freedom reaches its fullest embodiment. Let us imagine that we are members of a Hegelian civil society which appears to be fully rational and developed, in that it genuinely respects and promotes our particular interests and subjective choices through an appropriate system of laws and institutions. We fully enjoy what Hegel calls 'freedom in the common parlance' or civil freedom. Are we then *completely* self-conscious and self-determined or is there still some extra element or dimension of freedom which is lacking? Hegel would probably answer this question along the following lines.

(1) Civil society, although autonomous, is ultimately subject to the political state and its governmental authority ('state power'). Rights may be abrogated, as they are in times of war or civil disturbance; property may be taxed for public purposes; corporate rights may be curtailed or independent social activities taken over by public bodies.

In contrast with the spheres of private rights and private welfare (the family and civil society), the state is from one point of view an external necessity and their higher authority; its nature is such that their laws and interests are subordinate to it and dependent on it (*PhR*, §261).

When the need for the state's intervention arises there is no machinery within civil society to explain and justify the need, and without it the intervention has the appearance of an arbitrary, high-handed activity. The certainty that sacrifices for the sake of the common good or some other higher ethical principles are justified requires an exchange of views, an expression of opinions, an institutional channel for the debate of public issues. Although Hegel in the *Philosophy of Right* goes out of his way to stress the capricious and often trivial character of public opinion, and wishes to curb its 'excesses', he regards it as a necessary element of political life and the chief manifestation of 'subjective freedom' in the public realm.

> The formal subjective freedom of individuals consists in their having and expressing their own private judgments, opinions and recommendations on affairs of state. This freedom is collectively manifested as what is called 'public opinion' (*PhR*, §316).

The operation of public opinion presupposes the freedom of the press, publication and association, all of which can exist in civil society and indeed constitute essential civic freedoms. Hegel, however, argues — quite correctly — that such public opinion is either impotent or dangerous as long as it is not related to governmental authority. It is the function of a representative body to remedy this defect. This body, which Hegel calls, 'the Assembly of Estates', forms part of the governmental authority or 'state power', and is a specifically political, not civil, institution.

> The Estates have the function of bringing public affairs into existence not only implicitly, but also actually, i.e., of bringing into existence the moment of subjective formal freedom, the public consciousness as an empirical universal, of which the thoughts and opinions of the Many are particulars (*PhR*, §300).

> ...in them [the Estates] the subjective moment in universal freedom — the private judgement and private will of the sphere called 'civil society' in this book — comes into existence integrally related to the state (*PhR*, §301R).

It is well known that in the *Philosophy of Right* Hegel is extremely vague about the power of the Estates' Assembly, and in all his political writings he insists that rational suffrage is not universal, direct and individual, but limited, indirect and based on communities or organized interests. It should reflect the social articulation of the national and ethical community. Nevertheless, even in the *Philosophy of Right*, he treats the principle of representation as a rational feature of the modern state.[13]

(2) Hegel makes the further point that the representative assembly, like the rest of the supreme public authority, is concerned with laws and policies which are necessarily general and must be discussed in universal, rational terms.

> The state, therefore, knows what it wills and knows it in its universality, i.e. as something thought. Hence it works and acts by reference to consciously adopted ends, known principles, and laws which are not merely implicit but are actually present to consciousness (*PhR*, §315A).

In the final analysis such ends and principles are part of the general culture of a particular country and express its 'national spirit'. Public opinion and representative institutions are the means through which the principles are related to the practical concerns of the community, where fundamental issues of public life are raised and thrashed out in debate. This makes deputies and the country at large conscious of the principles underlying the actual ethical order, reveals possible inadequacies and contradictions, and generates demands for reform. As for J. S. Mill so for Hegel, representative government is an essential agency of national education (cp. *PhR*, §315A). Political institutions promote the kind of national and political self-consciousness which men do not acquire by being mere members of civil society, and they contribute to freedom because they clarify the principles on which the ethical, social and political life of their community is based.

(3) Another reason for Hegel's dissatisfaction with civil freedom as an adequate form of ethical freedom stems from the form of human interaction peculiar to civil society. Although 'burghers' come to depend closely on each other and form a relatively integrated society, their social interdependence is brought about to some extent by the external forces of needs, labour, the division of labour and the market and not merely through inner individual commitment or personal choice. Also, while performing their duties to each other and co-operating closely, men remain primarily their own private ends – they (or as Hegel would say, their wills) do not consciously pursue their 'substantial' end, which is the existence of an ethical community making complete freedom possible. They promote the interest of such community only implicitly, indirectly, unconsciously. To this extent they remain within the realm of necessity more akin to nature than to the spiritual realm of freedom. The unity of particularity and universality in civil society is achieved without the knowledge and will of its members and so

is not the identity which the ethical order requires, because at this level, that of division, both principles are self-subsistent. It follows that this unity is present here not as freedom but as necessity, since it is by compulsion that the particular rises to the form of universality and seeks and gains its stability in that form (*PhR*, §186).

By contrast in the political community or the state

the universal does not prevail or achieve completion except along with particular interests and through the co-operation of particular knowing and willing and individuals likewise do not live as private persons for their own ends alone, but in the very act of willing these they will the universal in the light of the universal, and their activity is consciously aimed at none but the universal end (*PhR*, §260).

Man as potentially free, self-determined agent, once he has become conscious of his nature, cannot allow himself to be determined by social forces operating on him externally, like natural forces, all the more so as those forces are in the last resort the product of his thought and will and so are potentially under his control. His proper end – the membership of a rational ethical community – must be his own conscious aim, otherwise he is not fully free. By participating in political activities, the public affairs of his state, the individual makes a direct contribution to the life and development of the community and thereby increases his self-determination. As we have seen, a start towards this kind of freedom is made already in civil society through the corporation, which changes the 'unconscious compulsion' of working for others in the market economy into 'a known and thoughtful ethical mode of life' (*PhR*, §255A). The modern state creates further opportunities for participation to its citizens although it allocates different shares according to education, property and status.[14]

(4) Hegel's final line of argument that political freedom is distinct from civil freedom, and represents the highest stage in the development of freedom, is his version of Rousseau's idea of the General Will. Rousseau insisted that the General Will had to express or manifest itself in the actions of individual citizens performing public functions, especially voting on laws. The General Will is the rational or moral will of citizens acting for the common good (the general interest of the body politic) rather than for their own personal good or private interest. For Hegel the common good or public interest is identical with the totality of rational laws and institutions of a community and constitutes the 'objective will' of the community.

Confronted with the claims made for the individual will, we must remember the fundamental conception that the objective will is rationality implicit or in conception, whether it be recognized or not by individuals, whether their whims be deliberately for it or not (*PhR*, §258R).

But although Hegel differs friom Rousseau by postulating a transcendent General Will which, as the 'objective will' of a rationally structured community is more than the sum of individual wills, he agrees with him that such will must express or manifest itself in the actual thinking and willing of individual citizens, consciously identifying their subjective will with the 'objective will' and its needs. This union of subjective and objective will constitutes 'concrete freedom' which is higher than the abstract subjective and objective freedoms taken by themselves. It is through the *political* institutions of the ethical community that the reconciliation of the subjective and objective aspects of the will is effected.

In the *Philosophy of Right* the necessity of the subjective will assenting to laws, and other requirements of the common good is argued by Hegel only with the reference to the monarch, as the official head of the political community, but in his *Philosophy of Mind*, the third part of the *Encyclopaedia of the Philosophical Sciences* (1830), this necessity is explicitly stated also with reference to the mass of citizens. In paragraph 544 of this work Hegel raises the question 'in what sense are we to understand the participation of private person in state affairs' and after ruling out superior intelligence or good will of the people as an adequate reason he answers his question as follows:

The desirability of private persons taking part in public affairs is partly to be put in their concrete, and therefore more urgent, sense of general wants. But the true motive is the right of the community (collective) spirit to appear as an *externally universal* will, acting with orderly and express efficacy for the public concerns. By such satisfaction of this right it gets its own life quickened, and at the same time breathes fresh life in the administrative officials; who thus have it brought home to them that not merely have they to enforce duties but also to have regard to rights. Private citizens are in the state the incomparably greater number and form the multitude of such as are recognised as persons. Hence the rational will (will-reason) exhibits its existence in them as a preponderating majority of freemen, or in its 'reflectional universality' which has its actuality vouchsafed it as a participation in the sovereignty.[15]

The meaning of this somewhat poorly translated passage is fairly clear: the rational will of the ethical community, public, affairs must be mediated through the wills of the multitude and must take the form of 'an externally universal (general) will', i.e. one embodied in the particular wills of the citizens exercising political rights or participating in sovereignty. Only then does the general will become fully alive and acquires universal existence.

We may therefore conclude that Hegel has largely justified his claim that 'the [modern] state is the actuality of concrete freedom'. Freedom defined as the self-determination of a rational, moral and ethical agent reaches its fullest development only in a politically organized modern community, in which he interacts with other citizens and the government through free public debate, suffrage and representation. Political liberty, involved in these activities, is distinct from civil liberty. The *raison d'être* of civil society and the justification of civil freedom is the private interest and subjective choice of the individual *bourgeois* which, mediated through a system of economic and social relations as well as laws, institutions and authorities, promotes the interest of the ethical community only indirectly and in the last resort. The *raison d'être* of political community and the justification of political liberty is the good of the ethical community itself, the common good or the public interest, which the fully self-conscious and self-determined *citizen* promotes for its own sake. In so doing he actualizes his own deepest freedom and realizes his nature not simply as a particular but as a universal, communal being. Political freedom, although roughly hewn, is the indispensible coping stone of Hegel's theory of freedom which (so to speak) is the obverse of his theory of political community. And the two theories taken as a whole represent Hegel's adaptation of Plato's idea of 'ethical substance' to the modern world and the solution of Rousseau's problem of political association — how to live in community with others and yet remain a free individual.[16]

Hegel's radical idealism: family and state as ethical communities

MEROLD WESTPHAL

Hegel's theory of the family is important both for its own sake and for the light it throws on his understanding of the state. On its own account his systematic discussion of the family stands out both for the illuminating interpretation it presents and by its mere existence, since the major modern philosophers have not paid much attention to the family in its own right. On the relation of family to state Hegel's view calls attention to itself by flying in the face of the tendency, strong in his own time and even stronger in our own, to view civil society as both the model and the goal (essence, telos) of the state.

It is the way Hegel makes the family the model (but not the goal) of the state which I wish to explore in this essay, hoping that something of the intrinsic importance of what he says for the theory and practice of family life will come to light as well. In the light of this modeling relationship between family and state Hegel's social theory can be called radical idealism, just as his metaphysics is called absolute idealism.

In this context the term 'radical' has both its etymological and its popular senses. In etymological terms Hegel seeks to be radical by getting us to the very root of what family and state are. Deviations from the essences he exhibits would have to be interpreted as 'untrue' or unhealthy approximations of the real thing. In popular terms he is radical by being sharply and deliberately out of step with prevailing attitudes and behaviors. To take him seriously would require fundamental change, both in his own times and in ours.

Similarly the term 'idealism' has a double meaning in relation to naturalistic or materialistic alternatives. In the order of explanation radical idealism denies that family and state can be accounted for in terms of sexual or economic needs as their basis, while in the order of evaluation it denies that these needs are the definitive standards by which family and state should be judged.

This preliminary sketch of radical idealism is too negative to be very satisfying. But Hegel's dialectical thinking is negative thinking, and our point

77

of departure will have to be what the family and state are not. Above all, they are not contractual relationships, and we will have understood most of what I am calling radical idealism when we fully understand why he writes: 'To subsume marriage under the concept of contract is thus quite impossible; this subsumption – though shameful is the only word for it – is propounded in Kant's *Philosophy of Law*. It is equally far from the truth to ground the nature of the state on the contractual relation, whether the state is supposed to be a contract of all with all, or of all with the monarch and the government' (*PhR*, §75).[1]

There are three reasons why Hegel thinks it shameful to think of family and state in terms of contract models. Contractual relationships are (1) abstract, (2) contingent, and (3) self-centered.

On the first point Hegel protests against the tendency in philosophy and legal theory to confuse 'rights which presuppose substantial ties, e.g., those of family and political life, and rights which only concern abstract personality as such'. In the notion that family and political life involve 'substantial ties' there lies embedded Hegel's distinctive understanding of community as an essential feature of human experience and fulfillment. But the meaning of 'substantial ties' comes to light through contrast with another kind of human bond, those 'rights which only concern abstract personality as such'. This type of relationship is exhibited above all in property-ownership and contract. In such contexts 'it is only as owners that these two persons really exist for each other' (*PhR*, §40). In a sales contract, for example, the only relevant factor in the relationship between two persons is that each is the owner of property he is willing to exchange for the other's property. Reciprocal recognition, which is so central to Hegel's understanding of human existence as spirit, occurs here.[2] But since each person is much more than an owner of property and all these other dimensions of who each is get left out of the relationship as irrelevant, it is a very thin or incomplete form of recognition. Hegel calls it abstract because it is arrived at by abstracting from so much of what makes up the identity of each person. The beautiful woman who wants to be loved for who she is and not just for her good looks and the wealthy man who wants to be appreciated for more than the benefits he can bestow know just what Hegel means by 'abstract personality', even if neither understands his terminology immediately. Whatever else defines the 'substantial ties' which Hegel finds essential to family and political life, they will have to be relationships of whole or concrete persons to each other.

In addition to being abstract, contractual relationships are contingent. They result 'from the arbitrariness [*Willkür*] of the parties' united by them. So far as the state is concerned, it 'does not rest on contract, for contract presupposes arbitrariness [*Willkür*]. It is false to maintain that the foundation of the state is something at the option of all its members [*in der Willkür aller*]. It is nearer the truth to say that it is absolutely necessary for every individual to be citizen.' (PhR, §§75, 75A). Returning to Kant's view of marriage as a contract, Hegel notes that in such a marriage 'the parties are bound by a contract of reciprocal caprice [gegenseitige Willkür], and marriage is thus degraded to the level of a contract for reciprocal use' (PhR, §161A).

The exercise of will exhibited by contract is described in the above passages as arbitrary, capricious, and optional. Of these three ways of rendering the German term Willkür, the last is most suited to Hegel's meaning. He does not mean to suggest that contractual relationships are arbitrary or capricious in the sense of being entirely random, unmotivated, or without reasons. In fact, as we shall see shortly, his third objection to contract is directed toward its underlying motivation. He rather means to say that contractual relationships are contingent or optional in the sense of being nonessential, extrinsic, or incidental both (a) in relation to the human condition as such and (b) in relation to the individual's own personal identity. It is not necessary to enter into such relationships to be fully human, and whether I do so or not does not significantly affect who I am.

Hegel views both family and state as necessary and essential rather than contingent and accidental in both of these senses. Regarding the first we have already noted him saying 'that it is absolutely necessary for every individual to be a citizen'. More boldly, he writes, 'Our objectively appointed end and so our ethical duty is to enter the married state' (PhR, §162). The point about personal identity is perhaps even more important. The family represents a unity unlike contractual unity because one has 'self-consciousness of one's individuality within this unity as the absolute essence of oneself, with the result that one is not in it as an independent person but as a member' (PhR, §158). Similarly, individual self-consciousness knows the state as its essence and 'it is only as one of its members that the individual himself has objectivity, genuine individuality, and an ethical life' (PhR, §§257–8).

In this way the non-contractual bonds which Hegel earlier referred to as 'substantial ties' are given further specification. Beyond being between whole or concrete persons, these relationships belong to the essence of the individuals related. The point is not that the I disappears before the We, for Hegel is answering the question how individuality occurs. His point is simply this. Who We are in the family and state to which I belong is an essential part of who I am, not some peripheral episode which takes place on the surface of my selfhood.

One practical consequence which Hegel is quick to draw from this view of 'substantial ties' is that marriage is indissoluble. His point is eloquently expressed by C. S. Lewis in a theological context. Noting that Christian churches have not agreed with one another on the subject of divorce, he points to a deep underlying agreement.

I mean, they all regard divorce as something like cutting up a living body, as a kind of surgical operation. Some of them think the operation so violent that it cannot be done at all; others admit it as a desperate remedy in extreme cases. They are all agreed that it is more like having both your legs cut off than it is like dissolving a business partnership or even deserting a regiment.[3]

What Hegel would appreciate most from this passage is not that Lewis happens to agree with him on the topic of divorce, but rather the phenomenological confirmation that certain kinds of relationship, of which marriage is a kind of paradigm, *are*, not merely ought to be, constitutive of our personal identity. That is the chief point of his polemic against *Willkür*. The irony is that while modern psychology and sociology illustrate and confirm this thesis again and again, we tend increasingly to view family and political relationships through contractual-contingent categories.

The third reason for repudiating contract thinking in our attempts to understand the 'substantial ties' of family and state is the self-centered motivation of contractual relationships. This is perhaps the most obvious of the three features Hegel targets for criticism. People enter into contractual relationships, not in order to share themselves with someone else or to create some new reality larger than themselves, but for the sake of the personal advantages they will gain. The heart of the contractual posture is simply, I'll scratch your back if you'll scratch mine.

Since Hegel views the family relation as an essential part of a person's identity, it is not surprising that he would oppose any model which treats it as merely instrumental to the private ends of the individual as such. This is why, as we have seen above, he complains that with a contract model marriage is 'degraded to the level of a contract for reciprocal use'. He acknowledges that there is something quasi-contractual about the way a marriage comes into being, in the agreement between the parties or their parents. Nevertheless, 'it is not a contractual relation. On the contrary, though marriage begins in contract, it is precisely a contract to transcend the standpoint of contract, the standpoint from which persons are regarded in their individuality as self-subsistent units' (*PhR*, §163; cf. §75A).

Just as Hegel extends his critique of the abstract and contingent nature of contract thinking both to family and state, in this case also he insists that the state, properly conceived, cannot be viewed as a means to my private ends. Hegel regularly insists that the state is to be viewed as an end, as the 'absolute' and 'final' end of individual self-consciousness (*PhR*, §§257, 258 and 260).[4] He is totally opposed to those who 'conceive the state as a mere mechanical scaffolding for the attainment of external, non-spiritual ends ... The state from this point of view is treated simply as an organization to satisfy men's necessities ... [It] is entirely deprived of any strictly ethical character.' Such states have occurred, Hegel notes, 'in times and under conditions of barbarism' (*PhR*, §270). It was, in fact, the principle of such a society 'which appeared in the ancient world as an invasion of ethical corruption and as the ultimate cause of that world's downfall' (*PhR*, §185). In other words, the internal barbarism of egoism which destroyed Rome from within before the external barbarians administered the *coup de grâce*, is the very principle of modern civil society.*

This alerts us to the fact that the passion of Hegel's critique at this point stems from his sense that the barbarism of which he speaks is anything but a thing of the past. Historically speaking nothing very noteworthy occurs when those in power view the state as a means to their personal ends.[5] The genius of social contract theory is that it teaches the ordinary citizen in the modern world to hold the same view.[6] Whether this becomes an ideological justification of the status quo, in which state power is accepted because it is said to serve the individual's interest, or becomes the revolutionary demand that the state actually serve those interests is not the primary concern from Hegel's perspective. In either case an assumption has been made to which he is totally opposed. It has been very succinctly expressed in our own time by an economist colleague who talks about the state as a kind of omni-insurance company. The crucial question, or, to be more precise, the only question to be asked is whether it is a good buy. Does a cost-benefit analysis reveal that the state scratches my back at least as hard and as long as I scratch its?

It is this sort of phenomenon which led to the earlier comment about the tendency, strong in Hegel's time and even stronger in our own, to view civil society as the model and goal of the state. For just as regularly as he denies that family and state can properly be understood in contract categories, he portrays civil society as the institutionalization of contractual relationships.[7] His opening description of civil society is the following:

an association of members as self-subsistent individuals in a universality which, because of their self-subsistence, is only abstract. Their association is brought about by their needs, by the legal system – the means to security of person and property – and by an external organization for attaining their particular and common interests. This external state... (*PhR*, §157).

It will be noted that civil society, by which Hegel understands the economic and legal organization of capitalist society, bears all three marks of contract thinking which Hegel has been denying to family and state. It is a means to the personal and economic security of individual property owners. For this reason its members are self-subsistent individuals related only by an abstract universality, a bond which relates them to each other only

---

* *Editor's note* – This is discussed more fully in M. J. Inwood's and G. Kortian's essays.

as owners of life, liberty, and property. This makes the resulting organization externally related to its members, not as something necessarily foreign or hostile, but as something essentially unrelated to who they are.[8] To belong to a different civil society would be like changing insurance companies or stockbrokers. If our immediate response to this is that we could not so easily exchange our citizenship for another, this only shows that Hegel is phenomenologically right, that the state is more than social contract theory allows it to be.

As a means toward the ends of its individual members, civil society's task can be defined both negatively and positively. It is necessary

first, that accidental hindrances to one aim or another be removed, and undisturbed safety of person and property be attained; and secondly, that the securing of every single person's livelihood and welfare be treated and actualized as a right, i.e., that particular welfare as such be so treated (*PhR*, §230).

The negative task of removing human interference with the individual's livelihood and wealth Hegel calls 'the Administration of Justice.' The positive task of affirmative action to assure the individual's livelihood and welfare he describes as 'the Police' or 'Public Authority' and 'the Corporation.' 'The Public Authority' is broader than what we today understand by police. For while it is concerned with crime control, and thus is directly related to the administration of justice, it also has responsibility for regulating prices, educating the citizens, and administering the anti-poverty programs which will inevitably be needed.[9] By the Corporation Hegel means those voluntary associations which 'come on the scene like a second family' for their members. The organized church is one example, but the primary model Hegel has in mind is economically oriented. It is something like a cross between a medieval guild and a modern labor union, assuring the livelihood of its members but also providing the recognition and respect that go with belonging. Thus, 'as the family is the first, so the Corporation is the second ethical root of the state, the one planted in civil society' (*PhR*, §§250–6, 270).[10]

The point to be noticed here is simply this: civil society is organized in the pursuit of the goals to which it is a means and of the three structures Hegel discusses, 'the Administration of Justice' and 'the Public Authority' belong to what we call government while only 'the Corporation,' which includes features of genuine community within it, belongs to what we call the private sector. This makes it very easy to identify the state with the self-regulating organization of civil society. This is what is meant by speaking of civil society as the model and goal of the state. For when (1) the state is viewed simply as the further extension of civil society in pursuit of the latter's own goals and (2) civil society is composed of the network of contractual relationships which make up capitalist society, it is natural to think of political life as essentially a contractual affair with primarily economic goals.

Hegel resists this tendency. Having affirmed that the state is like the family in being non-contractual, Hegel consistently denies that it is like civil society in being contractual, without overlooking how deeply ingrained the latter assumption is upon modern thinking. 'If the state is represented as a unity of different persons, as a unity which is only a partnership, then what is really meant is only civil society', he writes, immediately after noting that the creation of civil society is a distinctive achievement of the modern world.

In the course of the actual attainment of selfish ends... there is formed a system of complete interdependence... This system may be prima facie regarded as the external state, the state based on need, the state as the Understanding envisages it (*PhR*, §§182A and 183).[11]

In other words, what may appear to be the state is not really the state at all, not the state as it truly is, as Reason envisages it.

Individuals in their capacity as burghers in this state are private persons whose end is their own interest. This end is mediated through the universal which thus appears as a means to its realization.

But,

this unity is not the identity which the ethical order requires... It follows that this unity is present here not as freedom but as necessity (*PhR*, §§186–7).[12]

Neither the market nor the government regulation of the market can be experienced as the freedom in terms of which the state is to be understood. The second half of this essay, beginning on p. 84 with the quotation from *PhR*, §§149, shows how Hegel's theory of community is also a theory of freedom. The double liberation embodied in ethical life at the levels of family and state indicates that for Hegel freedom is neither the absence of restraint on natural inclinations nor the self-sufficiency of the independent individual but rather the overcoming of both of these conditions.[13]

Perhaps Hegel's clearest attempt to distinguish the nature of the state from that of civil society is the following:

If the state is confused with civil society, and if its specific end is laid down as the security and protection of property and personal freedom, then the interest of the individuals as such becomes the ultimate end of their association, and it follows that membership of the state is something optional. But the state's relation to the individual is quite different from this. Since the state is spirit objectified, it is only as one of its members that the individual himself has objectivity, genuine individuality, and an ethical life (*PhR*, §258).

We can summarize Hegel's negative thinking to this point with two claims: like the family the state cannot properly be understood in contractual terms, and therefore, the self-regulating organization of a capitalist economy, even in its public or governmental structures is only the appearance and not the true essence of the state. Negative results are always a bit frustrating, but these are likely to be more than usual for many of us moderns. For if this is not what the state is, what could it possibly be? We have been so thoroughly conditioned to think of the state as that which protects us from enemy and criminal interference in our personal lives and which manages the economy so as to maximize our wealth that we can think of little or nothing else in terms of which to understand the state. After all, do the politicians ever talk about anything else during election time but national security, crime control, and who can best manage the economy? If Hegel is going to say anything to us that we can understand, he will have to become more positive.

What Hegel has been trying to evoke through all his negotiations is the central notion of his social theory, *Sittlichkeit*.* It is the concept which underlies his talk about 'ethical substance' and 'substantial ties.' Its etymological roots are in the term *Sitten*, customs, and it is usually translated as ethical life, though for Hegel it connotes a whole theory of human community. There is perhaps no better brief summary of that theory than Charles Taylor's.

> '*Sittlichkeit*' refers to the moral obligations I have to an ongoing community of which I am a part. These obligations are based on established norms and uses, and that is why the etymological root in '*Sitten*' is important for Hegel's use. The crucial characteristic of *Sittlichkeit* is that it enjoins us to bring about what already is. This is a paradoxical way of putting it, but in fact the common life which is the basis of my *sittlich* obligation is already there in existence. It is in virtue of its being an ongoing affair that I have these obligations; and my fulfillment of these obligations is what sustains it and keeps it in being. Hence in *Sittlichkeit*, there is no gap between what ought to be and what is, between *Sollen* and *Sein*.[14]

It turns out that the parallel between the family and the state provides a positive articulation of what *Sittlichkeit* means as well as a negative evocation. Thus a closer look at what the family *is* will be our most helpful clue to understanding the kind of community Hegel understands the state to be.

As we have already seen, the institutions of ethical life provide 'the duties of the station' to which the individual belongs.

> The bond of duty can appear as a restriction only on indeterminate subjectivity or abstract freedom, and on the impulses either of the natural will or of the moral will which determines its indeterminate good arbitrarily. The truth is, however, that in

---

* *Editor's note* – *Sittlichkeit*, with special reference to its Greek origin, is the subject of M. J. Inwood's essay.

duty the individual finds his liberation; first, liberation from dependence on mere natural impulse...secondly, liberation from the indeterminate subjectivity which...remains self-enclosed and devoid of actuality. In duty the individual acquires substantive freedom (*PhR*, §149).[15]

The first instance of ethical life as this double liberation, from 'mere natural impulse' and from 'indeterminate' and 'self-enclosed', i.e., isolated subjectivity, is presented in the opening two paragraphs of Hegel's account of marriage.

Paragraph 161 describes the first moment.

Marriage, as the immediate type of ethical relationship, ... contains first, the moment of physical life; and since marriage is a substantial tie, the life involved in it is life in its totality, i.e., as the actuality of the race and its life-process. But, secondly, in self-consciousness the natural sexual union, which is only inward or undeveloped [*an sich*] and therefore exists only as an external unity, is transformed into something spiritual, into self-conscious love.

Alongside this notion that in marriage human sexuality is raised from something merely natural and biological to something spiritual and ethical, 'that the consciousness of the parties is crystallized out of its physical and subjective mode and lifted to the thought of what is substantive' (*PhR*, §164), Hegel places the idea of marriage as reducing the importance of sex and putting it in its place. In genuine marriage

physical passion sinks to the level of a physical moment, destined to vanish in its very satisfaction. On the other hand, the spiritual bond of union secures its rights as the substance of marriage and thus rises, inherently indissoluble, to a plane above the contingency of passion and the transience of particular caprice (*PhR*, §163).

The view that marriage as an official, public act is alien to true love 'is a travesty of the ethical aspect of love, the higher aspect which restrains purely sensual impulse and puts it in the background'. In the ethical bond of marriage

the sensuous moment, the one proper to physical life, is put into its ethical place as something only consequential and accidental, belonging to the external embodiment of the ethical bond, which indeed can subsist exclusively in reciprocal love and support (*PhR*, §164).[16]

Hegel is not at war with himself here. True to the dialectical spirit, he insists that marriage is at once the upgrading and the downgrading of sexuality. He units these two thoughts in a phrase when he describes sex as 'the external embodiment of the ethical bond'. The ethical bond of marriage is love, which is something spiritual. While Hegel defines spirit in inter-subjective terms as recognition rather than in metaphysical terms as incorporeality, it remains the case for him as for the tradition that the physical can never be fully adequate to the spiritual. Thus sexuality as a biological process can only be the *external* embodiment of the ethical bond. But since Hegel is no dualist, the spiritual is that which reveals itself through incarnation. Hence the ethical bond, though spiritual, is embodied. As the *embodiment of a spiritual relation* sex is caught up into the realm of spirit and is no longer something merely natural or biological. In marriage sex takes on a sacramental role, for it becomes the outward and visible expression of an inward and invisible love. This sacramentalism of the sex life is for Hegel the mean between the naturalism of the sex life, which views it only in terms of psycho-biological needs and their fulfillment, and the romanticism of the sex life, which views it as the be-all and end-all of human life and love.

If we ask about the spiritual or ethical bond of self-conscious love whose expression or embodiment sexuality properly is, we bring ourselves to the second moment of liberation. Ethical life in general and marriage in particular brings liberation not only from the merely natural but also from the isolation of autonomous selfhood. Paragraph 162 describes this second way in which social structure and duty belong to the story of human freedom.

On the subjective side, marriage may have a more obvious source in the particular inclination of the two persons ... But its objective source lies in the free consent of the persons, especially in their consent to make themselves one person, to renounce their natural and individual personality to this unity of one with the other. From this point of view, their union is a self-restriction, but in fact it is their liberation, because in it they attain their substantive self-consciousness.'[17]

Just as in traditional metaphysics properties, qualities, or accidents cannot be themselves apart from the substance in which they inhere, so Hegel claims that human individuals cannot be themselves apart from the social wholes to which they belong. This is why he calls the union in which two persons become one their 'substantive self-consciousness'.[18] Neither in isolated self-sufficiency nor in contractual interdependency (which presupposes a genuine self prior to the relationship) does this kind of relationship exist and it is only in such ethical relationships, and thus in community, that true human selfhood and freedom are achieved. In Hegel's abstract language neither particularity nor abstract and external universality can satisfy the Idea, but only the genuine universality of substantial unity.[19]

The power and authority of this kind of ethical substance is not something alien to the individual who belongs to it.

On the contrary, his spirit bears witness to them as to its own essence, the essence in which he has a feeling of self-hood, and in which he lives as in his own element which is not distinguished from himself. The subject is thus directly linked to the ethical order by a relation which is more like an identity than even the relation of faith or trust (*PhR*, §147).

Clearly the notion of contract would be even less appropriate for describing this relation of identity. I *am* who We are.

This is why Hegel says of the family in particular that

one's frame of mind is to have self-consciousness of one's individuality within this unity as the absolute essence of oneself, with the result that one is in it not as an independent person but as a member (*PhR*, §158).[20]

Commenting on this passage, Hegel adds

Love means in general terms the consciousness of my unity with another, so that I am not in selfish isolation but win my self-consciousness only as the renunciation of my independence and through knowing myself as the unity of myself with another and of the other with me . . . The first moment in love is that I do not wish to be a self-subsistent and independent person and that if I were, then I would feel defective and incomplete. The second moment is that I find myself in another person, that I count for something in the other, while the other in turn comes to count for something in me. Love, therefore, is the most tremendous contradiction; the Understanding cannot resolve it since there is nothing more stubborn than this point of self-consciousness which is negated and which nevertheless I ought to possess as affirmative. Love is at once the propounding and the resolving of this contradiction. As the resolving of it, love is unity of an ethical type (*PhR*, §158A).

In love I am who We are. This is why We cannot view our relationship or the entity We comprise together simply as a means to our separate, individual ends.

The ethical aspect of marriage consists in the parties' consciousness of this unity as their substantive aim, and so in their love, trust, and common sharing of their entire existence as individuals (*PhR*, §163).

Several things need to be noted about this passage. First, this unity consists not only of attitudes (love and trust) but of activity as well (sharing of their entire existence). It is something to do. Second, though individuality renounces its ultimacy it does not disappear. The parties share their existence as individuals, though in sharing they create a reality which is more than the sum of their individualities. Third, it is 'when the parties are in this frame of mind' that 'their physical passion sinks to the level of a physical moment', becomes but one aspect, important as it is, of their total sharing together. Finally, by calling this unity the parties' aim Hegel indicates not only that it is a task and not a fact, something to be done, but also that it is valued for its own sake. It is not simply the means to something other than itself, but is itself the end, the goal, the aim of the attitudes and activities which constitute it. In Aristotelian terms marriage is *praxis*, not *poiesis*, and the knowledge on which it depends is *phronesis* rather than *techne*. Like all forms of virtue, the We formed by love is its own reward.

In sum, marriage as a non-contractual relationship is a double liberation. It frees our self-consciousness from self-centeredness so it can participate in a We which is larger than itself but with which it remains in a relation of identity. And it frees our sexuality from its state of nature so it can be an expression of the committed sharing which constitutes that We and not merely a means for reproduction or physical pleasure. If the family is to be the positive model for the state in its non-contractual rationality, we can expect the state to be a similar double liberation. And this is just what we find.

To begin with the state is a We of the same sort as the family. There are differences, of course, most notably of scope. Hegel also suggests that while the family is based on love and thus feeling, the state is based on law and thus thought, though his discussion of patriotism as political sentiment (*Gesinnung*) complicates that distinction considerably.[21] Still the isomorphism is strong. The state is also a non-contractual unity in which the individual finds 'substantive freedom' (*PhR*, §257). Hegel makes this clear, I believe, in one of his first descriptions of the state.

The state . . . is the actuality of the substantial will which it possesses in the particular self-consciousness once that consciousness has been raised to consciousness of its universality. This substantial unity is an absolute and unmoved end in itself, in which freedom comes into its supreme right. On the other hand this final end has supreme right against the individual, whose supreme duty is to be a member of the state. If the state is confused with civil society . . . then the interest of the individuals as such becomes the ultimate end of their association . . . But the state's relation to the individual is quite different from this. Since the state is spirit objectified, it is only as one of its members that the individual himself has objectivity, genuine individuality, and an ethical life. Unification pure and simple is the true content and aim of the individual, and the individual's destiny is the living of a universal life. His further particular satisfaction, activity, and mode of conduct have this substantive and universally valid life as their starting point and their result (*PhR*, §258).

Hegel returns to this theme of unity as an end in itself and not merely a means only a couple of paragraphs later. The state is the actuality of concrete freedom because individuals

pass over of their own accord into the interest of the universal . . . they even recognize it as their own substantive mind; they take it as their end and aim and are active in its pursuit. The result is that the universal does not prevail or achieve completion except along with particular interests . . . and individuals likewise do not live as private persons for their own ends alone, but . . . their activity is consciously aimed at none but the universal end (*PhR*, §260).

In short, participation in the state is of value for its own sake and not instrumentally because the state, while transcending the individuals who make it up remains in a relation of identity with them. It's a matter of ontology. I the citizen am who We the people are. Like the family, the state frees self-consciousness from self-centeredness.

The identity which Hegel affirms here does not exclude difference. In the family difference was reconciled with identity partly through the attitudes of love and trust and partly through the activity of sharing the whole of life together. All three, love, trust, and sharing, pre-suppose difference, identity, and the harmony of the two, such that the identity in question requires difference and vice versa.[22]

It is the sentiment of patriotism which corresponds to the love and trust in the family. By patriotism Hegel does not primarily mean 'a readiness for exceptional sacrifices and actions', but rather an everyday attitude which 'habitually recognizes that the community is one's substantive groundwork and end'. He explicitly identifies this sentiment with trust, and though he has said that law is to the state what love is to the family, he continues to describe patriotism in terms similar to earlier descriptions of love. Obviously the sexual element is missing, but we have already seen that it is not the essence of the love which constitutes marriage. What is common to love and patriotism is that the other is perceived as not being other. We instinctively recognize this when we speak of patriotism as love of country.[23]

If the sentiment of patriotism is the individual's affective participation in the state, the active participation which would correspond to the sharing of life together in marriage remains to be determined. The We of marriage we have seen to be an aim or goal, not just because it is valued for its own sake, but also because it is something to do. How do we act in the state, so that, as Hegel insists, the individual self-consciousness finds the state to be not only its own essence and end, but also the 'product of its activity' (PhR, §257; cf. §258)?

Here it is necessary to distinguish 'the strictly political state' from the state without qualification, the state as a people's system of government from the state as the whole of their life together, including in the broadest sense, their culture.[24] Hegel writes

The spiritual individual, the nation – in so far as it is internally differentiated so as to form an organic whole – is what we call the state. This term is ambiguous, however, for the state and the laws of the state, as distinct from religion, science, and art, usually have purely political associations. But in this context, the word 'state' is used in a more comprehensive sense, just as we use the word 'realm' to describe spiritual phenomena. A nation should therefore be regarded as a spiritual individual, and it is not primarily its external side that will be emphasised here, but rather what we have previously called the spirit of the nation, i.e. its self-consciousness in relation to its own truth and being, and what it recognises as truth in the absolute sense – in short, those spiritual powers which live within the nation and rule over it.[25]

It is clear from Hegel's account of patriotism that such a sentiment can exist only on the basis of an active participation in both the strictly political and the cultural life of one's people. In the former case the central notion is that freedom involves 'self-determining action according to laws and principles . . . ' (*PhR*, §258). Hegel here echoes Rousseau's definition of liberty as 'obedience to a law which we prescribe to ourselves'.[26] It is debatable whether Hegel fully appreciates his own requirement for political participation and whether the constitutional monarchy he envisages provides sufficiently for it.* (It is also debatable whether the parliamentary and presidential democracies of today really fulfill his criterion of rational government fully.)

What is clear is that Hegel's view of freedom requires active citizen involvement in determining the laws which regulate individual behavior. It is the quality of that involvement rather than effectiveness in promoting economic growth and consumption by which the political state is to be measured. Political participation (pursued for its own sake and not just as an instrumental necessity) is part of the sharing of one's life with one's people which constitutes the state.

The other part is obviously a sharing in the cultural life of the nation. Just as Hegelian philosophy cannot conclude with a philosophy of objective spirit but must go on to reflect on art, religion and philosophy, so the active life of the individual must go beyond the narrowly political to the more broadly cultural aspects of national life.[27]

This is the first liberation which the state actualizes, participation in a We which frees the individual from the self-centeredness of natural selfhood. The other moment of liberation in the family is the transformation of sexuality from a natural to a spiritual activity by its incorporation into that community life (the family We) whose external embodiment it becomes. There is a human activity which undergoes a similar upgrading-downgrading by its incorporation into the life of the state. It is the economic activity which lies at the heart of civil society.

It should already be clear that the incorporation of economic life into the life of the state cannot mean government planning and regulation of the economy so far as these activities are determined by economic goals. For we have already seen that this dimension of government belongs conceptually to civil society and not to the state.[28] Just as sex for reproduction and pleasure does not belong to the essence of the family (though they get included in family life) so economics as production and consumption does not belong to the essence of the state (though they get included in political and cultural life). It is only as economic life is transformed by becoming an external embodiment of the We which is the state, rather than an end on its own terms which the political and cultural life of a society serve as means, thereby becoming its institutional and ideological superstructure, that the state

---

* *Editor's note* – The reasons for Hegel's failure in this respect are explained in K.-H. Ilting's first essay.

completes the freedom which is its destiny.* In this sacramentalism of economic life political and cultural values are the basis, production and consumption the superstructure of society.

Like social-contract theory, this one is capable of ideological or revolutionary readings. Hegel tells us that the state is rational because in the modern world it actually achieves these goals. Marx tells us it is irrational because the opposite is true. History has taken the side of Marx increasingly, as economic life has become more and more autonomous[29] and political participation and cultural expression have become more and more subordinate.

But let us linger with Hegelian theory long enough to notice the upgrading and downgrading of economic activity which it entails. Hegel is more explicit about the latter and is clearly as eager to put the pursuit of wealth in its place as he earlier was to put the pursuit of sexual pleasure in its. We have already seen him label barbaric any society which makes economic goals its ultimate goals.[30] The needs which economic life satisfies are in the first place merely animal needs. Beyond these there are artificial needs whose basis is culture and not biology. Still, the goal of satisfying economic needs, whether animal or human, is a goal so restricted, finite and particular that in the institutions of civil society which are given over to this goal we cannot hope to find the actuality of true human freedom.[31] One direct consequence of this is that it would be a travesty to conceive of education 'as a mere means to those ends... The final purpose of education, therefore, is liberation and the struggle for a higher liberation still' (PhR, §187), not the attainment of marketable skills.

There are perhaps two reasons why Hegel is less specific in discussing the elevation of economic life above the mere satisfaction of needs, natural and artificial, to the place where it is the external embodiment of the ethical bond of the state. First, the world he lived in, like our own, was not exactly brim full of instances where economic life had been subordinated to serve the political interests in shared decision-making, the aesthetic interests in beauty and equipoise, and the ethical and religious interest in justice. *Shalom*, the ancient Hebrew name for such a situation, has never been the most striking characteristic of capitalist society.[32] Second, Hegel regularly celebrates the freedom given the individual by the economic system of the modern world and focuses his praise of economic life on this feature. This is a constant theme in the *Philosophy of Right*, summed up in this claim:

The principle of the modern state has prodigious strength and depth because it allows the principle of subjectivity to progress to its culmination in the extreme of self-subsistent personal particularity... (PhR, §260).

* *Editor's note* – The ways in which Hegel's civil society achieves this – or fails to achieve it – are discussed in the essays of A. S. Walton and R. Plant respectively.

But the freedom of free enterprise receives only penultimate praise from Hegel, who completes the claim just cited with these words: 'and yet at the same time brings it back to the substantive unity and so maintains this unity in the principle of subjectivity itself'. Since it is the substantive unity of the state and not the abstract unity of civil society which Hegel mentions here, it is clear that he understands the state to be rational only insofar as economic life is transformed to become the expression of non-economic values.

If we compare Hegel's idealism of the community with the prevailing theory and practice of sexuality and economic activity in our own society we will be able to see how genuinely radical is the inner movement of Hegel's social thought.

Hegel's concept of the state and Marx's early critique

K.-H. ILTING

In the spring and summer of 1843, the young Marx wrote a critique of Hegel's philosophy of the state which had a decisive impact upon the history of marxism, and which is still influential today.[1] Although Marx could claim that he had, together with Arnold Ruge, adopted Hegel's intentions more wholeheartedly than anyone else, he decided at that point, under the influence of the Polish Count August Cieszkowski and Ludwig Feuerbach, to take a stand against Hegel and to subject his doctrine of the state to an apparently radical critique.[2] This inherently contradictory polemical *volte face* has not only left lasting traces in his own later writings. It has also continued to determine the marxist interpretation of Hegel until this very day; and in many and various ways it has obscured the degree to which Marx still remained a Hegelian even after his radical renunciation of Hegel.

This critique is centred upon Marx's objections to Hegel's concept of the state. He believes that, by a detailed discussion of the introductory paragraphs of Hegel's theory of the state in the *Philosophy of Right*, he can demonstrate that Hegel, in his political philosophy, had inverted subject and predicate; i.e. that he had understood and presented an independent entity as an attribute, whereas something occurring only as an attribute of an independently existing object was presented as being itself an independent entity. According to this interpretation, Hegel sought to comprehend the state as an object which existed independently of the individuals living in a state community and credited these individuals themselves with only a dependent existence. Finally Hegel had thereby reduced the state itself to no more than an embodiment of an abstract 'Idea'.

This picture of Hegel accords so well with the conceptions of conservative, liberal and even fascist authors that even today it is often accepted and transmitted without question. And under the auspices of marxist orthodoxy, there is a total lack of willingness to check its accuracy. Moreover, Marx's commentary is every bit as tortuous and obscure as the corresponding parts of Hegel's texts. Only on the basis of a careful investigation is it therefore possible to determine whether, and how far, the young Marx's interpretation and critique of Hegel's remarks on the concept of the state are justified. The following study attempts to clarify this issue.

I

Hegel expounded the concept of the state in §§257–70 of his *Philosophy of Right*, published in 1820. This text is an expanded version of the corresponding exposition in his lecture course on *Natural Law and the Science of the State* from the winter term of 1818–19, the wording of which is in essentials preserved for us verbatim in the notes taken by the law student Carl Gustav Homeyer.[3] For reasons which should become clear presently, it is convenient to clarify Hegel's concept of the state first of all by reference to this lecture of 1818–19. The passage on the state begins with the sentence: 'The ethical Idea, as that in which [individuals] are immersed as ideal along with their natural feeling and [also] the aims of personal singularity and particularity which tear them away from their unity and absorb them in themselves, and [in which they] only produce it as moments of this one mind, have it as their end and depend on it, is the state.'[4] In these introductory paragraphs, the state is described from the point of view of the individuals who together constitute a state. As members of their families and civil society, Hegel points out, these individuals have their own ends which differ from those of the state community to which they belong. But these private ends nonetheless link them with the ends of the state community, since the chief task of the state consists of the coordination of diverging social interests.[5] For individuals it is therefore vital to recognize that their private and personal ends do in the long run converge with the communal end, and to cooperate in the preservation of the state community. This is the 'ethical Idea' in which their private ends 'are immersed' when they have been recognized as 'ideal'.[6]

The fact that Hegel is here speaking of the state as the 'ethical Idea' is best understood from his usage in his early writings. In a jotting of 1795, he writes: 'In a republic it is for an Idea that people live; in a monarchy, they live for the individual. In the latter, men can nonethelesss hardly be devoid of an Idea; they make themselves an individual Idea, an Ideal. There we find an Idea as it should be; here (in a republic) an Ideal, that is, one which they have rarely created themselves, divinity.'[7]

So the 'Idea' of which Hegel speaks in the context of political philosophy is the political community, the preservation of which is the common purpose of free citizens. He found one such community actualized in Attic democracy, and another in the Roman republic: 'The idea of his country or of his state was the invisible and higher reality for which he (the free citizen) strove, which impelled him to effort; it was the final end of *the* world, an end which he found manifested in the realities of his daily life or which he himself cooperated in manifesting and maintaining.'[8]

The concept of the state which Hegel develops in § 114 of his natural law lectures of 1818–19 accords so patently with these and similar remarks in his Frankfurt and Jena writings that there can be no doubt as to its republican character.

With these preliminaries in mind, we can understand what Hegel says in the second part of § 114: the citizens of a free state are only 'moments' in the spirit of their people, and as such they produce the 'spirit' of their people; but this 'spirit' is just as much the end of their activity as their activity and their understanding of themselves 'depend on it' (have it for their foundation).[9] So it can be no surprise if, in the explanatory remarks to paragraph 114 of his lectures, Hegel says: 'The right [Recht] of the state is the highest law for the individual.' This is not, as one might suppose, a demand for the subordination of the individual to the interests of the state; it is, rather, a recognition of the right (Recht) of the citizens to take part in political decisions within the state.

In §§ 116–21 of the 1818–19 lecture course Hegel then faces the task of applying this conception of the state, based on Attic democracy and the Roman republic, to the institutions of the modern state; and of showing what implications it holds for the modern state. He begins with the idea that, in the modern state, freedom must be actualized in the citizen's right of self-determination:

Concrete freedom, the actuality of which is the state, lies in the circumstance that personal individuality and particularity not only possesses full development and recognition of its rights but also is partly absorbed into the interests of the universal and partly consciously and deliberately acknowledges this interest and is active on its behalf; so that the universal is never accomplished without the particular interest, knowledge and good will of the particular, nor do private persons live in and for this [particular interest], without at the same time willing in and for the universal and being consciously effective for it (§ 116).

The modern state is first and foremost distinguished from the political communities of antiquity by the fact that its citizens have the right to a private sphere.[10] But in Hegel's work these liberal civil rights are expanded into fundamental social rights (Dahrendorf): individuals are to be guaranteed not only the 'recognition of their rights' to a private sphere, but over and above that they are to have assured 'the full development' of their personal individuality and particularity. But according to Hegel's conception, these private civil rights must be complemented by political rights. Since the private interests of citizens are absorbed into universal and public interests, it is desirable for the realization of freedom in the state that the citizens should acknowledge 'the universal' (the organs of the state and their activity) 'both consciously and deliberately'. Without this acknowledgement, a modern state could not claim to be an institution in which concrete freedom is actualized. The crucial factor is, however, that, in addition to this recognition, citizens must be given the right to act on behalf of 'the universal'. Only by this means, Hegel believes, can the state be prevented from splitting into two mutually hostile sections, the political and the private. The unity of the state is thus, according to his conception, only guaranteed where the organs of the state are not independent of the particular interests of citizens, but act in public and with the consent of the citizens; and, conversely, where the citizens are not confined to the pursuit of private interests but can at the same time also act in accordance with the interests of the general community and with an eye to universal aims. If these conditions are met, then Hegel can indeed say of the citizens of a modern state that they too 'only produce it as "moments" of this one mind'. His republicanism, centred on antiquity, is thus clearly articulated into a conception of the modern free and democratic legal state.

The implications for the relation between the two spheres of private and public life are described by Hegel in § 117 of his lectures of 1818–19: from the standpoint of the citizen interested only in his private ends, the state appears to be an 'external necessity', inasmuch as its 'laws are subject to the nature of the state and dependent upon it'. However, from the point of view of a citizen conscious of his rights of political participation, the state acquires 'freedom in its actuality'. Only the actualization of these private and political civil rights gives the state 'its true vigour'; for the state can only make demands on its citizens inasmuch as it has given them rights.[11]

With this conception of the state, Hegel attacks two mutually incompatible one-sided views, as he explains in § 118.[12] The one hopes for the actualization of freedom through an awakening of political consciousness ('sentiment'), in particular, an awakening of an idealistic consciousness of freedom.[13] The other considers that only the creation of state institutions on the basis of a written constitution would be a proper and adequate means for the actualization of freedom in the state.[14] Hegel attempted to combine the justifiable aspects of these two one-sided views in his conception of the state as an 'organism'; the state should be internally structured according 'to its concrete estates' and fulfil its tasks through institutions the working of which was to be determined 'by the Idea'.[15] From these activities and interests, there would then result 'the universal interest and achievement, and therewith also the universal political sentiment'. Political sentiment and state institutions should mutually determine one another and so form the 'organic' constitution of the state. Hegel then describes their internal structure in the three following paragraphs, which conclude this section of his work.

The spheres of family and civil society together form the realm of private life, in which individuals pursue their particular and limited ends. As a part of this state, this realm is, as Hegel puts it, the 'spirit' of the state 'in its finiteness' (§ 119). There are clear echoes of the republican ideals of his youth in Hegel's interpretation of the limited character of private existence as a loss of free humanity which can only be justified as a sacrifice necessary for the preservation of the political community: 'It may seem hard that the totality of ethical life relinquishes a part of its individuals to the limitations of family life or to the need of civil life. On the one hand that is necessity; on the other [there is] reconciliation in that necessity.'[16] It is in this light, too, that we should understand the phrase that the 'mind of the state' (or spirit, *Geist*) 'relegates a part of its individuals – the mass – to the spheres of family and civil society'. Evidently he does not here envisage state recruitment of the work-potential of society, as suggested, e.g., by Plato in the *Republic*. But in order to eliminate any such misunderstanding, he immediately adds that the freedom of the state 'is only concrete and actual when channelled through the particular will (of its citizens)'.

However, unlike his early writings, Hegel's lectures of 1818–19 lay emphasis on the idea that even private spheres of life are already permeated by the institutions and laws of public life; they absorb 'the universal into themselves'. Moreover, the pursuit of private interests in the long run benefits all members of the political community. The private spheres are therefore, in the last resort, 'founded and justified in the universal end'. Even in the institutions of civil society, then, individuals can 'recognize and confirm as their substance' (§119) the universal end of the preservation and formation of the state community. In the following §120, Hegel names institutions which guarantee the actualization of freedom in the state: 'the freedom of person and property', the 'public laws', the magistrates' court, communal and provincial self-government, and the corporations of civil society, which 'directly provide a universal occupation for individuals'. But the actualization of freedom is completed only in the organization of state institutions. In §121, which brings his account to a close, Hegel attempts to develop this point.

In the organs of the state the 'universal' is the end of state action, both in the handling of public affairs themselves and in the supervision of the 'particular spheres' of civil society. Hegel now attempts to outline the structure of the organs of the state and the principle of the distribution of power by following Kant in using the model of rational action.[17] The establishment of universal norms is the task of the legislature, the 'subsumption of particular cases under these' is the task of the government; what remains are thus single acts of administration on the basis of universal and special norms. But at this point, Hegel, like Kant, is unable to apply the model of the practical syllogism to the distribution of state powers. He interprets those acts in the operations of state conduct which have direct bearing on particular circumstances as 'subjectivity of the final decision of the will', and ascribes them to an organ of the constitution which had never been mentioned before in this account – to 'princely power'. Yet it is perfectly clear that in Hegel's model of the distribution of power the activity of the monarch consists exclusively of single acts of administration, whose execution is left to the government.[18]

However, we cannot overlook the fact that at this point Hegel's republican conception of the state comes into conflict with the historical powers of his time. If individuals 'produce the state, have it as their end and depend upon it' (§114), then a monarch in this state can only play the part of a head of state who may in principle be deposed at any time; whereas at the time of the restoration, the monarchs of the European states claimed that they exercised underived rights of sovereignty. Hegel circumvents this conflict by accepting the 'monarchic principle'[19] of the restoration states, by attempting to justify it by reference to history;[20] and, for the rest, by trying to reduce the political significance of the monarch in his conception of the state to 'political nullity'.

II

In the spring and summer of 1819 Hegel was busy working out his *Philosophy of Right*; he intended to have it printed in September. Then the so-called Karlsbad Decrees were announced. They imposed strict political control on the German universities and extended pre-publication censorship to scientific works. In the winter semester of 1819–20, Hegel once again lectured on the philosophy of right; his book did not appear until October 1820.

These facts give some indication as to how the relationship between the philosophy of right lecture of 1818–19 and the *Philosophy of Right* which appeared in 1820 should be interpreted. Clearly, in the fifteen months beween the completion of the lecture and going into print, Hegel had expanded his manuscript considerably: the published book contained, not 142 paragraphs, but 360. They do, however, correspond very closely with the text of the lecture; for Hegel, as a rule, used the older manuscript as a basis when writing his full version. This is also evident in the corresponding sections on the concept of the state, as the following list shows:

1818–19	1820
§114	§257
	§258
§115	§259
§116	§260
§117	§261
§118	
§119	§262
	§263
§120	
	§§264–6
§121	
	§§267–73

Whilst §§114–17 of the *PhR* 1818–19 correspond closely with §§257–61 of the *PhR* 1820, Hegel reformulated the succeeding paragraphs during 1819–20.

Thus, in the *Philosophy of Right* of 1820, the section on the state begins with an exposition of that republican ideal of the state which is essentially centred on the political association of free citizens in antiquity. Hegel even goes so far here as to describe political association as something divine: it is, like the divine mind of Aristotelian metaphysics, 'an absolute unmoved end in itself' (§258)[21]; it is 'the absolutely divine principle' which has 'majesty and absolute authority' (§258R) and, with reference to the civic goddess Athene, the 'mind of a nation' is called 'the divine, knowing and willing itself' (§257R). In 1820, Hegel expressly applies all this to the modern state.[22]

However, in paragraph 258 of the revised *Philosophy of Right* the antiquity-orientated ideal of a republic of free citizens also appears expressly in the form of the modern democratic state, as first conceived by Rousseau; the state is at the same time 'the actuality of the substantial will which it possesses in the particular self-consciousness once that consciousness has been raised to consciousness of its universality'. The citizens thus recognize the political association of which they are members, not only (as Hegel puts it, modelling his formulations on the philosophy-of-right lectures of 1818–19) as their 'essence', and as the 'end and product' of their activity (§257), but also as an institution which they have jointly willed and created. It is therefore only consistent if Hegel, like Rousseau, rejects the liberalistic conception of the state which defines the purpose of the srate as being *merely* 'the security and protection of property and personal freedom', because it deprives the citizen of his political significance: 'the individual's destiny is the living of a universal life'. Thus he expressly accords Rousseau the merit of having established 'the will as principle of the state' (§258R).

Precisely at this point, however, Hegel shies away from the political consequences of his republican, or democratic, conception of the state. If the state is an institution willed and created jointly by the citizens, then the citizens also have the right to determine the constitution of their state for themselves. It is just this that Hegel will no longer admit in 1820, because by doing so he would call into question the monarchical principle of the restoration state. According to the doctrine of Rousseau, 'the dignity of the monarch' would, as he quite rightly remarks, be 'something reduced, not only in its form, but in its essence' (§279R). Hegel feels obliged to object to this conception by declaring that Rousseau's doctrine would result in 'logical inferences which destroy the absolutely divine principle of the state, together with its majesty and absolute authority' (§258R). It seems from this that Hegel means to assert the incompatibility of Rousseau's democratic theory of the state with his own republican conception of the state. But in

fact the conflict is between the democratic theory of the state and the
restoration doctrine of the monarchic principle, which Hegel now seeks to
justify and substantiate. It becomes clear that Hegel is fully aware of this when
he assures us: 'Hence the majesty of the monarch is a topic for thoughtful
treatment by philosophy alone, since every method of inquiry, other than
the speculative method of the infinite Idea which is purely self-grounded,
annuls the nature of majesty altogether' (§281R). The republican idea that
political association is something divine is of course thereby transformed into
the idea that monarchic power is something divine: 'Akin, then, to this
reasoning [Hegel's speculative "substantiation" of monarchy] is the idea of
treating the monarch's right as grounded in the authority of God' (§279R).[23]

But when Hegel, in order to be able to assert the conformity of his political
philosophy with restoration ideology, rejects the idea that the dignity of the
monarch is something deduced and belittles the doctrine of popular
sovereignty as 'a confused idea' (§279), he implicitly also calls into question
his own conception of the state according to which the citizens understand
the state as the 'end and product' of their activity. A monarch who possesses
state sovereignty (§278), and rules by his own absolute power, is alien to
Hegel's originally republican conception of the state. Thus the conflict, which
was still latent and meant to be played down in the philosophy-of-right
lecture of 1818–19, becomes apparent in the *Philosophy of Right* of 1820.

The conception which Hegel propounds in the two opening paragraphs
of this latter work does indeed accord entirely with the one he had put
forward in §114 of his 1818–19 lectures. But the basis of this conception is
destroyed by the intellectual context into which it is shifted in 1820.
Nevertheless, Hegel still attempts, in the second part of his introduction
(§§260–70), to show how the Idea of freedom is actualized in the modern
state. Thus he transfers almost word for word (§264f.) the two paragraphs
on liberal and political fundamental rights (§116f.) from his lecture of
1818–19. But in the Remark to §261 he practically withdraws what he has
laid down shortly before. The thesis that individuals in the state only 'have
duties to the state in proportion as they have rights against it' (§261)[24] turns,
in the Remark, into the idea that the rights of the citizen are entirely different
in content from his duties, as a subject, to prince and government. In his
'elucidation', Hegel inverts the idea that citizens' rights must be the
foundation of all duties in the state into its precise opposite by making the
fulfilment of the duties of a subject a precondition of all civil rights: 'The
isolated individual, so far as his duties are concerned, is in subjection; but as
a member of *civil society* he finds in fulfilling his duties to it[25] protection of
his person and property, regard for his private welfare, the satisfaction of
the depths of his being, the consciousness and feeling of himself as a member
of the whole; and, in so far as he completely fulfils his duties by performing

tasks and services for the *state*, he is upheld and preserved' (§261R). The political self-consciousness of the republican here appears reduced to the subject's awareness of and pride in himself as 'a member of the whole'. There is no longer any mention of the citizen's political rights of participation in the state, that is, of the idea that 'individuals... will the universal in the light of the universal, and their activity is consciously aimed at none but the universal end' (§260): Hegel mentions only liberal civil rights and a certain 'managerial and political sense' (§310).

The incompatibility between Hegel's explanations in the Remark to §261 and the wording of §260f. is typical of Hegel's elaboration of the *Philosophy of Right* during the years 1819–20. By far the largest part of the texts which Hegel seems to have composed after the publication of the Karlsbad Decrees in September 1819 are to be found in the Preface and in the Remarks – and, incidentally, they occur with striking frequency precisely at the end of a Remark. This points to the conclusion that Hegel left largely unchanged[26] the text which he wanted to have printed in September 1819 and made his corrections chiefly by deletions and supplementary additions. It thus becomes understandable that, in §§262–70, Hegel develops his conception of the state as 'the actuality of concrete freedom' (§260) with no hint of those authoritarian state ideas which appeared in the Remark to §261. That does not, of course, mean that the original republican conception of the state of the *Philosophy of Right* was developed without distortion in these paragraphs.

The fact that this section is a revision of §§119–21 of the philosophy-of-right lectures of 1818–19 is shown by the word for word correspondences between §262 of *PhR* 1820 and §119 of *PhR* 1818–19. There are nonetheless notable differences between these two versions. While in 1818–19, Hegel sharply distinguishes the 'spheres' of the family and civil society from the institutions of the state,[27] in 1820 he wishes to show particularly how the Idea of the actualization of freedom connects the institutions of society with the institutions of the state: individuals choose their own family and social position in the circumstances obtaining (§262); but the mutual interdependence of all members of civil society already displays 'the power of the rational in necessity' (§262). Thus individuals actualize their private and public rights to freedom in the social institutions (§264) which form the 'constitution' of the state 'in the sphere of particularity' (§265); but social institutions need unification[28]; in them, a political, civic sentiment of the citizens can develop (§267f.); the structure of the institutions of the state is based on rational principles (§269), and the end of the state is completely actualized in the activity of the organs of the state (§270). With this sketch Hegel indeed seems to have developed what he had declared programmatically in §260f. It is beyond doubt that, to this extent, the same intentions underlie both his text of 1820 and the earlier text of 1818–19.

These intentions, however, can only be discerned with great difficulty; and this leads to a further difference between the two versions. Whereas in 1818–19 Hegel in unambiguous terms describes the 'guarantee and actuality of the free totality' (§ 120), in 1820 he seems, in the corresponding passage, to be trying to shroud his intentions in obscure formulations:

The guarantee and actuality of the free totality therefore lies in the institutions of the freedom of person and property, public laws, public trial by jury; further in the constitution[29] of the particular branches of civil society, as well as of the individual spheres of the whole communal life of parishes and provinces, as in corporations which by independent right manage their own interests and resources, and directly provide individuals with a universal occupation.

Mind is the nature of human beings *en masse* and their nature is therefore twofold: (i) at one extreme, explicit individuality of consciousness and will, and (ii) at the other extreme, universality which knows and wills what is substantive. Hence they attain their right in both these respects only in so far as both their private personality and its substantive basis are actualized. Now in the family and civil society they acquire their right in the first of these respects directly and in the second indirectly, in that (i) they find their substantive self-consciousness in social institutions which are the universal implicit in their particular interests, and (ii) the Corporation supplies them with an occupation and an activity directed on a universal end.

Put more simply, but more clearly, § 264 of *PhR* 1820 may be summarized thus: in the state, individuals have private and public rights; their private rights they receive directly in the spheres of family and civil society; their public rights are actualized in two ways; in the social institutions which administer their particular interests, they have 'their substantive self-consciousness' (in so far as they see themselves represented in these institutions); to the extent that they are actively engaged in these institutions, they receive, in addition, the opportunity of 'an occupation and activity directed on a universal end'. It is thus clear that Hegel is here merely reiterating what he had already said in § 260 of *PhR* 1820 (§ 116 of *PhR* 1818–19).

However, it also now becomes clear that in § 264 he withdraws much of what was foreshadowed in § 260. For in § 260, as in the corresponding passage in the lectures of 1818–19, 'the actuality of concrete freedom' in the state means that individuals 'will the universal in the light of the universal, and their activity is consciously aimed at none but the universal end'; in § 264, by contrast, the 'occupation and activity directed on a universal end' is restricted to the institutions of civil society whose aim is precisely 'limited and finite' (§ 265). 'Political sentiment' is, by contrast, 'simply a product of the institutions subsisting in the state'; but this sentiment has, in Hegel's words, its basis merely in the 'consciousness that my interest, both substantive and particular, is contained and preserved in another's [here the state's]... interest and end' (§268). Thus the restriction of the citizen's freedom to the sphere of society is signed and sealed; for him, the state is no longer 'the end and product of his activity' (§257), but 'another'. There is still talk of the citizens' rights of political participation in the state in §260, and this text is taken over from the lectures of 1818–19. In the expositions which Hegel worked out after his lectures (§§262–70), this is passed over in silence. The 'universal life' which, according to Hegel, the citizens are destined to lead in the state (§257R) is, in the elaboration of his idea, reduced to the subjects' 'trust' that the organs of the state are acting in their interest (§268).

Once Hegel has, in this fashion, restricted the public rights of the citizens in the state to participation in the self-government of corporations, he can of course no longer envisage the 'organism of the state' (§269) as developing from the Idea of the citizens' freedom. From §266 onwards, therefore, the freedom of the citizen is replaced by the freedom of the state. It is not the freedom of the citizens that is actualized in the institutions of the state; rather 'the mind' or the Idea of the state becomes, in the organs of the state, '*aware* of itself as its own object and end' and thus 'a shape of freedom' (§266). If asked whose mind it might be which actualized itself as a shape of freedom in the organs of the state, Hegel would certainly have answered that it is the Idea of the state as conceived by free citizens. But, in the political conditions prevailing at the time of the restoration, he cannot maintain that it is the free citizens who are '*their own* object and end' in the operation of the political institutions of their state; and so he must leave unresolved the question of what foundation the 'mind' of his state has in political reality.

Hegel does emphasize, even at this point, that the 'end of the state' is 'the universal interest' and that the 'conservation...of particular interests' is catered for within this universal interest (§270); but this holds equally well even in a paternalistic state constitution. In the context of his republican conception of the state, Hegel should have shown how the citizens are themselves entitled to provide for the actualization of this universal end of the state. Instead, he contents himself with deriving the doctrine of the organs of the state from the concept of the universal end of the state: the concept of the end of the state 'is divided into the distinct spheres of its activity, which correspond to the moments of its concept' (§270); the structure of the state powers is 'fixed by the *nature of the concept*' (§269). With these formulations, Hegel is no doubt deliberately anticipating the rational model of the division of power which he later outlines in §273 following Kant's original[30] as he did in the lectures of 1818–19. But he does not make clear the purpose which this model is meant to serve in a rational theory of the state: namely, to derive the competences of state powers from the Idea of the institutionally guaranteed actualization of rights and to define them in these terms. Since this remains unclear throughout his work, Hegel cannot succeed in basing the institutions of the state on the Idea of the actualization of freedom. An impression is thus created that the abstract concept of the end of the state leads a kind of independent existence in that it 'is divided into the distinct spheres of its activity, which correspond to the moments of its concept' in accordance with conceptual necessity.

The dire consequences of this separation of the end of the state from the Idea of the actualization of freedom in a republican state are fully manifest when, at the end of his exposition, Hegel tries to bring the Idea of the state back into the area of political reality from which he had previously removed it. In the activity of the organs of the state, the 'spirit' or 'mind' of the state becomes a 'mind knowing and willing itself' (§270). The political consciousness of the bearers of state power, which is what Hegel is discussing here, remains separate from the 'political sentiment' of the members of civil society, which consists merely of the 'trust' that the possessors of state power are preserving their 'interest, both substantive and particular' (§268). At the end of his exposition of the concept of the state, Hegel is, therefore, referring only to individuals active in the organs of the state when he says: 'the state therefore knows what it wills' (§270). At the beginning of these observations, by contrast, he had declared that the state 'exists...mediately in individual self-consciousness, knowledge, and activity' (§257); and by this he certainly meant the citizens and not merely those holding office. Thus, in the course of his exposition in the *Philosophy of Right* of 1820, the state of the citizens has become the state of the office-holders, and the republican conception of the state has become the authoritarian state.

III

The results of the foregoing analysis appear to substantiate to a very large extent the critique which Marx, in 1843, put forward in his commentary on this section of Hegel's *Philosophy of Right*. But this impression proves deceptive as soon as one looks more closely at Marx's discussion. For it emerges that Marx is primarily concerned to substantiate the correctness of Feuerbach's critique of Hegel by reference to the text of the *Philosophy of Right*, and that he therefore almost consistently ignores Hegel's intentions and train of thought. Moreover, he seems scarcely to have understood the meaning of important parts of Hegel's text. He reproaches Hegel with mistakes which the latter simply has not made; and he overlooks deficiencies which it would have been decidedly in his interest to criticize. Thus he arrives at conclusions about Hegel's political philosophy which do justice neither to Hegel's intentions nor to his own purposes.

At the very beginning of the manuscript as preserved, in his commentary on §261 of *PhR* 1820,[31] Marx seems almost obsessively determined to push the obvious intentions of Hegel into the background. Whereas Hegel wants to make it clear that, in relation to the interests of individuals in civil society, the state is both 'the end immanent within them' and also 'an external necessity and their higher authority', Marx occupies himself exclusively with the idea of the dependence of private interests on the universal interest of the state and their subordination to it. Making this an absolute, he feels impelled to prove that Hegel has admitted that, in the state as he conceived it, 'relations, limiting and contrary to an autonomous being' prevail (404.24f.).[32] He goes on to assert that Hegel thus ascribes to the state a necessity 'which relates by opposition to the inner being of the thing' (404.27f.). In fact, Hegel had merely drawn attention to the point that the state does indeed seem an 'external necessity' to the individual who is limited to his private interests.[33] The fact that Hegel at the same time characterizes the state as the 'immanent end' of the private sphere of life (because the state guarantees its existence) is for Marx merely a symptom of an 'unresolved antinomy' in Hegel's thought, in so far as the state is supposed to be 'on the one hand external necessity, on the other hand immanent end' (405.1–3). He seems not to have realized that, in any state, private and universal interests coincide only partially. In his critique of Hegel, Marx thus adopts the stance (clearly without being able to account for it to himself) of an individual living only for the sake of his private interests, and refusing to pay a price for the political guarantees of his rights to freedom.

Marx has clearly overlooked the fact that Hegel, first, in §261, makes civil rights the foundation of all duties in the state, and then, in the Remark, presents the fulfilment of the duties of a subject as a condition for the preservation of civil rights. He passes, completely without comment, both over Hegel's thesis that the duties of a citizen in the state must correspond exactly to his rights and over Hegel's shrinking from the consequences of this doctrine.

All the more emphatically does he point out, in his discussion of §262, that at this juncture Hegel's 'logical, pantheistic mysticism' is 'very clearly' in evidence (406.21f.). 'The entire mystery of the *Philosophy of Right* and of Hegelian philosophy in general is contained in these paragraphs' (408.30–2). But Marx can arrive at this interpretation only by taking §262 out of context and completely misconstruing its significance in Hegel's exposition. Whereas Hegel wishes to show how the rights to freedom of the members of civil society expand to become rights of participation in social institutions (§§ 262–4), Marx simply fixes on the metaphysical tone of Hegel's style. He intends it to serve him as proof that in Hegel's exposition 'the producing' is conceived 'as the product of its product' (408.1f.), i.e. that Hegel is representing the activities of the individuals from which the state arises as the result of the activity of an abstract 'Idea'. And this critique, inaccurate as it is in itself (at this point, at least), also reveals that Marx is himself proceeding on the basis of inadequate presuppositions.

In §262, and similarly in §119 of his philosophy-of-right lecture course of 1818–19, Hegel begins by describing the political community of a state from the point of view of the whole and by emphasizing the actualization of the right to freedom in the state. He takes as his starting-point the fact that the acts in which members of civil society determine their social position under the prevailing natural and social conditions always have as their condition a pre-existing structure of society. From the point of view of the state as a whole, the establishment of a family and the individual choice of a vocation are to be interpreted as processes by which individuals enter into already existing branches and institutions of social activity. Hegel's metaphysical style notwithstanding, there is nothing at all mystical in this. Marx, however, feels it his duty to interject here that 'the political state cannot exist without the natural basis of the family and the artificial basis of civil society' (407.40–2) – as if it had ever occurred to Hegel to doubt the fact.

In his attempt to unmask Hegel as the representative of a 'logical, pantheistic mysticism', Marx first of all bases his assertions on Hegel's remark that 'the actual Idea is mind' and that it distributes to the spheres of family and civil society 'the material of this its finite actuality, viz., human beings as a mass'. Here indeed there would seem to be a 'subjectivization' of the Idea (406.37), and therewith a hypostatization of a universal concept. In fact, it is simply a matter of *façon de parler*; Hegel is speaking of processes described from the point of view of the state as though they were an activity of the state. The 'distribution' of individuals to the spheres of family and civil society means in concrete terms simply that individuals take on various social functions on the basis of personal decisions. This 'distribution' *is* in consequence, as Hegel particularly emphasizes, 'mediated by circumstances, the individual's caprice and his personal choice of his station in life'. He does not mean that this mediation is merely an appearance, or even an illusion, but rather that it is observed from a particular point of view.

Marx misinterprets this simple implication and objects that 'this fact, this actual situation is expressed by speculative philosophy as appearance, as phenomenon' (406.25–7) and that it thus becomes 'an inner imaginary activity' (406.37–9). But what 'speculative philosophy' is expressing here is simply the dependence of any description of facts on the standpoint from which it is made; an individual's choice of vocation *appears* from any given individual's standpoint to be a decision within his life history; from the standpoint of society (the 'Idea') it *appears* to be the assumption of a social function. The speculative interpretation of these processes is indeed intended to make clear that the active individual's way of seeing things is neither the only possible way nor the only 'true' perspective to describe social facts.

Marx, by contrast, is inclined precisely to the view that the perspective of actual individuals is the only 'true' perspective. He therefore lays considerable emphasis on the point: 'The fact is that the state issues from the mass of men existing as members of families and of civil society' (408,12–14). Now Hegel's intention in this section of his work is indeed, as our analyses above have demonstrated, to show the state as emerging from the activity of its citizens. But Hegel would certainly not just set this down as a 'fact'. Marx not only fails to see this intention in Hegel's account; he feels obliged to object that, in Hegel, 'the empirical fact in its empirical existence has a significance which is other than it itself' (408.23–5). This is only an objection if Marx assumes that empirical facts have no other significance in their existence than just that they *are* empirical facts. But this empiricism is hardly appropriate as a basis for argument when criticizing Hegel's speculative method.

The misinterpretations which Marx produces in this discussion also stem from his failure to consider the connection between § 262 and the following paragraphs. It is significant that he barely mentions §§ 263–8, which, both because of their obscurity and because of their importance, would have been well worth commenting on. He fails to see that, in these explanations, Hegel is aiming precisely at the goal which he had indicated at the beginning of this section of his *Philosophy of Right* (§ 257ff.): to develop the Idea of the state as 'end and product' of the activity of its citizens; or, to use Marx's words, to show that 'the state issues from the mass of men existing as members of families and of civil society'. Marx therefore fails completely to see how Hegel misses this goal and how in his account, the Idea of the state becomes, almost by way of compensation, an independent entity in certain respects. Instead, he merely objects that Hegel is here using abstract categories from his *Logic* to show the transition of family and civil society to the political state; this transition is, he says, 'not derived from the specific essence of the family, etc., and the specific essence of the state, but rather from the universal relation of necessity and freedom' (409.29–33). Hegel, he says, is exclusively concerned 'to discover, for the particular concrete determinations, the corresponding abstract ones' (409.38f.). But this reproach is surely unjustified. In § 266n Hegel does indeed use, as he so often does, a schematic interpretation from his *Logic* in order to describe the relationship between social institutions and the realm of the state. But he gives no indication whatsoever that the sequence of logical categories permits the 'derivation' of the state from family and civil society.[34]

Since, under the influence of Feuerbach's critique of Hegel, Marx is primarily concerned to follow up Hegel's alleged mysticism, he barely touches upon the political implications of Hegel's account. Consequently, the charge of abstraction which he constantly levels against Hegel rebounds on himself. Instead of working out the concrete political significance of what Hegel conveys by means of concepts and models from his *Logic*, and submitting it to a thoroughgoing political critique, Marx himself abstracts from the real political implications of this text so that he can dismiss it as a piece of applied logic. He then on several occasions reproaches Hegel with precisely the thing which Hegel was seeking to achieve.[35] For this very reason he fails to perceive where – by the criteria of his own and Hegel's intentions – the true weaknesses of this text actually lie. He thus praises Hegel's 'nice exposition concerning political sentiment' (410.29f.), but he takes no interest in the question which political rights of participation are, in Hegel's work, meant to be the basis of this sentiment. On the contrary, his objections are that 'what is not clarified is the way in which familial and civil sentiment, the institution of the family and those of society, as such, stand related to the political sentiment and political institutions and cohere with them' (410.13–17). But it is precisely Hegel's intention in §§264–6 to enlarge upon this connection. It has to be said that Hegel at this point barely goes beyond an authoritarian state patriotism of the Lutheran stamp, but he cannot be accused of not having explored the connection at all.

Marx turns this into its opposite when, in his detailed discussion of §269f., he attributes to Hegel the intention of deriving the constitution of the state from the abstract concept of the Idea. Hegel does indeed attempt to found the power of the state and the division of powers on the abstract Idea of the end of the state, instead of deriving it from the principle of the political freedom of the citizen in the state. By the criteria of his own intentions, this is certainly inadequate. When he argues that legislation, government and princely power are 'fixed by the nature of the concept' (§269), i.e. inasmuch as, for the actualization of the end of the state, the 'moments' of universality, particularity and singularity must be represented by special institutions (§273), one could reasonably expect him to make clear how this arrangement of state power was related to the universal end of the state ('the individual's destiny is the living of a universal life' (§258R)). But these omissions do not justify the criticism that Hegel had no intention whatever of describing this connection, but was rather attempting to give 'the political constitution a relation to the abstract Idea', to classify it 'as a member of its (the Idea's) life history' (415.6–8). In these two paragraphs Hegel is not speaking of the abstract Idea in general, but of the Idea of the state.

It would seem that Marx did not understand at all the formulation that the three powers are 'fixed by the nature of the concept'. He imagines that it can be dismissed with the comment 'the various powers do not have their specific character by reason of their own nature, but by reason of an alien one' (415.12f.).

Marx here takes for granted that the 'nature of the concept' and the 'own nature' of the powers of the state have nothing to do with one another, and this is surely incorrect. The attempts by Kant and Hegel to describe the distribution of power by reference to the model of the practical syllogism are admittedly inadequate;[36] but it cannot be denied that they intend to use this interpretative model to determine rationally and appositely the relationship of the powers of the state to one another. The rationality of the division of powers which Kant and Hegel seek to establish is not therefore alien to the 'own nature' of these powers; it is exactly and precisely what this 'own nature' *is*. It is not the attempt to establish the rationality of the division of powers which is at fault; the error lies in trying to do this by means of the over-simple model of the practical syllogism.

In view of these fundamental misinterpretations, it hardly comes as a surprise when, at the end of his remarks on this section of the *Philosophy of Right*, Marx reaches the conclusion that this work taken as a whole is 'only a parenthesis to logic' (419.17f.). Hegel employs the term 'organic' (§ 269) for a constitution in which the three powers of the state stand in the same relation to one another as the three propositions of a practical syllogism; that is, their various functions complement one another and form, as it were, a living whole. In the three powers of the state the universal end of the state is articulated (to keep this image to which Hegel had been so much attached ever since his Aristotelian studies in Jena) into an 'organic' constitution. By this interpretation Hegel seeks to overcome the liberalistic conception of the division of powers as a mutual 'check of powers'. Even Marx regards this as a 'great step forward' (411.17f.). But since he failed to recognize the theoretical basis of this conception, the model of the practical syllogism, he feels in good earnest bound to conclude that Hegel, in his concept of the state, wished to deduce the 'organic' nature of the constitution from the abstract Idea of the organism. He then criticizes this supposed mistake of Hegel's with arguments which are as obvious as they are superfluous (412.2–20; 413.34; 414.10; and 414.18–41).

Starting from the premise that Hegel had turned subject into predicate throughout, Marx is content for his own part simply to invert this relationship.[37] He thus considers that, in his theory of the state, Hegel should have presupposed the division of powers and should then have developed the organic nature of the constitution from that 'the actual differences, or the different parts of the political constitution are the presupposition, the subject. The predicate is their determination as organic. Instead of that, the Idea is made subject, and the differences and their actuality are conceived to be its development and its result, while on the other hand the Idea must be developed out of the actual differences. What is organic is precisely the idea of the differences, their ideal determination' (411.28–36). But these sentences reveal how little can be achieved in this context with the stereotype of 'subject and predicate'. In a theory of the state, the division of powers cannot simply be assumed as something given, as though it were an empirical fact. And it is to be doubted whether there is any point in calling the 'organic' nature of the constitution the 'predicate' of this 'subject'.

Marx continues to work with the same interpretative premises in his discussion of the final paragraphs of this section. Having attempted to derive the organs of the state from the universal end of the state, Hegel aims, in § 270, to show that the state is actualized in the bearers of state power as 'mind knowing and willing itself'. To this Marx objects that 'the true starting point' where Hegel should have begun is 'mind knowing and willing itself'; without it, the universal end of the state and the three powers of the state are nothing but 'illusions devoid of principle or support, inessential and even impossible existents' (418.4–7). When Hegel depicted the end of the state and the powers of the state as modes of existence of the 'substance', and distinguished between them on this basis (418.18–20), he was merely using the state to prove the *Logic* (418.34). But Hegel does indeed, just as Marx had demanded that he should, start from the premise that the end of political unification ultimately lies in the 'preservation of the particular interests' of the members of a state. Because individuals can pursue and actualize their particular interests only on the basis of state guarantees, he therefore regards the 'universal interest as such' (the end of the state) as the 'substance' of particular interests. This expresses quite clearly the idea that the state is not to be conceived of as separate from the particular interests of its members. When Marx objects that 'had the actual mind been taken as the starting point, with the universal end its content, then the various powers would be its modes of self-actualization, its real or material existence, whose determinate character would have had to develop out of the nature of its end' (418.10–14), then we must reply by pointing out that Hegel does say just that: the 'real mind' from which Hegel starts is the 'particular ends' of individuals.[38]

Since Marx misinterprets all this and proceeds to regard it as demonstrated that one must, throughout, reverse Hegel's inversion of subject and predicate, he asserts that Hegel should have begun where he ended: with the 'mind knowing and willing itself'. But in Hegel's account, this is the self-consciousness of those active in the organs of the state; for only of them is it true that 'the state, therefore, knows what it wills and knows it in its universality, i.e. as something thought. Hence it works and acts by reference to consciously adopted ends, known principles, and laws which are not merely implicit but are actually present to consciousness; and further, it acts with precise knowledge of existing conditions and circumstances, inasmuch as its actions have a bearing on these' (§ 270). When Marx says that Hegel's theory of the state should have started from this point, he confuses the political consciousness of the bearers of state power in state institutions with the political consciousness of the citizens at large. He fails to see that Hegel ascribes to the bearers of state power what he should, in accordance with his own republican approach, have demanded for all citizens of the state: political self-consciousness. And he fails equally to see that, in the course of his account, Hegel increasingly loses sight of his initial premise: in § 257 the state 'exists...mediately in individual self-consciousness'; in § 270 the 'mind knowing and willing itself' of the state exists in the self-consciousness of office-holders, while the political sentiment of the citizen and subject is reduced to the 'trust' that his 'interest, both substantive and particular, is contained and preserved in another's [i.e. in the state's] interest and end' (§ 268). Misled by his eagerness to verify in the text of the *Philosophy of Right* Feuerbach's thesis concerning Hegel's confusion of subject and predicate, Marx fails to see what is indeed the politically decisive defect in Hegel's development of his conception in the version of 1820.

IV

As early as 1841, in a note to his doctoral dissertation, Marx had written: 'Also in relation to Hegel it is mere ignorance on the part of his pupils, when they explain one or the other determination of his system by his desire for accommodation and the like, hence, in a word, explain it in terms of *morality*' (MEGA, I, i, 63). This remark is directed at the view, prevalent at the time amongst Hegel's followers, that in his Berlin writings Hegel showed a willingness to make many compromises with the Prussian state of the restoration era, and that these compromises obscure his true standpoint in current debates on the philosophy of law and religion.[39] Under the influence of Cieszkowski,[40] Marx counters this with the idea that 'this apparent accommodation has its deepest roots in an inadequacy or in an inadequate formulation of his principle itself' (MEGA, I, i, 64). Like Cieszkowski, he believes that in the contemplative nature of Hegel's basic approach, he has found that alleged inadequacy in the foundations of Hegelian philosophy.

This verdict clearly does not rest on an unbiassed assessment of the arguments which, to the minds of most of Hegel's disciples, seemed to suggest an 'accommodation' on Hegel's part. At no point did Marx attempt to invalidate these arguments. He is, on the contrary, of the opinion that it is 'more philosophical' to attribute the inadequacies of a philosophical work to the inadequacy of its philosophical premises, instead of explaining them in terms of a political reaction to topical and politically relevant questions. In the context of the idealist conception of history which Marx adopts[41] in his doctoral dissertation, this may appear compelling enough. But it is remarkable that neo-marxist authors, such as Lucio Colletti[42] or Jürgen Habermas,[43] should adopt this idealist conception simply because it is to be found in Marx, and reject the view of Hegel's political option in the era of restoration as a politically motivated decision. It would have been more in keeping with marxism's own image of itself as pre-eminently political philosophy if they paid more attention to the political significance of philosophical statements.

If we examine the arguments which support the idea that, in his Berlin period, Hegel was prepared to make concessions to the Prussian state of the restoration era, the view (especially prevalent among the Hegelian left) that Hegel in his time worked within the bounds of the possible for the transformation of political conditions immediately emerges as accurate.[44] But this demolishes the premise on which the young Marx, in his doctoral dissertation, based his verdict on Hegel; Hegel was by no means the contemplative philosopher primarily orientated towards the past that he purported to be in 1820 and afterwards. When, in face of the advance of the forces of restoration, he depicted the historical role of philosophy in the image of the owl of Minerva, which begins its flight only with the fall of dusk, this springs from a temporally conditioned political assessment of the situation. Hegel is more faithful to his historical image of himself when he compares the task of philosophy with the subversive activity of a mole.[45]

The present study only confirms this assessment. It has been shown in detail that, in discussing the concept of the state in his *Philosophy of Right* of 1820, Hegel in many instances undermines and retracts what he had advanced in the corresponding paragraphs of his lecture on the philosophy of right of 1818–19. These temporally conditioned concessions are indeed contrary to his basic conception; but his conception of the state, evolved in 1820, contains political aims which point far beyond Hegel's time into the future. Marx consistently ignores this in his critique of 1843, in order that, jumping on Feuerbach's bandwagon, he shall be able to unmask Hegel as the representative of a pantheistic mysticism. But, at least in the text discussed here, his interpretation falls wide of Hegel's intentions in every respect.

It is obvious that this result has a certain significance in the context of discussions currently going on, especially in Italy, on the connection between Marxist philosophy and Hegel.[46] The unpolitical approach of Marx's critique of Hegel in his manuscript of 1843 can be held partly responsible for the fact that, even in his later writings, Marx primarily concerned himself with questions of economy and society and largely neglected questions of legal and political philosophy.[47] In the firm belief that his critique of Hegel's political philosophy – in which German political and legal philosophy had 'been given its most consistent, rich and definitive form'[48] – had altogether demolished the standpoint of political philosophy, he felt it to be his duty henceforth to turn his attention primarily to the analysis of social and economic processes. The predominant tendency of marxists towards orthodoxy – even outside the pale of leninism-stalinism – has perpetuated this neglect.

This is the price which Marx had to pay for his urge to free himself, violently and prematurely, from Hegel's great shadow. Nonetheless, this unsuccessful attempt at liberation was politically a virtual necessity. When Marx set himself, with immense decisiveness and open visor, to enter the lists for the advancement of the very political principles which Hegel had defended with care and circumspection, the inordinate reflectiveness of Hegelian philosophy must have proved an obstacle. From the point of view of a 'philosophy of action' (Cieszkowski), Hegel's political philosophy might indeed appear as no more than 'pantheistic mystification'. Unjustified though this criticism is if one takes it seriously in a philosophical sense, it nonetheless appears justified in the political sense; Hegel's retreat into a metaphysical– sounding usage of language, clearly discernible when one compares the *Philosophy of Right* of 1820 with the corresponding formulations in the lectures of 1818–19, is in view of the political situation in that year a retreat from an unambiguous commitment to the political consequences of his doctrine – whatever additional philosophical meaning this usage of language may carry. As a political programme, Hegel's *Philosophy of Right*, then as now, is useless.

But any political programme, not merely the marxist one, needs to be founded on a political philosophy worthy of the name. No one with a knowledge of the debate over the fundamentals of political theory after Hegel will assert that we have progressed very far beyond Hegel's awareness of the problem. On the contrary, the history of political philosophy since Hegel shows a narrowing of the problem, which is counteracted only by more refined methodological analyses and by immensely increased empirical knowledge. Any serious reconsideration of the fundamentals of political theory must, therefore, eventually run the risk of missing its mark unless it bears in mind the questions which Hegel raised.*

* Translated from the German by H. Tudor and J. M. Tudor.

Towards a new systematic reading of Hegel's Philosophy of Right

KLAUS HARTMANN

Introduction

We live at a time of marked interest in questions of social order. This interest is not restricted to the observation of societal structures irrespective of whether they should be changed; intellectual, and indeed in many cases also public, opinion appears engaged in an open-ended process of pressing for solutions to what seem to be problems on the political or economic or, if we choose to deny the distinction, on the socio-political level.

There is room for disagreement about what prompts this process, but we can be sure that one fundamental motive is the impotence attributed to, or indeed actually felt by, the individual in the face of 'repressive' institutions which determine him (be they political or societal). Correspondingly, the interest in change in the social order is often focused on the universal participation of the individual in the structuring of society. People talk about 'democratization' and mean by this the setting up of a functional equality of all in the participation in any decision process, by analogy with the participation of all in the general elections of a political democracy. Here and there doubts have been voiced as to how such democratization can be reconciled with – perhaps necessary – hierarchical structures, or whether the exercise of collective self-determination will not be usurped by functionaries and activists so that a minority gets the better of the majority. And yet the slogan of equal participation and co-determination, which goes along with the levelling of the realms of economy, society and state, seems to have lost none of its impetus. Understandably, the slogan is variously expressed by the leading disciplines of the day such as marxism, sociology or neo-marxism.

It is surprising to note in surveying the scene how little reflection there has been on the part of social philosophy regarding the relationship between individuals and institutions; the dominant theoretical approaches do not seem to realize the need for affirmative theory. Now if, in spite of the socio-cultural situation sketched above, we propose to concern ourselves with Hegel, it will be with the intention of showing how the shortcoming of contemporary social philosophy might be made good. As opposed to neo-marxist approaches, which start out from human self-determination, social philosophy can be shown to be successful in its claim that institutions or institutional structures are necessary; this leaves us with the question of how the relationship between individuals and institutions can be couched in terms of *affirmative theory*.

The fact that this desideratum has remained largely unfulfilled can be explained by a basic assumption of current social theory which, as a remote inspiration of the dominant trends of the age, appears as something so obvious as not to be questioned. This basic assumption is that we should consider the social domain — society, societal structures and the state — from the vantage point of the *individual*, and regard institutions as a function of aggregates and indeed as themselves aggregates. This raises the demand for an equal footing of individuals and institutions, which themselves only consist of individuals: institutions appear as unjustified in their authority, in their *office*, to the extent that they, in operating, adopt subject-function over against the many, as the embodiment of the few who indulge in greater presumption than the other individuals (which is precisely what we accuse democratization of).

This basic *nominalist assumption* — Popper for his part speaks about *methodological nominalism* and *methodological individualism* — is a foregone conclusion for humdrum non-systems-theoretical sociology which in line with its empiricism regards institutions as a function of their individual bearers. Without an appreciation of its affirmativity, office can be no more than a legal exception to equality, or at best serve as a game-rule. The situation in systems-theoretical sociology is more complex in as much as supra-individual unity is allowed in the concept of system; but apart from society, the theory only provides for particular systems or sub-systems whose relations to each other can exhibit no affirmativity but only opposition. Nor does its thesis that institutions afford relief to the individual, a thesis shared by Gehlen's version of sociology, constitute affirmativity.

In the case of marxism, the fundamental nominalist assumptions seems to be in conflict with the fact that this doctrine postulates an overall totality — capital with its 'accessories', the exploited class — or, to put it another way, sets up a totality — capital — over against another totality — the working class. But this state of affairs is an object of criticism designed to lead over into species life in which human differentiation is eliminated. Species life is a totality, which at the same time constitutes an aggregate in line with the representational thought inherent in sociology. This has the theoretical bonus that the totality lacks an institutional frame even if the more developed notion of the proletariat reintroduces institutions such as state and party.

Neo-marxist theory, in turn, adopts the nominalist assumption when it embraces the notion of a 'communication community' where the inter-subjectivity of individuals goes to account for the priority of their community status. From here, the theory has to propose the equal relevance of each individual in decision processes; the structureless nature of a community of communicating individuals makes institutions impossible.

If it is justified to assume that nominalist social theory cannot deal with the problem of institutions, we are led to suggest that such theory turn to an approach which is not nominalist. It would then be necessary, but also possible, to understand social formations in their relationship to the individual as a *distinct type of unity*; furthermore, to introduce *structuredness*, a plurality of separate social formations in a common context; and to give a theoretical account of rational *affirmative relations* between the various social structures, including institutions.

I. Categorial social philosophy

We believe that in order to fulfil this task we shall have to have recourse to the concept of *category*. As opposed, e.g., to the concept of *rule*, which might be used in the interpretation of the law, the notion of a category has the advantage that with it one can achieve absolute comprehension of social structures as unities of specific content, provided that it is legitimate, as in the case of other categorial unities, to claim an ontological grasp of supra-individual unities. Categories are *unity claims* which can count as ontologically justifiable, in other words, claims without which the realm of actuality under consideration cannot be made intelligible. (We thus opt for wholes and claim that Popper's critique of 'holism' does not invalidate the categorial understanding of wholes; categories are not 'essences' in Popper's sense). With a multiplicity of social categories, structuredness, too, can be taken care of. And finally, it will be possible, by means of linking categories with one another in the dialectic, to establish affirmative relations between the various levels of social formations that may be legitimated. Over and above this, from a theoretical point of view the social domain would benefit from an ontology which can be articulated as a system, or as a systematic hermeneutic, affording, in a broad sense of the term, a thoroughgoing *transcendental* grounding.

One substantial attempt to achieve such a theory of the social domain is Hegel's *Philosophy of Right*. A systematic development of the theory type which we have called indiscriminately *categorial, transcendental* or *dialectical* has, however, been vitiated by the historical reception of its primary Hegelian statement. In some quarters, the *Philosophy of Right* has been subject to a reading which is theoretically inadequate, while in others certain features such as the monarchy, the estates, the rejection of a division of powers, primogeniture, etc., have been stressed so much as to permit of easy condemnation of the theory as a product of its age, although the distinction between society and state which is found in it has met with appreciation. (In the case of Marx, this distinction was judged to be the expression of a false actuality.) Anyhow, the task still remains of uncovering the deeper inadequacies of the *Philosophy of Right* that are not a product of historical circumstances. Despite all manner of inadequacies, however, its theoretical character must still rank as exemplary, for it does allow a statement of affirmative social relations.

In what follows we can only sketch some ideas towards a new systematic understanding of the *Philosophy of Right*; our aim will be partly a new sort of analysis, partly criticism, and partly the adumbration of corrections in line with a plea for social philosophy in categorial terms generally.

The theoretical foundations of Hegel's *Philosophy of Right*

An analysis of the theoretical fabric of *Philosophy of Right* has first to face the fact that it is a section out of a more comprehensive system. It covers the realm of what Hegel calls 'objective spirit', the subject-matter, together with the realm of 'subjective spirit', of a practical philosophy (*Realphilosophie*) valid for man. The statement as we have it in the *Encyclopedia* in turn points back to the *Logic*. So the *Philosophy of Right* benefits from the overarching rational structure of the system; it is ultimately grounded in the *Logic* which provides the determinations of universality, particularity and individuality so essential to any analysis of social structures.

As we have seen, social structures can be understood categorially as irreducibles with distinct status; the family, e.g., is something in its own right, not reducible to an aggregate of like individuals, and so likewise are society, corporation and the state. A second point is that the irreducibility and peculiarity of these formations does not prevent their distinct contents from being 'understood' by being related to each other and to a common basis. This is borne out by their reconstruction, a procedure through which they are related to earlier and later categorial levels and thus in keeping with a dialectical architectonic resulting from the *Logic*. Thus the family, e.g., appears as the immediate (natural) unity of plural spirit, society figures as reflective unity in disparity (as envisaged by the Understanding), and the state constitutes a unity which is for itself (self-comprehending, total).

A third point: the reconstructed categories form a context such that, in keeping with the linearity of the theory, a later stage is proved to be more *perfect* or *complete*, i.e., more rational or more true. An early stage such as the legal person and his property is deficient and as such demands further steps – contract, punishment, etc. – leading to the family, which in its turn requires the introduction of society, and this, by yet another move, calls for the state. The incompleteness of one stage leads on to a further, more perfect or complete one; the final stage is that of perfection or completeness to the extent that this is objectively possible. In systemic terms, such perfection is tantamount to a non-indebtedness to any further stage within the social realm.

This concluding stage has the logical meaning of what one could call a 'vertical' *inclusion* (Hegel speaks of *Aufhebung*, 'sublation') of the previous stage. The deficient stage is logically complemented by what, according to the organizing rational principle, it lacks to make up a whole; consequently it takes on a categorial novelty. At the final stage, there is no unintegrated opposite left over; the whole is presented as the result of imperfect antecedents, as *their* perfection and completion. The talk about sublation in the sense of 'preserving' antecedent determinations invites misunderstanding; when, e.g., society is transcended by or sublated into the state, society is still there as something not coincident with the state. What the state offers is the solution demanded by the fundamental theory of something that remained unsolved in the antecedent category of society, viz. an account of affirmativity. So the state presupposes society but has a content of its own. As a result, the concluding perfection must not only be taken for what it is in itself, but for what it is in relation to its antecedents. What is imperfect or abstract is complemented by the perfect or concrete which affords it affirmation; the affirmative is that which is affirmed by other categorial states. It is here that we can see a possible way of giving a theoretical account of *affirmative institutions*. The particular is fulfilled in the universal, which is concrete.

Now if the above account of social structures concerns a logical relationship between them which has its relevance in spite of the fact that we think of these structures as coexistent entities not subject to sublation, the question arises as to what extent Hegel does in fact intend a (vertical) inclusion of lower structures in a higher one (in the sense of an 'anomalous set', as N. Luhmann puts it, 'which includes itself as a part').[1] This is a problem to be kept in mind in relation to what follows.

Institutions in Hegel's *Philosophy of Right*

Having considered the type of theory represented by the *Philosophy of Right* in categorial (transcendental, dialectical) terms, we may now turn to an outline of the main institutions it reconstructs. What Hegel deals with first is the relationship between man and things (the latter being instances of what is immediately given in nature): property, either taken and possessed or formed and acquired, then rivalry for property and the settling of disputes over property in contract, together with wrong and its settlement, all under the title of *abstract right*. Hegel here adumbrates the law of property and of obligations, and the beginnings of criminal law, brought under abstract right because the subject-matter is abstract and because right is not yet grasped in its concrete social form.

If we pass over *morality*, a non-institutional sphere (much as Hegel had his systematic reasons for including it in his theory), we are left with the most important part of the *Philosophy of Right*, entitled *ethical life*, which thematizes the categorial state of affairs where the human subject is confronted with his fellows in such a way that this confrontation issues in unities of praxis, or, in other words, where the inclusion of one's opposite number constitutes (in a way we may call horizontal inclusion) a new content, or posits new concepts such as those of family, society, corporation and state.

The family, to comment on it briefly, is not simply to be thought of additively, in the sense that a man takes a wife (or, as of late, a woman takes a husband) and thus produces an aggregate, a companionship marriage. Rather we should view it as a 'concretely universal' unit whose constituents are its 'moments'. Logical tools are available to develop the concept of this concretely universal unit according to its moments of universality, particularity and individuality: the function of the man in public life, the inwardly directed role of the woman, and the totality of the family, posited as individual in the child.

Passing over the subtleties and the more dubious aspects of Hegel's interpretation of the family to a consideration of society as the next topic, we find as the fundamental thesis that it is an atomistic structure which can nevertheless be grasped as a unity (as is shown by economics, which deals with forms of societal rule-governedness). Unity in diremption is the logical scheme which makes intelligible a society of producers and consumers exhibiting a division of labour, a society which is also one that reflects upon itself with a view to its own survival and so establishes the administration of justice (redress in a given case of wrong-doing) and the police (redress in the form of continuous stabilizing, welfare and security.) Logically, then, we have a series of determinations covering the increasing unity of an atomistic system, from the parataxis of individuals to the reflection of a whole upon itself. Hegel is thus able to give a philosophical account of the economy, and, along with it, accounts of education as elemental to a community featuring the division of labour and of the societal organs required to regulate society in the acceptance of a 'state based on need'.

How is it that society is not the last category of social philosophy? Why does it lack something, so that Hegel thinks he has to move on to the *state*? Surely society already has everything – production and market, education,

administration of justice, welfare, self-stabilization? Hegel's exoteric answer
to this is that society cannot cope with itself, that it produces a polarization
of poverty and wealth, pauperization and colonialism (remarks in which
Hegel shows his reading of the English political economists). His esoteric
answer is that there must be a higher categorial structure, a structure with
a more affirmative relationship of the many to one another than obtains in
the antagonisms typical of society. The architectonic schema has a place left
for 'spirit's return to itself'. To put it another way, society is not yet
universal; it merely regulates the activities of the many bound up with their
atomism (thus implementing the typical task of Locke's 'political society',
which is the protection of the individual and his property) or provides
arrangements to accommodate particular, i.e., group interests. (Hegel is quite
modern in his grasp of the particular character of societal forces, even though
he did not fully realize the extent to which society is the realm of the
particular, as is shown by his reliance on corporations in a later context.) The
requisite level, not yet accomplished by society, that of the state, is not
sufficiently described in terms of the functions it has with respect to society,
compensating the deficiencies the latter cannot cope with; the state can fulfil
such a task only because, rather than being itself an instance of social rivalry,
it stands for the level of an identification of each and all or, in substantive
terms, for a universal community. To mediate the transition from society
to the state, Hegel adds a structure, the corporation, which to us seems to
be particular, a group centring on common interests within society, but which
Hegel regards as a type of identification with the universal, albeit a relative
one.

Logically, the state is the universal in which every individual is contained
as a 'moment'; accordingly, when individuals reflect upon each other as
citizens, the universal attains self-identity. The universal is the whole for the
many, who, included severally or horizontally, are its moments. The entire
structure can be read 'upwards', from the point of view of the individuals,
or 'downwards', from the point of view of the totality. The Hegelian
unity-oriented teleology favours the latter reading. Despite this, Hegel is at
great pains to show that in the modern age consideration must be given to
subjective freedom in the state. This he thinks is fulfilled in his concept of
the state.[2]

It is important to realize that Hegel's concept of the state is radically
different from an account in terms of non-categorial theories which try to
picture-think the state.[3] We are thinking here of Hobbes, Locke and many
others, including Rousseau, who wish to explain the genetic question of how
the atomic individuals in the state of nature establish a state. Hegel on the
other hand is interested in what the state is, regardless of how it arose.

However, the logical interpretation of the state as an organism in which the many relate to each other as to their whole, or in which the whole recognizes itself in the many and relates them to itself so as to be self-conscious (a theoretical model Hegel also uses to set up a concept of God, which is why the analogy between God and state so often occurs in Hegel) is not the last word, the introduction of individual satisfaction notwithstanding. A state on this interpretation would be a community of the many who have each other *qua* totality as a point of reference; it would be a community where this totality, as coincident with the many, is not separable from them as something possessing external existence. What we normally regard as an inevitable requirement, viz., leadership, a requirement refined later in Mill's idea that only a few can lead while the many must be judges of their leadership,[4] appears in Hegel as follows. The concrete universal called 'state' cannot figure as something concrete and actual unless its structure (which is its reflection on itself as universality) is shown to be something particular. From the point of view of dialectical logic, an undifferentiated and thus abstract whole is still a whole subject to its category. But in the present context we are dealing with a whole in objectivity, and this means that it must present itself to the universal as a universal turned objective.

In the political state, such a reflection is actual. In the state taken as an organization and hence as distinct from the politically constituted individuals, political universality is actual as an opposite, as a distinct and internally differentiated universal. Now the state as a whole, consisting of all politically constituted individuals, is just as much a universal as the political state. So for dialectical logic, the two, taken for what they are, are identical but for their different degrees of explicitness. But *qua* opposite of an other, the political state is particular, as are the many over against it.[5]

Only a short résumé of Hegel's conception of the political state is called for. The political state is divided into 'powers'. Among them, the *legislature* stands for universality, by virtue of its 'link' with the many who are represented by it. The *executive power* is, by force of dialectical logic, particular and as such 'linked' with the particularity of society; there are ministerial departments corresponding to societal differentiations. Finally, in Hegel's scheme, there is the *crown*, a unifying head, the fusion of universality and particularity in individuality. The monarch, advised by the executive and (indirectly) by the legislature, is the individual decision-maker. He is the bearer of sovereignty and as such modelled on the prince embodying the personality of the state in modern classical theory. Let us note that the judiciary is not a power in its own right, but falls under the executive; this is a Hegelian position hard to accept.[6]

Strangely enough, although the division of the material is as above, Hegel does not deal with it in this order (*PhR*, §273), but reverses it, beginning with the monarch (§§275ff.), who, as we noted, stands for the moment of individuality of the political state.[7] One would rather expect that the political state, as a universal, be grounded in its moment of universality, the legislature, to be developed next into differentiation by showing that the legislature can take on executive function only by way of certain organs, which might be specified according to the various tasks (taken care of by ministries) corresponding to the differentiations of society, all of which ought to be brought together in an executive head. This differentiation could ultimately terminate in the embodiment of the state in a figurehead.

But such a line of thought would conflict with the idea that the legislature is the least organic element in the political state. If logically subsequent formations were to be *functionally* dependent on this one, something relatively unorganic (even if preserved from the worst by pre-selection), or something comparatively irrational, would set the standard of rationality.

Clearly, then, Hegel has conflated a categorial (and that means systemic, architectonic) with a *representational* rationale. He wants to consider the various powers of the political state according to their degree of unity, and this is how they are being treated, but along with this there is the idea at work that a higher unity only comes about by the good grace of a lower one (in this case, the legislature). To forestall that Hegel rejects the sovereignty of the people (in §279 of the *Philosophy of Right*) with the argument that the people without a monarch are a 'formless mass' (a thesis that Marx was one of the first to criticize as a tautology: if the form, the constitution as a political body, is eliminated, one is left with formlessness).[8] Is it not rather the case that the dialectic ought to derive the necessity of further determination through the organs of state and the head of state from the very imperfection of what is merely universal (viz., the legislature)? For Hegel, however, such a progression of steps would imply a functional dependence of consequents on antecedents. His is a representational view of an untrue antecedent producing an existing untrue consequent, ignoring the dialectical rationale that what is more true results from what is less so. That is why he reverses the succession in his account of the political powers and starts with the gathering of the universal in individuality, as the dialectical truth in the monarch and then moves downwards. The development of the political state takes the monarch as its point of departure and establishes a 'linkage' with the many whose state it is via the executive (including administration) and the legislature. From what has been said it appears that there is a flaw in the dialectic.[9]

The state of estates

This flaw can be shown to be connected with a further problem. Confusing the *politically constituted many*, whom he regards as unorganic, with *society* — a dialectical mistake which ignores the novelty of political constitution – Hegel is of the opinion that the many as universal (as electorate) cannot set up a universal (the legislature) or, to discount any element of picturing, cannot recognize themselves and each other in a universal. Hegal regarded the formlessness of the many not only as *political amorphism*, but also as *societal pluralism* and *particularism*, neither of which he could accept as a political universal. His expression 'aggregate of private individuals'[10] covers both a political and societal state of affairs. Consequently he thought he ought to give political articulation to societal divisions according to their relative distance from, or closeness to, the state (cases in point being the so-called substantial estate of landowners, the representatives of the professional class, the so-called universal estate of civil servants). However societal, they occupy various levels of universality. The comparatively universally minded ones are more disposed to affirm what is affirmative than are the ones less so minded; they view the universal as non-alien to them, i.e., they are closer to the state, more convinced by it. (It may be left to sociology to judge on the plausibility of this thesis which has often been used to support policies promoting the acquisition of property on the part of individuals; there are undoubtedly reasons to believe that property ownership and behaviour at the polls go together.) The idea is not so much to sort out more or less rational individuals as members of the state; what Hegel means to say is that the comparatively less universal should play a more limited role in it, participate less in it, constitute it to a lesser degree. The universal is thus a product or function of the *partial universals* standing closest to it.

The relationship Hegel is thinking of here cannot be a purely logical one, for if it were, it would only pinpoint a relative affirmativity and its indebtedness to a higher universal, and thus the affirmation of the latter by the relative universal which reaches fulfilment in it. What Hegel has in mind is an institution of the state from below, and the best means available seems to him the relative degree of universality as a qualifying criterion for constituting the state, participating and holding positions in it. He also wants to show a continuity, and existential link, in the relationship between society and state. The result is a *state of estates* (*Ständestaat*).

The main thought behind Hegel's notion of a state of estates is not the coordinated participation or representation of all the particular interests relevant in the whole; granting a dialectical breakdown in terms of universality, exemplified in the various estates, what he claims is participation of those who are able to constitute a universal. Confusing the societal many with the politically constituted many Hegal brings the other, societal, factor into play, as, e.g., in the case of landowners who are accepted as born members of a chamber of their own. Representation is introduced for the more volatile professional class; they are to be represented by their most universal members who, in turn, are to be selected by the corporations engaged in the advocacy of particular interests.

The Hegelian version of the make-up of the political state according to stages of rationality or universality is designed to provide a reflective relation of the political many to the truly universal political state and, at the same time, preserve the rationality of the political state through selective recruitment. The Platonic problem of the rationality of the state arises again, if in a different form: the concrete universal of the political state figures as an entelechy; the many relate to it in a circle of reflection. But the solution is not a genuine one: it suggests identification with, or opportunities for participation in, the state on the part of voters, members of parliament or office holders, according to the degree of universality.

The difficulty in all this is that as far as the make-up of the universal is concerned, participation of the relatively universal in fact makes for the very opposite of what is intended, viz., for the *particularization* of the universal as a political agent. Hegel points quite explicitly to societal, and thus relative, universals as suited for political office (i.e., corporations whose representatives sit in ministries, partly on the basis of 'popular election' and partly on the basis of appointment) (*PhR*, §288). Hegel is blind to the particular social viewpoints which get into the government in this way. For him, there seems to be a continuous scale of universality, on which society already registers, so that certain parts of it overlap with the universality of the state. The dialectic and the categorial architectonic, according to which society and state are to be strictly distinguished, have all been forgotten. The notion that the relatively universal elements of society, trained as they are, are better able to take the step into the completely universal, also plays its role. However, as has been said, once the particular interests are involved in government, they will lead to the opposite of what is intended. The universal will become functionally dependent on the particular, although this eventuality was precisely the reason for rejecting the sovereignty of the people.

So the Hegelian model of the state of estates is either utterly irrational or constitutes – if suitable parities are maintained – an entity which, in its political result, passes off *compromises between particular interests* (and not all at that) as *political universality* (which is just what happens in the current debate about democratization). The result is unsatisfactory.

II. A proposal for methodological clarification

In search of greater dialectical strictness in these matters we are led to the following general consideration. As distinct from a concept of the state as a sub-system of the system 'society', Hegel views the state as a categorial level which is not as such compromised in its independence by its relation to society. State and society stand in a relation to one another, to be sure, but the question is how this relation can be determined whilst avoiding the above error. Let us take the simplest case, the state prior to any articulation of the political state, or prior to any stipulation as to its political constitution. On such terms we have to grant the political many, as distinct from the many taken in abstraction from their political constitution, the way Hegel takes them. What we have is a *political plenum*. The question how society and state are related amounts to the question how society, the *social plenum*, relates to the political many. The view that the two are the *same* because in Hegel's dialectic sublated levels or spheres are preserved in a consequent, and hence society in the state, is, as we have seen, untenable. Such a crude, *integrative understanding* of the dialectic overlooks the fact that the state would then involve the contradiction of rendering the non-political domains (economic, familial and private) political, whereas they form levels of their own. Hegel himself, we may say, is to blame for the confusion when, in adopting the vantage point of the political state, he identifies society and state taken abstractly; this is borne out by the expression 'aggregate of private individuals' which he uses for the many, without drawing a distinction between the social and the political many. It is precisely this point of view which leads him, with regard to the question of how society and state are related, to use relative universality as a criterion for access to constitutive or co-constitutive roles in the state, and so to allow the socially particular to penetrate the universal. What leads Hegel down this slippery path is his interest in the make-up of the state and his attempt to account for the fact that the two coexisting entities are not indifferent to one another.

By contrast, a categorial view should be given its due; methodologically, what we have in mind is a *stratificatory reading* of the dialectic which involves in our case treating the state as a *categorial novelty*, regardless of how it might be coordinated with other categorial levels. There are several distinct levels on which freedom or the will can be realized: the private and familial, the economic and societal, and the political. (Taking the individual human being as the point of orientation, this would involve a division of man according to aspects, something to which Marx took offence in his *Critique of Hegel's Philosophy of Right* (*Staatsrecht*) and elsewhere, whilst sociology, with its role-theory, tries in its non-affirmative way to do justice to the matter.)

The suggested reading does not involve rejecting the *inclusion* of the various levels in the highest one. Setting aside its fundamental theoretical dimension, this inclusion is of several kinds. Firstly, it is an existential inclusion: the individuals who lead their lives in the social and political realms are identical. There is — at least in developed states which have outgrown the stage of having *metoikoi* (resident aliens) and *perioikoi* (subjects of dependent communities) — extensional equality between the political realm and society and existential identity of their individuals. The state cannot exclude anybody who is a member of society. But this does not mean that society is in reality sublated in the state; it has not become the same thing as the state. Furthermore, the inclusion is a logical one, in the sense that the state will have to be determined by the way society is constituted. This raises the question to what extent the theory of the political state should respond to differences in the societal domain (e.g. in the breakdown of administrative structures). And finally, we have inclusion in the sense that the state is responsible for a remodelling of society which, however real, leaves society relatively independent. Let us postpone these points concerning an integrative reading of the dialectic for the time being and turn to the findings of a stratificatory reading.

According to these findings, the state as a political entity must, as a matter of principle, be understood *without recourse to societal entities*, albeit that, in logical or principal terms, the level of society is a presupposition for the establishment of its, the state's, concept. Structurally, the state has to be grasped as categorially distinct from its societal antecedents. Hegel certainly means to make this claim but at the same time he holds a peculiar theory about the transition of societal antecedents to political status. An assessment, though, of how the structure of the state is concretely affected by these antecedents cannot form part of a categorial account of the state, only of a correlative, integrative understanding of its nature. Such a conception must, however, rank second, as otherwise the specific categorial nature of the state, for all its 'real' entanglement with society, would be compromised. Thus the relationship between the political state (as an articulated entity) and the politically constituted many has to take pride of place.

Sovereignty of the people

In view of the above, we can offer a correction of the Hegelian model of a state of estates. On the political level, the question is not how relatively universal societal entities exert an influence on the state or have access to the offices of government, but rather, whether there are reasons for crediting the politically constituted many who, on the level of the state, have been accorded universality, with differences of political potential. Categorially, this is impossible in view of the requirements both of affirmation as the reflection on the universal in elections and practical implementation in terms of access to offices, for otherwise the political realm would turn out to be particular. The politically constituted many encompass all (with the exception of those not come of age); thus universality is also *universitas*.[11]

The consequences of a categorial account of the state is therefore the *sovereignty of the people*. It is the expression of the relationship of the political many, who are all, as unarticulated universal, to the political state as an articulated objectification of the universal. It is this sovereignty which alone affords the self-affirmation of the universal as affirmation of the universal by the universal.

Hegel does not make the mistake of the classical (English, French, German) theory which linked the concept of the state with its genesis and so tried to picture the transition from society, or the state of nature, to political organization. But he does make the mistake of rationalizing the state and people's access to its offices in terms of estates, thus rejecting the sovereignty of the people, or the self-reflection of all in the political state, with the argument that a people without its monarch (or, more generally, without being politically constituted or without a political state) is a 'formless mass'. Such a statement is, as we have already noted, indebted to picturing or abstract nominalist thinking. In categorial terms the argument is wrong.

The relationship of the politically constituted individuals to each other and hence to their state might, it is true, also cover the case in which a rational state is simply accepted by the many, without there being any sovereignty of the people. Categorial theory has no reason to deny statehood because of differences in participation of the many in the political state. However, if it is correct to say that the political constituted many make up the universal, universal participation (in the sense of Hegel's *Philosophy of History*, that 'all are free') is imperative. Otherwise, the political state would not only be socially or personally particular – which is unavoidable – but would be particular in substance and thus forego the chance of possible universality. In fact, it is surprising Hegel did not make the entelechy of his *Philosophy of History* the basis of his *Philosophy of Right* in the sense that the state in which all are free involves the sovereignty of the people.

One need hardly add that our plea of sovereignty of the people does not imply arguing for plebiscitary democracy. The state's universality does not hinge on an omnipotent plebiscite, nor is its *universalitas* assured by the *universitas* of the decision-makers. Rather, universality has to have the substantive content of an objective political constitution. To defend plebiscitary democracy would be tantamount to accepting as concrete what is substantially abstract and without objective constitutional content. This is precisely the error which Hegel's theory can help to pinpoint. What this theory argues for is not an abstract plebiscite – an amorphous state of affairs posited as concrete – but everybody's reference to the universal as to something objective: this option opens the way to universal suffrage in a *democracy* (in which everybody, through voting on party programmes and electing representative persons, reflects on the political constitution of the state).

Political particularity

But does it make sense to set up a political realm as such? If we except foreign policy, isn't politics concerned with regulations addressed to society? Surely; and yet, the political level has to come in for a stratificatory analysis first, and rather than arguing in terms of estates, one will have to proceed as follows. The politically constituted individuals will have political views concerning the societal and foreign-affairs activities of the state. Such views will – as a matter of contingency, not of implication – relate to their societal status; but however particular these views may be, they involve political recipes for society (and, if need be, for foreign policy) *addressed to everybody* or tendered for general adoption. These recipes are made explicit by *political parties*. Political parties and their programmes constitute the particulars amongst the many, whereas Hegel makes societal particulars falsely spill over into the political sphere.[12] Political parties, moreover, are the agencies responsible for the recruitment of holders of office in the political state. (For Hegel, this recruitment, insofar as it has not been made redundant by the birthright of landowners, is left to the corporations who pass delegates and office holders on to higher level.)

The stratificatory reading, or the stratificatory element in dialectical theory, or the emphasis on the respective category, demands attention to typically political differences of the many in as much as they are politically constituted as opposed to differences due to societal estates. The universality of the individuals who are politically constituted and particularized in party affiliation calls for universal franchise as an essential requirement allowing for the participation of all in the political state and establishing particularity as universality (the major party forming the government).

It follows that political parties, if interpreted as political particulars, should not focus on societal or class allegiance. Indeed, they should not be formed along any other non-political lines either, such as age-group or sex. Even the formation of youth organizations within parties appears undesirable.

Nor should we be in doubt to what extent *a one party state* could be covered by the theory. The imperfection of such a state is bound up with the fact that we are left with societal differences within the one party (bosses and the rest, the poor and the bigshots). At any rate, the case where typically political differences give rise to a multiplicity of political parties channelling the ways in which the electorate form their opinions, is a more advanced form of political life.

Sovereignty of the people and monarchy

It is scarcely necessary to elaborate upon the relationship between sovereignty of the people and monarchy. Such sovereignty could be reconciled with a constitutional monarchy, but hardly with monarchic sovereignty *à la* Hegel (although he calls his monarchy 'constitutional'), for he regards the monarch as a sovereign, as a power and indeed as the highest and all-inclusive one. A genuinely constitutional monarch, on the other hand, would be, in the words of Arnold Ruge, a 'constitutional person of state with the whole content of the three state powers'.[13] One might stipulate that the head of the executive be identical with the constitutional person of state, but in that case his office must, in contrast to Hegel's conception of hereditary monarchy, be subject to appointment in accordance with the sovereignty of the people and permit of change (as, e.g., in the presidential system). The question of whether to opt for a representational president or a representational monarch or to prefer an executive president who would for his part be subject to rules of alignment with a parliament, is a matter for substantive political theory or for the given political tradition to settle.

The terminal concept of the state

The theory of the political state still has one shortcoming: it views the political state as categorially identical with the state as a totality, as a universal for a universal, and thus also as an individual, and yet conceives it still as a particular. That is, as a differentiation of the state, the political state stands in a relationship of non-identity of the political many, the citizens. The latter do indeed indulge in reflection upon it as upon themselves (in elections), with the opportunity to form part of it by running for office. But the political state remains nevertheless an opposite, an independent power, something particular (in societal terms, a complex of civil servants as distinct from the other professions).

What suggests itself at this stage is yet another mediation between the objectivity of the political state and the citizens. That is to say, the unity of the state at large and the political state, so far claimed as immediate or *per se*, may stand in need of a reflection to assure that the politically constituted individuals acknowledge the political state as their own. In line with the dialectic and its demand, formulated in the abstract, this would constitute the developed expression of the sovereignty of the people, viz., the 'posited' unity of the political state and the state as the *universitas* of the politically constituted individuals or citizens. This unity could be interpreted as the trust of all (which Hegel argues for under the name of *patriotism*, prior to any associations this term may carry with regard to foreign affairs) (*PhR*, §268).

But on the other hand, the opposition remains; in the objective realm there is no absolute avatar of concept which could serve as the mediation of the opposition. The result is therefore a reflection of distrust and a tendency to check up on the activities of the state. The state may in turn pre-empt such misgivings through the division of its own powers, and, over and above this, through judicial review, public auditing boards and the guarantee of a free press.

One might wish to provide textual support for the further stage of reflection we have been considering by a statement Hegel makes in a section of the *Philosophy of Right* devoted to history, where he says that the opposition between reason and actuality 'has implicitly lost its marrow and disappeared [ist an sich...geschwunden]' (§360, adapted from Knox's translation) while he also says that 'the true reconciliation...had become objective' (ibid.). One could follow Ilting[14] in seeing in the word 'implicitly' the admission, veiled in Hegel's reference to a reconciliation which has 'become objective', that there is room for democratic or liberal progress. One may wonder, though, quite apart from the question of whether the passage permits of this interpretation, if it is satisfactory to introduce a non-systematic, historical dimension in order to extend and correct a systematic theory (just as Young Hegelians such as Ruge did, despite the latter's interest in a systematic re-interpretation of the *Philosophy of Right*).[15] Systematic theory must, so we hold, contain its affirmative closure in explicit terms. Following the lines suggested above, this would be secured by an express positing of a unity of political state and political plenum and would reach its final theoretical statement in terms of people's sovereignty. As will be clear, we are thinking of something rather different from what the Young Hegelians had in mind; they were still trying to extrapolate a sovereignty of the people, whereas we claim it as a systematic recipe resulting from a corrected statement of Hegel's theory. What we mean is, beyond that, an open-ended reflection playing between the political state and the political plenum once sovereignty of the people is granted.[16]

Incidentally, our position is consonant with the thesis that there will be *no* sovereign left within the constitutional state; it may be no longer meaningful to talk about sovereignty of the people there as a constitutional state does not allow for any isolation of the people as a sovereign within itself (a view maintained by Martin Kriele in his political theory).[17]

A further question concerns the state in relation to other states: should we attempt a final theoretical account of the internal relations of the state before we admit foreign relations, or should we deal with what Hegel calls 'internal constitution [taken] by itself', without the final reflection referred to, then turn to foreign relations, and only after that, in a move beyond Hegel, add a concluding reflection? The former, linear progression contains the problem that the position of the *military*, an organ of the state designed to cope with external relations, cannot be interpreted within the state's internal constitution. It is, however, desirable to account for it under such constitution (or, in concrete terms, to make the military subservient to the civil power). The question is whether there are categorial clues for a correct placement of the issue. Conceivably, a satisfactory categorization will exceed the resources of linear theory.

III. Society and state

Attention to the categorial level in a stratificatory reading – a reading we have adopted for the treatment of the state's inner structure made up of the politically many and the political state – does not exempt us from considering the integrative aspect and pinpointing the correlation of society and state. It would indeed be simplistic and misleading to regard the notion of a 'sublation' of society in the state as an adequate account of their relationship. Accordingly, we have sought to correct such an account by distinguishing the two readings, the stratificatory and the integrative, and also by offering a critical analysis of Hegel's attempt to bridge the gap between society and state in terms of recruiting procedures constitutive of the latter. What remains, then, is to give an account of the integrative aspect for which a catalogue of questions has already been set up. The problem cannot be treated in isolation: we have to understand how society is integrated into the state, but equally, how society is and remains something in its own right. What is required, then, is an integrative consideration of society from the point of view of the state and, to balance this, a stratificatory consideration doing justice to society as it is in itself, underlining its categorial uniqueness within a framework calling for unity. In what follows, stratification and integration must, therefore, go together, but in such a way as to avoid the 'misplacements' in Hegel's landscape of society and state which contradict the category of the state and have been criticized above.

The interdependence of society and the state:
subsidiarity

Granting the categorial status of society as a result of stratificatory analysis, what difference does it make to grant its integration in the state as well? The very distinction between society and the state within the requirement of unity gives rise to the question of whether the state could not take over all the functions of society, or at least their control. Or should one say that it has the power to do so, but simply releases certain functions from its grip? This line of questioning follows from the *subsidiarity principle*. According to this

principle, the issue is to what extent agents or competent bodies not subject
to central or state control can deal with matters as well as, or better than,
the central state. In this way the principle assures satisfaction through private
initiative which, under decentralization, is spread over wide circles (a view
shared by the Catholic social doctrine, Humboldt and J. S. Mill).[18]

Categorial theory provides reasons for urging a distinction between
society and the state: the two are ontologically distinct as diremption and
as affirmative unity. In one sense, then, the subsidiarity principle is
recognized; in another, though, it appears as something dispensable since the
state does not delegate or surrender to another level what it could equally
keep for itself. Accordingly, Hegel treats of groupings on a societal or pre-state
level not in terms of the subsidiarity principle, but in a linear fashion, viewing
them as stepping stones towards the universality of the state.

However, considering the coordination and co-existence of society and
state, we are back to the question of whether there is not a sphere of functions
to be fulfilled, one way or the other by the state or by society. For this
alternative not to remain too global we have to distinguish, in addition,
between *political* and *societal* subsidiarity. Political subsidiarity would be such
as to admit of non-central agents committed to universality (on communal
or federal-regional levels); societal subsidiarity, on the other hand, involves
the surrender of functions in matters of education, welfare, health and culture
to societal or private responsibility.

Hegel has next to nothing to say about *political subsidiarity*,[19] a fact not
to be construed, though, as an error but simply as an understandable case
of skirting the issue, given his intention to produce a constitutional theory
of 'the' state. A categorial theory of the social domain may dispense with
political subsidiarity since any ulterior issues may be settled in terms of such
casuistry as the balance between local and regional automony, the comparative
distance between the local, regional and central levels, etc. We must note,
though, that politically subsidiary structures introduce a level which resists
the simplified schema of society on the one side, and the state on the other.
The central state will have to allow politically subsidiary agents, and maintain
relations with them, which the oversimplified schema ignores. Of course,
the question of political subsidiarity always depends, among other things, on
the size of the social formation concerned, and Hegel can easily call on the
qualitative significance of quantity, without committing himself to structural
modifications as a consequence.

In the case of *societal subsidiarity*, it has already been suggested that Hegel
did not simply ignore it, but was not able to deal with it in any detail because
of the linearity of his theory. Our point is not that Hegel fails to discuss
welfare, private and public poor-relief, etc. He does this in the section on
'Civil Society' within the context of his discussion of the 'state based on

need', disregarding the political state as coming later in his linear scheme. What has to remain an open question in Hegel is whether the societal functions mentioned would, after his concrete exposition of the state, be left in the hands of society.[20] One could compare this question with the situation in the case of punishment which ranges from revenge, through self-protective measures of society to punishment imposed by the state, much as the latter notion remains implicit and is not explicitly treated.

It appears that Hegel's theory cannot give an explicit account of societal subsidiarity. We can extend this conclusion to categorial social theory in general: its guiding thought is nothing more than the claim that the state must arrive at some coordination of society and state and some remodelling of societal forces and institutions, a task which will have to come up for discussion presently under the heading of the *common good*. Whatever resists such coordination and remodelling would be subject to remedial measures on the part of the state. An assessment as to what may rightly be left to subsidiary elements, either unadulterated or as remodelled by political control, indeed, what could count as an optimum division of functions in the interest of the whole, is for heuristic endeavours, or for political topics, to determine.

The interdependence of society and the state: the common good

Having stressed the difference between society and the state within the framework of their interrelationship, we must turn to their integration in favour of a whole, an issue raised before in connection with subsidiarity. Though Hegel tends to deal only with society's one-way reference to the state, the converse, the state's reflection on society, also makes its appearance. It occurs, first of all, as has been seen, in the linkage between executive power and society – to the effect that this power, as a particular, corresponds to the particularity of society – and in the idea of the state as remodelling and influencing society. Thus it is that Hegel says: 'In times of peace, the particular spheres and functions pursue the path of satisfying their particular aims and minding their own business, and it is in part only by way of the unconscious necessity of the thing that their self-seeking is turned into a contribution to reciprocal support and to the support of the whole...In part, however, it is by the direct influence of higher authority that they are not only continually brought back to the aims of the whole and restricted accordingly..., but are also constrained to perform directly services for the support of the whole' (*PhR*, §278); in times of war, the restrictions may be far more extensive. As we can see, Hegel is thinking of *ad hoc* state interventions and of continuous policies to keep the economy in balance;

quite generally, what we have is an existential dependence of the whole on the substratum of society, and an ideal steering of the substratum from above, by the state. The phrase 'in part...in part' betrays an interplay of stratificatory and integrative interpretations. The state lets the societal domain go free, not so much as a subsidiary realm, but as something having its own status *qua* economy, and yet co-determines it.

In this way, societal satisfaction together with the maintenance of the universal, may count as assured. From a fundamental theoretical perspective we realize that the particular finds satisfaction in the universal which surpasses its own limitations, i.e., in something other than itself, in the political, not in the societal domain. But over and beyond that, we are pushed towards the view already indicated, that the state, by way of its political influence, remodels society in such a way that – however compromised by party-political factors or particularity – both society and the political universal achieve satisfaction by themselves.

Such a formulation addresses the theme of the *common good*, in fact it defines it. The common good will have to be the objective result of the dialectical tension between individual satisfaction in society and satisfaction in the universal, and thus figures as the self-affirmation of the state. The common good exhibits the tension between the two readings of the dialectic, the integrative and the stratificatory; their harmony constitutes its explanation: it is the restless unity of subjective and objective satisfaction. Empirically, this unity is never definitively achieved, nor is it subject to prescription on the part of a still higher unity-concept. An optimum state of affairs can only be aspired to in terms of a historical, not in terms of a categorial progression.[21]

One might find it objectionable to conceive of the common good in this way and say that on the basis of what is, in the final analysis, a liberal conception the state will establish itself as a class society (a society of the rich who find it easy to acquire education, wealth and political influence). Quite apart from the empirical facts which go to show that a wide spread of education over all classes is possible, but that a concentration of the educated in the middle classes is, albeit contingent, nevertheless probable, what has to be seen is that only acceptance of the political level, separated from societal divisions and available to all, avoids the prevalence of particular interest groups (parties, trade unions, other societally organized groups) or a mere compromise between them, and so affords optimum opportunities for all. The problem arising out of the fact that the state, through its impact on society as its existential basis, controls a considerable part of the middle class and helps to assure their reproduction need not be serious where sovereignty of the people is guaranteed.

Our proposal, then, is that, on the level of matters of principle, there is no getting around Hegel's distinction between society and state and his claim that society be included in the state, with its implications for the common good; otherwise, society would sit in judgment over matters of universal relevance and deliver them up to particular interest groups and their conflicts, compromises or dictates. What has been said on this point is not peculiar to Hegel, but belongs to western tradition in general. What Hegelian theory can do, however, is to give it a logical foundation. As for points where Hegel's theory proves defective, we think that a more rigorous categorial theory is possible which, within the limits imposed by this theory-type, can provide satisfactory solutions.[22]

Conclusion

We must break off here. A number of important questions remain, above all the question whether an ontological theory in terms of Hegel's *Philosophy of Right* can account for a state with constitutional guarantees of due process (*Rechtsstaat*), in other words, whether a categorial theory of social formations and their normative structures is sufficient in concrete cases to overcome legal positivism (committed as this is to an equation of state, law and right) or whether one has to posit an ideal level of the law (law as not exhausted to an ontological theory of social configurations). Although Hegel refers to a 'constitution a priori' which might be presented to a nation as '*ens rationis*' (*PhR*, §274), he indicates a solution when he relates states to the *world spirit* as a constitutional ideal, and so opens up an ideal sphere. We cannot take this question any further here.

Let us briefly sum up our 'ideas'. Our principal theses are that only a categorial (transcendental, dialectical) social philosophy can account for the *affirmativity of institutions*; and that a categorial social philosophy, implemented more rigorously than Hegel's own, can give an affirmative account of the *people's sovereignty* and of the *state* as the uppermost institution of the many. The possibility of such a correction need not be attributed to a desire for accommodation to the existing conditions, which appeal to us these days, but results from a reflection on how the dialectic should proceed in the region of *Realphilosophie*. In such a context, it can be shown that Hegel's concept of sublation involves an unclear, indeed misleading and incorrect theory: designed to enable one to talk about subjective freedom *and* state supremacy, it ends up by over-emphasizing the goal of the linear movement, the political state, and makes irresponsible claims about the links between society and state. Accordingly, important aspects of our analysis concern the linearity of the theory and its stratificatory and integrative readings.

From a categorial point of view, the thesis that the state is the highest affirmative objective entity is quite correct, but in the context of *Realphilosophie* it must be accommodated to the dualism of integrative sublation and stratificatory coordination of distinct spheres. To say this is not is to imply that a logical dialectic should take into account facticity as an element which may sabotage the affirmative universal (a view which has been propounded in another context by Kierkegaard and Sartre). We are saying that precisely in order to establish an affirmative universal, due consideration must be given to two readings of the dialectic (and, leaving behind the methodological aspect, to two co-existent states of affairs). The device suggested in our attempt at methodological clarification – the theoretical distinction of two dialectical states of affairs, tension between which is reflected in the problem of the common good – permits, indeed demands, the recognition of political universality as coincident with the sovereignty of the people; by the same token, we have to grant the state's reflection on society and its converse, society's subsidiarity. Dispensing with representational elements in thought which suggest a mistaken link between society and state and result in a state of estates or, more generally, in a particularized, societal state, categorial theory can fulfil the desire for an *affirmative understanding of political institutions*. Or, put still another way, categorial theory of the social realm is, in affirmative terms, what Niklas Luhmann sees critically when he talks about the 'anomalous set' which is both part of the whole and the whole itself. It is precisely this, or the sense of sublation in *Realphilosophie*, which we wish to understand from our point of view.

Clearly, what we have tried to offer is no more than a sketch of an affirmative *theory of institutions*; an excuse for this is that in view of its interface with substantive theory the limits of a theory concerned with principles ought to be respected with greater strictness than is the case in Hegel.

There remain, to take up thoughts of the introduction once again, queries, so current these days, concerning the *legitimation of the state*.[23] Empirically, complaints are a stock-in-trade as long as individuals and societal groups fail to appreciate the type of affirmativity discussed (in connection with political structure, common good and subsidiarity). No theory can eliminate this sort of contingency; all that theory can do in this respect is to ask whether appropriate institutional measures (to be determined by substantive theory) can help promote consent to the universal, or common cause, which can claim our allegiance.*

* Translated from the German by Stephen Bungay and the author.

Propaganda and analysis: the background to Hegel's article on the English Reform Bill

M. J. PETRY

Hegel wrote the article on the Reform Bill ten years after the publication of the *Philosophy of Right* and only a few months before he died. It was serialized in the official Prussian state paper, and the king himself intervened to prevent its being published in full. To clarify its background and his reasons for writing it is therefore to go a long way toward resolving many of the reputedly enigmatical aspects of his political thinking. We are surely obliged to assume that if he was ever clear in his mind as to the relevance of dialectical thinking to the solution of practical problems, he was so by 1831, that since he had then lived in Prussia for more than a decade he had formed certain well-considered opinions as to the political organization of the country, and that if he chose to point out the merits of a strong monarchy, he may have been insincere, but he can hardly have been developing wholly new ideas. The most important factor determining the background to the article is, however, the interplay of propaganda and analysis in both the writing of it and the composition of the sources on which it is based. This has not been investigated before, and is the main theme of the present article.

Hegel begins his analysis of the Whig proposals by placing them within the general perspective of the constitutional developments that had taken place in Europe since 1789. Paying particular attention to the Paris revolution of July 1830, he sees them as an attempt 'to bring justice and fairness into the allotment of the parts played by the different classes and divisions of the people in the election of members of Parliament, and to do this by substituting a greater symmetry for the most bizarre and haphazard anomalies and inequalities which prevail at present'.[1] He points out that although such an attempt is almost certain to clash with the '"positivity" which preponderates in the institutions of English law, public and private alike', it is progressive and necessary in that, 'at no time more than the present has the general intelligence been led to distinguish between whether rights are purely positive in their material *content* or whether they are *inherently* right and rational' (*PW*, 299). This leads him on, by a process of natural association, into a wide-ranging and detailed survey of the economic and social background to the Parliamentary manoeuvring involved in getting the Bill onto the statute book, and into calling attention to a multitude of anomalies and abuses in the administration of the national debt, tithes, Ireland, manorial rights, the legal system, etc.

Had the article ended with this dismal picture of the disorganized state of the country, one might have wondered where he had acquired his wealth of information, but one could hardly have regarded his reasons for writing as being in any way obscure or problematic. One would naturally have assumed that like so many of his English contemporaries, he regarded the Bill as a necessary first step toward thoroughgoing economic and social reform. At this juncture, however, the argument takes a new turn. In fact it changes direction to such an extent that the second half of the article seems to be very largely at odds with the first. Instead of building upon the premiss he had established and discussing the benefits to be expected from the Bill, he proceeds to condemn it, and in no uncertain terms, as subversive and dangerous, potentially revolutionary, 'downright illogical...a hotchpotch of the old privileges and the general principle of the equal entitlement of all citizens to vote for those by whom they are to be represented'. Criticism degenerates into something closely resembling polemic, and the inconsistency in the main drift of the argument enters into its details. On one page, for example, the English are characterized as being endowed with a 'so-called practical sense – concentration on gain, subsistence, wealth'. On another, they are said to be excelled by few other European peoples in the extent to which they are 'dominated by such dexterity of reasoning in terms of their prejudices and shallowness of principle'. Wellington's speeches, which can hardly be regarded as giving much evidence of his having been convinced that the Bill would bring 'justice and fairness into the election of members of Parliament', are praised for 'getting to the root of the matter'. Since the great majority of the members of Parliament are said to be 'incompetent and ignorant, with a veneer of current prejudices and a culture drawn from conversation and often not even that', it is difficult to see how any alteration in their manner of election could reasonably have been regarded as a change for the worse (*PW*, 312, 315, 323).

In the final section, he explores the practical implications of this analysis, and suggests that on account of the chaotic state of the country and the extraordinary weakness of the British crown, the challenge to the power of the traditional ruling class presented by the opening of Parliament to the radicals could easily give rise 'not to reform but to revolution' (*PW*, 330).

Rosenkranz thought that the apparent ill-humour and eccentricity of the article could have been the result of Hegel's having already been affected by cholera. Illness cannot account for its evident inconsistencies, however, and Rosenzweig almost certainly came closer to the truth of the matter when he suggested that, 'although the Reform Bill is referred to throughout, the article is not so much concerned with England as it is with the political problem of French and more particularly of Prussian liberalism'.[2] Before attempting to examine its merits as an analysis of what was taking place in Britain, it may therefore be of value to take a look at its Prussian and European background. It is certainly significant that Hegel should have chosen to publish it in the Prussian equivalent of the *London Gazette* and *Le Moniteur,* and that its criticism of British affairs and institutions should have been directly relevant to the problems then being faced by the administration in Berlin.

I

There can be no doubt that Hegel was justified in seeing a connection between the Reform Bill and the dramatic developments which had led to the downfall of Charles X in July 1830 (*PW*, 295, 303, 318, 325). The French king had abdicated while elections were in full swing in Britain, and although the news of what was happening in Paris reached England too late to have much influence upon the election results, it certainly had a very profound effect upon the Parliament which assembled at Westminster at the end of October, and upon the committee entrusted with the task of planning Parliamentary reform once the Whigs had taken office in November. Hegel was also justified in regarding what had taken place in France as having European implications, for England was by no means the only country to be disturbed by the Parisian turmoil. The sweeping constitutional changes which followed the rapid success of the revolution – the establishment of Louis Philippe as 'king of the French by the will of the people', the transformation of the Chamber of Peers into a council of officials, the abolition of the monarch's power to supersede laws by means of ordinances, the extension of the franchise and eligibility for election – provided the programme for liberal aspirations throughout the continent. It soon became evident, and nowhere more clearly than in north Germany, that the Parisians had initiated a movement which promised to be no less momentous in its long-term consequences than that of 1789. During the late summer and early autumn of 1830, popular uprisings in favour of constitutional reform took place in the kingdoms of Hanover and Saxony, where important concessions and far-reaching changes had to be made; in Brunswick, where the duke was driven into exile; and in Hesse-Cassel, where the landgrave was forced to summon the estates. The Brussels revolution, which was to result in the dissolution of the Kingdom of the Netherlands before the end of the year,

broke out in August; the Warsaw revolt, which was to give rise to war
between Poland and Russia, in November; and by December even
Switzerland was in the throes of violent constitutional disturbances.

Prussia, sprawling across the whole of north Germany, bordering upon
Belgium and Poland, including so many recently acquired territories,
consisting of so many potentially incompatible social, regional and religious
groupings, began to look increasingly vulnerable as this revolutionary
movement spread and gathered momentum. The country had no national
constitution at all, and for almost a quarter of a century Prussian liberals had
been pressing for a central diet or parliament. It was by no means
administratively or politically backward however. Stein and Hardenberg,
who had pioneered a number of basic reforms after the military collapse and
the disastrous Peace of Tilsit, had managed to bring into being an efficient
system of ministries and local government, as well as re-organizing the army,
abolishing serfdom and establishing the free exchange of land and choice of
occupation.[3] Both men had actually visited England, and to some extent had
drawn their inspiration from British institutions, the merits of which were
being effectively publicized in Germany during the early years of the century
by the writings of Friedrich von Gentz.[4] Both had seen the establishment
of a national assembly comparable in power and status to the British
Parliament as the final goal of their constitutional reforms and, during the
period of patriotic enthusiasm engendered by the War of Liberation, it had
looked as though their ideals were about to be realized. On 3 June 1814 the
king issued an order in cabinet promising a decision as to a national
constitution in the near future, a promise which he repeated on several
occasions during the May of the following year. By article thirteen of the
Final Act of the Congress of Vienna, passed on 9 June 1815, it was enacted
that there were to be 'assemblies of estates' in all the member countries of
the newly established German Confederation. Stein, encouraged by the
support of Russia, Great Britain and the Papacy at the Congress, had even
entertained the hope that the widespread popular demand for the restoration
of the Empire might be realized, and that the federal diet might be
transformed into an imperial parliament.[5] After the war, however, it became
increasingly apparent that centralized representative government no longer
offered a clear prospect of long-term stability and increased administrative
efficiency. What is more, the general attitude toward British institutions
changed. The statesman-historian Niebuhr, for example, in the foreword to
a work on the British constitution published in 1815, emphasized the
importance of self-government, not of centralization, of local institutions
functioning independently of the central authority. It was in this essay that
he formulated the much-quoted maxim that 'freedom depends more upon
administration than upon the constitution'.[6] Gentz, at the Carlsbad meeting

in the October of 1819, re-interpreted article thirteen to mean that the member countries were to establish assemblies representing corporate bodies such as the nobility, the clergy, the universities, the towns, not that they were obliged to institutionalize the sovereignty of the people.[7] The wildly romantic constitutional ideas of the patriotic pan-Germanic gymnastic societies and students' associations, of the demonstrators and haranguers at the revolutionary Wartburg Festival in October 1817, of the fanatical student who assassinated the reputedly reactionary Kotzebue in March 1819, confirmed the king in the view that a central Parliament could very easily result in the total breakdown of the country's administration. The promises made were not entirely neglected, however. Wilhelm von Humboldt was appointed Minister for Constitutional Affairs at the beginning of 1819, and soon produced a well worked out plan for a national assembly, but he had been dismissed by the end of the year, together with Beyme and Boyen, for making the supposedly revolutionary move of suggesting that a time limit should be set on the enforcement of the Carlsbad Decrees.[8] By an order in cabinet of 11 June 1821 the king finally put an end to all prospect of establishing a central representative assembly in the immediate future.

How was it then, that with absolutely no means of satisfying the liberal demand for parliamentary government, Prussia managed to ride out the storm which swept across Europe in the wake of the Paris revolution? The fact that the country remained almost totally undisturbed is even more remarkable when we remember that in 1831 no less than a quarter of the population of Berlin was dependent upon public assistance, and that in some of the large Rhineland towns the proportion was even higher.[9] To some extent the stability was undoubtedly due to the strength of the army and the militia, the censorship of the press, and the astuteness of the foreign policy being pursued. The government was certainly circumspect in its relationships with foreign powers. In spite of Prince Czartoryski's disclaiming all connection with Jacobinism and holding out the possibility of an independent Poland's accepting a Prussian prince as its monarch, the government refused to be drawn into the war being waged on its eastern frontier, and although Prussian troops in the Rhineland were mobilized with a view to supporting the Dutch king during the Belgian upheaval, they never actually crossed the frontier.[10] In the main, however, major disturbances seem to have been avoided because it was apparent that by and large the country was being administered with conscientiousness and efficiency. After the king had made it clear that there was no immediate prospect of his initiating a central Parliament, great attention was paid to building upon Stein's reform of local government, and developing the kingdom into a federation of provinces. Between 1825 and 1828, the administrative powers of the local authorities were standardized, the more egalitarian society of the Rhineland and

Westphalia being remoulded, together with the still predominantly feudal eastern provinces, by the establishment of councils, which tended to be dominated by the squirearchy, but which also represented the interests of the towns and farmers. Reform of the municipalities finally followed in March 1831, the mayors and councils being granted increased powers, and the property qualification for voters being removed.[11] On 30 October 1821 a council of state commission on the constitution was set up under the chairmanship of the crown prince, the outcome being the Provincial Estates Law of 5 June 1823, which divided the country into eight provinces – Brandenburg, Prussia, Pomerania, Posen, Silesia, Saxony, Westphalia and the Rhineland – each of which had its own single-chamber assembly. Gentz's interpretation of article thirteen was adopted in that estates and not the people were to be represented, but although the nobility were granted half the seats, the towns a third and the farmers a sixth, decision-making was by a straightforward majority, and in practice the members elected regarded themselves as representing the whole province rather than the estates. Although the assemblies could only advise the central government, their assent was required for bills affecting property or taxation, and they had certain powers of decision with regard to local affairs. Each was represented on the council of state by its marshal, who was appointed from among its members by the crown.[12]

This establishment of a federal instead of a centralized parliamentary constitution brought out the importance of the crown as the one constitutional factor guaranteeing the unity of the country. Stein had planned a council of state to advise the monarch, and such a body, consisting of princes of the blood, ministers of state, field marshals, crown nominees and representatives of the provincial assemblies, churches and universities was finally brought into being by ordinance on 20 March 1817. Although officially it had no governmental, administrative or legislative power, the legislation promulgated by the crown was prepared on its committees, and it was in fact not only the centre of policy making, but also an effective check on both the monarch and the ministries.[13] This lack of a central parliament also enhanced the part played by the ministries and the whole bureaucratic organization of the civil service in the co-ordination of the country. During the 1830s and 1840s the civil service was to become increasingly incapable of controlling economic, social and political developments effectively, but throughout the 1820s it morale and efficiency were high, and in 1830 the obvious success of its administration was probably the most important single factor in the creation of the public confidence which enabled the country to avoid political upheaval. In the economic field, for example, Bülow and Motz had turned out to be particularly effective at the ministries of commerce and finance, and Rother had managed to reduce the enormous national debt left by the war with remarkable efficiency, while in the cultural field equal success had attended Altenstein's educational policies, both in the schools and the universities.

II

In Hegel's article there are many instances of his giving direct expression to his views on particular political issues. When discussing the dangers of 'general ideas about the sovereignty of the people' for example, he makes no bones about referring to France. When pointing out the importance of the 'deep insight of princes' in the transformation of the law, he tells us that he is thinking of Germany (*PW*, 329, 330). Many of his observations involve references which are not so explicit, however, which would have been readily intelligible to his original readers, but which we can easily overlook. Unless we bear in mind the political context within which he is writing, for example, we can miss the approbation of Prussian policies implicit in his praise of such features of the British scene as the 'sense of justice' motivating the reform movement, the concentration upon altering institutions rather than admonition and exhortation, the representation of interests rather than the wills of individuals, the fact that the country is not lacking in 'men who make political activity the business of their life' (*PW*, 295, 297, 313, 324)..One we are aware of it, however, the apparent contradiction between the two parts of the article becomes more understandable. It seems reasonable to assume that since he had begun by making use of this oblique method in order to call attention to the merits of the Prussian establishment, he wanted to make quite sure, in the second half of the article, that he was not going to be classed with those who were in the habit of praising Britain in order to denigrate Prussia. It is important to realize that when he criticizes the general corruption of English political life, the high rate of taxation in England and France, the social distress in Ireland, he is also countering the way in which the German liberals of the times were censuring the Berlin administration (*PW*, 297, 303, 307). When he calls attention to the mishandling of the transition from feudal tenure to property in Britain, the way in which the careful analysis of social and political problems was being hindered by 'the pomp and display of formal freedom in Parliament', the arbitrary nature of the property qualification for voters, the incompetence and ignorance of the ordinary members of Parliament, he is also highlighting the most successful features of the Prussian reform movement (*PW*, 308, 311, 320, 323). By condemning 'that most stubborn of English prejudices, jealousy of the power of the throne', the overvaluation of the vote, the opening of Parliament to the radicals, he is calling attention to what he considers to be some of the reasons for Prussia's success in deactivating the revolutionary pressures threatening the disintegration of the country (*PW*, 300, 318, 330).

He was by no means alone in adopting such an attitude. By the end of the 1820s there was a fairly general awareness in certain circles that the long-term interests of Prussia were being badly served by the continued enforcement of the strict censorship introduced in accordance with the Carlsbad Decrees. Throughout the post-war years, the radical reform of land tenure, education, opportunities in the professions, finance, taxation and the customs had laid the foundations for the transformation of the country into a major commercial power, and by 1831 the corresponding constitutional reforms had enabled it to survive a general European upheaval unscathed. Since the policies being pursued had given rise to both prosperity and stability, what need was there for a censorship? The best antidote to the troublesome and pointless aspirations of the liberals was to call attention to the real benefits provided by the established order. What was required was simply an effective means for advertising what had been accomplished. Gentz had had the idea of setting up a popular paper to this end as early as 1828, but had been unable to get together a suitable team of journalists.[14] Two years later, the patriotic publisher Friedrich Perthes, who had served his country so well during the Napoleonic occupation and subsequently established a highly successful publishing firm at Gotha, called attention to the fact that 'it was not enough that the intentions and the administration of the country should be good', but that 'the general recognition of its merits was of almost equal importance' and that 'the Prussian government should therefore start publicizing itself'. He too saw the need for a popular paper, but the ministry turned down his proposal to start one with the observation that deeds were more important than words, and that if it started publicizing itself it could easily become dependent upon uncontrollable factors.[15] It concentrated instead upon launching Ranke's *Historical-political Journal*, a dignified and scholarly publication designed to appeal to dons, intelligent civil-servants and highbrow businessmen.[16] On 31 January 1831 the jurist Eichhorn wrote about the government's newspaper propaganda to his colleague Savigny: 'I cannot understand why the government should never have thought of arming itself more effectively. The *Austrian Observer* and the *State Gazette* are so dull, their didactic expositions are entirely lacking in zip.'[17]

Since Hegel had evidently been reading the *Prussian State Gazette* ever since his arrival in Berlin,[18] and shared a common background with Eichhorn and Savigny through the University, it seems reasonable to assume that he too had decided that something ought to be done about the paper's failings. It has always been evident from what has been known about the circumstances under which the Reform Bill article was written, that it was probably an attempt to overcome what he regarded as the deplorable ineffectiveness of the state paper in selling national policy. Direct evidence that this was in fact the case has, however, only recently come to light, through the discovery of a letter he wrote to Beyme some three weeks after the publication of the article in the *State Gazette*. Beyme had played an important part in carrying through Stein's reforms, as well as in supporting Humboldt's policies, and in 1817 had become a member of the council of state. He had evidently written to Hegel, congratulating him on the article, and asking why the last part of it had not appeared. The reply was a follows: 'It has remained unpublished on account of the main purpose of the article, which is to make use of the Reform Bill issue in order to deal with certain universally applicable principles, which are not only constantly giving rise to the misrepresentation and denigration of the constitution and legislature of Prussia, but which also act to the detriment of the latter in lending credence to the pretension and popular repute of English freedom. This could have been interpreted as an attack upon the British constitution, and as therefore suitable for the *Prussian State Gazette*.'[19]

A modern reader of the *Gazette* is not likely to dissent very strongly from the judgement passed upon it by its contemporary critics. It looks like a government publication. Foreign news is presented in accordance with the rank of the countries in the international hierarchy – Russia, France, England, the Netherlands, etc. – each section starting with an account of what is going on at the court. German affairs are reported in a similar manner, the emphasis throughout being upon their diplomatic, constitutional and legal aspects. There are no leaders as such, although the separate reports sometimes include a considerable amount of comment, and lengthy articles like Hegel's, serialized over a number of issues, are not very frequent. In certain fields, however, the quality of the reporting is high. On 16 March 1831, for example, the paper included a survey of the British press and of the attitudes towards reform being adopted by the various London and provincial papers, evidently no less than thirty of which were then being taken regularly in Berlin.[20] In a number of cases it is also distinguished by a remarkable degree of objectivity. Prior to the Paris revolution for example, it tended to give a fairly sympathetic coverage to French liberalism. Subsequent developments in France were reported in a rather matter-of-fact way, however, as were the Belgian and Polish uprisings, and although the Berlin riots of September 1830 were reported when they first broke out, the topic was soon dropped.[21]

News of the English Reform Bill first appeared in the *Gazette* on 9 March 1831, and from the outset the paper viewed the Whig proposals favourably, without looking very far beyond the issues actually being raised in Parliament. Major speeches against the Bill, such as those by Inglis, Wetherell and Peel were reported at length, but so was Spencer Perceval's fatuous effusion of Tory prejudices, together with a suitably acid commentary. Macaulay's powerful plea for the long-term constructiveness of the proposals was given the publicity it deserved, but the most notable feature of the reporting, considering the paper's basic bias, was the space and attention devoted to O'Connell and his colleagues. The Irish leader's erudite and masterly survey of the merits of the Whig proposals was judged by the London correspondent to be 'the best oration delivered during the last few days, and perhaps the most distinguished of the whole proceedings'. Sheil's fine maiden speech, with its spate of telling rhetorical questions, was printed in full: 'What are the obstructions that stand against Reform? Where are the petitions against it? Who are its opponents? They may be counted. Who are its advocates? Millions of Britons, with their Sovereign at their head.'[22] On 26 March the paper published a general commentary by its London correspondent which shows how well he had managed to size up the situation: 'There are of course many who are opposed to the ministerial plan because they are looking after their own interests, because they are prejudiced, because they are afraid that too much could be granted, or even that reform could follow reform until a revolution is under way. But although they regard revolution as possible if the plan is accepted, they are by no means certain that it is not *necessary* if it is rejected. This group tends to keep in the background however, they do not petition Parliament.'[23]

Parliament adjourned for Easter on 30 March, and the last reports of its proceedings appeared in the *Gazette* on 7 April. Hegel finished his lectures on the philosophy of world history on 26 March, and must have planned and written the article during the next few weeks. Judging from the way in which the paper had been reporting the topic, it looks as though his initial reason for doing so could well have been the desire to correct the broadly favourable impression of the Whig plan created by the London correspondent. The first two instalments of the article appeared in the morning and evening issues of 26 April, the third on 29 April.[24] On 2 May the concluding section had still not appeared, and Hegel wrote to the editor asking why. On the following day the king's private secretary also wrote to the editor: 'His Majesty has taken no exception to the article on the Reform Bill, but he finds it unsuitable for the *State Gazette*, and I must therefore request you to withhold the last part of it, which you so kindly forwarded to me, and which I herewith return.' Hegel was informed, by the editor, on 8 May. As we have already seen in the case of Beyme, the article was well received in court circles, and despite his intervention in the interest of international relations, the king evidently ordered that the last part should be printed separately and circulated privately.[25]

If we are going to avoid gross misinterpretation of this incident, it is essential to bear in mind the probable sequence of events. It looks as though the king must have asked to see the last section of the article when part three appeared on 29 April. He could hardly have found anything to disturb him in section one, and although some of the details concerning English society mentioned in section two were not what he was used to coming across in the *Gazette*, there was no reason why he should have seen any harm in them. In section three, however, Hegel criticizes the government and the constitution in such outspoken terms, that one can well imagine the king wondering what was coming next, and asking the editor to send him the following section before publishing it. But whatever happened, it was certainly not the case that the whole article was submitted for royal approval before publication began, and that the king only decided at the last moment against passing part four because it ended by mentioning the possibility of revolution.[26]

If we are looking for the more purely philosophical background to Hegel's assessment of the Reform Bill, it is natural that we should turn to his main work on political theory, the *Philosophy of Right*. Most of the topics taken up in the article are also dealt with in this earlier publication – the codification of the law (§216), the support of the poor (§241), the function of the monarchy (§275), the selection and training of civil servants (§289), taxation (§299), elections (§308), etc. Whereas the article is simply an essay in political journalism, however, embodying certain philosophical preconceptions it is true, but to a very great extent determined by the force of the particular circumstances under consideration, the *Philosophy of Right* is a systematic treatise on law, morality, sociology and statecraft, an integral part of the *Encyclopaedia of the Philosophical Sciences in Outline*, and essentially universal in its implications. The overriding consideration in the work is not pragmatic effectiveness, the influencing and moulding of a particular situation, but the analytical and synthetic procedures involved in eliciting from the given subject-matter the structure and interrelationships of a comprehensively dialectical exposition.[27] This is not to say that Hegel's political journalism is not philosophical or that his political philosophy is not pragmatic, but that they are not predominantly so, and that the connections between them are to be sought mainly in the subject-matter common to both, not in the general principles of his philosophical system. His journalism is therefore important to the study of his political philosophy not because it shows him putting his general philosophical principles to the test in practical political situations, but because it indicates, far more readily than the *Philosophy of Right*, his actual interests, preoccupations and prejudices, the ultimate sources of his empirical knowledge.

The article on the Reform Bill does, however, contain a number of general ideas which are deeply rooted in Hegel's whole manner of thinking. The very fact that he is attempting to put forward an apologia for the accomplishments of the Prussia of his day naturally calls to mind the main point made in the preface to the *Philosophy of Right*, the emphasis laid upon, 'the conviction that what is rational is actual and what is actual is rational, a conviction on which both the plain man and the philosopher take their stand, and from which philosophy starts in its study of the universe of mind as well as the universe of nature'.[28] An English reader unacquainted with the Prussian background and Hegel's other writings, might assume that his emphasis upon the constitutional disadvantages of a weak monarchy was simply the result of an anti-Whig prejudice. It can, however, be shown to be the outcome of a general concept of subjectivity which is also central to the dialectical structure of such purely philosophical works as the *Phenomenology* and the *Logic*, and the implications of which he had already worked out with respect to German imperial politics by the turn of the century.[29] Anyone familiar with the history of early nineteenth-century Britain might easily assume from Hegel's opinions concerning the rotten boroughs, the way in which he assesses the means by which the unreformed Parliament managed to represent 'the various major interests of the realm', that he was simply suffering from the same disastrous inability to size up the current situation as that which had brought about the downfall of the Wellington administration in the November of 1830. In fact, this preference for a constitutional system giving weight to the representation of interests rather than numerical majorities was not only in tune with Prussian policy after 1819, but is also to be found in Hegel's very early writings, and has its roots in his critique of logical atomism.[30]

Although the article's Prussian background and philosophical presuppositions play such an important part in determining the substructure of its thought, it is also what it appears to be, an attempt to analyse the situation in Britain. Since the main topics it raises are also classified dialectically in the *Philosophy of Right*, and its arguments are illustrated with such a wealth of concrete cases and specific instances, it is not surprising that Hegel should also have made use of this basic material in his university teaching. In the lectures on the *Philosophy of Right*, as in the article, he discusses the economic situation in Britain, the way in which the extremes of wealth and poverty were giving rise to class conflict, the anomalies and absurdities of the legal system, the functioning of Parliament, as well as such national institutions as the church, the press, the schools and the armed forces.[31] As in the article, the general tone is critical. As early as 1825, we find him suggesting that the healthiest feature of the British Parliamentary scene is that a change of ministry does not involve a change in the social background or fundamental constitutional ideas of those in office, and that the weakness of the situation in France is that the opposition consists of republicans, who would do away with the existing constitution if they came to power.[32]

III

To investigate the precise manner in which Hegel's philosophical presuppositions and dialectical classifications influenced his judgement of British affairs in the Reform Bill article, important though this is to an understanding of the whole corporate enterprise of thinking dialectically about politics, would be to go beyond the scope of this article. We now propose to confine ourselves to the rather more basic procedure of investigating the manner in which his analytical judgements were influenced by his sources of information.

He makes no mention of his sources in either the lectures or the article. This presents us with something of a problem, since although he could have derived much of his information concerning the constitution from the *Gazette*, this paper could not have provided him with his insight into the economic and social situation, or with his knowledge of the detailed working of the British legal system. Furtunately, we are able to trace the general pattern of his background reading from those of his notes that have been preserved in the Harvard College Library and the Staatsbibliothek Preussischer Kulturbesitz in Berlin. These scraps and scribblings show, for example, that he was acquainted with the Tory attitude to social and constitutional issues through the *Quarterly Review*. One of the articles he took notes on was Southey's 'Rise and Progress of Popular Disaffection', in which 'the causes which have tended to combine so many persons against the best government in the world' are sought in a general survey of English history from the fifteenth century onwards, which culminates in an eloquent condemnation of 'that brutal ruffian' Cobbett, and the assertion that 'the question is whether revolution can be averted till time be gained for educating the populace and improving their condition'.[33] Another *Quarterly* article he evidently read with some care was 'On the Means of Improving the People', in which the attempt is made to analyse the contemporary situation rather than the historical background. In this essay, particular attention is paid to the bad effects of rootlessness and social mobility, the prevalence of idleness, drunkenness, gambling and cruelty among the lower classes, the problems presented by the poor laws, mendicity, the prisons and the newspapers, and to the benefits that would accrue from improving religious education, repairing the stocks, enforcing the Sabbath, establishing savings banks and reforming the law. The article is naive and superficial by the standards of modern social analysis, but it does have the merit of calling attention to the complexity of the overall situation: 'The quack in politics, like the quack in medicine, prescribes one remedy for all the maladies of the commonweal; it is a sure criterion of quackery to do so.'[34] Hegel's knowledge of the corresponding Whig ideas seems to have been derived from the *Edinburgh*

Review, the basic attitude of which he evidently found more to his taste. It is certainly of the utmost importance to any analysis of his attitude toward the English legal system to know that he copied out the greater part of Samuel Romilly's review of Bentham's 'Papers relative to Codification', published in this periodical in November 1817. Romilly surveys Bentham's fruitless attempts to influence the legislatures of Russia, the United States, Poland and Pennsylvania, and then goes on to discuss the basic illogicality of the English procedure of expounding the law by analogy rather than drawing up a utilitarian code. 'The rule is not laid down until after the event which calls for the application of it has happened. Though new in *fact*, yet being of the greatest antiquity in *theory*, it has necessarily a retrospective operation, and governs all past, as well as all future transactions. Property, which had been purchased or transmitted by descent to the present possessor of it, is discovered by the newly declared law to belong to others; actions, which were thought to be innocent, turn out to be criminal; and there is no security for men's possessions, their persons, or their liberties.'[35]

It is clear from the notes that have been preserved, however, that by far his most important source of information concerning British affairs was the *Morning Chronicle*, which he seems to have read regularly throughout the greater part of the Berlin period.[36] It almost certainly interested him on account of the high quality of its journalism and its outspokenness. It had been founded in 1769, and by the time he was reading it regularly its general character was well established and widely recognized. It was obviously an opposition paper – critical, forthright, quite unlike the staid and conformist *Prussian State Gazette*. Although it had always been broadly Whig in its sympathies, it was financially independent of the party organization,[37] and did not hesitate to take a line of its own if it disagreed with current party policies. In 1817 the editorship had passed from James Perry (1756–1821), who had been secretary to the Fox Club and very much a part of the inner circle of Whig society,[38] to John Black (1783–1855), who was a close friend of James Mill, and something of a recluse. It was under Black, and during the period that Hegel was reading it regularly, that the paper reached the height of its influence, reputation and prosperity. As John Stuart Mill points out in his autobiography, during the early years of Black's editorship, it bid fair to become the main organ of the Utilitarian movement: 'During the whole of this year , 1823, a considerable number of my contributions were printed in the *Chronicle* and the *Traveller*; sometimes notices of books, but oftener letters, commenting on some nonsense talked in Parliament, or some defect of the law, or misdoings of the magistracy or the courts of justice. In this last department the *Chronicle* was now rendering signal service. After the death of Mr Perry, the editorship and management of the paper had devolved on Mr John Black, long a reporter on its establishment; a man of most extensive reading and information, great honesty and simplicity of mind; a particular friend of my father, imbued with many of his and Bentham's ideas, which he reproduced in his articles, among other valuable thoughts, with greater facility and skill. From this time the *Chronicle* ceased to be the merely Whig organ it was before, and during the next ten years became to a considerable extent a vehicle of the opinions of the Utilitarian radicals. This was mainly by what Black himself wrote, with some assistance from Fonblanque, who first shewed his eminent qualities as a writer by articles and *jeux d'esprit* in the *Chronicle*. The defects of the law, and of the administration of justice, were the subject on which that paper rendered most service to improvement. Up to that time hardly a word had been said, except by Bentham and my father, against that most peccant part of English institutions and their administration. It was the almost universal creed of Englishmen, that the law of England, the judicature of England, the unpaid magistracy of England, were models of excellence. I do not go beyond the mark in saying, that after Bentham, who supplied the principal materials, the greatest share of the merit of breaking down this wretched superstition belongs to Black, as editor of the *Morning Chronicle*. He kept up an incessant fire against it, exposing the absurdities and vices of the law and the courts of justice, paid and unpaid, until he forced some sense of them into people's minds. On many other questions he became the organ of opinions much in advance of any which had ever before found regular advocacy in the newspaper press. Black was a frequent visitor of my father, and Mr Grote used to say that he always knew by the Monday morning's article, whether Black had been with my father on the Sunday.'[39]

Admirable though it was as a popularizing medium and as a means for bringing the principles of Benthamism to bear upon current problems, Black's paper was clearly unable to accommodate the lengthy and elaborate articles and reviews that then constituted the stock in trade of any serious political or philosophical movement. James Mill saw the need for a periodical comparable to the Whig *Edinburgh* and the Tory *Quarterly*, and it was for this reason that he launched the *Westminster* in January 1824. In the decade or so during which Hegel was reading the *Chronicle*, the paper was therefore important to the Utilitarians not as a vehicle for the direct presentation of their philosophical views but as a means of general propaganda, and they were well aware that it was effective as such only in so far as it maintained its attitude of critical independence. It concentrated upon making its points by implication, by straightforward reporting of particular items of news, and Hegel almost certainly had no idea that there was any close connection between Benthamism and the sort of information the paper was providing on the law, elections, and the economic, social and religious background to the constitutional issues. Since he drew most of the conclusions the editors hoped he would, not only all the factual material but also many of the basic assumptions of the Reform Bill article are also to be found in the *Chronicle*. It is almost certain, therefore, that the line of argument he developed in order to advertise the merits of the Prussian government was originally suggested to him by the propaganda being disseminated by those intent on bringing about the social and constitutional reform of Great Britain.

On the central matter of the reform of the electoral system, the *Chronicle* had a consistent if somewhat devious policy, determined partly by changes in the Parliamentary scene and partly by James Mill's political tactics. Like Hegel, Mill was convinced that a powerful constitutional monarchy was essential to the effective and efficient administration of a country: 'A first magistrate is necessary; that is a fixed and undisputed point. The necessity of unity in matters of administration, the use of concentrated responsibility, and many other considerations, seem to place the balance of advantage on the side of the individuality of the first magistrate. He should be one, not two, or more.'[40] Like Hegel, he distrusted uncontrolled radicalism, and thought it essential that reform should be brought about by constitutional means. This gave rise to a certain amount of friction with the staff of the *Chronicle*, since from 1823 onwards Black's sub-editor was the anarchist Thomas Hodgskin (1787–1869), one of the leading lights of the Rotunda Radicals, the most extreme London working-class organization of the time. Hodgskin sometimes managed to insert his own brand of propaganda into the paper. On 25 October 1831 for example, Mill wrote to Francis Place enquiring about a group which had been attempting to influence Black: 'Their notions about property look ugly; they not only desire that it should have nothing to do with representation, which is true, though not a truth for the present time, as they ought to see, but they seem to think it should not exist, and that the existence of it is an evil to them. Rascals, I have no doubt, are at work among them. Black, it is true, is easily imposed upon.'[41] Place informed him that they were followers of Hodgskin, and when the chancellor, Lord Brougham, objected to the *Chronicle's* reporting of one of Attwood's speeches during the aftermath of the reform crisis, Mill passed this information on to him: 'The nonsense to which your Lordship alludes about the rights of the labourer to the whole produce of the country, wages, profits and rent, all included, is the mad nonsense of our friend Hodgkin [*sic*], which he has published as a system and propagates with the zeal of perfect fanaticism. Whatever of it appears in the *Chronicle*, steals in through his means, he being a sort of sub-editor, and Black not very sharp in detecting...These opinions, if they were to spread, would be the subversion of civilised society; worse than the overwhelming deluge of Huns and Tartars.'[42]

Mill and Black were convinced that any close identification of their support for the Reform movement with socialist radicalism was not only undesirable in itself, but would have alienated them from the Whigs and their supporters, and so reduced their effectiveness in helping to get the desired reforms through Parliament. They saw, however, as Hegel had seen during the Württemberg constitutional crisis of 1798 (*PW*, 243–5), that the threat of radicalism was useful in that it could be manipulated in order to frighten those in power into making concessions.[43] The general policy pursued by the *Chronicle* during the years immediately preceding the Reform crisis was, therefore, that of so reporting events that they contributed to the creation of a general impression of imminent revolution, while at the same time calling attention to the possibility of avoiding such a catastrophe by granting the constitutional reforms which Lord Grey had been advocating since the 1790s.[44]

Reading the *Chronicle* on the Reform Bill in order to overcome the obvious limitations of the coverage of the subject provided by the *Prussian State Gazette*, not being aware of the slant being given to its ostensibly straight-forward reporting, preoccupied as he was with the Paris disturbances and their repercussions, it is not surprising that Hegel should have drawn the conclusion that England really was tottering on the brink of revolution. During the French elections of July 1830, the *Chronicle* had paid a great deal of attention to emphasizing the relevance of the developments taking place to the situation in Britain, and when the liberal victory was announced, it asked if its effects would be confined to France: 'Will the other nations of Europe view unmoved this grand struggle of a great and enlightened nation to compel those to whose hands the powers of Government are committed, to be accountable to the people?' (20 July 1830, leader). Soon after the Reform Bill had been introduced into the Commons, it published a letter from Paris in which the correspondent informed his English readers that 'Our delight has originated in the pleasing thought that Great Britain will owe to the French Revolution of July 1830, the Radical Reform in her electoral system' (9 March 1831). Great prominence was given to reports of the Belgian and Polish revolutions, as well as to news of any other social or political disturbances taking place on the continent, the general tone of the articles being in favour of the insurgents. On occasions, the propaganda was a little too obvious to be really effective. On the day on which Lord John Russell's speech introducing the Reform Bill was reported, for example, the whole of the front page of the paper was covered with accounts of popular insurrections, Asian as well as European (2 March 1831). The machine-smashing, rick-burning and cattle-laming which spread throughout the agricultural districts of the home counties during the autumn of 1830 was exploited to the full, and once the trials began, the economic, social and legal background was explored in detail: 'It might be instructive to sum up the advantages which the lower orders of England derive from a Constitutional Legislature. They are not indebted to it for access to Justice, they are not indebted to it for Education. But they are indebted to it for the Game Laws, and in the Home Counties for the alternative of being starved to death, or becoming thieves.' (4 March 1831, leader).[45] The riots and radical meetings in the big towns were made to look even more ominous than they seemed to those directly threatened by them,[46] the interpretation of thoroughgoing class antagonism being put upon these events: 'There is not one country in Europe – not one – where the social ties have been so violently severed as in England. The accursed distinctions which run through English society teach men to hate, envy, and despise each other. The poor feel that they are not permitted to enjoy, and they are determined that the rich shall not. We have long raised our voice against the system which has so long been patronised by the English Aristocracy. That system has been gaining ground ever since the Aristocracy gained the mastery in 1688.' (30 October 1830, leader).

True to James Mill's conception of rational government and to the actual potentialities of the constitutional situation, but quite at odds with the traditions of the reforming party, the *Chronicle* laid constant emphasis upon the importance of the monarchy in furthering the interest of the whole people. The broad development since the seventeenth century Whig revolution was a recurrent theme in its leaders: 'In 1688 a new era commenced...The English constitution is merely a piece of machinery for enabling a certain number of rich individuals to take from the people as much as their patience will suffer to be taken. As long as the King wished to have exclusive mastery, and the proprietors of the boroughs and the people had a common interest, the Constitution might answer. But the moment the Crown and the Aristocracy combined, the people were utterly without protection. From thenceforward the Constitution was utterly worthless – existed only in name; for the check upon power at present is the same as that which the people of every country possess – the knowledge that the physical power is with them' (16 October 1830). Bentham's scepticism with regard to the truth or value of any kind of religion seems to have determined much of the *Chronicle's* reporting of religious issues, and it showed very little sympathy for the established church. When plans for the commuting of tithes were discussed in the Lords for example, it did what it might have been expected to do, and made use of the debate in order to call attention to the close identification of the Church of England with the interests of the aristocracy, especially in Ireland.[47] As James Mill and John Black saw it, the basic problem facing the reforming Whig ministry which came to power in the November of 1830 was, therefore, to find a middle way between the interests of the people and those of the aristocracy. 'With respect to Parliamentary Reform, Lord Grey's ministry is surrounded with still greater difficulties... There are two great antagonist Powers, the Aristocracy and the people – the Scylla and Charybdis of British politics. Clever must the politician be who can steer the vessel of State between these rocks, without damage... Whoever inclines towards the people is pursued by the Aristocracy, and whoever inclines towards the Aristocracy is pursued by the People. Whoever can solve the problem of distributing political power in such a way as shall leave the Aristocracy and the People satisfied with their respective shares, will be possessed of no ordinary skill.'[48] It is interesting to note that thinking in terms of social classes continued to determine the logic of their argumentation while the reform plans were being worked out in committee. 'To postpone Reform, in the present temper of the nation, would endanger the public tranquillity. On the other hand, we are satisfied, that if anything like universal suffrage were demanded, the higher ranks would be supported by a very large proportion of the middle classes in their refusal to grant it. It cannot be obtained. The only chance we have of obtaining Reform is in the union of the middle classes. The lower orders, though they contribute so much to the wealth of the country, are unable to make themselves felt by the Aristocracy. In times when society is thrown into confusion, and force decides, the lower orders are everything, but the signal must be given by the higher and middle classes before the lower can act.'[49]

As we have already noted, Hegel rounds off his article by suggesting that, if the reform of Parliament opened it to the radicals, 'The people would be a power of a different kind; and an opposition which, erected on a basis hitherto at variance with the stability of Parliament, might feel itself no match for the opposite party in Parliament, could be led to look for its strength to the people, and then introduce not reform but revolution' (*PW*, 330). This certainly seems to indicate that although he had taken seriously the *Chronicle*'s warning of impending revolution, he had not been convinced by its arguments for the general acceptability of the Whig proposals. We now know that he was mistaken on both counts, but since many of those actually involved in the events he was analysing sized them up in much the same way, it has to be admitted that he erred in good company. The king, for example, whose judgement seems to have been sharpened by his being presented with the proposed reforms on the anniversary of the martyrdom of Charles I, sent a long memorandum on them to Lord Grey in which he made it quite clear that he too doubted the wisdom of popularizing the Commons: 'All this would seem to point out the inexpediency, not to say the insecurity, of rendering the House of Commons more *popular* than it already is in the materials of its composition, by the substitution of a representation of *numbers* for one of *property*.'[50] Lord Melbourne, who as home secretary was responsible for dealing with the widespread civil disturbances, was worried enough by the agricultural riots to send military officers into the affected areas to supervise the disposal of troops and advise magistrates on the levying of local volunteers.[51] On the very day on which the last reports of the Parliamentary debates appeared in the *Prussian State Gazette* and Hegel probably sat down to plan his article, the London radical Francis Place wrote as follows to a friend: 'I hope with you almost against my conviction that we shall be able to avoid a violent revolution in working out our reformation. A violent revolution in this country would be dreadful in the extreme...Contemplate seriously what would be the consequences of the failure of supplies to this great metropolis...Do you think you can estimate with anything like precision the terrible consequences of a starving and enraged populace in London and its example on all parts of the county.'[52]

During the March and April of 1831 there were certain features, even of the parliamentary scene, which seemed to indicate that any reform, any concession to the radicals, could have precipitated a revolutionary landslide. Macaulay's argument that the Bill was the best possible guarantee against revolution in that it would bring the middle classes onto the side of stability and order, had incited Henry Hunt, the radical member for Preston, into asserting that it was entirely unacceptable to the working classes since 'it would give no satisfaction to those who were justly entitled to the exercise of their constitutional privileges',[53] an argument which he reiterated on several occasions during the following weeks. Reports of his speeches appeared in both the *Chronicle* and the *Gazette*, and Hegel's view of the disruptive effect which large numbers of radicals of this kind might have upon a reformed Parliament (*PW*, 324) was almost certainly based upon them. The people were, however, by no means so united in their condemnation of the Bill as Hunt maintained. They were not, it is true, particularly interested in adding to their constitutional ineffectiveness by helping their immediate social superiors to get the vote. On the other hand, many intelligent and constitutionally underprivileged people realized that they would gain nothing by standing aside and allowing the Bill to be defeated, and that if a beginning were made with limited reforms, this could easily and naturally lead on to more thoroughgoing measures. Even in the big cities, the sort of class consciousness subsequently cultivated by the Chartists and the Marxists had not yet been developed.[54] The red flag was, indeed, first raised in Britain as the symbol of rebellion only a few weeks after Hegel had published his article, but it was flown as the sign of a quasi-religious, not a political enthusiasm.[55] Modern historical analysis can demonstrate fairly conclusively that after 1818 there was never really any danger of the sort of revolution with which James Mill and John Black managed to frighten their readers. The closest Britain came to such a chaos during the sixty years following the first French upheaval was probably the spring of 1812, when there was a severe slump, the price of wheat was inordinately high, the Luddite riots were reaching a climax and the greater part of the army was engaged in foreign service.[56]

Subsequent developments showed very clearly that those who planned the Reform of Parliament during the midwinter of 1830–1, had assessed the potentialities of the current situation far better than those who were afraid that any such reform would precipitate an uncontrollable turmoil. By transferring parliamentary representation from the rotten boroughs to the new industrial towns, and dividing the representation of the predominantly rural counties from that of the exclusively urban boroughs, the Whigs satisfied those demanding a more reasonable degree of numerical representation, while preserving the more traditional principle of the representation of communities and interests. By abolishing all narrow rights of election and establishing universal property qualifications in both the countryside and the towns, while resisting the demand for universal suffrage, more frequent Parliaments and voting by ballot, they swept away enough anomalies to satisfy the radicals and preserved enough of the old system to pacify the conservatives. There was never any doubt in the Whig leader's mind about his overall objective. As he wrote to Princess Lieven, he wanted a reform which would 'take from the peerage a power which makes them odious, and substitute for it an influence which connects them with the people'.[57] This had been his policy since the 1790s, and he wrote as follows when considering it in its broadest setting: 'Everywhere, as far as I could form any judgement, this change required greater influence to be yielded to the middle classes, who had made wonderful advances both in property and in intelligence ... Without some such concessions the change alluded to will lead rapidly to republicanism and to the destruction of established institutions.'[58]

When first presenting the planned reforms to the king, Grey wrote that 'the great desideratum is to make an arrangement on which we can stand, announcing our determination not to go beyond it ... The plan of reform ought to be of such a scope and description as to satisfy all reasonable demands, and remove at once and for ever, all rational grounds of complaint from the minds of the intelligent and independent portion of the community.'[59] Like Hegel, the radicals, the king and the cabinet, Grey realized therefore that the proposed reforms could have initiated a landslide, but differed from them in being convinced that they would not do so. Although developments after 1832 certainly proved him right, it seems likely that if the Bill had become law soon after the sweeping electoral victory of May 1831,[60] the radicals would have persuaded the populace that the further stages of their programme could have been as easily achieved as the first, and would therefore have proved him wrong with a vengeance. It was the protracted manoeuvring and agitation necessary before the Bill finally became law in June 1832, which gave rise to the more thoroughly popular attachment to the Whig proposals, and to the widespread reaction against further change.

How are we to assess Hegel's article in the light of this background? As an analysis of the whole economic, social and constitutional situation out of which the Reform Bill issue arose, it was immensely superior to the parliamentary reports published in the *Prussian State Gazette*, and probably better than anything else written in German at the time. By modern standards, however, it is an unsatisfactory analysis, since by basing his approach upon what he regarded as the predominantly unbiased journalism of the *Morning Chronicle*, he allowed himself to be misled, on matters which were of central importance to his argument, by Utilitarian propaganda.[61] This is certainly interesting to the historian of ideas in that it brings together two of the most influential philosophical movements of the time, but since it resulted in Hegel's misassessing a situation he thought he was analysing objectively, it considerably reduced the intrinsic value of his work. As propaganda in its own right however, as an apologia for the Prussia of 1831, the result of an appreciative analysis of what had been accomplished during the quarter of a century following the disastrous defeat at Jena, the article can only be regarded as highly successful. Like all effective propaganda, and indeed like all thinking about human affairs, it was to some extent self-justifying in its pragmatic results. By calling attention, during a particularly critical revolutionary period, to the merits of the Prussian administration, the value of stability and security, it almost certainly helped the Berlin government to weather the storm in the way that it did.

But whatever conclusions we reach with regard to the merits or demerits of the analysis and propaganda the article involves, it is absolutely essential that we should not confuse its import with that of the dialectical exposition of law, morality and ethical life worked out in the *Philosophy of Right*.

Obligation, contract and exchange: on the significance of Hegel's abstract right

SEYLA BENHABIB

Since the publication of C. B. Macpherson's *The Political Theory of Possessive Individualism*, it has been a familiar argument that the models of political obligation and authority put forward by contractarian thinkers presuppose the institutions of a liberal market society.[1] Macpherson has also claimed that contract theorists smuggled into their conception of the state of nature historical and social presuppositions which could only characterize the behavior of men in modern market societies. Hegel in some way anticipated Macpherson's thesis when he analyzed the connection between the norms of personality, property and contract, and the structure of modern exchange relations, in his Jena writings. More significant is the relation, at the normative and methodological levels, between Hegel's *Philosophy of Right* and the contractarian natural rights tradition which began with Thomas Hobbes. J. Ritter, K.-H. Ilting and Manfred Riedel have referred to Hegel's discussion of persons, property and contract as evidence that the principles of Hegel's political philosophy are continuous with the tradition extending from Hobbes to Fichte.[2] In this essay, however, I will argue that Hegel's reception of the contractarian natural rights tradition rests on an irony which has been little appreciated until now. While he certainly analyzes contract in its specifically modern sense as the 'exchange of equivalents' in the market place, Hegel strongly denies the appropriateness of the contract metaphor for elucidating either the normative grounds or the historical-genetic origin of political authority. On the other hand, Hegel accepts the conclusions of the contractarians from Hobbes to Fichte insofar as they argue for a novel paradigm of political legitimacy. Following Max Weber, I use the term legitimacy to mean 'the grounds of obligation and authority relations among men'.[3] The novelty of the contractarian paradigm of legitimacy is that the recognition of the individual as someone entitled to rights becomes the necessary ground for accepting obligation towards a public authority. In the first part of this essay, I claim that Hegel transforms the contractarian paradigm of legitimacy into a philosophical justification of the rule of law

159

in the modern state. The legitimation function of forms of abstract right in
Hegel's *Philosophy of Right* is thus twofold: they serve as the philosophical
foundations of the rule of law in the modern state, and they justify practices
of exchange in the market place. 'Abstract right' is of course Hegel's term
for the traditional concept of 'natural right'.

In the second half of this essay I discuss the methodological divergence
between Hegel's *Philosophy of Right* and previous contractarian procedures.
Unlike the latter Hegel does not take as his starting point the condition of
an isolated self motivated to recognize the right of others through the fear
of death (Hobbes) or through an intuitive and presocial knowledge of the
natural law (Locke). Nor does Hegel understand 'persons' to be Kantian
moral agents endowed with the noumenal ability to act in accordance with
the categorical imperative. He proceeds from the condition of a society of
individuals who have recognized one another's entitlement to be persons in
order to describe the concrete forms of interaction compatible with this norm.
I argue that Hegel's methodology is based on systematic assumptions, which
sharply distinguish his political philosophy from the tradition known as
'possessive individualism' as well as the rationalist contractarian tradition of
Kant and Fichte.

In recent years both liberal and marxist thinkers have renewed their interest
in Hegel's political philosophy. On issues such as the nature of the modern
state, its legitimacy and the contradictions and crises of market societies Hegel
is seen as offering an alternative to mainstream liberalism and to orthodox
marxism. The opening arguments of the *Philosophy of Right* demonstrate this
contemporary relevance of Hegel's political philosophy most clearly. I
conclude that while Hegel challenges the individualist and ahistorical
presuppositions of the modern liberal tradition he confronts marxism with
a type of social realism that avoids reducing the normative dimension of
collective life to a positivist science of society.

I

Hegel's *Philosophy of Right* with its clearly articulated distinction between
state and civil society provides the first cogent analysis of the modern
organization of economic life. Hegel calls a 'system of needs' the form of
economic life which is arranged around the contractual sale and purchase of
goods among property-owners. This notion of a 'system of needs' as a
depoliticized sphere of commercial transactions had its forerunners among
the British political economists whose influence on Hegel has been well
documented.[4] However, if we distinguish between modern and premodern
exchange, and between modern and premodern norms of contract, I would
maintain that the uniqueness of Hegel's analysis, both in the Jena writing and

in the *Philosophy of Right*, consists (a) of depicting the structure of specifically modern exchange relations as the reciprocal transfer of proprietory rights among formally equal property-owners and (b) of clarifying the normative presuppositions of such exchange.

As early as 1802–3, in his essay on *Natural Law*, Hegel discusses the connection between the spread of formal, legal norms in social life and the emergence of market relations. In a passage which Lukács has made famous he describes the clash between the values of the *Politiker* (statesman) and the *Bürger* (burgher) as the 'tragedy and comedy of ethical life'. While tragedy is the conflict of values that are ends in themselves, comedy represents the usurpation of the status of an absolute by something that has merely relative value. The comic element must be given its due in the modern world in which the values of the feudal nobility have succumbed to those of the middle class within the ethical community of the nation. 'The principle of universality and equality had to take possession of the whole in such a way as to replace the particular classes with a mixture of the two. Beneath the law of formal unity what has really happened is that this mixture has cancelled the first class and made the second class into the sole class of the nation.'[5] When values like the security of property, the satisfaction of needs and the enjoyment of goods are universalized, relations in the ethical community come to be defined by the legal norms of formal equality among individuals. In the *Jenaer Realphilosophie* Hegel gives a more precise analysis of the relationship between the spread of monetary and commercial activity and the regulation of social life through legal norms. He has discovered the structure of modern exchange relations. In exchange, two distinct individuals engage in a monetary transaction to transfer their property rights over certain goods. Exchange relations are *formal*. As long as they do not violate the rights of ownership of the parties involved, their content and substance remain undefined. From the standpoint of exchange no characteristic of individuals is relevant apart from the fact that each owns a certain property desired by the other. The *equality* of individuals *qua* property owners is presupposed. Each can only expect from the other what the other can expect of him, namely, the mutual transfer of property rights. The *reciprocity* of the parties is thereby stipulated. Neither appropriates the property of the other by force, but respects the right of the other to dispose of it through a contractual transaction (the principle of formal freedom). The equality of the object of property is also thereby established. The acquisition by one person of the property of another can only occur through the exchange of equivalents. Property rights are transferred in return for the equivalent payment of the *value* of the property in money. 'This value itself as a thing', writes Hegel, 'is money...Each gives up his possession of his own accord...Only because the other sells his goods [*Sache*] that I also do so; and this equality in the thing as its interior [element] is value, which has my complete consent and the opinion of the other – the positive mine as well as his, the unity of my and his will...'[6]

In order to evaluate the significance of Hegel's analysis we should consider that in all economic systems exchange, or the 'mutually appropriative movement of goods between hands',[7] is regulated by certain norms of property and contract. Premodern exchange relations, however, are restricted only to certain groups of individuals, who on account of their special status in society enjoy certain privileges, among them the right to engage in exchange.[8] It is also characteristic of such premodern systems that the individual cannot truly dispose of all external goods as his property since his transactions with externality are restricted by magical, religious and other rules of social-symbolic significance. According to Claude Lévi-Strauss; 'For primitive thought...goods are not only economic commodities, but vehicles and instruments of an other order of reality: strength, power, sympathy, status and emotions.'[9] Taking place against a background of restricted status privileges and symbolically limited patterns of disposing of external goods, premodern exchange relations generate special bonds of obligation and reciprocity among individuals over and beyond the correct transfer of goods. By contrast the distinguishing feature of modern economic systems is that neither traditional relations of status and hierarchy among persons, nor the social and symbolic characteristics of externality can restrict the validity of exchange transactions. In his studies on ancient law and economy Sir Henry Maine characterized this difference by the pithy phrase 'from status to contract'.[10] Not only does Hegel anticipate Maine's conclusion, but in the *Philosophy of Right* he provides the most systematic analysis of the norms of personality, property and contract which are presupposed by modern exchange.

A contract results from the free initiative of two parties, each of whom is recognized as a legal person, to transfer rights of ownership in accordance with a formally correct procedure. The modern contractual relation is composed of three features: the free initiative (*Willkür*) of the contracting parties, their mutual consent and agreement, and the external (*äusserliche*) object over which the transfer of ownership rights is to be transacted (*PhR*, §75). The act of contract cannot generate the conditions of its own validity but presupposes background norms and rules the compliance with which confers validity on the contractual transaction. Hegel derives these background norms and rules from the rights of personality and property. First, valid contractual transactions presuppose the non-contracted and non-contractual capacity of individuals to be treated as beings entitled to rights. For only when individuals are recognized as persons can their free initiative and mutual consent result in a reciprocally binding transaction. The contractual relation generates obligation because, *qua* persons, individuals are entitled to be bound by such conditions as they would freely accept.[11]

Second, valid contractual transactions involve the transfer of rights over property. The proprietory rights of the individual are stipulated prior to the act of contract. The right of property entails the rights of possession (*Besitz*), use and alienability. Hegel rejects the possibility that the right of property (*Eigentum*) can be disassociated from that of possession and maintains that ownership is in essence 'free and complete' (*PhR*, §67). Without this latter stipulation alienability could not be a right, since the individual would not be entitled to transfer to another his full and complete rights of ownership. An object of property may be treated as such only when a person can enjoy full and unrestricted ownership rights with respect to it. Anything, capacity or activity 'external' to the person, can become an object of property. Externality does not mean simply that the thing is physically distinct from the person. Objects like books, works of art and mechanical inventions are external to the person, not in virtue of being physically distinct from him, but in virtue of being objectifications (*Entäusserungen*), i.e. concrete embodiments of human skills, talents and abilities. The use of such activities can be alienated (*entäussert*) to another for a restricted period of time. Since such activities are an intrinsic aspect of the individual, only the transfer of their use to another for a *limited* period of time is compatible with the non-alienability of personality itself (*PhR*, §67 and Addition). While ownership rights over what is physically distinct from the person can be alienated in full, ownership rights over activities that can be objectified are never relinquished completely; only their limited use and deployment for a period of time can be. The normative scope of modern contract is thus defined: contractual relations can generate duties of obligation among legal persons with respect to external or alienable goods and activities. That which is intrinsically non-alienable, first and foremost the public right of individuals to be recognized as persons, and all that personality entails, cannot be subject of contract.

It is usually assumed that Hegel rejects the use of the contract metaphor to define the authority of the modern state on conservative political grounds. Indeed, insofar as the 'contract' is construed as a historical or fictitious act through which the people come together to form a sovereign public body, Hegel denies the political thrust of contractarian arguments (*PhR*, §258).[12] The spontaneous consent of individuals can never constitute sufficient ground to challenge the legitimacy of an established political authority. But behind Hegel's rejection of contractarian arguments lies not only a conservative predilection. Having discovered the structure of modern exchange relations, and having specified the normative scope of modern contractual transactions, Hegel denies the *normative appropriateness* of this metaphor to define the grounds of specifically *modern* relations of obligation and authority. The contractarian tradition has confused a norm which has binding validity in the sphere of private transactions with norms governing the rights of political bodies like the state.

> Just as at one time political rights and duties were considered and maintained to be an unqualified private property of particular individuals, something contrasted with the right of the monarch and the state, so also in more recent times the rights of the monarch and the state have been regarded as subjects of a contract,...as something embodying merely a common will and resulting from the arbitrariness of the parties united into a state. However different these two points of view may be, they have this in common, that they have transferred the characteristics of private property into a sphere of a quite different and higher nature. (*PhR*, §75 and Addition)[13]

Behind the reference to that time 'when political rights and duties were considered and maintained to be an unqualified private property of individuals' lies the issue of German particularism. In his early essay on the *Constitution of Germany*, Hegel had written that the characteristic freedom of the German principalities was founded upon the confusion of their sovereign state power with their private civil rights: 'but the nature of this legal arrangement consists in this, that an estate's constitutional position and its obligations are not fixed by universal law proper; on the contrary, on the analogy of civil rights, the relation of each estate to the whole is something particular in the form of a property.'[14] Hegel's sensitivity towards the political fragmentation of Germany only partly explains his repugnance to contractarian arguments for it is a feature of all premodern systems of political obligation and authority and particularly of feudalism, that the obligation and duties owed to those in positions of power are regarded as the contractually guaranteed property of power-holders.[15] Prior to the formation of the modern state, the public rights and privileges of individuals are considered subjects of contract, transferable to others in accordance with certain regulations. The *tour de force* of Hegel's argument consists in pointing out that it is precisely because of the sense contract acquires in modern market societies that its use to define the grounds of modern obligation and authority relations becomes obsolete. If contract is understood in its specifically modern sense as 'the exchange of equivalents' in the market place, then it cannot be used as a norm to define the grounds of political authority in the modern state. These relations of obligation and authority derive their legitimacy from the fact that the public rights of individuals are *not* private property, and cannot be alienated to others at will, but are secured by the impersonal and general norms of the rule of law. Ironically, the paradigm of the rule of law in Hegel's political philosophy is the culmination of that specifically modern concept of legitimacy initiated by the contractarian tradition.

In order to substantiate this claim, I would like to begin with an analysis of the normative logic of contract methodologies.[16] The clearest case of the counterfactual of the social contract serving as an ideal paradigm is found in Kant's *Metaphysical Elements of Justice*. Kant calls the contract a 'juridicial fiction' of conditional validity.[17] The legitimacy of civil government can only be established if the principles on which it rests are such that free and rational agents in a hypothetical state of choice would accept them. Since all contract methodology begins by abstracting individuals from traditional relations of authority, hierarchy and inequality, it is thereby stipulated that the *equal* entitlement of such autonomous individuals to natural rights will be a pre-condition of the new civil government.[18] In the state of nature or in the hypothetical choice situation all individuals are equal: their reconstituted relations under civil government must uphold this equality. Upholding such equality means that all individuals have a claim to be treated alike in certain respects. Arbitrary and differential treatment of individuals, incompatible with their rights, would dissolve legitimacy. From moral equality there follows the stipulation of *generality* of treatment. Relations under civil government must be instituted to respect such generality. But the norm of generality can be respected only if obligations placed upon individuals and the rules regulating their social relations are issued in a *uniform* manner from a known public source.[19] The public character of these rules and regulations signifies that all stand under the strictures of a *common* political authority. The material content of these strictures is limited by the simple condition that they do not violate the original rights of individuals. Since all natural-right theorists proceed from certain prepolitical rights, these define a domain of privacy the boundaries of which public authority cannot transgress. Privacy means both privacy of conscience and intentions, and privacy with respect to certain relations to others. Public authority cannot bind the individual's conscience, but only his actions; neither can this authority encroach upon relations between father and child, husband and wife, master and servant.[20] Furthermore, as long as transactions among individuals do not violate the norms of equality, generality and publicity individuals are entitled to carry them out freely.

All contract theories, then, contain two elements: first, they prescribe a system of rights, conceptualized under the metaphor of the 'state of nature', and second, they specify a public institutional procedure – conceptualized as the 'social contract' – through which individuals can enjoy these rights as publicly guaranteed liberties. From Hobbes to Fichte natural or basic rights are defined as those inalienable claims of human nature or rationality the respect of which is a necessary condition of political obligation. Since, however, the unlimited exercise of such rights is incompatible with the peaceful and prosperous coexistence of all, the contract of civil government stipulates in *procedural* terms the necessary limitations to be placed upon these original rights and upon their exercise. This public institutional procedure should satisfy the norms of equality, generality, and uniformity, and should not violate the content of the original rights.

Though no comparable methodological fiction of a state of nature or of social contract is to be found in the *Philosophy of Right*, Hegel also begins his discussion of persons, property and contract with a conceptual abstraction. Proceeding from the single basic norm that each natural individual is a person, that is to say, a being entitled to rights, he seeks to define the content and relations among individuals consistent with this single norm. Unlike the contract theorists, Hegel does not pose the problematic of political obligation and authority: under what conditions would individuals endowed with certain basic rights consent to a system of public institutions as binding and legitimate? But the validity of the contractarian paradigm of legitimacy is not thereby rejected. Rather, Hegel claims that the right of individuals to a free and consensual acceptance of political obligation is satisfied by the institutionalization in the modern state of the rule of law. By the 'rule of law' is to be understood the regulation of social life through general norms issued publicly in a formally correct legal procedure, which also have the character of calculability and predictability.[21] The *Philosophy of Right* begins with the norm of personality precisely because the universal and alienable claim of every individual to be recognized as a person is the foundational norm of the modern legal system. 'Personality essentially involves the capacity for rights and constitutes the concept and the basis (itself abstract) of the system of abstract, therefore formal right' (*PhR*, §36).

Hegel thus initiates a shift from a contractarian theory of natural rights to a philosophical jurisprudence. With this shift the *Philosophy of Right* complements the early analysis of modern exchange relations with a systematic discussion of modern, positive law. In §211 of the *Philosophy of Right* we read '...in becoming law, what is right acquires not only the form proper to its universality, but also its true determinacy'. It should first be noted that Hegel understands 'right' (*Recht*) in its more general sociological sense as all normatively binding rules of conduct. Such binding rules of conduct can also exist in the form of religious precepts, prophetic utterances, customary rules and traditional sanctions. Individual needs, desires and inclinations can also be made the ground of public norms. By juxtaposing modern positive law to the first set of practices Hegel, like the contract theorists repudiates the normative power of traditional forms of authority and obligation. By arguing against the latter, he distinguishes the impersonal authority of the modern legal system from the authority of a charismatic or tyrannical leader.[22] With the formation of a positive legal system normatively binding rules of conduct assume their most adequate form and specification. What is right, argues Hegel, must have objective existence. It must be publicly known, and it must be valid and universally binding (*PhR*, §§ 212, 213, 215, 216). When norms of action are made obligatory through a legal system, they fulfill these characteristics. Laws have objective existence since they are publicly promulgated and posited. They are binding because they can be consciously adopted as a rule of their actions by all rational agents who stand equally under the jurisdiction of the same legal system. The public character and positedness of law upholds the *formal right* of persons as rational agents to be obliged only by those rules whose *cognitive* significance they grasp. On the other hand, the fact that laws are general principles of conduct binding all on the same grounds and in the same manner, upholds the *sub-stantive* right of the person to be obliged only by rules which are compatible with the *universal extension* of this obligation to all alike. Hegel concludes that it is only because of this identity between 'its implicit and its posited character that modern positive law has obligatory form in virtue of its rightness' (*PhR*, § 212). The modern system of posited statutory law satisfies the norms of generality, uniformity and publicity which are enjoined by the contract theorists as the necessary characteristics of the public procedure of legitimate authority. The right of privacy is interpreted by Hegel in a double sense as entailing the moral and the economic freedom of the person (*PhR*, § 114 and Addition to § 26).[23]

We can see now that in Hegel's political philosophy the norms of personality, property and contract fulfill a *double* function of legitimation: they serve as the philosophical foundations of modern positive law, and they justify modern relations of exchange in the market place. Hegel is aware of this double legitimation function of abstract right because he has grasped its 'rationalizing' force in modern society. Modern exchange relations and the institution of the rule of law initiate a break with the old order by introducing rationality into social life.[24] Both developments presuppose the establishment among individuals of the norm of formal equality. Both in law and in economy, hierarchical status and privileges sanctioned by tradition are rejected. The rejection of tradition implies the breakdown of the power of prepolitical communities and corporations, which had previously defined the public status of the person. These become private associations subjected to the centralized authority of the modern state. The rights and duties of individuals are now defined by the general norms stipulated by the state. The regulation of social life through general norms means that the content of exchange relations among formally equal individuals remains undefined. Furthermore, such general norms guarantee uniformity of treatment and render the behavior of the central authority predictable, from the standpoint of modern economic and legal actors. For the smooth functioning of modern exchange relations it is necessary not only that their content and substance remain undefined, but also that political authority does not arbitrarily interfere in the functioning of formal transactions among individuals. And I would add, it is precisely because he has rejected the atemporal methodological assumptions of the contract theories that Hegel can discover the rationalizing power of abstract right.

II

Hegel grasps the becoming of the modern state as a world historical process generated by the rationalization of tradition through reform or revolution and the spread of bourgeois market relations. He does not view the inalienable right of personality to be something either naturally given or dictated by the mere *a priori* of human rationality. Emerging in the course of a world-historical process the right of the individual to be recognized as a person defines neither the private property of autonomous individuals (as Locke and Hobbes would have it), nor the noumenal capacity of selves to act in accordance with the categorical imperative (as Kant would claim), but instead presupposes the resolution of the 'struggle for recognition'. In the *Phenomenology of Mind* the resolution of the struggle for recognition culminates in a community of universalistic morals.[25] This community develops out of the secularized Christian congregation who has come to see the divine not as natural creation or the Godhead but as the very spirit of those united by belief in the divinity of the community of worshippers itself. The secularization of the Christian congregation is preceded in the *Phenomenology* by the destruction of the ancien régime by the French Revolution and by the corrupting yet 'civilizing' norms of civil society. The *Philosophy of Right* does not trace the course of this education (*Bildung*) for the individual or for the collectivity, but begins from the standpoint of a social totality in which the right of individuals to be recognized as persons has become established as an intersubjective practice.[26]

The right of personality, which attains normative validation with the emergence of a community of reciprocal recognition, presupposes intersubjectivity in two respects. First, Hegel means more than simply that the norm becomes a practice in such a community. The claim is that the justification of this norm cannot derive from transcendental values of human nature or rationality but is grounded in the logic of relations of reciprocal recognition. Second, recognition (*Anerkennung*) defines both the Hegelian conception of self-identity and the social practice of individuals that are consistent with such a conception. 'Reciprocal recognition' is at once a theoretical term defining the constitution of self-identity in the human person and a normative practice among individuals who have reached self-knowledge.[27]* The claim that human identity is constituted through the theoretical and practical relation between self and other distinguishes Hegel's conception of subjectivity from Hobbes' and from Kant's.

Hobbes defines the condition of the modern self to be a basic drive for self-preservation. Self-preservation is a process of activity and assertion, as such it is not a final goal but the condition for a goal.[28] The power of the self to be what it is is revealed in the continual movement of human desire from one object to another. Infinite striving affirms a heightened sense of self-existence. The priority of self-assertion over otherness expresses in existential terms the precedence of freedom over nature. This unites Hegel and Hobbes. For Hegel too the basic drive of the modern self is towards the reaffirmation of self-certitude in desire. But infinite desire only serves to frustrate the self by generating dependence upon the object desired. Because desire has a telos, it can find genuine fulfillment. 'Self-consciousness attains satisfaction in another self-consciousness.'[29] Human desire is not infinite, since the self can attain satiation through the recognition of another. By claiming that self-expression can be achieved in the context of the human community, Hegel, unlike Hobbes, vindicates the beginning of classical political philosophy. The paradigm of subjectivity in Hegel is not self-preservation but spirit. When a self-consciousness has before it another self-consciousness, 'with this we already have before us the concept of Mind or Spirit'.[30] The structure of human self-consciousness is defined by the internalization of the original relation between self and other. This relation entails both theoretical cognition and a life-practice.

On the same grounds Hegel rejects the Kantian understanding of the person, which reduces intersubjectivity to the abstract and formal identity of all rational agents. Every agent capable of rational agency, according to Kant, is also capable of acting in accordance with the concept of such agency.[31] Action proceeding out of one's self-understanding as such an agent is sufficient to entitle those exercising it to a moral claim to be recognized as persons. Since only the moral law can formulate the correct condition of such rational self-understanding, by acting in accordance with the moral law one necessarily accepts the standpoint of all other agents as one's own as well. The moral law is guaranteed intersubjective recognition simply because formal identity among selves is assumed. Kant describes a condition of mutuality with no communication and of plurality with no interaction. The Kantian 'I' is tautologically equivalent to a 'we'.[32] For Hegel, the concept of the 'I' is not a universal simply because it is an abstraction formed in an

---

* The development of community through intersubjective relations, which Hegel portrays in the master–slave section of the *Phenomenology of Spirit*, is the subject of J. N. Bernstein's essay.

act of solitary self-reflection. Kant describes such universality in terms of the possibility that at any point the self can turn inwards and say 'I think that I think X.'[33] For Hegel, this return of the self inwards in reflection is not a movement away from object (*Gegenstand*) alone, but from an other who is likewise a self, and therefore, a partner (*Gegenspieler*). The abstract identity of persons is replaced by the concrete identity of mutually recognizing selves:

The concrete return of me into me in the externality is that I, the infinite self-relation, am as a person the repulsion of me from myself and have the existence of my personality in the being of other persons, in my relation to them and my recognition of them which is thus mutual.[34]

The completed structure of reciprocal recognition describes mutual acknowledgement among individuals that the others are not objects but selves in whose independence and autonomy my freedom lives as well.

Hegel did not develop this analysis of human intersubjectivity until his writings of the Jena period. Yet his earliest criticism of contractarian methodologies was that they ignored the condition of men in the human community, and began with an arbitrary abstraction called the 'state of nature'. The modern tradition falsely considers human nature or rationality to be a given, argued Hegel. As long as individuals are seen as complete and mature outside the bounds of ethical life, as long as their fundamental nature is juxtaposed to their life in civil society, the relation of the individual to the ethical community is perceived as accidental. Ethical life is viewed as if it were an external bond arisen to satisfy the basic needs of the individual. All features that belong to particular customs, history, cultural formation (*Bildung*) and the state are thereby regarded as accidental, inessential to human nature.[35] The individual and the community thus stand opposed, whereas it is only through the community that the individual attains spiritual significance. Hegel quotes Aristotle on this point: 'The positive is according to nature prior to the negative, or as Aristotle said, the people [*das Volk*] is according to nature prior to the individual.'[36]

In his early writings Hegel criticizes the arbitrariness of contractarian methodology on the basis of Aristotelian and Platonic presuppositions. After his discovery of the structure of human intersubjectivity in the Jena period, he will reject any methodology that posits human nature or rationality as a presocial given, ignoring the constitution and formation of human identity through interaction with other selves in the community. Whether it is on account of his Platonic and Aristotelian premises or because he accepts intersubjectivity as a basic human condition, Hegel in his political philosophy proceeds from the concrete historical and social conditions of the human community, and not from thought experiments.

The systematic oversight of the fundamental standpoint of the *Philosophy of Right*, which presupposes a community of individuals who have reached reciprocal recognition, has led to much confusion concerning Hegel's discussion of property and has obscured his divergence from the tradition of 'possessive individualism'. Hobbes and Locke share the fundamental assumption that the 'individual is essentially proprietor of his own person and capacities for which he owes nothing to society'.[37] But for Hegel the right of property, far from being a paradigm of the autonomy of the individual, is deduced from the right of personality. A brief comparison with Locke will clarify Hegel's position. Locke infers that appropriation through labor creates a title to private property from the following assumptions. Man appropriates the world by the 'labor of his body, and the work of his hands'. The activity is 'his' because every man 'has property in his own person',[38] that is to say in his body. And these means of appropriation are private – body, hand, and mouth – because they are given to man individually. It is important to note that Locke's inference is from the privacy of the means of appropriation to the privacy of the object appropriated. As is well known, Locke's criterion of appropriation shifts radically in the course of the *Second Treatise* from what each man needs to preserve himself, to what he can appropriate for his use and enjoyment, and finally to what becomes 'benefit and the greatest conveniences of life'. The invention of money, Locke admits, creates a source of value beyond use by making it possible for men to accumulate as much as they please.[39] Since gold and silver do not perish, but can always be exchanged for other more useful and enjoyable objects, there are no natural limits on how much men can appropriate and make their own. With the introduction of money, labor ceases to be the title of property. Locke's vacillation in the discussion of the *Second Treatise* between naturalistic and social constraints on the origin and extent of property indicates his commitment to the viewpoint that the isolated appropriator can be taken as a logical beginning of human history. In order to conclude that the privacy of the means of appropriation entails the privacy of the object appropriated, Locke has to assume (a) that every man has 'property' in his own body and labor, (b) that the instruments of labor are privately owned, and (c) that land and other previous objects of labor are also private property.

Already in the *Jenaer Realphilosophie* Hegel distinguished between 'possession' (*Besitz*) and 'property' (*Eigentum*).[40] Possession is man's physical and anthropological capacity to appropriate externality for human purposes. Property is *socially* recognized and *sanctioned* appropriation. Man as a species has a universal right to put his will 'into any and everything that cannot resist it by a will of his own' (*PhR*, §44). Individuals, however, are always situated in a context of social relations with others, and it is the reciprocally binding normative relations among them that legitimize the rights of persons to preempt externality for their own ends and purposes (*PhR*, §45). Laboring, forming, grasping or marking are patterns of appropriation or, in more abstract terms, various modes in which a subject can relate to objectivity. In the *Philosophy of Right* such human modes of appropriation are discussed under the heading of 'taking possession' (*Besitznehmung*) (*PhR*, §54). But taking possession confers the title of property only if the individual is situated in a context of social relations that legitimize this act.

Though Hegel's position may seem surprising at first, the issue becomes clearer once it is taken into account that his starting point is not an isolated individual, appropriating an equally isolated nature or external world. For individuals situated in an intersubjective and social context, nature or externality is already socially significant. If property relations are to be viewed as the behavior of individuals in a social context, the myth of the primordial relation between self and object must be replaced by a conception of individuals interacting through modes of appropriating an externality that is laden with social significance. For individuals who constitute a community of reciprocal recognition, the object of property serves as a medium in and through which such recognition is manifested and given presence as a public sign. The object of property is not a physical thing but a socialized or spiritualized object (*Sache*), for only another person, only another social being, can take cognizance of the thing as 'embodying' another's will. Thus Hegel writes: 'The thing (*Sache*) is the *means* by which the extremes meet in one. These extremes are the persons.'[41]

Nowhere is the social dimension of property more evident than in Hegel's discussion of the legacy of reformed Christianity. In modern property relations, nature is reduced to an external other that can be freely appropriated by the person.

It is about a millenium and a half since the freedom of personality began through the spread of Christianity to blossom and gain recognition as a universal principle from a part, though still a small part, of the human race. But it was only yesterday, we might say, that the freedom of property became recognized in some places (*PhR*, §62).

By shifting the locus of the sacred from the exterior to the interior, from object to subject, and from nature to spirit, reformed Christianity speeds the dissolution of those religions, world-views and cosmologies for which nature is still imbued with sacred significance.[42] Reformed Christianity is a rationalizing force, for it destroys the 'enchanted garden' of those world-views and religions in which the confusion between nature and spirit often means the subordination of the individual to the will of another. The transformation of nature into an object of the will of free personality presupposes the categorical distinction between subject and object. Only that which has no will of its own can become the property of another. When spirit leaves nature and finds its realization in the human community, nature loses meaning and is reduced to the merely external. Since Hegel rejects the myth of the isolated appropriator, as well as the myth of noumenal, ahistorical rationality, he views free property relations as an indicator of the rationalization of tradition and of the desacralization of nature.

Earlier Hegel had compared modern economic life to the motions of a 'blind' and 'elemental' animal.[43] The spread of legally regulated exchange-transactions throughout the community was perceived by him as the subjection of ethical life to the forces of 'nature'. Economic relations replaced the telos of men, the praxis of political life and action, by another form of life, dedicated to the satisfaction of the needs of life itself. But for men the goal is the transcendence of mere life in the name of the good life. In the *Philosophy of Right* Hegel compares modern economic life again to an inanimate natural system (§189 Addition). Here it is not the animal-like motions of economics, but those motions of the market unintelligible to the naked eye of the observer, which are emphasized. Modern economic life retains its opacity for the observer, and is in this sense not thoroughly rationalized. However, the nonrationality of the invisibly functioning economic laws is ontologically of a different order than the naturally pre-scribed systems of traditional economies. The imperceptible motions of the market are viewed as nonrational only by comparison with the criteria of formal equality, generality and predictability initiated by modern exchange and the modern legal system.

To recapitulate: having grasped the becoming of the modern state as a world-historical process generated by the rationalization of tradition through reform or revolution, the spread of bourgeois market relations and the spirit of reformed Christianity, Hegel does not resort to methodological thought experiments, but proceeds from the standpoint of a community of individuals who have come to recognize one another as persons to specify the form of social interaction through which such recognition is concretized as a practice. Individuals do not *choose* these practices in virtue of their being consistent with their entitlement to be treated as persons. On the contrary, *situated* in a community whose members have historically attained the standpoint of reciprocal recognition, individuals engage in social practices upholding the validity of property rights and contractual transactions. Hegel's methodo-logical movement is from an abstract concept – personality – to the con-crete forms of actuality that instantiate this concept as a reality in the social world. The stage of abstract right in the *Philosophy of Right* corresponds to the 'immediacy of free will', and to its unrealized or negative actuality. Since the actualization of free will designates the transition from concept to Idea (*PhR*, §§1 and 2), and since the exposition of freedom as Idea is the task of the science of right, the logical development of this section offers a key to the logic of the whole. 'An existent of any sort embodying the free

will, this is what right is. Right is therefore by definition freedom as Idea'
(*PhR*, §29). The free will is first actualized as Idea when the person by
appropriating the external world as property gives the human activity of
transforming externality a concrete embodiment. Actuality (*Wirklichkeit*)
designates the humanization of the given and the external (*Dasein*). But
appropriation alone is not paradigmatic of free activity. The transformation
of the existent into the actual proceeds through human activity that not only
transforms the world in appropriating it, but which, in virtue of being
situated in contexts of social interaction, imports social significance to the
thing appropriated.

The *Philosophy of Right*, by a method of successive conceptual elaborations,
moves from the sphere of abstract right to the sphere of moral interaction
and to institutional ('ethical') life. The meaning of 'actuality' is transformed
through this methodological movement. Actuality becomes not only the
external thing that embodies the free will, but also the intention of the moral
subject realized in his deeds in the world, and finally the objectively given
world of institutions in which modes of appropriation and patterns of
interaction combine to yield the matrix of social life. It is only when actuality
assumes the form of a world organized in socio-historical institutions that
'the system of right as the realm of freedom make actual, the world of mind
brought forth out of itself like a second nature' (*PhR*, §4). The oneness of
the rational and the actual implies that Hegel's *Philosophy of Right* is neither
a recounting of the empirically given and historically contingent facts, nor a
dismissal of the empirical in the name of criteria that derive their validity
from the *a priori* structures of human rationality or human nature. The
transition from concept to actuality is made possible by the transformation
of the existent into the actual. This transformation is the legacy of modernity
and of world history: the rise of the legal-rational paradigm of authority,
the spread of homogenizing market relations, and the spirit of reformed
Christianity alter the socio-historical world in such a way as to make it an embodiment of human thought and intelligence. The *Philosophy of Right* claims
to grasp the socio-historical order of modernity at the point when the
determinations of this world correspond to the unfolding of a 'science of
free will'.

III

Hegel's political philosophy gains a new significance as the current dis-
enchantment with the theory and practice of liberalism on the one hand,
and that of orthodox marxism on the other, deepens. It is argued that, if
not Hegel's conclusions, then at least his process of reasoning remains vital
for today: in the face of the inability of liberal thought and action to develop
a coherent sense of community that would overcome apathy, anomie and

alienation, or put an end to the continuing domination of natural and social processes in the name of scientific objectivity. Charles Taylor has recently written the continuing relevance of Hegel's philosophy depends on a single issue: his radical critique of the modern tradition in the name of its most cherished principle of freedom.[44] While appropriating the modern conception of freedom as self-dependence or autonomy in a non-teleological universe, Hegel is able to situate freedom in a concrete human and spiritual context that gives it an objective expression. Hegel's political theory is seen as a brilliant attempt to accommodate the demands of modern freedom – autonomy, privacy, and self-expression – within the continuing integrity of a communal structure.

The opening arguments of the *Philosophy of Right* illustrate this aspect of Hegelian thought most visibly. Since Hegel does not begin with the condition of individuals who *choose* their conditions of existence but instead takes as his starting point, the *context* of interaction in which these individuals are placed, his political philosophy can *in principle* accommodate a wealth of historical and sociological insights that the liberal contractarian tradition cannot. By considering norms in the context of social interactions that instantiate them, Hegel suggests how the limits and hidden presuppositions of norms can be illuminated. The pitfalls of formalist moralizing, which juxtaposes *a priori* norms to social structures, and of descriptive positivism, which juxtaposes given social structures to norms, can be avoided by examining how norms become instantiated as individual and collective practices, and how social practices reinforce and contradict prevailing norms. Since for Hegel freedom is defined by the structure of a social practice, the evolution and transformation of social institutions create new conditions of freedom, while destroying older ones. The interdependence between social and historical possibility and normative validity is intrinsic to freedom as Hegel understands it. Freedom becomes a continuous dialogue between norm and structure, activity and process, identity and conduct in the life of the individual and of the collectivity.

Until recently twentieth-century marxism, while acknowledging its Hegelian heritage, had not revised its critical rejection of Hegel's political philosophy. Critical marxists from Horkheimer to Merleau-Ponty, from Korsch to Sartre, insisted that human freedom could find concrete fulfillment only in the social and historical world.[45] For this world, they agreed with Hegel, is not a dead and objective weight, but a living and subjective counterpart that remains impervious to human subjects only to the extent that they collectively fail to discover the doer behind the deed, the process of objectification behind the object, and human interaction behind the nature-like objectivity of social life.

It was accepted wisdom about Hegel's political philosophy that the critical edge of Hegel's early writings gave way to the stifling conformity of the mature thinker. Jürgen Habermas was the first to initiate a re-examination of Hegel's social and political thought from the standpoint of the dilemmas of twentieth-century marxism. In an essay entitled 'Labor and Interaction: Remarks on Hegel's *Jena Philosophy of Mind*' Habermas wrote that without any knowledge of the Jena manuscripts Marx had discovered the interconnections between labor and interaction within the dialetic of the forces of production and the relations of production. 'But to set free the technical forces of production is not identical with the development of norms which could fulfill the dialetic of moral relationships on the basis of a reciprocity allowed to have its full and non-coercive scope.'[46] By conflating the liberating potential of the development of the forces of production with the development of *social relations freed from domination.* Marx's work left room for fatal ambiguities. A technocratic and authoritarian socialism could thus appoint itself the true interpreter of the motor forces of history. The mute but ineluctable logic of forces of production would provide the norm by which a bureaucratic elite could legitimize its power. It would be foolhardy to suggest that reconsideration of Hegel's political philosophy alone would suffice to resolve problems posed by historical materialism or by the development of authoritarian socialism. But insofar as marxism can be seen as lacking a theory of norms on both the systematic and political levels, and more specifically, a theory of normative political and legal structures, the road back to Hegel seems inevitable. As we have seen Hegel provides us with the first typology of modernity where the spread of modern exchange relations, the legal-rational state organization, and the world-view of reformed Christianity combine to yield a unique normative and social structure. Having a clear insight into the complexity of this process Hegel, unlike Marx, does not reduce the legitimation function of norms of abstract right to a mere ideological justification of bourgeois property relations. The genetic and functional 'fit' between the norms of the rule of law, and the structure of modern exchange-relations, emphatically does not mean that the normative significance of the first can be reduced to a mere epiphenomenon of the second. And for a renewed marxist normative theory of legal and political structures the clarification of this confusion is an essential beginning-point.

One can be less sanguine about the political cogency of Hegel's political philosophy in the light of today's tasks posed by the crisis of liberalism and marxism. The *Philosophy of Right* is the most articulate expression of the unique predicament of liberalism in nineteenth-century Germany. As Marx in his *Critique* and Leonard Krieger in his brilliant discussion of *The German Idea of Freedom* have both argued,[47] the condition of Germany in the last century resulted in a unique, and at times not too felicitous, reconciliation of freedom and authority. This reconciliation is amply evidenced by Hegel's reception of contractarianism: in disclosing the relations between the emergent practices of exchange and the norms of the rule of law Hegel scored a Pyrrhic victory. He confined the validity of contractual transactions to the civil or private sphere alone, and robbed contract arguments of their political significance. What makes Hegel's political thought so cogent and attractive in view of the legitimation problems of late capitalism, and the socially and psychologically disintegrating effects of commodity relations on a mass scale is, I would argue, precisely this Pyrrhic victory: Hegel's paradoxical reconciliation of modern freedom and authority, of a liberal market society with an authoritarian political state. Today some find in Hegel's theory of the corporations a basis for reviving such 'intermediate associations' as would provide the social and psychological function of reintegrating a society of atomized individuals.[48] Others view the relations between state and society in Hegel's *Philosophy of Right* as offering a model for an ethically oriented welfare state.[49] But Hegel's solution for securing the legitimacy of norms of abstract right in light of the destructive and disintegrating effects of civil society was at the price of sacrificing the concepts of participatory democracy and citizenship. Hegel replaced political democracy in the modern world by participation in non-political organizations such as corporations or professional associations, and never accepted the radical implications of the rights of the citizen as distinct from the rights of men. An alternative to the social integrationist or ethical ameliorist approaches to today's tasks would be to revive norms and values peculiar to a culture of participatory democracy, and to 'repoliticize' the public sphere of late capitalism.[50] In view of this task Hegel is a formidable opponent, but no guide.*

* Z. A. Pelczynski and K.-H. Ilting both take a more sympathetic view of Hegel's attitude to political participation. K. Hartmann suggests a restatement of Hegel's theory of the state which would make it compatible with the modern democratic state.

Hegel on work, ownership and citizenship

ALAN RYAN

1. Hegel is so much a writer whom every commentator turns to his own purposes that some initial account of my purposes is, I fear, not to be avoided. What follows is in part a matter of *explication de texte*, though my aim is not primarily exegetical. What I hope to do is to show Hegel combatting both a utilitarian and a strictly Kantian account of the connections between work, ownership and citizenship, with the ultimate aim of showing how various tensions which commonly beset theories of property bedevil Hegel's account also. This is partly a contribution to understanding Hegel, but partly a contribution to arguments about property rights today. For example, there is a tendency for writers today to describe such things as job-security and the ability of trade unions to influence management decisions as 'new property' rights;[1] but, there is a strong case for saying that they are not property rights at all, but rights of a different kind, which demonstrate that non-property based substitutes for property rights can readily be created or can evolve. A man who has tenure in his post, say a university teacher of a certain rank, does not *own* his job; he cannot sell to anyone else his right to the job, he cannot bequeath his position to his son, he cannot stipulate, even, who should succeed him. In all these ways, his position is quite different from that of, say, Montesquieu, who did own his position of *Président à mortier* at Bordeaux, in the straightforward sense that the post had been sold by the Crown; he could sell it himself, or leave it by will, and the new owner would have the same property right in it.

Hegel certainly saw the importance of the distinction between owning one's job and having security of tenure during good behaviour; indeed, he argued that the transition from medieval to modern constitutional arrangements necessarily brought with it a transition from private ownership of public positions to crown appointment on the basis of qualifications and performance: '...it is only in an external and contingent way that these offices are linked to particular persons, and therefore the functions and powers of the state cannot be private property' (*PhR*, §277). As so often, the untidiness of the English came in for reprobation: 'In France seats in parliament were formerly saleable, and in the English army commissions up to a certain rank are saleable to this day. This saleability of office, however, was or is still connected with the medieval constitution of certain states, and such constitutions are nowadays gradually disappearing' (PhR, §277A). All the same, Hegel stretched the notion of property in other contexts in much the same way that theorists of the 'new property' do. Thus, the family exists in part to look after family possessions; the 'family, as persons, has its real external existence in property' (PhR, §169). This 'property' is then widened to include anything that amounts to 'means' – Hegel calls them Vermögen, which Knox translates as 'capital' to avoid the misleading connotations of 'estate'; I incline to think that 'resources' might be the better translation for reasons which will emerge almost at once. When Hegel is well into the discussion of what property a family possesses in civil society, he counts both skills and security of income as forms of Vermögen, as when he remarks; 'In the corporation, the family has its stable basis in the sense that its livelihood is secured there, conditionally upon capability, i.e. it has a stable capital' (PhR, §253). To which the reply might well be that while we might generally agree that a man's abilities were part of his 'resources', we would not describe a man who owned no property as 'a man of means', no matter how great his skill; nor would we want to say he was a man of property even though he could guarantee that those skills would find employment.

2. The point is not one of merely jurisprudential or antiquarian interest – arguments about the existence or non-existence of a 'new class' in socialist states have often hinged about the question of what to count as property. For we might find a class of functionaries who have the de jure right as well as the de facto power to control the use of state-owned property in the means of production, and at a certain point be puzzled whether to say that they did or did not own them.[2] To say that the property in question is 'state-owned' begs the question, of course, against saying that the 'new class' owns it, too; clarity seems to dictate that we should say that what we have is a class which has the powers over investment and employment that formerly depended on ownership, but that these powers now depend upon bureaucratic position, or party rank, or whatever. Since the 'new class' has not got the crucial legal capacity, that of alienating the state's property to new owners at will, it does not have property rights in the state's property. One might then conclude, as Trotsky did, that the so-called new class cannot be a class after all, since a class is only such in virtue of its ownership or non-ownership of the means of production.[3] Or one might conclude instead that whether a group of people constituted a class was a question which ought to be detached from the question of what they owned; it might plausibly be argued that what we had always been interested in was power, and that once power and property were divorced, as they had been in the Soviet state, nothing was to be gained by insisting on tying classes to ownership. What is new about the new class is just that its power depends on its access to the state and its apparatus of coercion and indoctrination, not on its ownership of anything.[4] Or one might suggest that the concept of property needed stretching to include the new case; sufficient control over the state's resources, in effect, amounts to ownership of them. So, if some official or other could secure that he both derived an enlarged income from, say, his management of a chemical plant, and that he could dictate the terms on which people worked in that plant, and could dictate both the terms on which he left his post as manager and the succession to his position, he would be to all intents the owner of the plant.[5] Of course, all such arguments are bedevilled by further problems about the extent to which what is being alleged is that individuals in the new class have taken the means of production back into *de facto* private ownership as opposed to the new class having collectively taken the state's property into joint – that is, exclusive of everyone else's – possession, without there being any question of individual members of the class having more than a share in the proceeds. Hegel would have sided with anyone who argued that the concept of property was open-textured; at any rate, he certainly held that there was no distinction between a right to ownership and a right to the whole and entire use of something (*PhR*, §61). So, no doubt, if the 'new class' either jointly or severally get the entire use of the Soviet Union's means of production, then the 'new class' owns them, whatever the law says; if the law says something else about the legal title, the law is a dead letter.

3. Still, this is to run ahead of a proper exposition of Hegel's case. To take this at a proper pace, something must be said about the intellectual context of Hegel's exposition. This amounts to a recapitulation of themes associated with four authors, Locke, Rousseau, Kant and Hume.* It goes without saying that although Hegel in effect stalks Kant throughout the *Philosophy of Right*, the other three writers appear by implication rather than in their own persons. The themes I have in mind are these: in the work of Locke we find an account of the right to property which rests that right on human labour, and which further depends on the claim that everyone has a right to his own person, a property in his person; this right is a natural right, depending on no convention for recognition, and it follows that there can be private ownership of particular things in a state of nature.[6] Hegel sets out to deny most of this account; to some extent he intertwines his objection to what we may call

* *Editor's note* – A detailed analysis of the intellectual context of Hegel's concepts of right and property is to be found in S. Benhabib's essay.

Lockean naturalism with objections to a very different sort of naturalism, namely that which treats the laws of an organised political society as if they are natural, organic products, but here it is only the distinctions which he makes in opposition to Locke that concern us.

Rousseau is important, not as a theorist of natural law, but because Rousseau's *Discourse on the Origins of Inequality* provided one of the most rhetorically compelling cases against private property that the eighteenth century possessed. The true founder of civil society and the great author of all our ills was the man who put a fence round a piece of land, declared 'this is mine' and found an audience credulous enough to believe him; had his hearers retorted 'the goods of the earth belong to all, and the earth itself to nobody', all the evils of civilised life would have been averted. Nor was Rousseau impressed by the argument that without property rights nobody would have had any inducement to work harder and live better; on Rousseau's account, the idle savage was a happier man than we, and the smiling fields of wheat to which the apologists for private ownership of the land were accustomed to point were fields which had been watered by our sweat.[7] Hegel's relationship to this dystopian tradition was interesting and awkward; he did not deny outright that there was a great deal of misery and injustice attributable to the existence of private property. He did not even try to argue that civilised man was happier, healthier and better fed than the idle noble savage; he claimed instead that reason required that things should have owners. To put it less strikingly, Hegel's conception of freedom as the goal of human history was a conception which required that men lived in a constitutional state, where they had a certain sort of equality of rights as citizens; to have rights hinged upon the existence of property, because men could not act in the world as free agents unless they had the right to possess and use mere things. 'A person has as his substantive end the right of putting his will into each and every thing and thereby making it his, because it has no such end in itself and derives its destiny and soul from his will. This is the absolute right of appropriation which man has over all "things"' (*PhR*, §44).

Kant had already taken a not dissimilar route in justifying private property.[8] He had taken Rousseau's anxieties to heart, and agreed that human history presented a grim spectacle if looked at in the terms Rousseau had set. Yet if it was viewed as a sort of education, a roundabout route to the development of human faculties and to the universal rule of reason and justice, history was a process with which rational men could identify after all. However, Kant's conception of what it was for individuals to have rights against each other was altogether too abstract and too individualistic for Hegel. Kant's emphasis on the coercive element in law, his stress on the independence of each individual, together with his willingness to include some rather odd relationships within the sphere of possessory rights antagonised Hegel. Kant's picture of individual independence, although not founded on traditional natural law, inevitably led to the doctrine of the social contract. The way in which a system of rights integrated men into society, the way in which recognised social roles gave men their moral ideals and ambitions – what Hegel called *Sittlichkeit* – was thereby misrepresented by Kant, although, of course, his central offence, that of reducing our relationship with the state to a contractual relationship, was one Kant committed with innumerable others.

Hume stands here for the entire utilitarian tradition. In that tradition, the role of property rights is simple, though the working out of that role is not. The starting point is the observation that human wants exceed what nature willingly supplies; this is partly a brute fact about the meanness of nature, but partly a result of the way in which human wants change and expand, so that what once satisfied them soon fails to do so. In consequence we have to work, and adapt nature, in order to satisfy our wants; but work is in itself unpleasant, and we only engage in it in order to reap the reward of more and pleasanter things to consume. As rational creatures, we shall not work if there is no prospect of enjoying the results of our efforts; so some way of ensuring that our efforts are rewarded is needed, if there is to be any incentive to effort. Property rights are, in essence, rights to dispose of things and efforts; they are not 'natural' in that they exist only insofar as they are recognised, though they are certainly natural in the sense that human and non-human nature together explain why all societies from the very simplest have rules about property. The fact that these are not *natural* rights distinguishes utilitarian theories from a theory like Locke's; individuals are the *source* of labour, but they are not naturally its proprietors. That the most effective way of exploiting human effort and natural resources is by giving everybody a right to his own efforts – i.e. a right to choose whom to work for and so on – and by enforcing property laws much like those of eighteenth-century England, is a claim of the utilitarian theory. There may well be times and places when utilitarian considerations would support slavery and/or some sort of common rather than private ownership.

The heart of the doctrine is that the justification of property rights is that they foster economic cooperation at the degree of efficiency possible at a given time and place. Government exists primarily in order to defend such rights. The existence of government sets problems, however, for governments acquire power which may tempt its possessors to act in ways which undermine the goals government is set up to defend. The utilitarian theory of government, especially as presented in James Mill's *Essay on Government*, is the theory of how to avert these unpleasant side-effects. Hume, on the whole, looked to the power of the landed gentry to restrain the crown, where

James Mill looked to universal suffrage to restrain both the landed gentry and the crown.[9] Of a concern with citizenship, there is something in Hume and almost nothing in James Mill; nonetheless the theory of political rights can be sketched swiftly enough. Persons whose interests are identical with the general interest should possess enough power to prevent persons whose interests are hostile to the general interest from acts hostile to it. A working class content to follow middle-class leaders might have the vote; middle-class property-owners should certainly have it. Workers who were likely to pursue their short-term gains by expropriating the possessing classes had better not have the vote.[10] There were, of course, no pure exponents of what I here offer as the utilitarian theory though James Mill comes close. Hume was more influenced by classical notions of the senatorial virtues than the ideal type utilitarian would have been.[11]

Hegel was emphatically anti-utilitarian; he did not remark as Nietzsche was later to do that man cares nothing for happiness, only the Englishman wishes to be happy, but he came close to it.* We have already seen that he would not tackle Rousseauist critics of civilisation on the ground of utility, and this was a general rule. He was unimpressed by utilitarian arguments in principle; happiness was too indefinite a goal to rationalise a legal system; the utilitarian conception of happiness as a surplus of pleasures over pains was in addition inadequate, since happiness, as opposed to a string of sensation, demanded some judgment about a whole life; finally, the ordinary man's pleasures were essentially heteronomous, a matter of trying to keep up with the Joneses. Over and over, Hegel insisted that the rationale of a system of rights is freedom, not happiness; it might be prompted into existence by the need to satisfy one or another impulse, but its goal was freedom. This, of course, meant also for Hegel that its basis was essentially rational, since it is only if the will is determined by reason that it can be determined at all, and yet be free. The difficulty here, as more generally, is to see in what sense a system of law in which there is a good deal that is accidental, local and matter of arbitrary choice can none the less be a dictate of reason.[12]

4. One further preliminary observation about the argumentative context of Hegel's account of property is needed. There is a sense in which the whole of Hegel's philosophy is a possessory philosophy, and a sense in which the whole of Hegel's philosophy is obsessed by a kind of work. In the *Economic-Philosophical Manuscripts* Marx offers a famous rewriting of Hegel's *Phenomenology of Spirit* in which he says that Hegel was right to see work as the essence of history, and to see the appropriation of the products of work

* *Editor's note* – Hegel's critique of utilitarianism, in the context of civil society, is discussed in A. S. Walton's essay.

as its central task, but that Hegel was an idealist who thought of work only in terms of the work of the mind, that is, thinking, and who thought of the products of work only in terms of the products of thinking, that is, ideas. That the central question of philosophy is that of how we may appropriate our own products Marx thought of as a position he shared with Hegel.[13] Now, there is an undeniable charm to this interpretation; there is certainly a sense in which the *Phenomenology* describes a process of creation, loss and retrieval; and it is certainly true of Hegel as a stylist that he plays on the imagery of the German language. Objects, or *Gegenstände*, are so to speak standing out against us, as if opposing and resisting us; concepts, or *Begriffe*, aid us to seize them and grasp them, to hold them and therefore subdue them. The question remains, however, of the extent to which this illuminates Hegel's own thinking — we can agree that he came to provide Marx with an apt starting point, and that he provides Professor Kojève with an exciting topic for his lectures,[14] but does this suggest that work and appropriation are the hidden key to Hegel's own philosophy? It is hard to believe that they are; there is certainly a sense in which the wider philosophical concerns *haunt* the *Philosophy of Right*, but that seems to be almost as far as it goes. That is, there is no suggestion that work plays a peculiarly important role in our philosophical mastery of the world; there are a couple of small jokes at Kant's expense about the way in which work and consumption both deny the reality of thing-in-itself (*PhR*, §44R and §44A), but this is intermingled with an attack on philosophical realism, too, and there is no suggestion that Hegel intended anything very substantial to follow from these observations.

5. The starting point of the derivation of property rights is the claim that the object of right is freedom; rights are derived from the free will, not from their serving needs. The first and fundamental rights are those of persons, and persons exist in the first place as property-owners. It may seem odd to start from this end of the doctrine of rights; most modern writers would begin with some sort of statement of basic human rights, which everyone was supposed to have and to recognise in others, and then derive property rights, if at all, after some process of deciding which basic rights were of primary importance. Thus Professor Dworkin lays down a right to equal concern and respect as *the* basic right, and from this deduces the political institutions of liberal democracy — the right to equality in voting, for instance — as a political corollary, and to a more limited extent the institutions of the market — as a device which treats all wants indifferently — as an economic corollary. The right to property has to come in, to the extent that it comes in at all, as a result of, or as a means to, securing equality of concern and respect.[15] Now, Hegel is evidently not engaged in a process of the same sort; property rights do not in any obvious sense provide the premises from which one can deduce political or other rights. It seems, rather, that Hegel's aim is to start from what we might call the minimum characterisation of a person; this minimum characterisation is as someone capable of distinguishing what is him from what is not or, in Hegel's terms, capable of externalising his will. This minimal, and thus abstract, personality allows two crucial distinctions to be made, between myself and other persons and between myself and what I can have an effect upon. Thus, the first rights are rights to control external things, they are assertions of the right of my will to determine the behaviour of things, and demands for the recognition of this right (*PhR*, §§ 39 and 40). So eager is Hegel to insist that this first right of the will over external things is the basis of rights that he repudiates the familiar Roman-law distinction between *jus ad rem* and *jus ad personam*: 'To be sure, it is only a person who is required to execute the covenants of a contract, just as it is also only a person who acquires the right to their execution. But a right of this sort cannot for this reason be called a "personal" right; rights of whatever sort belong to a person alone. Objectively considered, a right arising from a contract is never a right over a person, but only a right over something external to a person or something which he can alienate, always a right over a thing' (*PhR*, § 40R). My will cannot occupy another person; hence Hegel sees in a right a relationship of occupancy between a person and a thing which other persons are called on to acknowledge. This is contrary to the utilitarian tendency to say that all rights are *jus ad personam* on the ground that *jus ad rem* is simply a right good against an indefinite number of persons as opposed to a right good against some specific person or persons. And this is important because it makes the relationship of *possessing* important in a way it simply cannot be for any utilitarian writer.

The obvious question which this raises is why Hegel thinks that the relationship between the will and the thing is of such central interest; in a way, the simplest answer is that it is one instance of the relationship between mind and nature, and that Hegel's philosophy is predicted on the urge to eliminate the independence of seemingly brute and alien stuff by showing that everything is an aspect of mind. But this answer is too simple; the basic philosophical task is itself so difficult to render intelligible that assimilating Hegel's social philosophy to it is to explain the less obscure by the more obscure. The account which one might try to give is something like this. In the search for freedom we distinguish ourselves from objects in the outside world which merely interact with each other in a mechanical, causal fashion; we use, alter, make, consume and control things. In doing this, we also alter the status of those things; they cease to be objects with no point or purpose, and come to reflect and embody our purposes. The world literally takes on human purposes. The doing of this both presupposes and demonstrates that we have a right to do it; or, rather, it makes it clear that the suggestion that we do not have a right to do it is incoherent. Only if there were already a will like our own opposing our will would we have no right, which is why we cannot, in principle, make slaves out of other persons (*PhR*, §§ 57R, 57A). *Ex hypothesi*, what makes things merely things is that they are will-less and not self-owned (*PhR*, §§ 44, 52). Whether there is also some suggestion that the world of pointless things in some sense *needs* to be owned it is hard to say; in a philosophy so permeated with Christian reminiscences as Hegel's, it would not be surprising to find echoes of the view that the world itself shared in the Fall and that its better nature is to be elicited by our efforts. When Hegel says that a thing has no ends of its own and 'derives its destiny and soul from [its owner's] will' (*PhR*, § 44), the redemptive tone is marked.

6. Hegel does not, as Locke did, derive the right to property from the right to the use of our own bodies. Rather, he puts on a par our occupation of our own organism and our occupation of things outside it. To be more accurate, what he does is argue as follows: our own bodies are in one aspect things like other things, and although it is true enough that my existence as a moral agent hangs upon the continued operation of a particular body, none the less it is only really *my* body in so far as I put my will in it (*PhR*, § 47). My body only answers to my control so long as I choose to control it (*PhR*, § 48). Hegel has the good sense to see that this line of reasoning has to be treated with care; there is a difference between theft and assault, and the person who hacks off my hand and runs away with it has not stolen my property but has injured me. Because we feel in our bodies, says Hegel, there arises a distinction between personal injury and damage to property (*PhR*, § 48R). What this threatens, however, is to assimilate human beings and animals, since animals certainly possess their bodies to the extent of controlling them and feeling in them. Hegel avoids this assimilation by agreeing that animals possess themselves – that is, they have *de facto* control of themselves – but he claims that they are not objects to themselves. Paradoxically, he expresses this by claiming that animals are external to themselves, where one might suppose that the obvious point was that they do not see themselves as external objects in the way humans do. As worryingly, Hegel also seems to think that this leaves room for slavery; persons who do not have the appropriate sort of possession of themselves can be the property of other men. If they withdraw their wills from themselves, they are occupable by the wills of others. In fact Hegel is ambivalent on the subject. As one might expect in view of the role played in the *Phenomenology* by the 'dialectic of lordship and bondage', he thought that slavery was justified at a particular point in human history, but he was unwilling to go as far as to claim that slavery might be right. As did Rousseau, he held that the blame for a man's enslavement lay with him as well as with his master – 'the wrong of slavery lies at the door not simply of enslavers or conquerors but of the slaves and the conquered themselves. Slavery occurs in man's transition from the state of nature to genuinely ethical conditions; it occurs in a world where a wrong is still right. At that stage wrong has validity and so is necessarily in place' (*PhR*, §57A). This, however, goes beyond Rousseau in limiting the claim to a particular point in ethical evolution. Again, however, its interest lies less in that than in the way in which Hegel's case is fundamentally anti-utilitarian; once humanity has reached a certain point of culture then it is absolutely wrong to enslave anyone just because the institution of slavery is inconsistent with that developed moral consciousness. Taken in the abstract, slavery is not a matter for utilitarian calculation but for prohibition outright; even when it was in place, it was only 'right' in the thinned out sense in which a necessary evil may be said to be right.

Hegel's distance from a Lockean view of our property in our own persons extends further than this, however. Locke's account of property rights in oneself was essentially defensive; property was that of which we might not be deprived without our own consent. Our lives and liberties were our property only in this negative sense; there was certainly no suggestion that since our lives and liberties were our property we might alienate them at will. We could not sell or give ourselves into slavery, and suicide was an infringement of God's prerogative, for it lay in His hand not ours whether we should live or die. Hegel evidently wishes to tie property rights much more tightly to the right to alienate than did Locke, and he cannot safely count life and liberty as part of our property, since he, like Locke, wants to deny that we can alienate these at will. Yet, the first moves he makes include the claim that our bodies, on which our lives depend, become ours when we put our will into them. In essence, what Hegel does is to deny that personality itself, religious liberty and the like *are* really external in the requisite sense: 'I may abandon as a *res nullius* anything I have, or yield it to the will of another and so into his possession, provided always that the thing in question is a thing external by nature' (*PhR*, §66). From which it follows that 'those goods, or rather substantive characteristics, which constitute my own private personality and the universal essence of my self-consciousness are inalienable and my right to them is imprescriptable. Such characteristics are my personality as such, my universal freedom of will, my ethical life, my religion' (*PhR*, §67). The upshot of this might well be to conclude that lives and liberties simply are not property in any useful sense of the term, but if we draw this conclusion there is some difficulty in hanging on to Hegel's claim that it is as property-owners that persons first exist.

7. What is equally distinctive in Hegel's development of the right to property is the treatment of the relation between work and acquisition. Evidently, in any developed legal system there will be many ways of acquiring property-rights other than by working; gift, bequest, transfer by contract or by purchase are obviously all of them relevant. For simplicity's sake, we can distinguish between rights acquired by transfer of whatever sort and rights by original acquisition. The suggestion of a great many writers is that there is only one principle of original acquisition, and that is acquisition by labour; Locke's claim that mixing our labour with unowned things gives us ownership of them, subject to our not preventing others doing the same thing, and subject to our making proper use of them, is no doubt the best known.[16] But a version of the same doctrine is a feature of Professor Nozick's *Anarchy, State and Utopia*[17] and a commonplace of nineteenth-century radicalism. It is a doctrine which has many internal difficulties and obscurities, one class of which involves the grounds of the claim that labour gives a title and another related class of which involves the extent of the rights thus claimed. Sometimes Locke seems to suggest that it is a matter of justice to give him who takes pains to get something the thing he takes pains to get; sometimes he seems to suggest that because there is something new that was not there before, it self-evidently belongs to him who brought it into existence. Again it is not clear whether Locke thinks that a man who clears the waste should have a bequeathable freehold in the land he has cleared, or whether some more limited right say a longish lease with a right to compensation from his fellows when he vacates − is what is got.[18]

Hegel follows Kant in avoiding these anxieties by denying that the title springs from labour; rather it springs from the will to possess. This is not to deny the role of labour, for it is no good merely wishing that one were the owner of whatever it is. The object must be *occupied*: 'Since property is the embodiment of personality, my inward idea and will that something is to be mine is not enough to make it my property; to secure this end occupancy is required' (*PhR*, §5). Here we find a characteristic difficulty in Hegel. For there are two sorts of claim about occupancy which we need to balance. Hegel says that being able to mark something as ours is the way which most clearly demonstrates the mastery of things by mind; and this is evidently true in the sense that a conventional mark, simply because it is conventional and not natural, must preserve the difference between mind and matter particularly acutely − we alter the destiny of a thing without so to speak lowering ourselves to its physical level; it was mine, it is yours, its destiny has switched tracks without my or your embroiling ourselves with it. Yet Hegel also stresses the role of forming things. Now this, which is the Roman-Law doctrine of *specificatio*, sticks to the same line of argument.

Working on things changes their form, shows that the way in which they were initially and naturally presented is to be negated. 'To impose a form on a thing is the mode of taking possession most in accordance with the Idea to this extent, that it implies a union of subject and object, although it varies endlessly with the qualitative character of the objects and the variety of subjective aims' (*PhR*, §56R). To the question of the extent of the right that we get over things, Hegel insists that we do not own only the difference we make to things, what we own is the things themselves, and we own them outright. This seems to settle the matter decisively in favour of the view that for Hegel ownership is absolute not only in the sense that somebody or other is always to be identified as *the* owner – which is in essence the Roman Law as opposed to the common law view of ownership – but that the owner has full and complete rights of disposal over the object owned.[19] This seems to commit Hegel to holding that the very concept of property implies freedom of testamentary disposition, and that insofar as we stand our own selves as owners to owned, suicide and self-destruction are implicitly licensed by the very concept of property. Yet Hegel denies that we have the right to commit suicide; we may sacrifice our lives for something higher than mere existence, so that we may lose them in a war, say (*PhR*, §70A) if and when the state demands it, but he emphasises that even the Roman hero in committing suicide is acting against his personality, not in accordance with its rights. We ought not, therefore, be surprised that Hegel did not think that unlimited freedom of testamentary disposition was part and parcel of the right to property: 'the recognition of a man's competence to bequeath his property arbitrarily is likely to be an occasion for breach of obligations and for mean exertions and equally mean subservience; and it also provides opportunity and justification for the folly, caprice and malice of attaching to professed benefactions and gifts vain, tyrannical and vexatious conditions operative after the testator's death and so in any case after the property ceases to be his' (*PhR*, §179R). Whether Hegel intends to distinguish, as he might, between rights of alienation during one's lifetime and rights of testamentary disposition is not entirely clear, for the remark on bequests occurs during the discussion of the family, and by then there has already occurred one of the several baffling shifts which Hegel makes, from the claim that property is essentially private and individual property to the claim that what we 'own' as members of a family is in some sense family property (cf. *PhR*, §§46 and 170–1). The whole issue is further confused by the fact that Hegel's most famous remark about the way in which 'restrictions on ownership (feudal tenure, testamentary trusts) are mostly in the course of disappearing' as being 'not in accordance with the concept of property' (*PhR*, §63A) occurs in a context where it is the right of a family to sell or pawn its goods that is at issue. So, whereas one might assume that restrictions on testamentary freedom were a feudal relic, whether they affected families or individuals, and that outright ownership was the only true form of ownership, the subsequent discussion seems to imply that the preservation of the family justifies restrictions at least on the making of wills; and whereas one might have tried to argue that Hegel thought that an individual without family ties might leave his property to whom or to what he wished, while the family man must not consult only his own whim in these matters, the context in which the point is made suggests that Hegel's distinction is between feudal and modern property law,* not between bachelors and husbands and fathers.

8. Having begun to pursue Hegel on such points, we may broaden the scope of our anxieties a little. The case we have so far been making is that Hegel's account of property rights is one which seems to stress their 'expressive' dimension; we express our status as free subjects by occupying mere objects. Again, there is an expressive aspect in the picture of work; things we transform by our efforts come to express our purposes in the world. They form, as it were, a record of our intentions and actions, and this is why, although work is not a title to ownership of the unique kind Locke claimed, it is a very complete way of occupying things, closing the gap between us as subjects and things as objects. There are some corollaries of all this which are of considerable interest, although we cannot pause for them now: Hegel's account of the ownership of ideas, for instance, offers a way into discussions of copyright quite different from utilitarian considerations about offering incentives to writers and inventors who would be deterred by unchecked plagiarism. Again, he says little on the vexed topic of the difference between the work of the innovative artist and the everyday labour of the manual worker, but he offers hostages to more romantic theorists in the same tradition who would distinguish between *labour* and *work* along the same lines by claiming that work involves the transcendence of mere nature, as mere labour does not.[20]

What is more important is that Hegel's picture of the abstract individual making his mark on the world by owning it and working on it already contains the seeds of a slide towards something different. This different thing is the claim that as we fill out the conception of freedom which grounds the *Philosophy of Right*, so we come to a more and more complete freedom, because what it is that is free is less and less the abstract individual and more and more the citizen of the rational modern state. However, as we pursue this course, various troubles arise. A very familiar one is that there seems a near contradiction between Hegel's account of the way in which feudal restrictions on property are vanishing (*PhR*, §63A already cited) and his

---

* *Editor's note* – S. Benhabib's essay deals at length with this distinction.

defence of those restrictions as something which makes the landed aristocracy fit to occupy political office (*PhR*, §306).[21] Nor is it enough to cite his observation that if it were not for the political purpose served by such restrictions they should be abolished as mere restrictions (*PhR*, §306A); for that reduces Hegel's account to the perfectly decent but entirely common-sensical claim that restricted property rights may have useful indirect effects, e.g. if they mean that elder sons of landed families will be guaranteed an income which will allow them to take part in political life without anxiety about making a living. What Hegel seems to be committed to is the development of the concept of freedom in such a way that something implicit in our free use and transformation of the world in our barest guise as property owners is more adequately revealed and realised in our activities as members of families, participants in the economic life of civil society, and as citizens of a rational state. Much that Hegel says about life in a modern society makes entirely adequate sense; but it makes so to speak common sense. This is, I think, not true of the initial exposition of the right to property, much of which captures an important human aspiration, and much of which suggests ways of analysing everyday phenomena which are not themselves everday ways. The same thing seems to me to be true of Hegel's account of the alienation of property, which again hangs on the thought that if we could not dispose of what we had once acquired, and so to speak restore it to its unoccupied status, we should be trapped in and dominated by the natural world after all. Whether this image is persuasive to all Hegel's readers is dubious no doubt, but at any rate the stress on the individual's mastery of the world, and on his ability to read the success of his purposes in the world is a stress which many of his readers have responded to. The difficulty is to discover whether this stress remains once we move from abstract right to the realm of *Sittlichkeit*.

Some doubts have already been ventilated in the context of the family. Hegel argues as if once there is a family, property is the family's property, and the head of the family is its administrator and supervisor; but, since not all families do have property in the usual sense, Hegel also broadens out the notion of property to include anything that is a part of the family's means of survival. Now, one can agree that between mere arbitrary behaviour and genuine freedom some distinction needs to be drawn; one can also agree that the shaping of the will needs a moral context, that of the family *inter alia*, in order that we should acquire steady aims towards which to direct our actions and so on. But, this should not lead us to gloss over the extent to which someone who supervises the family's property really is supervising its property and not his own; conversely, if it is his by legal title, but he feels that the family's claims upon it limit his freedom to treat it as he wishes, this is hardly an extension of his freedom. A person may certainly find that the existence of family ties provides a framework without which his work and his stewardship of his own or its property would be aimless. But he may not, and there is nothing gained by burking the fact that the initial account of man's relationship to the unowned thing suggests an exuberance in the mastery of nature that is quite at odds with the patient labour of the salaried, commuting paterfamilias of contemporary folklore.

9. The problem evidently gets more acute once we contemplate civil society. In one sense we are back where we started, for civil society is the market place; it is where we turn up with what we have got and see what we can get with it and for it. We come onto the stage as owners of our skills, our labour and our property in the narrower sense, and we do our best to maximise our take (*PhR*, §§ 183, 187). Here we are certainly individuals and we relate to each other as property owners. However, we are by this stage of the argument concrete, particular persons, and to say that we are in civil society is to say that we are selfish persons not by choice, and not because this is the final account of what we are, but because in the modern world we have to get our living by coming to the market economy. Such an economy presupposes that people may buy and sell what they have got; it operates only because they can do so, and because they treat one another as means to their own ends. It is here that the problems of deriving Hegel's results by conceptual expansion really begin. We can tackle the problem from perhaps three angles. The first is the difficulty that arises when we see that Hegel begins to suggest that collective interdependence is a form of property; the second is the difficulty that arises when we press the claim that work is a way of occupying things with our will and confront the division of labour; the last is the familiar difficulty of squaring what Hegel says property is with what he says about the various social classes which arise in civil society.★

(i) The simple point that one needs to make is that although it is of course true that the person who has nothing but his labour to sell must indeed rely on the fact that there is an interdependence between each and all, it is stretching the notion of capital a good deal to refer to 'the complex interdependence of each on all' as 'the universal permanent capital which gives each the opportunity, by the exercise of his education and skill, to draw a share from it and so be assured of his livelihood' (*PhR*, § 199). It is not that Hegel is not making a number of perfectly plausible points here. He is, as the first part of § 199 shows, intrigued by the way in which each person's pursuit of his own wellbeing becomes a means to the wellbeing of others, and he is certainly right that their needs provide us with opportunities we should not otherwise have. It is not unduly fanciful to suggest that Hegel's

★ *Editor's note* – The difficulties are also discussed in R. Plant's essay.

readiness to follow the line of reasoning from individual ownership to market interdependence is to be explained by the extent to which mind subordinates mere things. If we take our eyes off the individual's success in permeating any particular thing with his purposes, and look instead at the extent to which a society's environment now reflects the impact on it of the interplay of everyone's purposes, the transition from one sense of property to the other is not hard to follow. Yet, it obviously raises the question of whether the total effect of social interaction *is* a result with which we can identify. The result of the 'invisible hand' may be in one way a result we approve, but if it is the doing of the invisible hand, it surely has lost some of the charms that the doings of more visible hands may be said to possess. Hegel's own position is, notoriously, one that many people have refused to accept; he seems to want to admire the doings of the invisible hand, while also insisting that only the visible hand of the state is ultimately satisfactory. But quite how the workings of the invisible hand are to be embedded in the self-conscious and rational control of society by the state is not clear.

(ii) The same problem arises with work and the division of labour. Treated as a claim about the need to acquire new skills as more and more elaborate wants emerge, Hegel's argument is unexceptionable. Again, treated as part of an argument against Rousseau's praise of the idle savage, Hegel's insistence on 'the element of liberation intrinsic to work' (*PhR*, § 194), his characterisation of work as 'practical education' (*PhR*, § 197) and his defence of the skilled man 'who produces the thing as it ought to be and who hits the nail on the head without shrinking' (*PhR*, § 197A) all make good sense. They also hide a problem. The problem is whether the self-expressive aspects of work really are consistent with the division of labour. One can see why Hegel's own account is not in serious trouble here; since his conception of the will is a rationalist one, he can so to speak move back and forth between a view of the will which suggests that individual mastery of a whole task is what is wanted and a view which suggests that an understanding of and an endorsement of the process to which one contributes a small part is even better. But does it make sense to say that the man who performs some small task in an elaborate process really come to *occupy* the thing which forms the end result of the process? Should not the metaphor of occupation be given up, and would we not be clearer if we admitted that some of the satisfactions available to, say, craftsmen in a pre-industrial setting simply cannot be had at a later stage of the division of labour – even if we then went on to explain how something like them might be found in other settings?

(iii) Lastly, then, one needs to show how the same problems spill into Hegel's account of the formation of social classes. It ought not to pass without mention that Hegel's account of the class system which founds the modern state is a very reputable piece of sociology. One may complain, as I am about to, that it is rather loosely derived from anything he has to say about property-rights and work, but it can hardly be denied that the divisions to which he called attention were more important until long after 1848 than the division between owners and workers which Marx insisted was the only one worth attending to. Hegel's division between classes is a cultural rather than an economic distinction; he writes as if it is based on property, but in reality the question on which the distinction turns is one about the way in which people relate to the sorts of resources which give them a living. Thus, the agricultural class is not divided into owners and farmworkers, or into large landowners and three classes of peasants; rather, the agricultural class is defined by its attitude to the land from which it gets its living, and the naturalness of its behaviour (*PhR*, §203). This provides Hegel with one of the rare occasions when he is forced to characterise some actual state of affairs as contrary to nature: 'In our day agriculture is conducted on methods derived by reflective thinking, i.e. like a factory. This has given it a character like that of industry and contrary to its natural one' (*PhR*, §203A). He appears to have thought that this was largely an English vice, and that the patriarchal, God-fearing and trusting character of agrarian life was not much disturbed in Prussia at any rate. Again, the business class, embracing the activities of craftsmen, industrialists and their workers, and merchants is defined by the way it treats what it creates. Members of the business class regard their property as *assets*; a man may be in cotton today and wheat tomorrow but always he is trying to make the most of his assets. It is not inappropriate to describe this as treating one's property reflectively or formally. For what matters is not what it is, but what it is worth; and equally the worker who treats his time and his abilities as interesting not in themselves but in terms of what they will fetch on the market may be said to display the same attitude. Once Hegel tackles the third of his classes all suggestion that its importance is how it relates to its property has gone; for the third class in Hegel's system is the class of civil servants. They are distinguished by the fact that their interest lies in the promotion of the general interest. So far from there being any suggestion that their resources are their property, Hegel insists, as we saw earlier, that they must be appointed by the crown and must make their way by promotion on merit.

We must avoid the temptation to go on at length about the class system, and about the curious stratum which is half in and half out of the classification, namely the *Pöbel*, what Knox translates as a 'rabble of paupers' (*PhR*, §244). The simple points which I wish to make here are only two. The first is that the very good sense of Hegel's account of what social divisions we need to understand undermines any suggestion that a division along lines of property alone makes much sense; but, the price of accepting common sense here is again that the claim that class divisions can be developed out of basic conceptions of rights over things is decreasingly persuasive. It may be said that the complaint is ill-founded, and that all we can do is follow Hegel in two enquiries, the first being into the preconditions of the state, the second being into the variety of ways in which the search for rational principles of self-direction yields its results. To fight off such a reply would be a lengthy task, and in any case unnecessary, since I do not wish to deny that Hegel is indeed doing this. But, what I do want to say is that we have had two shifts from the starting point of the argument about the will's expression in the outer world; we have shifted from the recognisable individual human subject to something that is either a collective subject such as society, or else is not so much a subject as a role – so that we might say that a doctor realised his will *qua* doctor by doing the duties of a doctor conscientiously, without this bearing on the question of what satisfaction Smith or Jones would get from doing the job of a doctor. The second simple point I want to make is that Hegel lays himself wide open to just such a critique as Marx later launches against him: he suggests that whatever it is that a class masters is its property, though he retreats because he evidently does not want to say that whatever keeps civil servants alive is their property. Marx is working in the same framework when he asserts that what Hegel reveals is that the bureaucracy has in some sense 'appropriated' the state; political life has become the property of the civil service and its masters. One may flinch at Marx's claim that political life can be property – though we would not usually flinch at saying that a group had 'monopolised' it – but one could hardy flinch at his seizing on Hegel's apparatus for his own purposes.

10. What, then, ought one to say by way of conclusion? Perhaps something like this. Hegel's account of property is engaging and persuasive in all sorts of ways; viewed sociologically, as on the whole it has not been viewed here, the theory picks up some of the social and psychological consequences of different sorts of property rights very acutely, and in ways which most instrumental and utilitarian accounts do not – the way in which people identify with what they own, for instance, or the likelihood that a mercantile and industrial bourgeoisie will regard the state in contractual terms only, unless various corporate institutions are created to breed patriotism and public spirit in them. It is persuasive in linking work to self-expression, catching the way in which people want something like a record of their effects on the world, not just an income. It requires us to pay attention to the way in which both working and consuming in any developed society are processes with a high symbolic content. We do not just eat food, we eat 'cheap cuts' or buy 'the cereal that caring mothers give their children' or whatever. The richness and the complexity of economic relations are well caught by the way Hegel tackles his subject. In distinction both to the classical economists

who could not see how governments might manage civil society without wrecking it and to the Marxists who shared their blindness; Hegel has at least a few suggestions about the extent to which a capitalist economy is manageable by an effective state with adequate authority. Viewed philosophically, the theory is part of two enterprises: one, an account of how we come to be rational and free agents by becoming citizens of the modern state, and the other an account of how the world itself comes to be rational by being drawn into civilised intercourse.

I have complained that the internal coherence of these projects is not all that it might be; sometimes forms of control which do not seem to have anything to do with property are talked of as if they are property and sometimes not; nor is there any adequate account of how individual control of the environment and social control of the environment tie into each other. Perhaps as alarmingly, there is a tension between reason and self-expression, such that it is never quite clear whether we are being asked to believe that the satisfaction yielded by the daily round is akin to that of the artist's unpredictable creative spurts or not. There is no attempt to demonstrate that *social* control of the world is as impressive as the artist's control of his materials; whether Hegel thought that Berlin was as impressive a testimony to Prussia as Moses or the *Pietà* were to Michelangelo is undecidable, but it is a question raised by the form of analysis. This sounds grudging, but it is not. In a thinker with lesser aspirations than Hegel's, we should gratefully accept most of what Hegel has to say about rights of ownership and their place in the world; we might think that modern sociologists had taken it all in, and that we had nothing much to learn from Hegel, but we should hardly complain of his account on those grounds. It is only because of Hegel's apparent determination to reveal a coherence quite other than the limited coherence accountable for at the sociological level that one complains. It is perhaps much the same experience as Marx had: Hegel offers to show us that the whole world is satisfyingly *ours*, but he can't. Unlike Marx, I do not claim to have any idea of what it would be like for the world to be like that; but, then, anyone who did have would owe it to us not to spend his time wrestling with Hegel, as I have just been doing.

Subjectivity and civil society

GARBIS KORTIAN

Since the immutable vantage-point fixed for philosophy by almighty time and its culture is reason subject to the senses, what philosophy must pursue is knowledge not of God, but of Man (Hegel, 'Glauben und Wissen', *Sämtliche Werke*, Stuttgart 1927–30, vol. 1, p. 291).

The present study is an attempt to examine in its contemporary form the relationship between subjectivity and civil society as it is set forth in Hegel's *Philosophy of Right*.[1] Insofar as experience of this relationship in the present time has become crucial to the normative self-understanding of Critical Theory, our discussion must at the same time be seen as contributing to a clarification of this self-understanding.

I

The tripartite division of this work into Abstract Right, Morality, and Ethical Life, derives from Hegel's philosophical method as expounded in the *Science of Logic*. Right (*Recht*) is given a metaphysical foundation by means of the dialectical self-development of the practical concept,[2] i.e. the Idea of freedom of the will. The inherently free will is first of all determined in the abstract moment of its attitude to external existence – its concept remains here abstract and its 'existence an immediate external thing'; secondly, it is determined in an abstract moment of its relation to inwardness 'as reflected into itself away from external existence' and as subjective particularity... over against the universal'. Finally, it is determined in the concrete mediation of the spheres represented by these two abstract moments, a form of mediation which yields the objectified form of the inherently free will (*PhR*, Intr. and § 33). Only because the latter, which constitutes, as it were, the ethical life organically conceived, is concrete and therefore prior, can abstract right and morality be regarded as abstract spheres of the determining moments of the free will. They are seen as dissolved and separated from the binding forces of the substantial ethical life, simply to be re-absorbed into the latter and therein resolved. For Hegel relations between ethical life and abstract right and morality are of fundamental importance from both the systematic philosophical and historical viewpoints.

In the *Philosophy of Right*, Hegel describes ethical life as the inherently existing will, the 'circle of necessity whose moments are the ethical powers which regulate the life of individuals' (*PhR*, § 145). It is that 'actual spirit' which encompasses the ethico-political condition of man and unites the individual with the 'ethical powers'. The right of individuals achieves its first fulfilment in this order, for it is here that individuals come into true possession of their 'own essence', their 'inner universality' (*PhR*, § 153). Since the right of free subjects is one aspect of the substantiality of the ethical order, so freedom and necessity as well as rights and duties coalesce in this 'identity of the universal and particular will': 'in the ethical order a man has rights insofar as he has duties, and duties insofar as he has rights (*PhR*, § 155).

It seems as if Hegel is harking back in this definition of 'ethical life' to the cluster of concepts which he propounded in 1802 under the heading of 'absolute ethical life' in his two works: *System der Sittlichkeit* and *Über die wissenschaftlichen Behandlungsarten des Naturrechts*. In the latter we find the following words: 'Since the true absolute ethical life contains united within itself infinity or the absolute concept and pure individuality in its highest abstraction, it is hence the ethical life of the individual; and, conversely, the essence of the ethical life of the individual is simply the true and therefore universal absolute ethical life'.[3] Hegel's equation of the subjective individual and the universal in the sphere of absolute ethical life, an equation which rests on the presuppositions of Schelling's philosophy of identity, bears a greater resemblance to an ancient polis than to the contemporary situation, and Hegel makes polemical use of it in combatting modern natural-law theory. This harmonious condition adheres closely to the Aristotelian conception of the people or the community to which, among other things, Hegel directly alludes. For if the individual, writes Aristotle in his *Politics* (1253a), 'is nothing in isolation, then, like all parts, he must stand in a relation of unity to the whole; but whoever is unable to live the communal life, or whoever, because of his independence, has need of nothing, is no part of the community, and hence either a beast or a god'.

Despite Hegel's reversion in the *Philosophy of Right* to the concept of the absolute ethical life of 1802, which I shall deal with later, it yet reveals a new difference of content. This may be seen in the fact that civil society is discussed for the first time under the heading of ethical life, whereas in the earlier essays words like 'people', 'government', 'state', 'estate', had been used. Civil society appears in the ethical life of the *Philosophy of Right* as a 'stage of difference' between family and state (*PhR*, § 181). It should be observed that these are the only two concepts drawn from traditional political philosophy, which originated in Aristotle and which equated civil society and the state: *civitas sive societas civilis sive res publica*. Hegel, on the other hand — and this is made quite clear in the *Philosophy of Right* — emphasizes the difference between civil society and the state, and ascribes the discovery of this difference to the modern age (*PhR*, § 182A).[4] So we must now ask ourselves: what significance does this 'stage of difference' have for the determining moments of the free will mentioned above, and especially for the idea of subjectivity? The latter, which is a characteristic notion of modern thought, runs like a *leitmotif* through German Idealist philosophy since the time of Kant. In the *Philosophy of Right*, by turning it into freedom of the will, Hegel made it the basis of his metaphysical system of right.

At the point of transition from 'morality' to 'ethical life' and from 'family' to 'civil society', Hegel offers an anticipatory definition of this 'stage of difference': 'an association of members as self-subsistent individuals in a universality which, because of their self-subsistence, is only abstract' (*PhR*, §157). This universality had the self-subsistence of individual particularity as its starting-point and hence the substantial nature of the ethical world incurs a loss of unity (*PhR*, §181A). The concrete person reduced to his natural will, which is expressed in 'a mixture of caprice and physical necessity', is one principle of this society; the particular person, related to all other particular individuals in universal reciprocal dependence, is the other principle (*PhR*, §182). The 'selfish purposes' of the individual and their satisfaction through communal effort determine the system of mutual interdependence in which the 'welfare and rights of all are bound up with one another' (*Philosophy of Right* §183). Hegel designates this system as 'the state based on need, the state as the Understanding conceives of it', in which individuals, as its citizens, enjoy the status of private persons in accordance with the condition of abstract right (ibid.). 'The interest of the Idea' is conceived in this system as emancipatory: it is that 'process', determined 'in a universal way', of 'knowing, willing and acting' by which individuals are raised to 'formal freedom' and their 'particularity is moulded into subjectivity' (*PhR*, §187). Work is held to be a means of liberation from natural necessity and therefore stands as a positive force against both the 'immediacy of desire' and the 'vain subjectivity of feeling'. Through work the subjective will acquires objectivity and is raised to universality, to 'true individuality' (*Fürsichsein*) and 'infinity'.[5] From an anthropological standpoint, this marks the birth of freedom from alienation.

But contradiction remains immanent in civil society. In the separation of subjective particularity and objective universality the Idea imparts to each of these moments a characteristic right: 'to particularity the right to develop and strike forth in all directions; and to universality the right to prove itself not only the ground and necessary form of particularity, but also the authority standing over it and its final end' (*PhR*, §184). This dialectic within civil society transforms its emancipatory freedom into a negative form. The liberated subject, guided exclusively by his 'natural will' and the satisfaction of his needs, extricates himself from all ethical bonds and descends to the level of arbitrariness and whim. Hence society offers the spectacle of 'extravagance', of 'misery', of 'physical and ethical degradation'; it is transformed into 'the system of the ethical order split into its extremes and lost' (*PhR*, §§ 184, 185).

In the Remark to § 185 Hegel points by way of explanation to the fact that the 'self-subsistent development of particularity' appears in the ancient states as the 'moment of ethical dissolution' and 'ultimate cause of their decline'. These states, founded on 'simple ethics' and 'primitive unsophisticated intuition', 'could not withstand the disruption of this state of mind when self-consciousness was infinitely reflected into itself; . . . they succumbed to it . . . because the simple principle underlying them lacked the truly infinite power to be found only in that unity which allows both sides of the antithesis of reason to develop themselves separately in all their strength and which has so overcome the antithesis that it maintains itself in it and integrates it in itself'. The basic principle of modern states, on the other hand, so Hegel seems to assume in the *Philosophy of Right*, does not lack the force necessary to achieve a positive resolution of the antithesis of reason, the disruption of the simple ethical life and the subjectivity liberated by the latter.*

II

With the express introduction of civil society, this subjectivity appears under the aspect of emancipation, through co-operative work, both from the primary nature and from the 'second nature' (for caprice, pleasure and ethical corruption may be thought of as negative aspects of emancipation from the 'second nature'). If we wish to appreciate the full significance of subjectivity in the thought of the young Hegel we must turn to a remark he made in the *Early Theological Writings*. Here Hegel conceives subjectivity as the moment of decline in the absolute ethical life of the Greek polis precipitated by the rise of the universal Roman Empire. Hegel finds its socio-political expression in the abstract and formal nature of Roman private law. The freedom of the private citizen codified in that law is equated with the loss of substantial universality and the binding ethical life of the Greek polis. The formal universality of the law leads individuals as private persons to withdraw from the ethical immediacy of the ethico-political structure of the state and to live an atomized existence as separate individuals.[6] However, the common source of subjectivity and abstract private law in no way leads Hegel to reject the former. On the contrary, the enlightening and emancipatory character of 'living subjectivity' is beyond dispute. He attempts to gain some idea of it in his critique of 'bad positive law', which occurs particularly in the institutionalized legal rigidity of Judaism.[7] Nevertheless, Hegel asserts that such subjectivity betokens 'a tragedy for the ethical life'.

---

* M. J. Inwood's essay discusses this idea more fully.

In Hegel's essays on natural law and on the system of ethical life the connection of these two ideas is once again predominant. Moreover, under the influence of Schelling's philosophy of identity, Spinoza's conception of nature and Aristotle's notion of 'ethical nature', Hegel ignores the positive value of his 'living subjectivity' and considers it to be of no significance. The principles of the abstract private law of the modern citizen, emancipated by his freedom of property and acquisition, are anchored in the natural-law doctrines of the modern age. This private law, according to Hegel, owes its historical birth to ethical corruption and 'universal degradation'. He reproaches both types of modern natural-law theory – the empirical of the seventeenth century and the formal of the eighteenth century – for their negation of 'ethical nature' in the traditional Aristotelian sense. The negation of the idea that man is a political animal by nature emancipates the self-interest and subjective particularity of the individual. Furthermore, it even goes so far as to make them the philosophical basis of society and the state, when expressed in formal legal relationships. The individual's 'separate existence' is thus posited as 'the very first and highest factor'. Yet 'the principal factor is not the separateness of the individual but rather the living ethical nature, which is divine'.[8] The subjective individual as an utterly negative force sets the stage for destruction in a literal sense. In the *System of Ethical Life*, therefore, Hegel treats devastation, robbery, oppression, revenge, war, etc., under the heading 'negativity or freedom or crime'.[9]

Not until the Jena lectures on the philosophy of spirit of 1803–4, and especially those of 1805–6, does subjectivity, and hence also private abstract law, cease for Hegel to be a product of the disrupted ethical life. These lectures reveal both Hegel's thorough study of classical political economy and his repeated attempts to come to terms with modern natural-law theory, above all with Hobbes, Rousseau, Kant and Fichte.[10] Admittedly, civil society is not explicitly mentioned as the proper sphere of subjectivity and abstract right; nevertheless their material foundation is supplied by the specifically modern aspects of civil society as it emerges in history. The work process, which goes hand in hand with the struggle for recognition, leads to the emancipation and education of the subject. 'Abstract work', produced by social division of labour for the satisfaction of the needs of all through exchange, leads to the emergence of contract as a mutually guaranteed principle of commerce between liberated subjects. Subjective individuals acquire objective recognition by means of these two factors (exchange and contract), and this recognition transforms their fortuitous possessions into property, and themselves into persons, i.e. legal subjects.[11] All the categories upon which abstract right is founded in the *Philosophy of Right* – recognition, person, property, contract – are in these lectures closely bound up with the material conditions of society. Abstract right acquires validity as the guarantor of the modern citizen's emancipation, which is won through co-operative work in society.

Moreover, it is no longer as in 1802 the 'ethical nature' of the Athenian polis which provides the foundation for a system of right. Right is rather the product of negativity, freedom, the Ego (*Ich*) of Fichte, which Hegel equates here with the concept, and it is the concept's development which expresses the multiplicity of self-conscious individuals, who are ranged against and yet recognize one another. 'Right is the relation of one person in his behaviour to another, the universal element of his free existence, or the determination, the curtailment, of his empty freedom. This relation and this curtailment are not something which I have to devise for myself; on the contrary, the object is the production of right itself, *i.e.*, of the relation of recognition. In the process of recognition the self ceases to be an isolated individual; it achieves legal status in the process of recognition, *i.e.*, is no longer in a state of mere immediate existence... What the self recognizes, it recognizes as *immediately* valid through *its existence*, but this very existence is produced out of the concept.'[12]

The inevitable consequence of Hegel's insight is the incorporation of the modern era and its principle of subjectivity – 'the infinite reflection of the self-consciousness' – into his political thought as a positive factor. This signifies a retreat from both the Aristotelian tradition and Schelling's philosophy of identity. In the Preface to the *Phenomenology of Spirit* of 1807, Hegel gives metaphysical expression to the transformation in the following words; 'the living substance is that being which is truly subject'.[13] That this transformation of the metaphysical substance into subject has historical and social implications beyond a merely theological and Christian interpretation cannot be denied. Substance is also the present age reduced to its philosophical concept, the present determined by the historical emergence of modern civil society, whose political expression is the French Revolution. The *Philosophy of Right* presupposes this philosophical transformation as well as the characteristic feature of the present age, which corresponds to it. Since his essay on the difference between Fichte's and Schelling's philosophical systems of 1801 Hegel has designated this feature as 'cleavage' (*Entzweiung*).[14] The *Philosophy of Right* seeks to overcome this 'cleavage' by conceiving itself as the philosophical theory of precisely this present era.

Hegel's insight into the dual aspect of subjectivity and abstract right as simultaneously forms of emancipation and moments of corruption is paralleled by his attitude to the forms of the material and intellectual world which determine the present age, *i.e.* the new-born epoch of bourgeois society, the closely related French Revolution, and the philosophy of the modern era, the Enlightenment. All share in common the gnostic-theological category of 'cleavage' and the dialectical nature of the concept. Bourgeois society is the objective ground of the modern citizen's emancipation and of modern subjectivity. Subjectivity, the abstract principle of civil society ('the state based on necessity and Understanding'), is the origin of the force which disrupts the concrete universal of the substantial ethical life as it is grounded in the web of inherited tradition, in the family and the state; and finally brings about the loss of ethical life. The political expression of this society, the French Revolution, is the historical event which moulded society according to rational principles and enforced modern abstract natural law (*code Napoléon*), thus laying the foundations of the modern state. It is also the manifestation of subjective terror, which the *Phenomenology* treats under the heading 'Absolute Freedom and Terror': 'The sole work and deed of this universal freedom is death, and moreover, a kind of death which possesses no inner scope and fulfilment, for what is negated is the unfulfilled punctual entity of the free self; and so it is the most chillingly banal kind of death with as much meaning as the cleavage of a cabbage-head or a gulp of water.'[15]

Modern philosophy is the expression of the metaphysical substance which conceives itself as subject. But as the abstract, analytic, atomizing and crystallizing thought of the Enlightenment, it is at the same time that formation of the spirit which called in question the living unity of the one and undivided reason of the Western tradition. Against the background of this cleavage the analytical philosophy of the Enlightenment set up subjectivity and objectivity as rigid opposites.[16] Thus, along with the gnostic-theological implications of the term, 'cleavage' takes on the meaning of a politically and culturally antagonistic condition. 'As the moulding influence of the epoch', it is 'the given, unfree aspect of the form', the universal crisis which is felt by the young Hegel to be 'the source of our pressing need for philosophy'. To resolve this crisis by overcoming philosophically the rigid opposites in the intellectual and material world is the avowed interest of reason, of philosophy itself.[17]

III

The young Hegel's early aspiration is finally fulfilled by his completed system of spirit. The *Philosophy of Right* must be understood as the specific and detailed execution of this task of overcoming the cleavage in the practical realm, *i.e.* in the socio-political sphere. It is achieved by way of the affirmative and conciliatory dialectical method dictated by the *Science of Logic*. The 'absolute ethical life' sketched in the essay on natural law and in the *System of Ethical Life* reappears as freedom of the will in the dialectical self-development of the practical concept. The way for reconciliation has been cleared once the modern subject had been raised to principle in the form of free will; and once the development of the 'absolute ethical life' and the reduction of time and history to a logical category (according to the dictates of the *Science of Logic*) have been accepted. But reconciliation – and this is the tenor of the criticism which takes its source in Left Hegelianism and is repeated by Critical Theory – does not occur of its own accord and without some degree of force. Hegel, Critical Theory objects, does conceive the two spheres of modern subjectivity – abstract right and morality – as historically independent forms of behaviour, which refer respectively to the external world and to the intimate interior world of the subject. Although both in their uniqueness owe their rise to the modern world, Hegel is able to soften the critical potential of the former *vis-à-vis* mere positive reflection.

In the *Philosophy of Right* the section on abstract right deals with the contents of the modern code of civil private law whose principles are rooted in the modern natural-law theories and become positive 'ethical life' through 'the administration of justice'. Another section deals with morality, both revolutionary morality and the morals of the modern subject which spring from the depth of his self. The overall conception of the *Philosophy of Right* offers scarcely any insight into the social and material context of its birth.[18] Instead abstract right and morality are reduced in it to the relatively inferior levels of the realization of right, and conceived as determining moments of the free will which are abstract in comparison with ethical life. We therefore cannot avoid the following conclusion: the first mode of overcoming and resolving the two abstract moments of the determination of the will consists in raising subjectivity, the 'infinite reflection of self-consciousness', to the status of theoretical subject of Hegel's philosophy.[19]

The sphere of objective spirit as actualized right, and hence of freedom, can be subsumed even less than abstract right and morality under the merely logical development of the absolute concept (the 'absolute ethical life'). And it is even more difficult to reduce history to a logical dimension. What least resists such reduction is that which seems devoid of history: civil society. Of course, looked at as an abstract, a-historical 'state based on need, ...as the Understanding conceives it', it did indeed occur in the framework of history. And under civil society Hegel deals thematically with all those phenomena which were produced by the modern industrial and political revolutions. With all its characteristic features like division of labour geared to production and consumption, civil society impinged on the ethical life as conceived on the pattern of the antique polis; and its self-contradiction, as well as its contradiction of the historical tradition and the web of institutions that determine history, became apparent. Civil society, on the logical level a 'stage of difference', produces historically contradictory conditions. The subjectivity that it liberates is opposed to the objectivity immanent in it as a remorseless fate; the dead socio-political structures of antiquity and the

Middle Ages are opposed to the society and state of the modern age. Hegel is thus able to reconcile the contradiction between the traditional past and the modern age through the idea of time, conceived as the culmination of the centuries long struggle of the concept to raise itself to the level of concept, and to overcome itself as such. So an eschatological construction of world history, whose teleology is derived from a theologizing logic, is used to resolve these acute problems of contemporary social and political life. Turning retrospectively towards the currents of world history, Hegel identifies his own gaze with that of the world spirit and sees the outcome of history as reason actualized in the modern state. With this idea of the state as the 'species and absolute might' Hegel is now satisfied (*PhR*, §258).

Nevertheless, the empirical facts of history belie the contemplative view which attempts to resolve contradictions and to work an unreal reconciliation. Thus, in the face of empirical reality, Hegel is compelled to think differently: considering the antagonism inherent in the structure of the rising bourgeois society, with its system of needs where private interests enjoy untrammelled expression, he is forced to evoke powers which are not ideal agents of reconciliation, but mere empirical forces. The public authority ('police') and corporations come on the scene as those powers which, on the one hand, support the state as the guardian of the traditional ethical life, and on the other, restrain the disruption of ethical life. The public authority becomes an administrative power and, as the force representing the universal and public interest, fights against arbitrariness, injustice, deception, and softens the collision arising from differences of interest between producers and consumers (*PhR*, §§230, 232, 233, 236). Moreover, it controls the boundless growth of society which, caught up as it is in a 'continual expansion of population and industry', leads both to 'amassing of wealth' and to the 'creation of a rabble'; in short, to poverty and misery. For 'it...becomes apparent that despite an excess of wealth civil society is not rich enough, *i.e.* its own resources are insufficient to check excessive poverty and the creation of a penurious rabble' (*PhR*, §§243–5). As for the corporation, it represents a substitute for the ancient family or *oikos*, which lost its traditional economic function with the rise of civil society. For the latter is that 'vast power which draws man to itself and demands of him that he should work for it, and be and act exclusively through its medium' (*PhR*, §238A). The common interest inherent in the corporation is capable of uniting the individuals whom their respective trades have isolated from one another, and of preserving the ethical element which has passed to it from the ancient *oikos*. In this way 'ethical life returns to civil society as something immanent in it' (*PhR*, §§249, 253). Hence both public authority and corporation pursue empirically the goal of restoring the ethical life which civil society lacks, and of transcending the 'stage of difference' by carrying it over into the state.

This state, which is the concrete form of the 'organic totality', the 'actuality of the ethical Idea', the 'final end' (PhR, §§256–7), is in Hegel's conception specifically modern. As such the state has the 'strength and depth to allow the principle of subjectivity to progress to its culmination in the extreme of self-subsistent personal particularity and yet at the same time to bring it back to the substantive unity and so to maintain this unity in the principle of subjectivity itself' (PhR, §260). It is clear, however, that in the empirical context this characterization is valid only of the monarch who represents the priority of the traditional ethical whole. The monarch apart, subjectivity goes no further than mere opinion. 'Subjectivity is manifested in its most external form as the undermining of the established life of the state by opinion and ratiocination when they endeavour to assert the authority of their own fortuitous character and so bring about their own destruction. But its true actuality is attained in the opposite of this, i.e., in the subjectivity identical with the substantial will of the state, the subjectivity which constitutes the concept of the power of the crown' (PhR, §320). Subjectivity, which in the Enlightenment was understood as an emancipatory and critical application of reason to public events, is now reduced to mere opinion.[20] What is positive about subjectivity is embodied in the figure of the monarch ruling over the traditional institutions which represent the substantial ethical life.

This is the empirical counterpart of the excessive claims of subjectivity, analogous to the trimmings of the absolute concept in philosophy in the sense of a 'repetition of conditions for securing an as yet unaccomplished goal [i.e. the concept of goodness] after the goal has actually been achieved'.[21] In the substantial ethical life of the Philosophy of Right, just as in the form of the 'absolute Idea' in the Science of Logic, 'the pre-existing actuality' must be recognized by the thinking and reasoning subject as the already 'accomplished goal', as that which is objectively good. This form of good has only the name in common with the true good and really represents nothing more than the bare authority of the state. And yet the good represented by this state and modelled on antiquity is nevertheless compelled to guarantee itself empirically through the organic division of political estates found in pre-civil society. The inner contradictions of civil society, however, reduce their function of mediation between society and state to a feeble attempt at political restoration. For these political states were – as the Left-Hegelian Marx was soon to observe – truly political only in the framework of medieval politics; the emergence of civil society had robbed them of their political function. They will therefore inevitably be revealed as social estates, i.e. must be resolved into social classes.[22]

The unrelenting self-development of bourgeois society into a universal industrial society after Hegel's death has shown his utter lack of success in using the substantial ethical life of the state to force a reconciliation between society and the subjectivity it necessarily liberated. The negativity and abstraction which are associated with a bourgeois industrial society based on the division of labour, and which arise from the peculiar nature of the 'system of needs', have on the one hand enlarged the gap between the traditional past and the present. On the other hand they have encouraged the destruction of the ethical life and the ensuing 'atheism of the ethical world'. At the same time they have sharpened the contradiction immanent in his society and then, in the late-capitalist phase of development, have attempted to absorb it. At the present time this development has once again apparently rendered relevant — and upon this the normative self-understanding of Critical Theory rests — a Marxian approach to society which goes back to Hegel: social reality in its totality is viewed as a contradiction, as Hegel was wont to put it, between 'determination of the concept and existence of the object'. Man is now seen as a creature whose task is to liberate himself as an autonomous subject, in order to find a historical alternative to self-destruction.[23]

IV

The peculiarity of the development of bourgeois society into an industrial-technological world-society is connected with that abstract rationality which is expressed in the interaction between experimental science, technology, capital investment, mass-production, trade, regimented bureaucratic administration, etc. Since the abstract rationality of the social system is geared exclusively to production and consumption, it reduces man to the naturally determined needs of his species in even greater measure than Hegel visualized. This reduction amounts to the abstraction of man from all the cultural and historical influences, all the normative bonds, which determined his historical evolution. Thus, technological and industrial society affirms itself as a kind of ultimate value to which everything is relative, and its negation of those objective binding forces — institutions, traditional organizations and orders — leads inevitably to their disintegration and dissolution. The negative results of this socio-historical process is, in the first place, the undermining of the practical conduct of men whose norms of action and world views have been derived from those stabilizing forms of objective customary morality. It is, secondly, the isolation, atomization and herding into masses of individuals who have been reduced to their brute naturalness. Man as producer, consumer and competitor is compelled to submit to the abstract social system whose claim to legitimation is all-embracing; to use the language of Freud, it declares itself to be the sole 'reality principle'.

But precisely this contemporary 'destruction of the ethical life', this 'atheism of the ethical world', has been, from the point of view of the

social criticism of Critical Theory, a position which engenders its dialectical opposite, namely the possibility of the liberation of man. From two
points of view technological industrial society offers all the conditions of
man's liberation as a subject. Firstly, it offers emancipation from external
nature in the sense of relieving men from nature's immediate hardship
through scientific and technological mastery over it. This entails an increase
in the degree of human productivity and an extension of the area of man's
endeavour. Secondly, it offers emancipation from the 'second nature', in
Hegel's sense, *i.e.* the haphazardly evolved irrational institutions, the self-
contained social structures, and stereotyped, dogmatically rigid forms of life
which are taken over from the traditional past and whose disintegration and
dissolution Hegel deplored as involving the loss of ethical life. Admittedly,
this second aspect of emancipation is purchased at the price of negative forces
which determine the life of modern man. Once removed from the normative
framework of stabilizing institutions and their influence on action and
orientation, the emancipated subject shows signs of insecurity, chronic
introspection and a consequent paralysis of the will. His uncertainty and
disorientation cause him to be thrown back entirely upon himself.

This new form of the 'unhappy consciousness' provides fertile soil for the
sublimated impotence of an existential attitude, and for a blind, subjective
and irrational cult of decisions for the sake of decisions, irrespective of
consequences. In the phenomenon of mass society the destruction of patterns
of behaviour and of the highly selective social moulds of traditional
institutions by the negative forces inherent in technological and industrial
society leads to a distortion, a de-stylization and de-sublimation of man's
biological urges. From this there arises a directionless, 'libidinous' life of the
instincts and a liberation of the 'fearful naturalness of man'. This means
that man, existing in a state of complete rootlessness (*Nichtfestgestelltsein*,
Nietzsche), of negative freedom, is once again made primitive and
elemental.[24]

This negative freedom nevertheless contains the seeds of a self-discovery
which on a higher plane of consciousness expresses itself as reflection, and
thus creates a hiatus between the subject and the cultural-historical context
which has moulded him. Because of its ability to distance itself from these
forms of the 'objective spirit', the reflective consciousness no longer takes
its relation to them for granted. Thus in the era of the modern consciousness
the vast analytical and abstract power of the negative understanding has
placed objectivity and subjectivity against one another, and has liberated the
latter as reflection.[25] Because of the distance won through reflection, the
liberated subject can now posit all objects, natural as well as historical and
social, as objective, as appropriate material for scientific study. He is also able
to regard those objects from a Kantian point of view as produced by himself,

for according to Kant reason perceives only what it has produced to its own design. Once these objects are conceived as produced by the subject, and an insight gained into their complex interaction, critical reflection is able to work towards a resolution of these forces for the purposes of human emancipation.[26]

In the contemporary world the activity of modern understanding has been still further intensified by the massive development of 'bourgeois society' into the technological and industrial universal society. Thus, according to Critical Theory, because of these new forms of objectification which arise from the activity of the understanding, there is an increased likelihood of release, freedom and emancipation from the institutionalized forms of domination. Hence, if the subjectivity so liberated by the dissolution of traditional institutions does not become exclusively submissive to the technological and instrumental understanding, and to the ensuing forms of objectification which verge on loss of human identity – a process which is actually already under way at the present time – then it may take stock through critical consciousness of its real historical and social possibilities, and sketch forth the theoretically explicit concept of man who is to realize himself autonomously.

On the level of self-reflection, subjectivity gains insight into the objective forms of social and political domination in the process of theoretical enquiry. In practice it acquires an interest in liberation and independence. Here knowledge and interest become identified with one another as an anticipated unity of theory and practice which is consciously accomplished through the mediating activity of the whole of society.[27] Self-reflection gives insight into the possibilities of man which the forms of social domination have suppressed, inhibited and buried. It also sees through the pseudo-objectivity of a positivistic scientific activity. In all its programmatically explicit neutrality and value-freeness, the latter fails to take systematic account of its own social consequences. And finally it questions the purity of the merely contemplative conception of philosophy which, raised above the common world of practicality, transfigures the antagonistic structures of society and the corrupt condition of man by the deceptive aura of absoluteness and pure being.*

Critical Theory avers that, seen from the level of the fully developed concepts of subjectivity and of reflection which is aware of its historical and social situation as a negatively dialectical one, the idea of the autonomous fully realized man is not merely a piece of utopian transcendence. It is the historical transcending of existing negativity and blind tradition in the light of the contradiction which has become apparent between concept and existence. In this manner, a standard is set up which, in accordance with Marx,

---

* The essays by K.-H. Ilting and A. S. Walton dispute this interpretation of Hegel.

reduces all previous history to the status of pre-history, for such history has not been consciously made. In Hegel the 'movement of self-realisation' (*Realisierungsbewegung*) of the Idea issues from an affirmative dialectic of reconciliation. In this dialectic universal history is thought of as possessing an inherent guarantee of fulfilment, and as coming to a final close in accordance with the dictates of teleology and logic. It is in short the hypostasized subjectivity which has not yet achieved its historical realization: man. Henceforth man's reason, affected by the senses, strives towards the realization of itself.

Here it is plain that Critical Theory, by its normative moral attitude, accepts uncritically the prejudice concerning the all-embracing power of a concept of consciousness; and this is a legacy of the ontology of subjectivity of the modern age. That the power of human reason is thus morally overestimated constitutes the Kantian element in the Critical Theory, despite its claim to rest on the work of Marx. Such overestimation of morality, as well as reaction against it, is strictly a *problem* for a philosophical theory of our time, which Critical Theory, following Hegel, also claims to be.*

* Translated from the German by Roger Hausheer.

The dialectic of civil society

K.-H. ILTING

In his *Critique of Hegel's Philosophy of Right* (1843) Karl Marx took the view that the so-called 'actual Idea' was presented in the *Elements of the Philosophy of Right* 'as though it acted according to a determined principle and towards a determined end'.[1] However, Marx himself is in no doubt that in reality it is only to human individuals that principles and ends can be attributed; Marx takes the 'Idea', of which Hegel speaks, to be a 'predicate' whose actual 'subject' is acting men. He finds himself obliged to attribute to Hegel a metaphysical re-interpretation of this relationship; and he terms it 'logical, pantheistic mysticism'.[2]

Nobody who has studied the text of the *Philosophy of Right* can deny that in countless passages Hegel seems to speak the language of such a 'logical mysticism'. He calls the family, civil society and the state moments of the 'Idea', which passes through the 'ethical substance' *en route* to its objectification (*PhR*, § 157). In his account of this process, he attributes to the 'Idea' an 'interest' 'of which the members of civil society are as such unconscious' (*PhR*, § 187). This 'development of the Idea' he expounds 'as proper activity of its rationality' which 'thinking, as something subjective', merely contemplates 'without for its part adding to it any ingredient of its own' (*PhR*, § 31R).

Equally, an intelligent reader will have no difficulty in detecting the conception of such a self-propelled motion of the Idea. And it will not help to point out to him that Hegel has systematically developed this language of a 'pantheistic mysticism' in his *Logic*. He will insist that Marx is right to reject this metaphysical way of talking as misleading. Consequently, it seems perfectly understandable that the vast majority of commentaries on Hegel's political philosophy should simply ignore what appears to be its fantastic wrappings.[3]

Against this we must, of course, set the fact that Hegel himself rejects any such separation of thought and presentation, of content and form; it is precisely 'unity of form and content' that he claims for his philosophy.[4] As

Hegel himself sees it, the truly philosophical element in his *Philosophy of Right* is just that dialectical form of presentation which is consistently ignored in most commentaries on his political philosophy.[5] If we are to understand Hegel's thought expressed in his metaphysical way, as Marx did and any contemporary intelligent reader at first understands it, then it is Hegel's political philosophy itself and not just its form of presentation that is seen as fantastic. Only an exposition of the dialectical structure of his *Philosophy of Right* will make clear whether or not this is the case.

This essay, then, is concerned with examining the dialectic within Hegel's account of civil society. However, we shall not be discussing the dialectic of class antitheses which Hegel discovered in the historical development of early capitalist society (*PhR*, §246); we shall discuss the dialectic which governs the structure and progress of his presentation of civil society in the *Philosophy of Right*.[6] We shall soon find, of course, that the 'unity of form and content' at which Hegel aimed is not immediately apparent in his account. Our question will therefore be: what is the most appropriate and comprehensive standpoint from which Hegel's dialectic of civil society can be understood? The standpoint proposed here is the interpretation of the *Philosophy of Right* as a phenomenology of the consciousness of freedom. Just as Hegel attempts in his *Phenomenology of Spirit* to depict the path by which human consciousness can attain to awareness of the conditions of its unreflected existence, so he also explains in his *Philosophy of Right* how the free self-consciousness of man may come to understand the institutions of law, morality, family, civil society and state as conditions of his freedom.

1. To begin with, it is not clear precisely wherein this 'unity of form and content' is meant to lie in the *Philosophy of Right*. Hegel emphasizes at several points that he is basing his account on the method developed in the *Science of Logic*:[7] viz. that in philosophy the concept develops itself out of itself so that the concept is 'a purely immanent progress, the engendering of its determinations' (*PhR*, §31). So the *Philosophy of Right* is, like the *Logic*, intended 'to develop the Idea – the Idea being the rational factor in any object of study – out of the concept' (*PhR*, §2). The content treated by the *Philosophy of Right* is, then, no longer to be 'extraneous material culled from elsewhere' (*PhR*, §31), but content produced from within the determinations of the concept (*PhR*, §31R; 176, 1f.). According to these comments of Hegel's 'unity of form and content' therefore means that the content of the *Philosophy of Right* is to be developed by the dialectical method of the *Logic* out of the concept of right.

Hegel expresses himself very much more cautiously in the Preface. Here he concedes that he has 'only added an explantory note here and there about procedure and method' (58, 27f.; Knox, p. 2) and has made no attempt 'to bring out and demonstrate the chain of logical argument in each and every detail' (59, 1f.; Knox, p. 2). This methodological incompleteness is apparently due to the 'concrete and intrinsically so varied character of the subject' of the *Philosophy of Right*, i.e. to its material (58, 30; Knox, p. 2). If this is what he means, then Hegel is implying that the content of his work has certainly not been developed from the concept of right but is encountered as something already given. And indeed he does confine himself in this context to the thesis that in speculative philosophy 'content is essentially bound up with form' (59, 9f; Knox, p. 2). He constantly asserts that 'the whole, like the formation of its parts', is based 'on the logical spirit' (59, 5f.; Knox, p. 2). It follows from these comments that the 'unity of form and content' (73, 4; Knox, p. 12) aimed at is realized in the *Philosophy of Right* only in this limited sense.

2. How well justified these reservations are, by comparison with the much more positive remarks in the Introduction, is apparent in the transition from the family to civil society (*PhR*, § 181). Here Hegel distinguishes between two modes of transition. 'In the natural way' the family makes the transition to civil society when it separates into a plurality of families; whereas in a speculative interpretation this transition is necessary, because 'the moments found together in the unity of the family...must be released from the concept to self-subsistent objective reality'.

We may take Hegel's all too sketchy remarks to mean that, in historical development, the enlarged family gives rise to kinship within which relations become increasingly external as time goes on. In this natural process of development,[8] the legal 'principle of personality' will bring about the transition to an essentially different formation of society where many blood relations are connected with one another 'as independent concrete persons'.[9]

The transition from family to civil society is entirely different when seen from the speculative viewpoint. Here the point is that in a family the 'moments' of the 'ethical Idea' are not yet released into independence; rights and duties are only indeterminate and vaguely delimited, and the members of a family still constitute a community in which individuals are not fully independent in their dealings with one another. If they do nevertheless become so, then the family has in fact already been dissolved (cf. *PhR*, § 159). By contrast, the dialectic of civil society begins at the point where many members of different families enter into relations with one another as independent persons and where these relations produce a 'system of complete interdependence' (*PhR*, § 183). The individuality which, in the family, is still tied to the community and to common interests and aims is thereby 'released into self-subsistent objective reality' (*PhR*, § 181). As independent persons the individuals are now 'particulars' who are related to a 'universal', i.e. the system of mutual dependence, in so far as they wish to realize their aims. It is this 'differentiation' between 'particularity' and 'universality' which, according to Hegel's speculative interpretation, determines the nature of civil society.

   This explanation of the transition from the family to civil society has, Hegel claims, the character of necessity; he understands the family as the ethical Idea 'which is still in its concept'; but the moments bound up within its unity 'must' be released from the concept into self-subsistent reality (628, 13). If we ask wherein this necessity lies, we immediately recall the criticisms Karl Marx levelled at Hegel's 'logical mysticism'. Hegel's account of the development of the 'ethical Idea' in the *Philosophy of Right* obviously corresponds to his account of the Idea as such in the *Logic*. Just as there the Idea at the stage of the concept is described as the Idea of life, so here it appears as the institution of the family.[10] There the Idea at the stage of differentiation appears as the process of cognition, and here as the process of the formation of civil society; and the fully developed Absolute Idea of the *Logic* appears in the *Philosophy of Right* in the shape of the state. Marx is, therefore, apparently proved right: Hegel has not developed the 'necessity' of the transition from family to civil society from the concept of the family; he has imported it from his speculative logic into the *Philosophy of Right*.[11]

   Faced with this admittedly obvious accusation, we should note that, according to Hegel's formulation, the individuals 'bound up' within the community of the family are 'released into self-subsistent objective reality' in civil society. Now the theme of the *Philosophy of Right* is the development of the Idea of freedom.[12] So we should not forget that it is precisely in connection with the development of this Idea that Hegel asserts the necessity of the transition from family to civil society. Whatever the ways in which early capitalist civil society may have developed historically from a patriarchal social constitution, and whatever the explanatory models which Hegel took over from the *Logic* to describe the family, civil society and the state, his decisive argument for the transition from family to civil society is that this transition is to be explained as a liberation of the individual into 'self-subsistent objective reality'. In the context of the development of the Idea of freedom, civil society appears to him to be a stage of development which leads beyond the actualization of freedom already attained within the family. The parallels between the development of the Idea as such in the third part of the *Logic* and the development of the Idea of freedom in the third part of the *Philosophy of Right* can be explained thus: both in the *Philosophy of Right* and at the corresponding point in the *Logic*, on Hegel's view, there takes place a liberation of the moments which were not yet released into independence in the preceding stage of development.[13]

   It seems, then, that the transition from the family to civil society confirms what Hegel told us in his prefacing remarks on method: the concept of freedom here develops 'from within itself' in such a way that its development 'is a purely immanent progress, the engendering of its determinations' (*PhR*, §31). At all events it is clear, even by now, that this cannot mean some mystical self-propulsion of the concept. For this movement is not that of a free-floating concept whose development Hegel and his readers have 'only to watch' (cf. *PhR*, §31R; 176, 8f.); we are, rather, dealing with a philosophical reconstruction of the Idea of freedom, which Hegel, as author, undertakes to carry out in his *Philosophy of Right*.[14] This reconstruction is based on the concept of freedom; and in the dialectical development of this concept, which Hegel describes in the transition from the family to civil society, the progress consists of an 'immanent development of the thing itself' (*PhR*, §2).

It would not, of course, be true to say that Hegel had likewise developed the institution of the family or early capitalist society from the concept of freedom. One of the 'determinations' of the concept of freedom, which emerges from Hegel's dialectical reconstruction of the development of this concept, is indeed the independence of individuals in a 'system of complete interdependence'. But Hegel did not develop this system itself from the concept of freedom (as one might suppose) but from the anthropological and historical conditions for the satisfaction of human needs (cf. *PhR* §§190 ff. and §185R). In his reconstruction of the development of the concept of freedom, the historical existence of early capitalist society is presupposed as a given content.

This appears even more clearly at the beginning of his account of civil society (*PhR*, §§182 ff). Hegel identifies 'the concrete person who is himself the object of his particular aims' as a 'principle of civil society' and he immediately adds:

but the particular person is essentially so related to other particular persons that each establishes himself and finds satisfaction by means of the others and at the same time purely and simply by means of the form of universality, the second principle here (*PhR*, §182).

Hegel thereby accepts as given the existence of a society in which there is a highly developed division of labour, and thence everything required for its continued existence: civil and criminal law, peaceful conditions secured by police, a system of justice which works adequately, and institutions for the protection of individuals and for the development of their capacities. But Hegel's account does not mention these necessary conditions for the existence of early capitalist civil society until very much later; and not until he moves on to his account of the state (*PhR*, §256) does he make clear that such a society can unfold only within a modern state.

3. Only with strong reservations, then, can we endorse Hegel's claim that he did not import the subject-matter of his account in the *Philosophy of Right* from outside, but developed it from the concept of the thing in question. If the concept with which this work is concerned is the Idea of freedom, then we cannot expect Hegel to succeed at all in developing the contents of his account of family, civil society and state from the concept of freedom. His dialectical method of an immanent conceptual development simply can not, contrary to his assurances in the Introduction to the *Philosophy of Right*, be transferred directly from his metaphysical *Logic*, which is concerned with pure concepts, into political philosophy which is a part of 'empirical philosophy' (*Realphilosophie*).

However, at the end of the Preface to the *Philosophy of Right*, we find a different and more 'concrete' indication of how the desired 'unity of form and content' is to be understood in a philosophical account:

Form in its most concrete signification is reason as speculative knowing, and content is reason as the substantial essence of actuality, whether ethical or natural. The known identity of these two is the philosophical Idea (73, 15–19; Knox, p. 12).

Here he no longer speaks of reconstructing the content from the concept of the thing itself by means of a dialectical development of the concept; here content is 'intrinsically' rational reality, and form is the knowing which grasps the rationality of the actual. Thus, in fact, two distinct philosophical tasks emerge: the reconstruction of actuality as rational, and the exposition of the route by which speculative knowing arrives at this insight. In both cases, according to Hegel's methodological idea, dialectical development would proceed immanently and would produce the conceptual determinations immanently; but only at the end would the result be the same. In that way the 'philosophical Idea' would then have been realized.[15]

The fact that we do indeed have two different tasks here can easily be demonstrated in the case of rational natural law. The philosophical reconstruction of a universally binding law is a normative discipline; it must, as e.g. Hobbes, Kant or Rawls have argued, begin with the concept of a rational natural law itself, and from that concept develop the conditions for a legally ordered communal life.[16] Conversely, an exposition of the path by which speculative knowing arrives at its insight into the universal validity of the norms of right would have to begin with the everyday consciousness of right; it could even be described as a 'phenomenology of the consciousness of right'.

It is equally clear, however, that in his *Philosophy of Right*, Hegel does not attempt to find separate solutions to these two philosophical problems. His dialectical development of the concept of freedom is intended both to show that the conditions of common life in a modern state meet the requirements of reason, and also to indicate the path by which speculative knowing can attain to this insight into the rationality of the modern state.

4. We can see very clearly from the end of Hegel's account of civil society

that this inevitably leads to highly undesirable difficulties. Here the reader is suddenly informed that the state is the 'true ground of the family and of civil society' (*PhR*, §256R; 691, vide 11.16). Although in the *Philosophy of Right* the state makes its appearance only after family and civil society, it is, in Hegel's words, 'in reality' prior, since the family can develop itself into civil society only within a state.

Nor should this be taken as merely an assertion about the course of history. For in civil society as Hegel describes it the assumption is always made that there is a state which establishes the law, gives the law validity, maintains peace and order, pursues a social policy and guarantees the effectiveness of social institutions. Only when all this is taken as assured can members of early capitalist society pursue their private ends, without taking cognizance of the liberal legal state in which they live. It is, then, not only in historical reality, but also in Hegel's theory, that the state is seen to be prior to the family and civil society and to be their 'true ground'.

In a philosophical reconstruction of common life in a modern state, what is 'in reality' prior[17] would be the foundation and as such would be dealt with at the very beginning. Since this is so, we must ask ourselves why, in Hegel's *Philosophy of Right*, the state does not appear until the end. It is the knowing described by Hegel which through its progressive insight into the rationality of the ethical world at last comes to grasp the reality of the state. This also shows which of the two problems distinguished above takes precedence in Hegel's work; in its structure, the *Philosophy of Right* is not a deductive theory of the institutions of a modern state, comparable to the theories, say, of Hobbes or Kant, but a phenomenology of the consciousness of freedom, i.e. a philosophical reconstruction of the way by which an individual might become conscious of his freedom as it is realized in a modern state.[18]

However, since Hegel tries to develop, within the framework of a phenomenology of the consciousness of freedom, a theory of the modern state as well, it is quite inevitable that endless difficulties should arise from the linking of these two distinct problems. What is fundamental in the theory does not emerge in the exposition until the end because an individual who becomes conscious of his freedom arrives at the consciousness of the institutional foundations of his freedom only at the end; and what is fundamental in a theory of the modern state can only inadequately be treated within a phenomenology of the consciousness of freedom. In his exposition, Hegel is therefore constantly forced to start from premises the justification for which he is unable to explain; and even when he does reach these premises in his exposition, he frames his questions in such a way that he can not give satisfactory reasons for these premises.

Hegel usually makes the tacit assumption that early capitalist society can only develop when the state has set up an effective legal system for the protection of private property.[19] But even where he turns his attention to the exposition of this legal system (*PhR*, §208), he can only assert that 'the right of property...' is already in existence 'in its recognized actuality'. He simply declares that 'the principle of this system of needs' possesses 'the universality of freedom'; this universality is, he says, admittedly present only 'abstractly', as 'right of property'; but this right is, in civil society, 'no longer merely implicit but has attained its recognized actuality'. Likewise in the next paragraph, he can only reinforce this observation, not justify it. 'It is this very sphere...which gives abstract right...determinate existence' (*PhR*, §209). Whereas all the discussions from Hobbes down to Kant and Fichte made quite clear that the right of property, which had only 'provisional' validity in the state of nature (i.e. Hegel's 'implicitly valid right'), becomes a 'peremptory' right only in the state,[20] we certainly can not say the same for Hegel at this point.[21] Rather, he obscures the matter by attributing to civil society the power to give right 'determinate existence'. What he means is this: only as civil society 'develops' (*bildet*) do the historical conditions arise in which the Idea of unrestricted equality of rights can be actualized. But a modern state is the first prerequisite for this – a point which Hegel cannot discuss or justify here; nor does his way of putting his question within the framework of his theory of the state permit him to supply the missing justification.

Hegel's account of civil society leaves the origins of public authority (*Polizei*) and corporations just as vague as the origins of positive right. Hegel treats them as something already given, and turns immediately to the functions which they are meant to perform in civil society (cf. *PhR*, §§229–31). Here, too, the reasons for this striking omission lie in the fact that in his exposition the phenomenology of the consciousness of freedom takes precedence over the actual theory of the modern state: Hegel wishes above all to expound the doctrine that members of early capitalist society should acknowledge the realization of their freedom within positive civil and criminal law, in the public authority and in the corporations. This interest is so prominent in the structure of his exposition that one is tempted to think that he occasionally loses sight of the other problem, the development of a theory of the modern state. He wishes, however, to do justice equally to both problems, as is evident from his remark that his account of the family and of civil society contained the 'philosophic proof of the concept of the state' (*PhR*, §256R; 691, 12f.).

5. It is fairly clear that Hegel's account of civil society primarily outlines the path which individuals who have already attained self-subsistent reality must travel to become citizens 'capable and worthy' of being 'the actuality of the Idea' (*PhR*, §187R; 639, 2f.). Of course, Hegel does also describe this development as a process which must be undergone not by individuals but by the 'principle of particularity'.

But in developing itself independently to totality, the principle of particularity passes over into universality, and only there does it attain its truth and the right to which its positive actuality is entitled. This unity is not the identity which the ethical order requires, because at this level, that of division (§ 184), both principles are self-subsistent. It follows that this unity is present here not as freedom but as necessity, since it is by compulsion that the particular rises to the form of universality and seeks and gains its stability in that form (*PhR*, § 186).

But if the 'principle of particularity' transforms itself into 'universality' in the way which Hegel describes, then this means, in his own words, that at the same time 'the particular' (individuals) raises itself to the 'form of universality.'

It is the dynamic of civil society itself as a system of mutual interdependence that necessitates the creation of institutions which limit the private autonomy of individuals bent on their 'selfish ends' (*PhR*, § 183). The 'principle' of these institutions and of their activities (administration of justice, police, communal and social policy, corporate bodies) can no longer be the private interests of individuals; indeed these institutions must at the same time act in the public ('universal') interest. But if, in this way, the 'principle' of particularity thus turns more and more into 'universality', then this means, for individuals who are active in these institutions or who depend on their activities, that they too, as 'particulars', are also increasingly raised 'to the form of universality' the more they are forced to consider public interests while pursuing their private ends.[22]

The necessity of the development which determines the dialectical structure of this account of civil society is based, according to Hegel, precisely on the point that the principle of particularity 'develops itself independently to totality'; inasmuch as the principle of private autonomy asserts itself in modern society with increasing force, this society is increasingly obliged to relinquish its exclusive devotion to private interests. In Hegel's view, it is in the last resort this dialectic of particular and universal which has necessitated and determined the development of institutions for the administration of justice, for the protection or creation of peace and order, and for the realization of a communal and social policy in the historical development of the modern state.

But when Hegel, in the dialectical structure of his account of civil society, describes how the 'particular' raises itself stage by stage to 'the form of universality', the necessity for this historical development remains just as obscure as does the fact that these institutions and activities can only develop their effectiveness within the modern state. Hegel presupposes both the dialectics of this historical development and the existence of the modern state in order to describe through the structure of his account, how the relationship of particularity and universality develops dialectically, stage by stage.

Whereas in early capitalist society, as a system of mutual interdependence, private interests and general economic necessities still stand in unmediated opposition to one another (*PhR*, § 18); but the administration of justice already represents a first step towards overcoming this 'level of division' (*PhR*, § 186). It already leads back towards 'the unity of the implicit universal with the subjective particular' (*PhR*, § 229). But this unity is developed only imperfectly in the administration of justice; for 'the universal' here signifies civil and criminal law, and it actualizes this unity only 'in the single case', namely, in annulling 'offences against property or personality' (*PhR*, § 230). The activity of the public authority extends this unity 'to the whole ambit of particularity' (*PhR*, § 229) by effectively protecting the right to 'undisturbed safety of person and property' (*PhR*, § 230). Nonetheless, this 'unification' of particular and universal remains 'relative' (*PhR*, § 229) inasmuch as the separate interests of individuals are placed under state protection. Only in the activity of corporations does this unification extend to the entire existence of individuals, namely, to the 'securing of every single person's livelihood and welfare' (*PhR*, § 230). This does, indeed, actualize the 'concrete totality' of the unification of particular and universal; but even here, as in civil society at large, this totality is limited to the private existence of individuals (*PhR*, § 229). According to Hegel, the full unity of particular and universal is therefore achieved only in the state as 'the absolutely universal end and its absolute actuality' (*PhR*, § 256). The 'level of division' of particular and universal, characteristic of civil society, is thereby overcome.

This dialectical development of the relationship of particularity and universality which determines the course of the exposition does, however, presuppose a subject which undergoes this development and changes its 'standpoint' stage by stage. This subject is, strictly speaking, civil society itself as an ordering of common human life, which is divided into several 'spheres' or 'systems', namely, the system of mutual economic dependence ('system of needs'), the system of civil and criminal law, and the system of social welfare. Accordingly it is in this sense that Hegel calls the subject which, in its development, passes through these spheres 'Spirit' (*Geist*). It is Spirit which

attains its actuality only by creating a dualism within itself, by submitting itself to physical needs and the chain of these external necessities, and so imposing on itself this barrier and this finitude, and finally by maturing [*bildet*] itself inwardly even when under this barrier until it overcomes it and attains its objective reality in the finite (*PhR*, § 187R; 637, 23–7).

But, translated into an interpretation of concrete relations, this only means that in the economic system of early capitalist society individuals facing the general conditions of their common life find themselves at a standpoint of division and consequently at the standpoint of limitation and finitude; but this very finitude of their standpoint obliges them to overcome the limitations of their initial condition and to develop their subjective interests further towards 'objectivity'. This is why Hegel also describes this process as the course of development through which 'the subjective will itself attains an objectivity in which alone it is for its part capable and worthy of being the actuality of the Idea' (*PhR*, §187R; 639, 1–3). What Hegel describes as the dialectic of civil society is, according to this, a process of 'education' (ibid., 638, 18), in which the subjective will raises itself from the standpoint of the particular to the 'form of the universal' (ibid., 21).

It is, however, possible to speak of such an educational process in two quite different senses: as a historical progression in which private persons in early capitalist society increasingly develop a political consciousness, and as a hermeneutic process which Hegel traces in the dialectical construction of his account of civil society. Whereas Hegel goes into this historical educational process only in his account of the economic system (cf. *PhR*, §197), his account as a whole should be understood as a description of the route by which 'speculative knowing' must travel in order to get from the standpoint of the particular (or the *bourgeois*) to the 'standpoint of the ethical life' of the state (or the *citoyen*) (cf. *PhR*, §33R; 182, 16). When the reader realizes how the principle of particularity, 'in developing itself independently to totality', transforms itself 'into universality', then it becomes clear to him that the principle of particularity can have 'its truth and the right to which its positive actuality is entitled' (*PhR*, §186) only in this universality. He recognizes herewith that the limitation of self-awareness within which private persons are confined in the economic system is increasingly removed in the system of justice and in the system of social welfare, and is finally removed altogether when the standpoint of ethical life is reached. Hegel indicates in advance that the reader, from the standpoint of the *citoyen*, will then be able to see that the standpoint of the private person is justifiable within certain limits.

6. In a phenomenology of the consciousness of freedom as it has just been described, we must always distinguish the standpoint adopted by the observer from the standpoint of its object, i.e. of consciousness on its route to self-consciousness. In his *Philosophy of Right*, Hegel has unfortunately omitted to specify in each instance the standpoint from which his formulations are to be understood. It is therefore often possible for misunderstandings to arise as to whether he is speaking from the standpoint of phenomenal consciousness which is the object of his observation, or whether he is speaking from the

standpoint which he himself adopts for his observation and description. In his account of civil society, this difficulty is less formidable than in other parts of his work. But even here the reader must be clear in his own mind that many of Hegel's statements formulated in the language of a 'logical mysticism' become comprehensible once we distinguish these two standpoints.

When, for instance, Hegel distinguishes between the interests pursued by the members of civil society and the 'interest of the Idea, an interest of which these members of civil society are as such unconscious' (*PhR*, § 187), we are in no doubt that the expression 'Idea' simply denotes the standpoint adopted by Hegel in his account. As long as the members of civil society are pursuing their private ends, economic and social relations appear to them to be no more than the conditions to which they must submit in order to attain the fulfilment of their needs. But when they 'determine their knowing, willing and acting in a universal way and make themselves links in this chain of social connections', then they see (and so do we who are observing this process with regard to the formation of a consciousness of citizenship) that they thereby raise themselves 'to formal freedom and formal universality of knowing and willing'[23] (ibid.). This is the viewpoint from which the 'formal' education (*Bildung*), accomplished in civil society, is of 'interest'.

A similar interpretation can be given to passages in which Hegel speaks as though the 'Idea' works in civil society by 'imparting a characteristic embodiment' (*PhR*, § 184) to the 'moments' of particularity and universality. From the standpoint of the state, which we adopt for our observation of civil society, it is clear to us that the members of early capitalist society can only pursue their private interests because the modern state gives them the opportunity to do so. We also see that individuals pursue their aims under the conditions of prevailing social relations which, for their part, presuppose a modern state as their basis. This is the modern liberal state which guarantees its citizens the right to a private existence and which allows social relations to develop freely so that they can prove themselves to be the 'ground', 'necessary form', and 'power' over all private ends of individuals. It is in this sense that Hegel can say that the state or the (ethical) Idea imparts 'a characteristic embodiment' to individuals and to social relations.

Up to this point, this interpretation of the relationship of 'particularity' and 'universality' in early capitalist society is clear enough; but Hegel goes beyond it when he characterizes this social structure as an 'ethical order, split into its extremes and lost' (*PhR*, § 184). For this amounts to a declaration that civil society is a stage of development through which the ethical Idea passes on the way to its actualization. Just as he explains the family as the ethical Idea 'still in its concept' (*PhR*, § 181; 628, 12f.), so he now establishes civil society as 'the Idea's abstract moment, its moment of reality'[24] (*PhR*, §184).

This interpretation becomes comprehensible if, from a historical point of view, we apply it to the development of the Idea of the modern state. The 'immediate substantiality of mind' in the family (*PhR*, §158) then corresponds to the kingdoms of the ancient Orient, built on the 'patriarchal and religious principle', and also to the 'substance of ethical life' of the Greek polis (cf. *PhR*, §185R; 645, 3. 17); the historical origin of civil society as a 'system of the ethical order, split into its extremes and lost' is, then, to be sought in the era of the Roman emperors.[25]

However, this transference of diachronic stages of development to the synchronic structure of the modern state does cause a difficulty. The ancient Oriental kingdoms, the Greek polis and the Roman empire are actual political communities, whereas the family and civil society, as Hegel describes them, presuppose a state as their basis, and specifically the modern state. This difference is obscured when Hegel characterizes civil society as a 'system of the ethical order, split into its extremes and lost'.[26] The impression can arise that he means to interpret civil society as an independent stage of development of a mystical subject, of 'Spirit' or 'Mind', occurring between family and state.

It is in this sense that we can understand the proposition, 'Mind attains its actuality only by creating a dualism within itself' (*PhR*, §187R; 637, 22f.). But the context tells us that Hegel, from a historical point of view, opposes the Rousseauistic 'idea that the state of nature is one of innocence and that there is a simplicity of manners in uncivilized [*ungebildeter*] peoples' (ibid., 13f.) to the formation of a society based on the division of labour in which men overcome their original 'crudity' (638, 1) and raise themselves to 'the form of universality' (ibid., 5). What Hegel thus describes, in a semi-mystical way of speaking, as the history of the development of 'Mind', thereby shows itself to be the result of a paradigmatic reconstruction of the development of social systems from the standpoint of the Idea of freedom as actualized in the modern state.

When Hegel elsewhere speaks of a 'development of ethical life from its immediate phase through civil society, the phase of division, to the state' (*PhR*, §256R; 691, 9–11), he yet again seems to envisage the idea of an identical subject which undergoes this process. But when he asserts that this development is 'the philosophic proof of the concept of the state' (ibid., 12f.) it is immediately clear that he is speaking not about a real process but about his own dialectical reconstruction of the concept of the state. In this reconstruction, family and civil society emerge as derivative formations ('ideal moments', ibid., 5) which are always dependent on the state for their existence. But, above all, it is apparent in Hegel's account of civil society that the union of the particular with the universal, which is achieved in the corporation, is still incomplete because the aim of the corporation 'is restricted and finite' (*PhR*, §256). The notion that this unification is not fully completed until the members of civil society have raised their 'particular self-consciousness' (*PhR*, §258) to the universality of an 'absolutely universal end' (*PhR*, §256) is therefore crucial for the transition from civil society to the state. Since Hegel regards the state as the 'absolute actuality' of this end, the only 'philosophic proof of the concept of the state' which is worthy of the name lies in the demonstration of the necessity of this transition.

7. When Kant attributes 'truth' to the 'concept of morality', he means that this concept has 'application to any possible object' inasmuch as the highest principle of morality is binding for this entity.[27] Thus Kant also speaks of a 'deduction' of the categorical imperative, what is meant is the 'justification of its objective and universal validity'.[28] Hegel, too, with similar implications, speaks of the 'truth' of the 'proof' or of the 'deduction' of the concept of right (*PhR*, §2).

The 'philosophic proof of the concept of the state' is thus intended to demonstrate that reason is the 'substantial essence' (*PhR*, Preface, 73. 17; Knox, p. 12) of the modern state. But the modern state proves itself as rational when it can be presented as an institution in which the Idea of freedom is actualized. Accordingly, when Hegel claims that he has proved the 'concept of the state' in his account of civil society, he must mean that he has shown that the Idea of freedom is actualized only in the modern state.

Now Hegel made no attempt whatsoever to conduct his proof by expounding the actualization of the Idea of freedom in right and morality as well as in the family, civil society and the state itself. On the contrary, he traced the various degrees to which individuals had attained to consciousness of freedom at the 'standpoint of right' (*PhR*, §§45R; 216, 8; and 57R; 242, 3. 26) and morality (*PhR*, §105), and also as members of the family, civil society and the state. In so doing he constantly tried, though often only by giving obscure hints, to show that the 'individual self-consciousness' had not yet risen to its full 'universality' (cf. *PhR*, §258), and had therefore still some way to go beyond its present stage of development. At the end of his account, then, Hegel has not actually proved the 'concept of the state'. What he *has* done is to show that, for members of civil society in their corporations, freedom is indeed actualized as the right to an assured private existence (cf. *PhR*, §255), and yet that this exclusive devotion to their private interests must be relinquished if the actualization of freedom is to reach perfection in activity for the 'absolutely universal end' of the state. The argument that members of civil society must, in the interests of the Idea of freedom, progress from the standpoint of the *bourgeois* to that of the *citoyen* is, however, no 'proof of the concept of the state'.

Only when we give a historical interpretation of the 'development of ethical life from its immediate phase through civil society, the phase of division, to the state' (*PhR*, §256R; 691, 9–11) does this account take on the character of a justification of the Idea of the modern state. It then appears as the historical development of that concept of the state which has its origin in the Greek polis, and which, owing to the Christian religion and the de-politicized society of the Roman imperial era, has absorbed the principle of particularity. In this way the combination of the Greek principle of a free political community (*PhR*, §124R; 446, 20) with the 'right to subjective freedom' in the institutions of the modern state may be understood as the product of previous history. In so far as Hegel's account, thus understood, shows reason to be the 'substantial essence' of the 'ethical world', it may be allowed to count as a 'philosophic proof of the concept of the state'.

8. Two reservations must nevertheless be made, and both concern Hegel's form of presentation, namely, his conceptual language and his dialectic.

Our interpretation has shown that, contrary to all appearances, Hegel is not presenting us with a metaphysic which one could characterize as a 'logical, pantheistic mysticism'. Where he does use metaphysical conceptual language, we can translate his formulations into ordinary conceptual terms so that his way of speaking acquires a readily accessible meaning. Indeed, there can be no doubt that this is the intended meaning of these often profoundly obscure formulations. Futhermore, we can recognize that Hegel's difficult conceptual language has an immeasurably great advantage: it enables him to express incredibly complex conceptual relationships in a few words. In this respect, Hegel's texts resemble in many ways the fragments of the pre-Socratic philosophers; and indeed a work such as the *Philosophy of Right* must be interpreted in much the same way as the aphorisms of a Heraclitus.

However, these gains in complexity and richness of reference are purchased at a price, namely, the need for interpretation. This comes not only from the fact that it is necessary to translate Hegel's conceptual language into a rendering which displays its manifold meanings. In the interpretation it also becomes clear that this conceptual language itself has multiple meanings. This holds not only for Hegel's terminology – if one wishes to allow this expression for those conceptual terms in his philosophical language which have characteristic meanings divergent from ordinary speech. The significance which interpretation can attribute to his arguments is often also multiple. It is certain that Marx is wrong in attempting to tie Hegel's metaphysical mode of expression to its apparent mysticism; but it is equally certain that Hegel undeniably gives some grounds for such misreadings.

This is the reason why we cannot accept Hegel's claim to have given a 'philosophic proof of the concept of the state' in his account of the family and civil society, although we can make that claim comprehensible. Hegel is unable to produce a philosophical proof in the strict sense of the word because his conceptual language is not suited for the purpose. In fact, he has shown only that the modern state — i.e. the state of his time with regard to its remote future possibilities — is essentially rational because it can be, and should be, conceived as an institutional actualization of the Idea of freedom. This is an explanation with a practical purpose, not a philosophical proof.

There is an additional reason why Hegel can not produce a kind of 'proof' of the Idea of the modern state, i.e. a theoretical demonstration and justification of the principles on which it rests. His dialectical method as practised in the *Philosophy of Right* is unsuitable for the purpose. Proceeding by way of a phenomenology of the consciousness of freedom brings Hegel only to a 'reconciliation with the actuality' (*PhR*, Preface, 73, 7; Knox, p. 12) of the modern state, not to a rational theory which would have made the state in its historical forms an object suitable for a critique. If, in his political philosophy, Hegel has in many ways 'accommodated' himself to existing political conditions,* this can doubtless be explained not merely by the pressure of these conditions but also by the weaknesses of his dialectical theory of the state as a phenomenology of the consciousness of freedom. For it has already reached its goal when 'reason as speculative knowing' and 'reason as the substantial essence of actuality whether ethical or natural' are brought into a 'known identity' (ibid., 73, 16–18; Knox, p. 12). Having, reached this point, the question should rather be: how may Hegel's insight that reason is 'the substantial essence of actuality,' be formulated and established in a rational theory of the modern state? Only in such a theory, it seems to me, would the problem posed by Hegel be truly solved.**

---

* *Editor's note.* This 'accommodation' and its consequences for Hegel's *Philosophy of Right* are the subject of K.-H. Ilting's first essay in this volume.

** Translated from the German by H. Tudor and J. M. Tudor.

Hegel on identity and legitimation

RAYMOND PLANT

Several important recent works in politial theory have focussed attention once again on the relationship between the state and the economy. *The Legitimation Crisis* by Jürgen Habermas,[1] *The Fiscal Crisis of the State* by James O'Connor,[2] W. D. Narr and Claus Offe's *Wohlfahrtsstaat und Massenloyalität*,[3] C. Offe's *Strukturprobleme des kapitalistischen Staates*,[4] and *The Politicised Economy*[5] by M. Best and W. E. Connolly have all raised fundamental problems about the nature of the state in capitalist society from a broadly marxist perspective, but which incorporate within the critical account of the modern state a richness of empirical detail, for example about the development of welfare institutions and the management of the economy in the post-Keynesian era which are, of course, absent from the classical marxist texts. Nevertheless, these studies are all well within the marxist tradition of theorising about the state and it is perhaps not surprising that Habermas at least has seen the basis of one central aspect of the modern relationship of the state of the economy — what he calls the legitimation crisis — in the work of Hegel. This essay will attempt to throw some light upon neglected facets of Hegel's view of the relationship between the state and the economy partly for their intrinsic interest, partly because these views of Hegel do point towards Habermas's conception of the legitimation crisis and partly because Hegel's own partial failure to perceive the consequences of his own theorising poses significant questions not only about his own account of the relationship between the state and the economy, but also problems which are central to the political agenda in our own day.

Perhaps a word could be said first of all about the nature of legitimacy in question here and why in Habermas's view there is a crisis of legitimacy in modern capitalism. The crisis arises basically because of what Habermas sees as the dysfunctional effects of the economic market which seem to require some kind of state intervention to correct. The extent of this state intervention however, goes far beyond the role allocated to the state in what Habermas sees as the political theory of liberal capitalism within which the

activity of the state is seen largely in terms of securing the general conditions
of production. A good recent statement of such a view would be Hayek's
The Constitution of Liberty[6] and *The Mirage of Social Justice*.[7] Yet this increased
state activity and responsibility for the direction of the economy, irrespective
of its theoretical justification, has been a major feature of the modern capitalist
world. Partly because of the extent of the contemporary coupling of the
political with the economic sphere there is pressure to secure some firm
normative foundation for this interdependence. At the same time, the state
cannot call upon traditional, precapitalist views about the appropriate role
of the state just because, as Habermas says, these have been 'undermined and
worn out by the very development of capitalism'. In addition this process
of legitimation of the modern interventionist state has to be linked with the
mass franchise: 'legitimation can be dissociated from the method of elections
only temporarily and under extraordinary conditions'. Where is the rationale
for collective action to come from in a culture deeply marked with
individualism, an individualism which has close connections with the very
forms of economic life which collective action in pursuit of some conception
of the common good is designed to curb and control? In a crucial sense for
Hegel this is the problem of political *identity*: is there a coherent set of values
which can link the economic and the political and thus provide the moral
basis for political identity and thus for a secure political community? Indeed,
can there really be a political community given what might be thought to
be the radically discordant features of the market on the one hand and the
state on the other? In a paper 'On Social Identity' Habermas points out
the extent to which Hegel was confronted in his own political thinking by
questions of much the same sort:

> It was in the course of the development of capitalism that the economy broke out
> of the limits set by household production, *and in general out of the boundaries of
> normative regulation*. The primitive sphere of 'bourgeois society' separated from the
> state as well as the family is primarily under the control of the imperatives of the
> market, i.e., of economic mechanisms and not norms of action and value orientations
> of the actors; that is why for Hegel this sphere represents the 'loss of morality'.
> Hegel, of course, was convinced that the economic system 'the system of
> needs' – notwithstanding its internal conflicts – would retain its connection with
> ethical life through the mediation of the legal system.[8]

Hegel is certainly centrally concerned with this problem in *Jenenser Realphilosophie* I and II, in his 1801 essay on *Natural Law*[9] and, of course, in the
Philosophy of Right.[10] One thread which runs through all of these works is
that which Habermas mentions: how can collective action, or what Hegel
calls the 'universal', be developed and legitimated within the system of needs
or the economic market which is highly individualistic – as Hegel says, lost

both to universality and lost to morality? How can collective intervention in the economy come to appear as more than the 'external state' as Hegel calls public authority at one point in the *Philosophy of Right* (§256)?

Of course this is only a problem for a political theorist who envisages a large role for the state in economic activity. At the moment it is fashionable to try to solve the problem of legitimacy of state economic management by taking the issue off the political agenda, at least as far as possible. Such economic libertarians as Friedman and Hayek argue that since there is no agreed moral basis on which political intervention in economic activity can proceed – for example in the sphere of the distribution of economic rewards – the problem of legitimation is bypassed by radically restricting the role of the state, and the economic outcomes of the market are legitimised paradoxically not in terms of any moral principle but rather (as Hirsch cogently argues) as something in principle unjustifiable.[11] Hegel, however, is very far from seeing the system of needs as Hayekian catallaxy, as a self-equilibriating system of production, distribution and exchange. In all of his writings from *Jenenser Realphilosophie* I to the *Philosophy of Right* he is insistent that the market has to be controlled by some kind of state intervention. As a young man Hegel had been particularly impressed with accounts of modern society given in the work of Smith, Steuart and Ferguson and also by the more critical writings of Schiller, Herder and Hölderlin. In *Letters on the Aesthetic Education of Man*, which Hegel regarded as a masterpiece, Schiller produced a vigorous critique of the modern economic order and, drawing upon this basically romantic critique of modern society, Hegel saw the need for state control in two forms.

(1) He was worried about the enervation of human capacities and powers in the working environments characteristic of modern production. In his Sixth Letter on the *Aesthetic Education of Man* Schiller had been bitingly critical of modern society on just this point:

Eternally tied to a single fragment of the whole, man himself develops into nothing but a fragment. Everlastingly in his ear is the monotonous sound of the wheel, the wheel he turns. He never develops the harmony of his being, and instead of stamping the imprint of humanity upon nature, he becomes no more than the imprint of his occupation and specialised knowledge.[12]

Hegel echoes some of these themes in *Jenenser Realphilosophie* I where he discusses Adam Smith's example of the pin factory:

The particularisation of labour multiplies the mass of production; in an English manufacture 18 people work at the production of a needle; each has a particular and exclusive side of the work to perform; a single person could not produce one hundred and twenty needles, not even one...But the value of labour decreases in the same proportion as the productivity increases. Work becomes thus absolutely more and more dead, it becomes machine labour, the individual's own skill becomes unjustly limited and the consciousness of the factory worker is degraded to the utmost level of dullness. The connection between the particular sort of labour and the infinite mass of needs becomes wholly imperceptible, turns into blind dependence...The spiritual element, the self conscious plenitude of life becomes an empty activity. *The power of the self resides in rich comprehension*; this is being lost.[13]

Modern labouring processes thus lead to the enervation of the personality, but not only this. Hegel argues in the *Philosophy of Right* that when the products of labour are entirely owned by others this has severe consequences for the individual's sense of his own worth just because of the important role which labour plays in human self-development. The point is made in the context of a discussion about slavery, but the consequences of this position are radical:

...those goods, or rather substantive characteristics which constitute my own private personality and the universal essence of my self-consciousness are inalienable and my right to them is imprescriptible...Single products of my particular physical and mental skill and of my power to act I can alienate to someone else...[but] by alienating the whole of my time as crystallised in my work and everything I produced, I would be making into another's property the substance of my being, my universal activity and actuality, my personality (*PhR*, §66, §67).

Hegel sees state intervention in the market as necessary to mitigate as far as possible the personal consequences of the tendency for this to happen in the modern world.

(II) More generally Hegel argues that while the modern economy, as Say, Smith and Ricardo have shown, does exemplify a very high degree of mutual interdependence, these patterns of interdependence, secured by 'the hidden hand', or 'the cunning of reason' are, in Hegel's view, highly insecure and highly unpredictable. As he argues: 'Society becomes a vast system of mutual interdependence, a moving life of the dead. The system moves this way and that in a blind and elemental fashion and like a wild animal calls for permanent control and curbing.'[14] As we have already seen, Hegel takes the view that the power of the self resides in 'rich comprehension' and the network of relationships within which the individual lives in the modern economy can only be rendered comprehensible in so far as it is subjected *to rational control*. Instead of a rationally constrained market, individuals are at the mercy of arbitrary changes in economic activity; 'Whole branches of industry which supported a large class of people suddenly fold up because of a change in fashion or because the value of their product fell due to inventions in other countries: whole masses are abandoned to poverty which cannot help itself.'[15]

Only a constrained and controlled market Hegel thinks will be able to obviate these painful and irrational consequences of economic activity. It is clear that Hegel is concerned with a moral critique of unconstrained markets, a critique with two facets: (1) the enervation of the individual in modern market society; (2) the social cost and the unpredictability of the unconstrained market. But both of these facets are part of the working out of the same basic vision: the need for human beings to have a sense of identification with their own central life-activities and a sense of solidarity and significance within the broader society of which they are members. It is the failure of the system of needs to provide its own means whereby these values can be achieved that Hegel refuses to condone the outcomes of unconstrained economic activity. Paying more attention to the consequences and disadvantages of what Adam Smith calls the 'commercial spirit' than did classical political economists, Hegel refuses to admit the predilection of those economists for a minimal state.

The disadvantages of the system of needs meet in Hegel's view in the problem of poverty in modern society. Poverty became a preoccupation of his from the late 1790s and he is clearly aware of the problem which it poses both for the modern economy and the modern state.

In the *Philosophy of Right* Hegel argues that poverty is an endemic and ineradicable feature of modern society. In other words, it is a feature not just of particular societies in a state of decline or disintegration, but precisely of society when it is running smoothly, when in Hegel's own words 'civil society is in a state of unimpeded activity' (*PhR*, §243). The mechanics of this process are rather obscure, but the main outline of his argument seems to be clear enough. When industry produces goods to satisfy the incessantly increasing pressure of men's wants, it may well find that in a particular case there are not enough consumers for its products (*PhR*, §245). In such circumstances, the bottom will drop out of the market for a particular commodity; those who, because of the continuing refinement of the division of labour within the system of needs, are entirely dependent upon the industry producing that particular product will be thrown into idleness. The poverty resulting from such an economic slump will have two distinct sides: the actual level of physical deprivation involved and the social attitudes of those who are deprived.

In Hegel's view, the level of poverty is not fixed by some neutral or objective standard based upon a notion of absolute or basic need but rather by some notion of need relative to what is necessary to be a functioning and integrated member of a particular society, with a specific standard of living and pattern of consumption: 'When the standard of living of a large mass of the people falls below a certain subsistence level – a level regulated automatically as the one necessary for a member of the society... the result is the creation of a rabble of paupers' (*PhR*, §244). In a comment on this

paragraph Hegel gives a pithy and practical application of this point of view:
'In England, even the poorest believe that they have rights; this is different
from what satisfies the poor in other countries' (*PhR*, §244A). In other words,
poverty is relative deprivation. In this view, of course, Hegel was strikingly
modern in his outlook.

It is precisely at this point that poverty as a relative state makes contact
with Hegel's other view that there are social attitudes which are characteristic
of poverty. Because of their deprivation, men become cut off from the
various advantages of society – the acquisition of skill, education, access to
justice and even to organised religion (*PhR*, §241) – all of which are
mediating activities and institutions which link men to the social order. Bereft
of these mediating links, men become estranged: 'Poverty in itself does not
make men into a rabble; a rabble is created only when there is joined to
poverty a disposition of mind, an inner indignation against the rich, against
society, against the government, etc.' (*PhR*, §244A). When modern society is
functioning normally therefore, in Hegel's view a group of people are pressed
to this internally posited poverty floor, and within such groups there is
generated a profound sense of alienation and social hostility.

There is ample evidence that Hegel was greatly exercised by this problem.
Rosenkranz reports that Hegel was an avid reader of the English press, and
closely followed debates in Parliament on the Poor Law. His account of
Hegel's relationship with Steuart portrays the former's particular interest in
the problem of poverty.[16] The state cannot be indifferent to the outcomes
of the market and while it is, of course, part of Hegel's view that a major
task of the state is to provide a framework of law within which individuals
may pursue their own ends in the market without interference and to protect
property, this by no means exhausts the role of the state. On the contrary
in fact, it has the responsibility to secure 'every single person's livelihood'
and welfare has to be 'treated and actualised as a right' (*PhR*, §230). Within
civil society each individual has a right to promotion of his welfare: 'I have
a right to claim that in this association with other particulars, my particular
welfare too shall be promoted' (*PhR*, §233A). It is also clear that by 'welfare'
Hegel does not just mean the consumption of consumer goods but also the
realisation of those powers and capacities which Hegel, in common with the
Romantics, regards as being threatened by an unconstrained system of needs.

It is in these terms therefore that Hegel rested his case for state intervention
in the system of needs. At the same time, however, it is extremely important
to realise that Hegel does envisage an important function for the economic
market in the pattern of human development. In economic activity
individuals realise in a concrete and external form that sense of subjective
freedom which dawned originally in the Romano-Christian world. This
'satisfaction of subjective particularity' is traced in world history by Hegel

through Christianity, Roman law, the growth of Protestantism, the Enlightenment, Kantian moral thought and the French Revolution, which, as Ritter[17] points out, was for Hegel the working out in the political sphere of the principle of subjectivity in the modern world the economic counterpart to which is the system of needs. So Hegel does endorse many of the features and achievements of modern civil society, particularly the independence and personal liberty which the modern economy has both enhanced and reinforced. At the same time Hegel does see civil society as being devoid of an agreed, concrete morality. Morality, such as it is, consists in the pursuit of personal self-interest which yields a situation in which 'ethical life is split into its extremes and lost' or, as Habermas says, 'individuals become oriented to purely private norms'.

On the one hand, therefore, the system of needs is characterised by its individualism, its particularity and this, as we have seen, is the culmination of a long process which has been quite central to human liberation; at the same time the economic market produces unacceptable outcomes both for particular individuals and also for society as a whole and it has to be constrained by the state. However, Hegel is keenly aware that in imposing some sort of order on the system of needs the state is likely to appear to be authoritarian in its actions and its policies are likely to appear as external impositions. Indeed from the time of writing 'The Positivity of the Christian Religion' in the 1790s Hegel was haunted by the fact that the state might appear as alien and imposed.[18] This issue is rendered particularly acute by the character of civil society. How can individuals lost in particularity, in this individualist ethical framework, develop both a sense of the legitimacy of, and identification with, the regulative activities of the state? What basic rationale can be seen within the system of needs for the collective action necessary to constrain the system? The problem here is clearly indicated by Hegel's calling the police or regulative functions of the state the 'external state' in the *Philosophy of Right* and as one which involves a separation and merely 'relative indentity of controller and controlled' (*PhR*, §256).

Here we seem to be faced with Hegel's own early version of what might be called the legitimation crisis and it is a crucial problem for anyone wishing to claim that at least in principle the modern state can provide the basis for a political community to which its citizens can relate and with which they can identify. Hegel does make the claim that the state is an 'ethical substance' and surely part of what is meant by this difficult term is that there is no fundamental discontinuity in values between the state and the wider institutions and practices of society over which that state exercises authority. Only if there is such an 'ethical substance' at the basis of the modern state can the state have a rational identity.

Hegel's own solution to the problem, which his own forthright description of the political economy of the modern state has posed for the theory and practice of modern politics, is complicated and as we shall see is at least a partial failure in terms of his own criteria, but broadly speaking it consists in trying to give a redescription of the system of needs: that is providing an account in terms of Reason (*Vernunft*) rather than the Understanding (*Verstand*). This redescription is a *dialectical* account so that the economic activities of modern society come to appear in less unremittingly individualistic terms. He tries to pass from an immediate to a mediated description, and through this to a change in consciousness about the operation of the market.* In an attempt to see a role for corporations Hegel tries to provide a broader understanding of the social context within which individuals in their economic activities come to form a conception of their own interests. As Heiman says: 'Hegel uses civil society as a means of achieving a higher degree of mediation.'[19]

The first part of the solution to his problem was to provide a transfigured understanding of the role of the system of needs in order to bring into focus more fully the extent to which the modern economy, while certainly generating a considerable sense of personal freedom and independence, equally leads to complicated and to much less completely comprehended forms of mutual *interdependence*. The central motif for this account is given in the *System der Sittlichkeit* when Hegel says that 'nobody is for himself regarding the totality of his needs'[20] and he seeks to demonstrate the profound forms of *Gemeinschaftlichkeit* at work in the modern economy and which are only taken incompletely into account in works of political economy. In what follows I have selected a number of themes in terms of which this *Gemeinschaftlichkeit* is shown by Hegel to be developed within the system of needs.

Labour is a central category in the system of needs and a conception of labour is central to any political economy which seeks to explain economic activity, but it is much more than this for Hegel. Labour is crucial to human self-consciousness and being in the world and as such it has a central place not just within political economy but also within the philosophy of mind and epistemology. At the same time these transcending features of labour have consequences within the system of needs. Needs become multiplied beyond bare necessities as a result of the manipulative power of labour and the development of self-consciousness and this multiplication of needs is the vehicle for economic development. Hegel also used labour to help to solve the deep philosophical problems which preoccupied him and which he had inherited from Kant, Fichte and Schelling. It was in labour, in Hegel's view, that the reconciliation between subject and object was achieved, for labour

---

* *Editor's note* – A. S. Walton in his essay analyses this process as well as the role of corporations in it. His interpretation questions that given in this essay.

developed both the subjective consciousness of the agent and also involved the manipulation of external objects. The problem of man's relationship to the external world was thus for Hegel to be seen in much more *active* terms than had been the case since the time of Descartes.

All these features of labour, both within the sphere of political economy and beyond, stress the extent to which labour is a personally liberating facet of human activity, but it is also much more than this. The development of self-consciousness through labour also involves the labour and thus the consciousness — intentions, purposes and projects — of others because no man can satisfy all the range of his needs through his own labour. Each person requires in some degree the labour of others in order to satisfy his needs. Within the apparently subjective process of labour there is generated a very complex system of mutual interdependence.

When men are thus dependent on one another and reciprocally related to one another in their work and the satisfaction of their needs, subjective self-seeking turns into a contribution to the satisfaction of the needs of everyone else. *That is to say by a dialectical advance, subjective self-seeking turns into the mediation of the particular through the universal, with the result that each man in earning, producing and enjoying on his own account is* eo ipso *producing and earning for the enjoyment of everyone else* (PhR,§ 54, my emphasis — R.P.).

Labour in this sense is, as Marx clearly saw, social in its essence. So, while it is central to Hegel's thesis that labour is personally liberating, this element of personal emancipation is mediated socially. Thus labour, the crucial concept in classical political economy, which had yielded a vision of society which was radically individualistic, is used by Hegel not just as a category within political economy, but within a broader framework. Hegel tries to show that labour leads to personal liberation, a growth in self-consciousness and to the manipulative power over nature, but also that it is *gemeinschaftlich*. This organism may not be the *sinnliche Harmonie* of the Greek polis; but nevertheless there are patterns of mutual interdependence in modern society which are by no means peripheral but rather generated naturally out of one of the central active powers of the human person. Political economy has itself provided the basis for this account, but Hegel seems to have thought that writers such as Smith, Say and Ricardo had not given sufficient weight to this aspect of their work. However, the political economist is in Hegel's view 'trying to find reconciliation here, to discover in the sphere of needs this show of rationality lying in the thing and effective there' (PhR, § 189).

Herein lies the difficulty of this version of the market theory of community. It makes the existence of community a matter of the upshot, of the unintended consequences of a sequence of actions undertaken for different reasons. Community is a matter of grasping these unintended consequences; it is not a matter of relating to persons in terms of fraternal feeling and attitude. However, it is difficult to see how a concept of community can operate without making some reference to the values in terms of which members of the community perceive themselves in relation to one another. Community is not just a matter of particular outcomes, but of right intentional relationships, relationships which involve benevolence, altruism, fraternity. The obvious answer to the difficulty, and the one which Hegel, in so far as he sees the problem, appears to give, is that once we comprehend the facts of our interrelationship this knowledge will enter into our motivations in the market and we shall consciously work for the satisfaction of the needs of others.

The labour of the individual for his own wants is just as much a satisfaction of those of others as of himself, and the satisfaction of his own he attains only by the labour of others.

As the individual in his own particular work *ipso facto* accomplishes unconsciously a universal work, so again he also performs the universal task as his *conscious* object. The whole becomes in its entirety his work, for which he sacrifices himself, and precisely by that means he receives back his own self from it.[21]

This is now a different claim. The first claim was that private profit-maximising activity in the market produces forms of community and mutuality as an unintended consequence of such activity, which there is a need to grasp in thought. The second claim is that when this is understood, individuals will pursue such forms of *Gemeinschaftlichkeit* in a self-conscious way and actively seek to promote the satisfaction of the needs of others. This second claim has the advantage from the point of view of community theory that it does make reference to the conscious relationships between individuals.

Tools too play a central part of the transformative and therefore consciousness developing aspect of labour. As Hegel said in *The Science of Logic*: 'In his tools, man possesses power over external nature.' However, there are aspects of tools which go beyond the role which they play in personal self-development, and these were equally stressed by Hegel. A tool is a public instrument which is in principle available to all, and thus allows mastery over nature secured specifically by it to be repeated at least in principle, by anyone: 'In the tool, the subjectivity of labour has been elevated to something universal; everyone can initiate it in precisely the same way, thus it is the constant rule of labour.'[22] Tools help the routinisation of the mastery of nature and make both its transformation and the self-development which goes along with it available to all men. Again, there is the same dialectic at work: that which develops individual self-consciousness has a universal element simultaneously present within it. At the same time tools link generations, in the sense that a new generation inherits from the old certain techniques of production involving tools. This is another important social dimension of the use of tools; a tool 'is inherited in the traditions while that which desires and that which is desired only subsist as individuals and individuals pass away'.[23]

Hegel, therefore, did not see the system of needs necessarily generating a radically individualistic vision of society; rather, the activities characteristic of the economic sphere both in production and exchange presuppose very intricate patterns of mutual interdependence. These forms of interdependence are not predicated upon peripheral features of human life. On the contrary, labour and the use of tools are central ways in which human beings come to self-consciousness; as such, the forms of mutuality to be found within them are of very great importance. But as I have suggested these forms of mutuality are external. Similar features are characteristic also of the division of labour within the system of needs. As needs develop, so productive processes have to meet them. This requires an increasing division of labour; 'the sub-division of needs and means thereby *eo ipso* subdivides production and brings about the division of labour' (*PhR*, § 198). Again, this is in a sense a gain in self-consciousness, in that an individual's specific skills increase; at the same time, this complex division of the productive process leads once again to extremely intricate forms of mutual dependence and 'reciprocal relation in the satisfaction of their other needs'.

Correlated with the division of labour are the most important social groups within the system of needs, namely classes (*Stände*) of which Hegel distinguished three: the agricultural class, the business class and the civil service. Hegel did not define classes in terms of relationship to the means of production, but rather to types of work, the general skills required for its performance, and the kind of ethos or consciousness which it produces among those who perform these tasks. His agricultural class, for example, contained both landowners and peasants and this emphasis upon ethos or modes of consciousness linked with skills in production was to permit Hegel to claim, once again, that the system of needs yields social integration. It did this in two ways: in the first place, an individual is bound together with members of his society with whom he has certain things in common, based upon labour and the skills attendant upon it; secondly, these specific classes yielding different types of consciousness and ethos stand together, not in opposition but in a system of mutual or functional interdependence.

At the same time, membership of a class equally relates to the individual's growth of consciousness as much as it does to social integration. As an individual in the system of needs, a man seeks to satisfy his own needs or those of his immediate family; his motivation is entirely selfish, whatever patterns of social integration emerge from it. However, Hegel regarded self-consciousness as marked by universal features and not just by particularity.

Each man's consciousness is formally universal: 'Every self-consciousness knows itself as universal.' In other words, an individual man, unlike an animal, is aware that he has desires and is able to choose which he will pursue. Each individual is aware of his own identity, despite the changing flux of his desires and interests. At the same time, this sense of the universality of self-consciousness was purely formal for Hegel. The universality of the content of mind has to be developed, otherwise man will be an inwardly bifurcating being: a sense of universality on the one hand confronting a mass of episodic, particular desires on the other – the position into which Kant had been driven in his moral psychology. It was therefore vital, in order to give a coherent account of self-consciousness on his own terms, that Hegel could explain how the claims of universality could be made to equate with the particularity of desire and need, where Hegel says all is 'lost to particularity'. His answer to this problem was a developmental one. Man learns through participation in specific institutions to take into account a wider and wider range of values and membership of a social class is one way in which this educative or socialising process takes place. By being a member of a class, a man will come not only to have a sense of solidarity with others, but will also learn to take into account the claims and desires of others in forming his own intentions and purposes. Membership of a social class is, therefore, yet another way within the system of needs in which there is a dialectical relationship between the growth of self-consciousness on the one hand and the generation of forms of social integration on the other. Equally, participation in corporations is also vital to the development of an overall sense of community because they act as educative institutions, developing within individuals a consciousness of the claims of others which transcends the purely personal level. A sense of overall community in society has to be developed, or mediated (*vermittelt*) through specific supportive institutions. As G. A. Kelly argues, 'the corporation...harmonises man on a small scale and renders him apt for the fraternity of the state as he is naturally for the family'.[24]

At the same time, though they transcend the personal level, these institutions are rooted in specific economic functions and interests. As a result, they do not embody any sense of personal identification with an overall universal normative order in society, a feature which Hegel regarded as central to human life in the sense that man as a self-conscious being is open to universality. This universality is supplied in the political state proper and in the general cultural life of the community, particularly its art, religion and philosophy. Only within the state and in the culture of the community as a whole can the universal be realised. In the strictly political sphere, the particular individual is related to the state *via* the specificity of his social and class position within the Assembly of Estates. Although the modern world has realised most of all, and in many divergent directions, the values of freedom and autonomy, Hegel thought that the French Revolution and the subsequent Terror had demonstrated the undesirability of direct participatory democracy in the modern world. But, at the same time, despotism, however enlightened, was incompatible with the autonomy developed particularly within the economic activity of modern society. A political system had to be commensurate with the sense of freedom and individualism characteristic of economic life and in Hegel's view, while there could be no return to the direct participatory system of the Greek polis, a state representing individuals *via* classes or estates and thus minimising the disruptive political effects of particularity, was the most appropriate form of political community for the modern world.

Through the partial communities of the system of needs, and the representation of the most basic of these – the class or estate – through the Assembly of Estates in the political arena, both the enervation of the individual so characteristic of the productive processes in the economic sphere is diminished and in addition, civic ties are forged out of interests engendered naturally out of the economic sphere. As Kelly says, 'Hegelian politics is a healthy circulatory system and not an inert *pousse-café*.'[25] Universality is not imposed from above, but in Hegel's view exists in close relationship with interests and activities developed within the sphere of political economy. Hegel seemed to be confident that this is in fact how the institutions of the modern state would appear to its citizens once they had correctly understood it.

The principle of the modern state has prodigious strength and depth, because it allows the principle of subjectivity to progress to its culmination in the extreme of self-subsistent particularity [of the system of needs] and yet at the same time brings it back to the substantive unity and so maintains this unity in the principle of subjectivity itself (*PhR*, §266).

Hegel's state transcends the egoism of the market place but at the same time is not to be seen as an alien institution imposed upon the market.* In Hegel's view the system of needs is not just the 'realm of otherness'; on the contrary there is the basis for collective action to be found there. The market does have certain basic social orientations which, while not sufficient to allow it to be a self-equilibrating system, nevertheless act as mediating links between the state and the market itself. Without this soil within which the universal can grow, the state in its police functions would appear as external and imposed on the system of particularity present within the system of needs.

However, I want to argue that if we look back to the problem of poverty which was mentioned earlier in the paper we can perhaps test this general

* *Editor's note* – A different account of how the state, as an ethical community, transcends the market, is given in M. Westphal's essay.

thesis about the proper relationship between the state and the economy, and it is arguable that in seeking solutions to the problem of poverty the state, in Hegel's conception, is perhaps inhibited from effective action because of the residual but necessary role of individualism within the market.

As was argued earlier, Hegel sees poverty as an endemic feature of modern society and its consequences as devastating for those who are pressed down into poverty as the result of the operation of the market. Such individuals exist on the periphery of society; so can anything be done to relieve their condition? Certainly within the Hegelian framework that state has a responsibility here: after all part of the justification for his view of the role of the state is that the market gives rise to socially dysfunctional effects which require state intervention to mitigate. In the *Philosophy of Right* Hegel discusses a number of solutions to the problem. The first is the stimulation of the economy by state intervention, which despite its obvious attraction, Hegel did not see as feasible since the problem of poverty is caused by the tendency of the economy to produce too many goods for two few consumers, and a stimulation of the economy on his view would therefore only make matters worse (*PhR*, §245). Much more interesting though, in the present context, is his study of charity. His argument here is that while a state charitable system would alleviate the physical deprivation of poverty such a solution would fly in the face of those principles of self-maintenance and independence which are central to civil society. In such a welfare system: 'the needy would receive subsistence directly, not by means of their work, and this would violate the principle of civil society and the feeling of independence and self-respect in its individual members' (ibid.). This is precisely one of the sorts of features which are central to Habermas's argument. In seeking to legitimate itself to its citizenry the state is forced to pursue integrative policies but these policies are likely to provoke other kinds of system-crises – in this case a motivational crisis. The crisis of identity and citizenship can only be solved in a manner which undermines the work ethic. The state cannot impose such a system on everyone because in so doing it would undermine a central principle of civil society, namely the principle that a person's well being and social position should reflect his effort and contribution in the process of labour, production and exchange. Here is a crucial context in which the integration of a particular group of citizens into the political community is at stake and yet the state is prevented from effective action because it cannot find within its own civic culture a range of values which would legitimate its attempt to provide welfare and the benefits of citizenship for its members. The values of particularity characteristic of civil society militate in this case against the possibility of collective action to secure welfare, the promotion of which, as we saw earlier, is supposed by Hegel to be a right of citizens.

Of course, it is well known that in the *Philosophy of Right* Hegel argued that the problem of poverty required a solution which involved imperialism: the search for captive markets for overproduced goods and for land to settle poverty-stricken elements of the home population. However, while this conception has a great deal of interest, standing as it does in a tradition of writing upon imperialism and political economy which includes the work of Bukharin, Lenin, Rosa Luxemburg and Hobson, it is really irrelevant for the purposes of the problem posed in this paper because it is an explicit admission that the modern state cannot provide a home in the world for its citizens and that its identity and legitimation problems are intractable.

Hegel's problem is a central one for modern society as a number of recent writers, particularly Habermas, Offe, Bell and Hirsch have made clear to us. Our rationale for state intervention in the economy has to draw upon and make sense in terms of the values and motivations present *within* economic activity. However, on his own account, because he realistically sees that these legitimating resources are not present Hegel tends to see the modern state as being unable in the end to provide a way of integrating significant numbers of its members.

However, there are ways of finding solutions to the legitimation of state intervention for welfare purposes within the general framework of Hegel's system. The first and most obvious of these is that the economy can be stimulated and work found for those in poverty in such a way as not to exacerbate the problems of overproduction. This of course is the Keynsian answer and one which would allow the relationship between reward, welfare and work to be retained. This would be achieved by state intervention to secure economic activity so as to produce public works, roads and other utilities which would provide paid employment for those engaged in such projects, but at the same time such activity would not lead to the overproduction of consumer goods. However, the interesting difficulty here is that the Keynsian approach to economic management, which seems to be the most obvious solution open to the Hegelian, has recently been brought into question by those whose work has been a major source for posing the current problem of legitimation, namely Friedman, Hayek, Hirsch and Offe.

Another solution would be a welfare state based upon an insurance principle. In such a system the link between effort and welfare would be retained. Welfare benefits would depend on contributions which would reflect the effort in terms of labour and production of the contributor. Such a principle has, of course, been the one most clearly favoured within existing welfare states and a good account of the theoretical underpinning of such an approach and one which emphasises the way in which it coheres with an individualist political outlook is to be found in *The Calculus of Consent* by Buchanan and Tulloch.[26] The main difficulty within the Hegelian framework for such an understanding of the legitimacy of state welfare activity is that it still leaves out of account those who are unable to contribute to the welfare premiums: the chronically handicapped, the sick and the disabled. If the alleviation of this condition is a matter of private benevolence then clearly their integration into the state, granted what Hegel says about the social disadvantages from which the deprived suffer, is going to be a private arrangement (*PhR*, §253), which no one can demand as a *right*; or this group is going to be seen as having a right to have their welfare promoted irrespective of the fact that they have been unable to act as contributors within an insurance framework. The basis for such a claim would be that their deprivation and poverty is in no sense their own fault and that therefore they should not bear the costs of the arbitrary misfortunes of nature.

However, at this point we can perhaps see how there are grounds within Hegel's own position for a far more radical approach to the problem of poverty. If those who suffer from deprivation did so in a way that is not the result of their own action then, as was argued above, they may not be held responsible for the consequences of their position or for the costs to society in providing a remedy for it. This seems clear in those cases where deprivation is the result of physical infirmity for which the agent is not responsible. In Hegel's view though, poverty in general is a structural phenomenon in society, the result of the operation of civil society when it is in a state of 'unimpeded activity' and not the result of some *personal* failing on the part of the poor. Hegel clearly regarded the study of the structural causes of poverty in society to be of prime importance in social theory (*PhR*, §242) and on the basis of his own views on this issue it might be thought that the deprivation and humiliation characteristic of poverty are quite undeserved and unmerited. From this point it might then be argued that *if* poverty is the result of the operation of civil society and not a personal failing, and that civil society on the whole works for everyone's advantage, both in material terms and in terms of the independence and freedom which it yields the ordinary citizen, then a welfare system designed to compensate those who are made poor by the operation of the system could be seen as part of the necessary cost of maintaining the system. Although in a particular case the operation of such a welfare system might drive a wedge between welfare and labour and thus possibly cast doubt on what Hegel sees as a central principle of civil society, this could be seen as a necessary concession required to maintain both civil society and therefore this principle more generally.

Thus it is certainly true, as Avineri argues, that 'Hegel's concept of civil society and hence his whole political philosophy, is premised on an integration of the major tenets of modern political economy into his philosophical system'[27] and this attempted integration on Hegel's part is an extremely fertile aspect of his political theory. On the one hand Hegel claims to do full justice to the egoism and particularity of civil society; at the same time he rejected the view, currently fashionable, that the state should not intervene in the market and leave it to secure its own equilibrium. The state has a responsibility to the community as a whole and in embodying the collective will of its citizens it acts as an ethical substance, as a community. But at the same time, Hegel maintained – and we have some reason to doubt this – that this collective action of the state can be legitimated in terms of the values and motivations which characterise human economic activity. It is the opinion of those who have raised the problem of the contemporary legitimation crisis that this is not the case and that the integration which Hegel claims to achieve between the particularistic values of the market and the collectivist values of the state is illusory because his insistence that civil society, as the system of needs, encapsulates at a deep level a communitarian relationship is mistaken. It is mistaken because a sense of community has to make reference to the attitudes and intentions of those in the communitarian relationship, and while he does say that my labour for others becomes my conscious object he does not explain how this is to come about, nor does he explain the effect that such a recognition would have on the market economy. Community is not just an *effect* or a consequence of basically private, maximising activity: it has rather to depend upon a real sense of involvement with others, valuing those others and acting with fellow-feeling towards them. Because those motivations are not characteristic of the market and because a sense of solidarity cannot exist without them, it is not surprising that the real motives required by the market activity reappear and render impossible in certain crucial areas state action for the common good.

Economy, utility and community in Hegel's theory of civil society

A. S. WALTON

1. Introduction

Disillusionment with the effects and failures of capitalist societies has typically, and most forcefully, been expressed within the marxist tradition. The criticisms offered have been of various kinds, but have included at least two general propositions. First, that capitalist economic forms are inimical to the development of human powers and capacities; that is, they are alienating, reducing both worker and capitalist to a condition of spiritless interdependence. Second, that the rectification of this state of affairs is dependent upon a total restructuring of society in such a way that the capitalist form of economic organisation is transformed. Marx expressed this point in relation to Hegel by urging the abolition of civil society on the grounds that it did not, as Hegel supposed it did, express the claims of individual freedom and personality. Rather, Marx construed civil society as the means by which freedom and personality were negated.

In this essay, I shall attempt to examine Hegel's account of civil society with a view to elucidating its distinctiveness from both the utilitarianism of classical political economy and marxism. In doing this I shall hope to show that Hegel offers an account of civil society and the place of economic activity within it which contains features of both classical political economy and marxism, but in such a way that it presents an alternative to both of them. The alternative which Hegel proposes is derived in part from a criticism of both political economy and his observations of economic practice and organisation in England. What Hegel offers, therefore, is a sharply critical perspective on certain features of the way capitalist economic organisation had developed. However, his own theorising of the place and structure of the economy does not presuppose the abolition of private ownership of the means of production, and indeed of civil society *in toto* as Marx subsequently recommended, but rather certain changes within capitalist economic organisation and the structure of civil society. What, precisely, this involves will be taken up in the course of this essay.

In the interpretive literature it has been usual to suppose that Hegel speaks of civil society, and particularly of the role of economic activity within it, as an autonomous sphere of experience governed by its own inexorable laws, and subject, inevitably, to persistent and endemic crises and problems which can only be alleviated, although not substantially resolved, through the intervention of the state. According to this view the main difference between Hegel and the political economists is his recommendation of a more extensive role for the state in the economic life of the community,[1] but he is seen to be in agreement with them in so far as the main feature of civil society is the individual's drive for personal satisfaction.[2] Moreover, Hegel is often depicted as having been unable to find any solutions to the major problems confronting civil society, for example crises of overproduction and poverty. It is supposed that he reckoned these problems to be insoluble.[3] In this essay I shall suggest an alternative approach to Hegel's theory of civil society. I shall try to indicate some of the ways in which he treats economic activity as an integral feature of the development and expression of essential human capacities, and the implications this has for the internal structure and consciousness of civil society. Furthermore, I shall suggest that Hegel was not as pessimistic about finding solutions to the problems facing civil society as some of his interpreters have suggested.*

In order to defend and present this interpretation I shall draw to some extent on recently published texts. Hitherto, readers of Hegel interested in his theory of civil society have only had available to them, apart from the early writings, the published version of the *Philosophy of Right* and the section on Objective Spirit in the *Encyclopedia*. More recently further evidence of Hegel's views has become available in the form of his students' lecture-notes taken during his various Berlin lectures on the philosophy of right. Of particular interest are the notes of Hegel's student Griesheim who recorded in some detail Hegel's sharply critical opinions concerning the development of laissez-faire utilitarian economic liberalism in nineteenth-century English society.[4] From this critique there emerges a clearer picture of his model of a rational economic society. This critique, seen in the context of some of Hegel's general arguments about human powers and capacities, enables us to see more clearly why he thought economic activity was important, how he thought the implications involved in it for human development could be fully realised, and how civil society could be re-organised so as to overcome the major problems of crises of overproduction and poverty.

* R. Plant's essay in this volume represents such a pessimistic interpretation.

2. Hegel, political economy and marxism

Some general features of the utilitarian model of the political economists can
be briefly sketched. According to this model society is conceived atomistically
as an aggregate of individuals each pursuing his own satisfaction. Economic
activity and the relations associated with it possess a strictly instrumental
significance in so far as they are a means to the achievement of individual
satisfaction. The individual is taken to be a rational calculator of the means
to satisfaction in a competitive situation. The rationality involved in this
calculative process is free from value considerations since it is technical
rationality; that is it specifies the empirical and analytical conditions of
satisfaction.

This instrumental view of rationality is closely associated with an
empiricist philosophy of mind. For the empiricist there are certain irreducible
psychological states of individuals which can be identified as the ends of
human activity;[5] rationality involves the determination of the means most
appropriate to the securing of those ends. In utilitarian economic theory this
philosophical outlook issues in a model of economic man as a rational
calculator of optimum satisfaction.[6]

The utilitarian economic theory to which Hegel addressed himself in the
first part of the nineteenth century was the laissez-faire theory of the classical
political economists. Influenced by hedonistic and associational psychology
the political economists supposed that it was possible to identify general laws
of human nature which governed economic activity. Moreover, they argued
that there was a natural harmony of interests which could be realised through
a minimum level of government intervention. Economic progress would be
assured by allowing rational self-interested individuals to pursue their own
interests in the free market.[7] In the *Wealth of Nations* Adam Smith spoke
of the 'system of natural liberty' which needed to be preserved except for
the purposes of protecting society from invasion, protecting one individual
from the oppression of another, and providing public utilities. Hegel was
familiar with the writings of Smith and Ricardo, but he was not concerned
only with the laissez-faire aspect of their conception of the economy. He was
also exercised by the model of man on which their thought was based and
which gave rise to their laissez-faire position. I shall in due course attempt
to indicate some aspects of Hegel's critique of this model.

The utilitarian model contrasts markedly with the marxist position,
according to which rational economic activity is dependent upon the
transformation of contemporary society and its concomitant utilitarian
individualism. Rational economic activity is held to be expressive as opposed
to instrumental, and mediated by co-operative rather than competitive social
relationships. It is expressive because it is the manifestation of men's essentially

human powers and capacities and is a condition of their development. It is mediated by co-operative social relationships because the development of human capacities is dependent upon the realisation of men's *species-being*: rational economic activity embodies men's ability for social harmony and co-operation rather than individualistic competition. These arguments emerge clearly in the philosophical anthropology of the 1844 *Paris Manuscripts* and provide the basis for a fundamental criticism of capitalist socio-economic forms.

In the 1843 *Critique of Hegel's Philosophy of Right*,[8] Marx offered a critical onslaught against Hegel's conceptualisation of civil society as a distinct and identifiable aspect of a rational and harmonious community. In the *Philosophy of Right* Hegel had argued that the claims of particularity required concrete embodiment in a complex of practices and institutions geared to the pursuit of personal goals and projects. Thus, he speaks of the 'development of particularity to self-subsistence' (*PhR*, §185). It is the emergence of civil society as a sphere of individual freedom and choice which provides one of the most crucial features of the modern world, and which differentiates it from classical Greece as Hegel interpreted that society.

Hegel's characterisation of modern civil society and the function of the economy within it clearly reveals the influence of both the theoretical framework provided by the classical political economists, above all Adam Smith, and his knowledge of nineteenth-century economic development as he observed it in England. He recognises, and accepts, the development of a system of competitive economic relationships, but he presents his acceptance with a number of crucial qualifications, some of which will be taken up in more detail later in this essay. First, he denies that the pursuit of personal satisfaction is an end in itself as it is for the utilitarian political economist. This argument is developed in the context of a consideration of the role of education:

Similarly, the feeling that needs, their satisfaction, the pleasures and comforts of private life, and so forth are absolute ends, implies treating education as a mere means to these ends (*PhR*, §187).

Second, he argues that the individual's relationship with the external world is an aspect of the development of the powers of the mind:

Mind attains its actuality only by creating a dualism within itself, by submitting itself to physical needs and the chain of these external necessities, and so imposing on itself this barrier and this finitude, and finally by maturing [bildet] itself inwardly even when under this barrier until it overcomes it and attains its objective reality in the finite (*PhR*, §187).

The individual's relationship with the external world is, thus, not only a means to satisfaction, but is constitutive of the growth of his essential powers and capacities.

This argument is further developed in the theory of private property. It is denied that property ownership has only instrumental functions:

> If emphasis is placed on my needs, then the possession of property appears as a means to their satisfaction, but the true position is that, from the standpoint of freedom property is the first embodiment of freedom and so is itself a substantive end (*PhR*, §45; see also §489).

Third, Hegel denies that the social relations involved in the pursuit of personal satisfaction have *only* instrumental significance; and, further, he denies that economic rationality consists in the application of criteria which are determined through strictly empirical and analytic enquiry and therefore divorced from considerations of value.

These various qualifications distinguish Hegel's position from that of the utilitarian, but not in a way which shares Marx's concern to see civil society transcended. Hegel shares with the utilitarian the view that economic activity has a rationale in the pursuit and satisfaction of individual needs, but denies that an explanation of rational economic activity is reducible to an account of the satisfaction of individual needs as the ends of activity. He shares with Marx the view that economic activity is both expressive of essentially human powers and capacities, and integrally tied to men's social being. He wishes to demontrate the respects in which the pursuit of personal satisfaction in a competitive situation has expressive as opposed to merely instrumental significance, and that it implies his social as well as his particular being.

Hegel states these points in relation to civil society through an application of the notion of appearance (*Erscheinung*).

> The right of individuals to their particular satisfaction is also contained in the ethical substantial order, since particularity is the outward appearance of the ethical order – a mode in which that order is existent (*PhR*, §154).

In the *Logic*, Hegel's comments on the notion of appearance arise within the doctrine of essence, and there are several ideas which directly bear upon the theory of civil society. First, appearance in particularity is intimately connected with the universal essence which it expresses. Secondly, there is an important sense in which appearance *is* essence in so far as the latter can only be developed and actualised in the former. Third, the particularity of appearance cannot be understood except in terms of the whole of which it is a part and an expression; the particular does not have independence.[9]

The description of civil society as the 'outward appearance of ethical order' carries with it significant implications. An understanding of civil society requires an appreciation of the 'essence' it expresses. Civil society is thus a critically important aspect of the expression and development of human powers and capacities in so far as they are developed within the 'ethical substantial order'. Since appearance is the manifestation of an underlying essence, and civil society the 'outward appearance of the ethical order', it is important to identify the bearing of that order on the particularity of civil society. Civil society must be understood as being decisively mediated by the general ethical and social context of which it is a part.

3. Human powers and capacities

In this section of the essay a number of aspects of Hegel's theory of human powers and capacities will be outlined as a prelude to a further consideration of the theory of civil society. The theory of civil society can only be understood in the context of Hegel's theory of man and the respects in which the social world is necessary for his self-realisation.

(a) Hegel develops a theory of human capacities in which the ideas of self-determination and expression are central. A man has developed his capacities to the extent that he is self-determined and has expressed himself in his activities. This argument is given substantial elaboration by Hegel and has a number of elements, but one particularly important aspect for the purposes of this essay is the significance attaching to the pursuit of personal satisfaction. In Hegel's view, as we have noted, personal satisfaction is not an end in itself, but an aspect of the individual's capacity for self-determination; it is important, however, since only when a man has related to the external world through the medium of what is peculiarly his own, namely his desires and interests, has he fully expressed *himself* in his activities. 'Pursuant to the moment of the particularity of the will, it has in addition a content consisting of determinate aims and, as exclusive individuality, it has this content at the same time as an external world confronting it' (*PhR*, §34). The satisfaction of personal desires and interests therefore has a significant individualising function.

(b) Hegel takes the view that men are beings who develop their capacities in using them; their capacities develop through the medium of their activities. What is merely potential is rendered actual through action.[10] In this respect the constitutive significance of men's relationship with the external world is crucial. The external world exists as something alien and external, and a fully satisfied and self-conscious being is one who has overcome all externality in the sense of subordinating it theoretically and practically to his will. Speaking of property ownership, Hegel says that 'a person must translate his freedom into an external sphere in order to exist as Idea' (*PhR*, §41). Modern civil society is significant because it makes possible the extensive mastery of nature. Emancipation from primitive dependence on nature is not only a way of being more satisfied in the utilitarian sense; it is a way of furthering one's spiritual powers, of mastering and controlling the external world and shaping it through the medium of peculiarly human values and conceptions. Like Rousseau, Hegel deplores some of the consequences of modern civil society, but unlike Rousseau he welcomes material progress because it offers, potentially, an important sphere for human expression. Like Marx, Hegel recognises the potentiality contained in men's relationship with the external world for the development of men's rational powers and capacities.

(c) In Hegel's view, human capacities and the potentialities contained in economic activity, can only be fully actualised in the context of a properly ordered social context. The norms and values of the social context are constitutive of the individual's capacity for rationality:

> The right of individuals to be subjectively destined to freedom is fulfilled when they belong to an actual ethical order, because their conviction of their freedom finds its truth in such an objective order, and it is an ethical order that they are actually in possession of their own essence or their own inner universality (*PhR*, §153).[11]

This involves the claim that men are essentially social beings and that they only develop fully when they live in communities which are characterised by norms and values which adequately embody that social being. The implication of this is that a community which is dominated by the ethic of utilitarian individualism is not adequate.[12]

This argument has important implications for Hegel's theory of rational economic activity. The application of empirical and analytical criteria in respect of the determination of means to ends is rejected as a sufficient condition of rationality. Economic rationality is, rather, dependent upon the clarification of the norms and values of ethical life. A coherent ethical life is thus a condition of economic rationality.

(d) There is a final aspect of Hegel's theory of human capacities that I should like to consider. It is usual in the interpretive literature to stress Hegel's theory of community and the value he places on cultural coherence. One recent interpreter has suggested the following:

> To restore the harmony of personal experience and to recreate a closely-knit community in contrast to the fragmentation of the person and growing social divisions were the two basic aims of members of [Hegel's] generation.[13]

This is undoubtedly a central feature of Hegel's thought, and it would be a mistake to underestimate its importance. It is important, however, not to exaggerate this aspect, or at least it is necessary to view it in the right perspective. That is to say, there are compelling reasons why we should focus on Hegel's theory of the individual as the subject of social action, and therefore on the respects in which the theory of community is related to the theory of subjectivity. This is a complex issue which needs to be seen in the context of Hegel's theories of will and subjectivity and in the detailed context of their relationship with the community. There is no opportunity here to consider these issues in detail, and it is possible to do little more than assert a number of propositions about Hegel's thought.

Hegel is primarily concerned with the individual as the subject of social action and as a pursuer of personal goals and projects. Undeniably he speaks of the respects in which men's characters are formed by the community, and of how the community presents ethical demands upon them and is constitutive of the obligations pressing upon them; he speaks of men occupying particular roles within society, and of being socialised into the norms and values which underpin the role structure of the society. He rejects an atomistic conception of the individual and theories of ethics and politics which rest upon deductions from alleged characteristics attaching to individuals. Nevertheless, he does not speak of ethical life as a structure of norms and values demanding unreflective commitment on the part of individuals. He does not speak of the end of ethical conduct as the maintenance and promotion of the community. He speaks of society as the source of morality in the sense that ethical obligations arise within it; but he does not hold the further view, which is not entailed, that society is also the end of morality.[14] The ends of human action are the freely determined personal goals and projects of individual subjects. For Hegel the community constitutes a *medium* which is drawn upon by individuals, which is a source of their obligations, and which is reconstituted through their use of it. The community stands, analogously, in relation to the individual in much the same way as the rules and conventions of language stand in relation to particular statements; the rules and conventions of language do not determine what one says, but they are conditions of intelligibility and standards of excellence which are, in addition, transformed in being used.[15]

If it is correct to emphasise the importance of the individual in Hegel's theory and to give the pursuit of personal goals and projects a more prominent place, then it follows that civil society is invested with greater significance than is sometimes suggested. It has to be seen less as a problem which Hegel has come to terms with, but rather as a solution to a problem, namely the problem of how individuals can develop their capacities as active subjects whose development is in part dependent upon personalised control over the external world.

4. Hegel's critique of utilitarian political economy

In the context of the theory of civil society, the essential attributes of
Hegel's account of human powers and capacities can be captured through
a consideration of his criticism of utilitarian economic liberalism. It is clear,
particularly from the Griesheim notes, that Hegel is attacking all of the central
propositions of classical political economy. He rejects the view that the
economy possesses an essential harmony and coherence of its own which is
realised through allowing individuals freely to pursue their personal
satisfaction.[16] He rejects the view that rational economic activity takes place
when individuals live in a society which encourages them to pursue their
personal satisfaction as the major end of human activity. Furthermore, he
rejects the view that economic relationships have only instrumental
importance in so far as they are a means to personal satisfaction.

In his Berlin lectures Hegel speaks at length about the problems of
economic liberalism. He stresses the precariousness of contemporary economic
life in England, and regards this as a direct effect of the application of the
laissez-faire principle that individuals prosper best when left free to make their
own rational calculations. In Hegel's view the economy is not a self-regulating
mechanism the dynamic of which is individual rational self-interest. On the
contrary, the practical consequences of laissez-faire are frequent crises of
overproduction resulting in enormous hardship for those who cannot survive
the ups and downs of economic life.

Hegel regards the growth of inequality as one of the most disastrous
consequences of English economic life. He speaks particularly of the great
wealth of London, and of how wealth has become concentrated in fewer
and fewer hands. He makes the point that the larger one's capital the smaller
the proportion of its return is required for subsistence, whereas the man with
a small stock of capital requires a larger proportion of it for subsistence and
is therefore more vulnerable in times of crisis (Ilting 4, p. 494). This point
is associated with a criticism of monopoly capitalism. He speaks of the
progressive crushing of the smaller capitalists by the larger ones and of the
resulting monopoly, and remarks that the monopoly of capital is the 'worst
kind of monopoly' (Ilting 4, p. 627).

Hegel focusses on the psychological effects of laissez-faire capitalism.
Modern civil society depends so much on contingency that men are forced
to live for momentary luxury (Ilting 4, p. 627); their lives lack order and
design, and their control over the external world is precarious and unstable;
it is not subject to the self-conscious control which, as we have seen, is for
Hegel a condition of human self-realisation.

Hegel is much concerned in his lectures, as he is in the published version
of the philosophy of right, with the issue of poverty. In §245 of the published

version he argues that charity is an inadequate way of dealing with poverty since the individual does not derive subsistence from his own efforts, and this militates against the 'feeling of individual independence and self-respect' (*PhR*, §245). In his lectures he develops this argument in the context of a consideration of the importance of labour as an activity (Ilting 4, p. 497), arguing that labour is an aspect of self-determination and freedom. If there is poverty individuals lack the opportunity for self-conscious control over the external world. He argues, furthermore, that a commercial (rather than charitable) relationship between individuals is a more adequate one because it involves recognition of the other's freedom. Commercial relationships therefore have an expressive as well as an instrumental significance; they express recognitive social relationships and are not merely a means to personal satisfaction. This expressive significance is lost, however, in the presence of great inequality and poverty.

The issue of inequality has important implications for Hegel's view of the causes, nature, and significance of poverty. It has been suggested by some interpreters[17] that poverty is an endemic feature of modern civil society because a critical aspect of it is the phenomenon of relative deprivation. That is to say, poverty cannot be understood in purely quantitative terms, but concerns differentiations in wealth between persons. Undoubtedly Hegel does employ the relative deprivation argument, and identifies relative deprivation as a feature of English civil society, but it is far less certain that he regards it as an inevitable feature. The implication of his analysis is that relative deprivation is a significant problem only in a situation of immense inequality, when the poor are presented with the spectacle of the great wealth of the rich. Thus poverty arises from 'the luxury of the business classes and their passion for extravagance' (*PhR*, §253), which also involves a monopoly of the 'broader freedoms and especially the intellectual benefits of civil society' (*PhR*, §245).

The task, then, is to find ways in which massive differentiations of wealth and opportunity can be adjusted. In this respect it is significant that Hegel says that the extravagance of the business classes provides the 'ethical ground of poverty' (*PhR*, §253). As an 'ethical ground' it does not have a determinate and ineradicable existence in social life; it is not simply given. It is subject to human evaluation and control. The causes of poverty lie in men's attitudes towards one another and in the grossly unequal society to which they give rise. Poverty is not the effect of wholly determinate psychological states of individuals, or of fixed structural conditions of society. Hegel is clearly not an egalitarian, but he does recognise the deleterious effects of inequality on social harmony and mutual recognition. And he traces the origins of inequality to their source in the unrestricted and unmediated drive towards personal accumulation which results in crises of overproduction, the weakest losing out, and hence increasing divisions between rich and poor.[18] Towards the end of his life, in the *English Reform Bill*, Hegel further expressed his concern about inequality. 'In England the contrast between prodigious wealth and utterly embarrassed penury is enormous.'[19]

These issues can be given further clarification by considering Hegel's account of the significance of colonisation. There is an extremely interesting observation in the Griesheim notes concerning England and the issue of colonisation. It has been supposed that Hegel speaks of colonisation as an inevitable feature of civil societies[20] in view of recurrent crises of over-production and increasing poverty. This view of Hegel is associated with the general view that he is unable to find internal solutions to the problems of civil society, which is seen to be a complex of relations possessing its own internal dynamic which drives men beyond the boundaries of the state. In his lectures Hegel considers the question of colonisation in the context of whether or not laissez-faire is a cause of economic progress. He notes that England has experienced great economic progress under laissez-faire, but argues that this is because it has experienced rather special conditions. Of particular importance is the fact that England has a world market and through colonisation has spread its economic influence to all parts of the globe thereby achieving an unprecedented monopoly of economic resources. He remarks that 'everywhere in the world one finds Englishmen' (Ilting 3, p. 626). His argument is, then, that England has only prospered under laissez-faire because of these special conditions.

The issue of colonisation is taken up again in the context of a discussion of whether or not the closed character of the corporations is a cause of colonisation. He admits that it may be, but argues that under unlimited free enterprise colonisation is even more necessary because so many people lose out in the competitive process (Ilting 4, p. 629).

Several significant points emerge from these arguments. First, when Hegel speaks of colonisation as a solution to the problems of civil society it is clear that he regards it as a solution which only one especially well placed country has been able to take advantage of, namely England. Second, it is clear that he does not regard English civil society as a paradigm instance of how civil society in the modern community should be organised; the problems he identifies in modern civil society are not reckoned to be inevitable features of it, but rather problems to which solutions need to be found. Third, the solutions to the problems of civil society lie at a deeper level than the palliative of colonisation. The deeper level at which the solution to the problems of civil society must take place lies, for Hegel, in a fundamental restructuring of the culture and organisation of the community, and the creation of a different model of society from the one which he observed emerging in England, and thus the creation of conditions under which colonisation is no longer necessary. In particular, the solution offered involves the growth of different attitudes towards the conduct of economic life and the character of economic relationships. For Hegel, the problems of civil society cannot be dealt with by changes at the economic level alone; it is not sufficient simply to make adjustments to economic activity through state action or by seeking new venues for economic activity abroad. The problems of civil society are an expression of more fundamental and pervasive problems of society as a whole. Thus, the problems of the economy must be tackled at the level of society in general. This means challenging the dominance of utilitarian individualism and the practices and institutions supportive of it; it means advocating a social structure and institutional framework more conducive to the growth of fundamentally different attitudes and values thereby harnessing economic activity as an aspect of the development and expression of essentially human powers and capacities.[21]

5. Hegel's model of civil society

In the preceeding section an attempt was made to outline some aspects of Hegel's criticisms of the pervasiveness of the utilitarian ethic in English civil society. This section will be concerned with the kind of model of civil society that Hegel recommends, and with the forms of consciousness which he regards as necessary for rational economic life.

He begins by identifying the 'system of needs' as a distinct level of experience within civil society. The 'concrete person who is himself an object of his particular aims, is as a totality of wants and a mixture of caprice, and physical necessity, one principle of civil society' (*PhR*, § 182). The system of needs is the complex of reciprocal relationships which promote the satisfaction of individual interests; men become dependent upon one another for mutual satisfaction. The satisfaction of personal interests involves using others as a means and competing with them.

This raises the question of the significance of the system of needs. It has been suggested[22] that an important aspect of Hegel's theory of the system of needs is the respect in which he contrasts animal with human needs (*PhR*, § 190). It is this which is said to differentiate Hegel from political economy and which establishes the satisfaction of needs as an aspect of self-consciousness; individuals are not tied to particular needs but are free to develop new needs and 'mental needs arising from ideas' (*PhR*, § 194). This in itself, however, is not sufficient to establish Hegel's distinctness from utilitarian political economy. First, there is nothing to prevent a utilitarian from arguing that the needs men experience are socially developed and are not fixed and given in nature; a utilitarian need not deny that men can develop new needs and that they are capable of the kinds of mental processes described by Hegel

(*PhR*, §§ 190, 191, 193, 194). Second, Hegel himself argues that the growth of the sophisticated system of needs can lead to a kind of dependence in which 'dependence and want increase ad infinitum' (*PhR*, § 195). This is dependence on luxury which has no 'qualitative limits' (*PhR*, § 195). Hegel is sharply critical of the respects in which men become grossly dependent upon the pursuit of luxury which gives rise, in his view especially in London, to a kind of depravity.[23] This is seen by him to be a consequence of the relentless drive towards personal satisfaction and of men's ability to create for themselves more and more needs in contrast with the fixed and given needs of the animal.

Why, then, is the system of needs important, and how does it relate to the previous discussion of Hegel's theory of human capacities? In his early Jena writings Hegel was deeply pessimistic; he sees men trapped in the mutual dependency of economic relations and driven on by the pursuit of personal satisfaction which gives rise to unintended consequences over which they have no control. He speaks of their alienation and degradation and is unable to find a solution. In the later writings he is unable to solve the problem of alienation in the labour process,[24] but there is a shift away from the hopeless tone of the Jena lectures. In the earlier writings it is clear that Hegel believed that economic relationships provided insuperable barriers to human development; in the later writings the system of needs is firmly established as a condition of human development. In this respect we need to examine its significance for individuality and its intimate relationship with the norms and values of ethical life. It becomes clear that the distinction between Hegel and the utilitarian lies less in the respects in which the former speaks of human transcendence of natural needs than in his rejection of the utilitarian view that personal satisfaction is the end of human activity.

Of particular importance in Hegel's later views is his attempt to consider the system of needs against the background of a theory of law, rights and personality. In this respect his attitude towards Kant is significant. In his early writings, for example, the *Natural Law* essay, Hegel takes a largely negative attitude towards Kant's practical philosophy which is treated as abstract and devoid of content. In his Nürnberg period and after, the influence of Kant is marked, in particular regarding Kant's insistence on the integrity of the individual and the respects in which law is a condition of personality. For Kant, law was not a restriction upon individual freedom, but rather its condition. Hegel's theory of the system of needs must be seen in the context of this view of personality and law. The system of needs is also a set of relationships between property-owning individuals whose rights are secured through law (*PhR*, §§ 211, 213). In the early writings and lectures the legal presuppositions of the system of needs are not fully appreciated by Hegel. In the later writings, under the influence of Kant, he is concerned with the system of needs in so far as it involves relations between free persons possessing property as the embodiment of their personality.

The establishment of individuality is, further, intimately connected with the social aspect of experience, and a number of arguments are employed to demonstrate this. As was noted above, Hegel distinguished between animal and human needs, and it was suggested that this distinction by itself did not enable us to clearly distinguish Hegel from the utilitarian. This distinction does, however, bear upon Hegel's view of the importance of the social context and the respects in which the individual's development is dependent upon his ability to realise his essentially social being. The utilitarian can speak of needs being socially developed, but this does not have any special significance for him since the end of activity is personal satisfaction. For Hegel, on the contrary, the identification of the social character of needs is the identification of a significant constitutive feature of the growth of human capacities which has important ethical implications. The advances of modern civil society in releasing men from primitive dependence upon nature and natural needs results in the growth of shared concepts and ideas regarding needs. Needs are socially developed; to have needs is to have social needs and to draw upon shared concepts. The needs men experience do not arise within them as basic naturally given wants which require satisfaction; they are the result of shared concepts which the individual learns in the course of living in a society:

Since in social needs, as the conjunction of immediate or natural needs with mental needs arising from ideas, it is needs of the latter type which because of their universality make themselves preponderant, this social moment has in it the aspect of liberation, i.e. the strict natural necessity of need is obscured and man is concerned with his own opinion, indeed with an opinion which is universal...(*PhR*, §194).

The ethical implications of the contextual character of the individual's needs are brought out through the notion of recognition. Hegel's arguments about recognition are usually associated with his treatment of the master/slave relationship in the *Phenomenology of Spirit*, but it is important to notice that he uses arguments about recognition in a number of other contexts. In the *Philosophy of Right* Hegel says that when 'needs and means become abstract in quality, abstraction is also a character of the reciprocal relation of individuals to one another. This abstract character, universality, is the character of being recognised and is the moment which makes concrete, i.e. social, the isolated and abstract needs and their ways and means of satisfaction' (*PhR*, §192). In the system of needs men are able to recognise one another as common participants in a scheme of reciprocal relationships; the other's needs and interests are comprehensible because they are informed by a common system of concepts which provides the basis for social recognition.

The apparently atomistic system of needs on closer inspection can be seen to generate the basis of common understanding and ethical ties.

The social character of the system of needs is further developed through groups and classes. The level of groups and classes provides a major aspect of Hegel's theory of the rational organisation of civil society and is decisive in the overcoming of utilitarian individualism as the dominant ethic in economic activity. Utilitarian individualism is transcended by the mediation of attitudes and values which give expression to the individual's social being. Groups are integral to the growth of a social medium adequate to the rational pursuit of personal goals. They provide a sphere of social relationships which enable the individual to identify with others, thereby fundamentally altering his attitude towards his economic activity and the relations involved in it.

In his Berlin lectures on the philosophy of right Hegel describes the social whole as a *totality*, and distinguishes a totality from a *collectivity*. He speaks of the need for a community to be differentiated into groups and classes which are themselves totalities. He says that the 'true totality is not a collectivity, but one which is necessary in itself. A collectivity exists only where individuals are externally related. In a totality the bond between men is essentially internal' (Ilting 4, p. 510). A community requires subordinate spheres for the development of ethical relationships; it requires specific social groups with which the individual can identify. A totality can only sustain itself and realise the essentially internal character of its relations if the differentiations within it are themselves internally related and constitute ethical totalities rather than collectivities.

In this respect Hegel pays particular attention to the corporations which overcome the extreme particularity of the business class. On one level they are organisations which are instrumental in helping and supporting their members by ensuring their livelihood. However, they are also important in so far as they are vehicles for the development of forms of consciousness which are radically different from the extreme particularity of utilitarian individualism. In a rational community economic activity is informed by a sense of common values and ideals which are not reducible to rational self-interest. In a rational civil society men pursue their own goals and projects, but in a manner mediated by shared values adequate to their essentially social being. In order to stress the ethical character of the corporation Hegel says that it is ethical like the state; it mediates between the family and the state, and like them possesses ethical characteristics (Ilting 4, p. 619). The corporation is a 'little state' (ibid. p. 621).

Hegel's theory of the corporation involves a direct attack upon the model of man as an individualistic calculator of economic satisfaction. For Hegel rational economic action cannot be divorced from a consideration of shared social values:

The so-called 'natural' right of exercising one's skill and thereby earning what there is to be earned is restricted within the Corporation only in so far as it is therein made rational instead of natural. That is to say, it becomes freed from personal opinion and contingency, saved from endangering either the individual workman or others, recognised, guaranteed, and at the same time elevated to conscious effort for a common end (*PhR*, §254).

In his lectures Hegel takes up this theme in the context of a discussion of the argument for the abolition of the corporations. He notes that it is often claimed that trade and industry would improve in the absence of the corporations (Hotho's notes, Ilting 3, p. 711). Once again his remarks on England are critical for an understanding of his position. He argues that unlimited free enterprise is only conducive to great progress because of England's command of world markets. 'The example of England should not be quoted since England has the whole world as a market in a way in which no other people has' (Ilting, 4, p. 625). He continues by advocating the corporations as institutions which would modify the ethic of unmediated self-seeking, and develops the argument about the ways in which the corporations modify the principle of self-interest through further analysis of the notion of recognition. He argues that social atomism is conducive to unmediated self-interest, and that the pursuit of material satisfaction becomes a substitute for genuine social recognition:

Unless he is a member of an authorised Corporation...an individual is without rank or dignity, his isolation reduces his business to mere self-seeking, and his livelihood and satisfaction become insecure. Consequently, he has to try to gain recognition for himself by giving external proofs of success in his business, and to these proofs no limits can be set (*PhR*, §253; cp. Ilting 4, p. 626).

The lack of social recognition, the failure to develop stable ethical relationships, drives men perpetually to increase their material wealth; they are trapped in an infinite movement towards further accumulation and take wealth as a measure of their worth as human beings. Hegel does not see this as an inevitable feature of civil society; it is only characteristic of civil societies, such as England, in which ethical ties and values fail to enter into and inform economic activity.

Membership of the corporation is, in addition, of great importance for a man's relationship with the rest of the community, and once more raises the issue of recognition. To be a member of a corporation is to be a member of a social group which has the recognition of other members of the community. It is recognised that the individual 'belongs to a whole which is itself an organ of the entire society, and that he is actively concerned in promoting the comparatively disinterested ends of this whole. Thus, he commands the respect due to one in his social position' (*PhR*, §253). The corporations are vehicles for the development and expression of the general social values of ethical life, they mediate between the individual and the general community, and are decisive in the overcoming of the ethic of utilitarian individualism.[25]

6. Conclusion

In this essay an attempt has been made to suggest a number of closely related themes in Hegel's theory of civil society. First, it has been argued that the satisfaction of needs is not an end in itself, but an aspect of the individual's self-conscious control over the external word. The system of needs is a complex of relationships between persons embodying their personality in legally recognised property. As such it is incorporated as an element within Hegel's theory of expressive action in which personal control of the external world is crucial.

Second, it was suggested that the individual's self-conscious control of the external world is dependent upon incorporating into economic activity within the system of needs ethical values not reducible to self-interest. It was not suggested that for Hegel personal satisfaction should be abandoned or subordinated to some other end; the system of needs is a sphere in which individuals can seek their own satisfaction and compete with others. Nevertheless, the ways in which satisfaction is sought is informed by ethical considerations. In a rational civil society, economic relationships are not merely instrumental to personal satisfaction; they also express, and are mediated by, the individual's sense of community and identity with others. In this respect the corporations perform the important function of engendering recognitive social values. Furthermore, to be a member of a particular social group is to have the general recognition of the members of other social groups since groups are generally recognised elements in a common ethical life.

Third, a central concern of the preceeding discussion has been the argument that Hegel does attempt to identify solutions to at least some major problems of civil society. It was argued that the problems he observes are ones which in his view arise only in a particular kind of civil society, namely one dominated by the relentless pursuit of personal wealth. Economic crises are a result of the persistent drive towards personal satisfaction. They in turn are a cause of increasing poverty, thereby creating a society in which there are immense inequalities in which only the strongest are able to survive. The drive towards increasing personal wealth, crises and poverty forms a vicious circle which can only be broken through a fundamental re-orientation of consciousness which modifies the ethic of personal accumulation, and which complements and reinforces the intervention of the state in economic life. In Hegel's view, the problems of modern civil society lie deep in people's attitudes and consciousness, and cannot therefore be solved by external technical control alone.

Hegel's critics have claimed that his failure to solve the problems of civil society represents a major fault in his system[26] which aims at the overcoming of all contradictions and alienation. I have not attempted here to suggest that Hegel's solutions are necessarily appropriate or that he develops them with perfect clarity. But I have suggested that he does attempt to offer solutions to at least some of the major problems of civil society, that these solutions derive from the fundamental presuppositions of his thought, and that he is not as quiescent about the problems of modern industrial capitalism as has sometimes been supposed.

Nation, civil society, state: Hegelian sources of the Marxian non-theory of nationality

Z. A. PELCZYNSKI

The failure of Marx (and his friend and collaborator Engels) to explain the nature of nationalism and to account for its place in the historical process is well known. In an authoritative French anthology *Les marxistes et la question nationale 1848–1914* one contributor, Michael Lowy, has summed up the position in this way:

> One does not find in Marx either a systematic theory of the national question, or a precise definition of the concept of 'nation', or a general political strategy for the proletariat in this field. His writings on the subject constitute, for the most part, concrete political positions on specific cases.[1]

Perceptive though the comment seems to be, Lowy fails to give a reasoned explanation for this remarkable gap in Marxian theory. How (we may ask) could Marx, who was such an acute observer of contemporary history as well as a social theorist of genius, have been so theoretically unconcerned about one of the dominant political phenomena of nineteenth-century Europe, and apparently blind to its significance for world history?

In the literature on the subject one can detect two main types of answer to this puzzle. The first focuses on Marx's personal background. He was Jewish by origin and presumably not firmly rooted in his native Germany, then transplanted abroad, to live a life spent largely in a cosmopolitan world of exiles and revolutionaries of various nationalities. The second type of answer focuses on the heritage of the Enlightenment thought, which Marx was undoubtedly steeped in. As Isaiah Berlin has persuasively shown in his 1972 *Foreign Affairs* article, 'The Bent Twig,'[2] Enlightenment thinkers assumed that national loyalties and conflicts would inevitably disappear with the progress of rationalism, liberalism and free competition. There is something to be said for both types of explanations. However, I wish to suggest that Marx's and Engels' 'blind spot' may have been also due to the specific heritage of Hegel, which (in this particular respect) has gone virtually unnoticed.

Hegel's social and political philosophy (to the extent to which it is relevant to the problem of nationalism) can be analysed into four main elements: (1) the conception of the state as a political community or a politically organized nation; (2) the conception of civil society as a unique and prominent aspect of the modern state; (3) the conception of world history as the formation, development, decline and dissolution of political communities which are also in some sense nations; and (4) the conception of a self-realizing spirit which develops to full consciousness and freedom through the activities of individuals and the interaction of national communities in time and space. Of the four, Marx and Engels wholeheartedly accepted only the second element, the conception of civil society; indeed, as I shall attempt to show in this essay, they made it the basis of their whole theory of society and social development. They took up a polemical, often extremely hostile, attitude to the other three elements, although it could be argued that the wider Hegelian influence was not wholly without trace, e.g. in Engels' distinction between 'historical' and 'unhistorical' nations in the 1849 *Neue Rheinische Zeitung* article on 'Democratic Panslavism'.

In the Preface to *A Contribution to the Critique of Political Economy* (1859) Marx clearly acknowledges his debt to Hegel's conception of civil society.

> The first work which I undertook for a solution of the doubts which assailed me [about the adequacy of existing German theories of society] was a critical review of the Hegelian philosophy of right... My investigation led me to the result that legal relations as well as forms of state are to be grasped neither from themselves nor from the so-called general development of the human mind, but rather have their roots in the material conditions of life, the sum total of which Hegel... combines under the name of 'civil society', that, however, the anatomy of civil society is to be sought in political economy.[3]

Nothing could be clearer than this well-known passage as a testimony that the Hegelian conception of 'civil society' was the foundation of Marx's social theory and decisively shaped his ideas about politics and history. We must, therefore, begin by taking a look at what Hegel meant by 'civil society'.

For Hegel civil society was an aspect of the modern state which emerged in Western Europe in the eighteenth century and became strikingly apparent after the French Revolution of 1789. It was a specialized and highly complex network of rules, institutions, agencies, groups, practices and attitudes evolved within the legal and political framework of the nation-state to satisfy individual needs and safeguard individual rights. It was bound up with the conception of an abstract, atomistic individual, pursuing his selfish interests through work, production, contract and exchange and enjoying morally and legally guaranteed rights to free activity in the economic, social and cultural sphere. An essential part of the rational system of rights (which Hegel called

'Abstract Right') existing within civil society was the right to acquire and amass property and the consequent inequalities of wealth and the rise of a pauper class, something Hegel recognized as one of the crucial problems of civil society for which no solution had been found in his own time. Another feature of civil society which he noted was its dynamic character, e.g. the drawing of traditional rural relations into its orbit and its expansion through commerce or conquest to less developed or wholly uncivilized parts of the world. But the most important characteristic of civil society from our point of view was its universalistic, cosmopolitan character.

The material bases of civil society for Hegel are basic human wants, grounded in certain biological features of human nature such as the need for shelter, clothing, food and drink, but tending to become increasingly complex and sophisticated as civilization progresses. While political relations are in Hegel's view predominantly shaped by historical tradition and express national peculiarities and differences, social relations are simply human. 'Here at the standpoint of needs...what we have before us is the composite idea which we call man. Thus this is the first time, and indeed properly the only time, to speak of *man* in this sense' (*PhR*, § 190). Civil society, in other words, has what might be called a homogenizing tendency. It creates a social world in which national, cultural and historical considerations are secondary or irrelevant, where 'abstract universality' reigns supreme, a world theoretically epitomized by the rational economic man of the classical political economists and the happiness-maximizing individual of the Benthamite utilitarians, as well as the burgher or member of civil society as Hegel portrays him in his *Philosophy of Right*.

This homogenizing tendency of what Hegel calls 'the system of needs' (i.e. market, production and exchange) is reinforced by the conception of universal human rights, irrespective of race, nationality, religion or social status, which forms in Hegel's view the normative basis of modern civil and property rights. The recognition of the universality of such rights (expressed e.g. in the French declaration of the Rights of Man or the *Code Napoléon*) Hegel regarded as a tremendous achievement of the modern era and a ground for justifiable pride of the modern Europeans.

It is part of education (*Bildung*), of thinking as the consciousness of the single in the form of universality, that the ego comes to be apprehended as a universal person in which all are identical. A man counts as a man in virtue of his manhood alone, not because he is a Jew, Catholic, Protestant, German, Italian, etc. This is an assertion which thinking ratifies and to be conscious of it is of infinite importance. It is defective only when it is crystallized, e.g. as a cosmopolitanism in opposition to the concrete life of the state (*PhR*, § 209).

The last sentence of the quotation warns us that the validity of civil society's standpoint is only relative and has definite limits for Hegel. It does not contain the whole truth about man and society, only a part or element of the truth which is much richer and comprehensive (as truth always is for Hegel). The modern man is not only a member of the abstractly universal civil society, of producers and consumers or contracting legal persons, but also a member of a specific, historically formed national community existing within a political framework. He is also a member of the 'concrete universal' of a political community and in one way or another participates in (as Hegel has put it) 'the concrete life of the state'. Hegel thus sees civil society and the national political community as conceptually different, in practice even antagonistic, forms of social life which are nonetheless dialectically related. The abstract universality of civil society provides a vital but incomplete environment for human or spiritual development. It enables man to become fully an individual by acting primarily on his personal, subjective opinions and by promoting his private happiness. It is, however, inadequate for man's complete development because it ignores his capacity for *public* action, on behalf of *shared* interests and ideals. Hence only by belonging to a national community and taking part in its political life does a man fully realize himself. To put it differently, in ontological rather than ethical terms, civil society for Hegel is not a self-subsistent entity or reality, still less something fundamental and prior to the state. It is part of a wider whole, a sub-system conceived by reflective thinking, a mere aspect of a genuine and concrete totality. Civil society as a system of interdependence created by the pursuit of essentially selfish ends is only an aspect of the national community. 'This system may be prima facie regarded as the external state, the state based on need, the state as the Understanding envisages it' (*PhR*, § 183) – to quote a well-known phrase.

We might note in passing that Hegel's notorious justification of war as something necessary for the 'ethical health' of nations is closely bound up with the distinction between the state conceived as civil society and the state conceived as a national community which is politically organized. By making sacrifices for the sake of the state's integrity or independence, including the supreme sacrifice of life itself, men show themselves capable of virtue and heroism which have little or no scope in the prosaic and mundane world of civil society.

An entirely distorted account of the demand for this sacrifice results from regarding the state as a mere civil society and from regarding its final end as only the security of individual life and property. This security cannot possibly be obtained by the sacrifice of what is to be secured – on the contrary (*PhR*, § 324R).

Man reaches the height of ethical life in Hegel's view not as a member of a cosmopolitan civil society, existing to promote his private wants and interests, but as a member of a specific, individual national community, which forms an independent state and exists to promote a shared conception of the common good.

In the *Philosophy of Right*, and in far greater detail in the Introduction to the *Lectures on the Philosophy of World History*, Hegel argues that the network of governmental and political institutions of the state – its constitution – is typically a product of history and expresses the culture of a particular nation – its values, religious beliefs, views about the world, traditions and customs. That culture (or 'spirit') of the nation permeates also other human relations (least of all, however, those which have come under the relative sway of civil society) and gives the whole unity, and cohesion.[4] The values of the national community and the operation of its central government are linked together through mediating institutions (such as corporations, estates and the representative system), which ensure that the activities of the government broadly express the basic ideals and interests of groups within the community or its individual members. If such mediating links do not exist or cease to perform their proper function the nation or its important sections become alienated from the government and the integrity or independence of the political community is jeopardized.

The constitution is thus the mechanism which in practice ensures the identity of the national spirit with the attitudes and actions of the multitude of groups and individuals composing a nation. In this respect Hegel believed that the modern monarchical state of his time had an advantage over earlier political communities because it linked the individual to the community in an organized institutionalized way while, for example, the ancient republics relied mainly on non-institutional factors, i.e. sentiment, character and education. Hegel's concept of nationhood, unlike that of the contemporary German Romantics, is thus heavily political in character. Pure culture or common ethnic and linguistic characteristics are not, in his view, sufficient by themselves to weld a large human group into a nation and to provide a firm focus of loyalty; only the possession of a common government and the tradition of political unity can do so. This theme is particularly strongly stressed in the first of Hegel's political writings, the unpublished pamphlet on the constitution of the German Empire.[5]

Marx never challenges this political conception of nationality. Like Hegel he has no interest in nations as merely cultural, ethnic or linguistic communities. Nations for him are always either past or present political entities or peoples struggling to be states.[6] For him the national question is *par excellence* the question of political independence or self-determination. In other respects, however, he and Hegel disagree fundamentally. One can trace the growth of this disagreement in Marx's writings of the 1840s. Marx parts company with Hegel first of all over the issue whether the modern state is, in a meaningful sense of the word, a political *community*. In his first work on political philosophy, the *Contribution to the Critique of Hegel's 'Philosophy of Right'* (1843) Marx does so rather obliquely. He is primarily concerned to expose the falsity of Hegel's philosophical treatment of political concepts such as the state, civil society, the people, monarchy and bureaucracy. Applying Feuerbach's so-called 'transformational criticism' to Hegel's political philosophy he seeks to strip these terms of their supposedly 'mystical' character and to ground them in what he takes to be a real structure of social relations instead of a structure of mere concepts determined by the philosophical method of the dialectic. In Hegel's *Philosophy of Right* (Marx argues) family and civil society are portrayed as 'moments' of the state or stages in the development of the ethical Idea. In fact they are the realistic basis on which the state is grounded.

The fact is that the state issues from the multitude in their existence as members of families and as members of civil society. Speculative philosophy expresses this fact as the idea's deed, not as the idea of the multitude, but as the deed of a subjective idea different from the fact itself... The fact which is taken as a point of departure is not conceived as such, but as a mystical result (*MER*, 17–18).

In the various commentaries on this early work attention has generally focussed on Marx's criticism of Hegel's philosophical method which he first develops here, but in the context of this essay certain other points arising out of the *Contribution* are rather more significant.

First, Marx asserts that family and civil society are in some sense more basic than the state. As he says: 'Family and civil society constitute *themselves* as the state. They are the driving forces' (*MER*, 17). We see here the earliest formulation of the view, as yet asserted without any proof or argument, that civil society (like the family, which afterwards rather drops out of the Marxian picture) is a more fundamental or prior form of social life than the state. Although Marx's thinking is rather undeveloped and obscure he seems to be implying that in the family and civil society we deal with real, concrete human beings ('the multitude') whereas the state for Hegel and other German philosophers is an idea or abstraction which somehow transcends them. If so, he is of course mistaken. For Hegel 'family', 'civil society' and 'state' all involve real human beings. They are simply different forms of social life, involving different human ends and different means of realizing them – specific patterns of human relations such as practices, rules, institutions and so on.

Marx reveals more of his thought when he goes on to discuss the relation of the people to the state, and asserts the primacy of democracy over monarchy. The nature of this primacy is not at all clear. He says: 'The state is an abstraction. The people alone is what is concrete' (*MER*, 18). This of course is true only in one sense of the people, viz. as a mere multitude of human beings. Without such a multitude no social life and social organization, and hence no state, are possible. But the people (*Volk* in German) can also mean a concrete, historically formed community in the sense in which, say, the people of Athens constituted the Athenian polis. In that sense the state (or polis) is not an abstraction; it is the sum total of specific relations which bind the multitude in a certain way and give it this form of social life. What Marx probably wants to say is that in a democratic type of the state there is strictly speaking no 'political state' and no 'constitution'.

In democracy the political state is itself merely a particular *content* and particular form of existence of the people... The French have recently interpreted it as meaning that in true democracy *the political state is annihilated*. This is correct in so far as the political state, *qua* political state, as constitution, no longer passes for the whole (*MER*, 21).

In a democracy, then, there is no organized institutional framework and no body of men (kings, ministers and civil servants) controlling it and separate from the general body of citizens. The public good or general interest is determined by the people as a whole, the assembly of citizens; it is the outcome of their personal activities, not the product of the activities of the 'state' as an organization over and above the multitude.

Marx's well-known attack on the Hegelian concept of bureaucracy as a 'universal class' is inspired by his belief that direct democracy, without any officialdom, is a more adequate form of political life since it is closer to the immediate, 'natural' existence of the people.

We may note that Hegel's interpretation of the historical experience of the Greek polis is almost identical with Marx's, but Hegel rejects the idea of modern men returning to a democratic or republican form of government as utopian. In his view there is a radical difference between the culture of the moderns and that of the ancients. Political life in ancient Greece or republican Rome presupposed the spontaneous identification of the citizens with the polis. Laws, customs and traditions as well as art, religion and philosophy shaped the social consciousness of the citizens in such a way that they saw themselves as merely parts, organs or instruments of the whole and regarded political life as a service to the community, a way of life superior to their merely private existence and personal concerns.[7] The highly institutionalized form of modern political state (or the modern state power, *Staatsgewalt*, as he generally calls it) is a consequence of the wholly different economic, social and cultural conditions of the modern world.[8] The modern man conceives his private life to be more important than his public life. As Marx puts it, in a wholly Hegelian way, 'the abstraction of private life belongs only to modern times' (*MER*, 22). For Hegel this 'abstraction' (made concrete in the realm of civil society) is overcome in the rational organization of the modern monarchical and representative state which draws men into the public, political arena without abolishing civil society. For Marx the overcoming of the private/public dichotomy requires the destruction not only of the political state, but also of civil society – the throwing away of the baby with the bathwater, so to speak.

Third, an idea apparently at variance with his mature position seems to be implicit in young Marx's viewpoint. He rejects the fact of a highly institutionalized form of government, based on fixed legal and constitutional relations, in favour of an ideal of political life in which people participate directly and spontaneously. But such participation is only possible when a certain political culture (or, as Hegel would have put it, 'national spirit') is present and accepted. It seems that what Marx was shortly to call 'social consciousness' is therefore not necessarily secondary to 'social existence'. Marx presents the development of political life from a simple ethical community into an ever more complex and institutionalized form as 'estrangement' or 'alienation'. But it is not clear that such an 'objectification' of culture is either avoidable or intrinsically bad. It is the essence of social and historical progress.

In the *Contribution to the Critique of Hegel's 'Philosophy of Right'* Marx's divergences from Hegel on the subject of the state are not yet explicitly stated. Their full theoretical development first occurs in the article *On the Jewish Question* of the same year (1843) and in the *Economic and Philosophical Manuscripts of 1844*. In *On the Jewish Question* Marx scarcely alludes to Hegel by name, but the polemic against the Hegelian distinction between civil society and the state forms the dominant part of the essay.

Marx points out that in the feudal epoch the civil and the political spheres are intertwined, and the boundaries between them are blurred; civil rights entail political obligations; estates are social groups with distinct political privileges; suffrage is based on social status rather than on such abstract qualities as property and manhood. The French Revolution ends this intermingling in theory and in practice; it postulates both universal civil rights and universal political rights, but it conceives the realm of civil relations as something distinct from the realm of political relations. The republic (which, contrary to Hegel's view, Marx claims to be a typical form of the modern state) is seen by the Jacobins as the realm where the citizens' idealistic motives (Rousseau's 'general will') should prevail over the selfishness and material interests of civil society members. This historical separation of the two realms Marx sees as producing an ideological and alienating effect.

Where the political state has attained to its full development man leads, not only in thought, in consciousness, but in *reality*, in *life*, a double existence – celestial and terrestrial. He lives in the *political community*, where he regards himself as a *communal being*, and in *civil society*, where he acts simply as a *private individual*, treats other men as means, degrades himself to the role of mere means, and becomes the plaything of alien powers (*MER*, 34).

Marx points out, with a good deal of justification, that the so-called rights of man proclaimed by the French and the American Revolution were really the rights of members of civil society, egoistic men, separated from the community, withdrawn into themselves and preoccupied with their private interest. To call such rights 'natural' in his view is to imply that the egoistic man, man as a bourgeois rather than a citizen, is the true and authentic man. 'The sphere of human needs, labour, private interests and civil law' is thus conceived as the natural basis of society 'whereas *political* man is only abstract, artificial man, man as an allegorical, moral person' (*MER*, 46).

For Marx this is the actual historical condition of modern Europe. A true political community is impossible even under a republican constitution as long as legal, social and economic conditions in civil society are what they are. Marx therefore concludes that true human emancipation cannot be equated with political emancipation while true community cannot be found in a democratic republic. Only when civil society, as the primary source of egoism and conflict, is abolished will real community life be possible. Then, incidentally, will religion also cease to play a significant role in society and history and Jews and Christians will become equal and integral members of community. The solution of the problem of religious division and intolerance lies in destroying the material roots of religion which for Marx lie in civil society.

But how is civil society to be destroyed? In the *Introduction to the Contribution to the Critique of Hegel's 'Philosophy of Right'*, written shortly after *On the Jewish Question*, Marx for the first time attributes the mission of human emancipation to the proletariat, which he defines as

a class in civil society which is not a class of civil society, a class which is the dissolution of all classes, a sphere of society which has a universal character because its sufferings are universal, and which does not claim a *particular* redress because the wrong which is done to it is not a *particular wrong* but *wrong in general*...a sphere of society which claims no *traditional* status but only a human status (*MER*, 64).

Hence civil society has for Marx not only a historical beginning but an end, which lies in the foreseeable future. As a form of social life civil society loses its raison d'être and disintegrates when the numerous class of factory workers that is produced by its development fails to secure the material and spiritual conditions for a human life. The society's own dynamism, impelled by economic forces, carries the universalizing and homogenizing tendencies within it to an extreme. In the daily life of the modern industrial proletariat human nature is reduced to its utmost simplicity and naturalness, but at the same time, through a dialectic twist, it is made capable of a higher form of communal, altruistic existence after the proletarian revolution and the establishment of socialist society.

In the Paris *Economic and Philosophic Manuscripts of 1844* Marx temporarily sets aside the topic of civil society and discusses the more fundamental problem of the nature of society in general. He views it as the creation of men seeking to satisfy their needs by labour and adapting nature to their ever-growing needs through a variety of practical and theoretical activities. In the process men develop their inherent powers and realize their specific human essence, which Marx calls 'species being' (*Gattungswesen*) — a capacity to think of man's nature and the nature of everything else in universal categories or (in Marx's terminology) scientifically.

Perhaps the best example of his approach to the subject of society is the section of the *1844 Manuscripts* given the title 'Estranged Labour' by its editors. In that section Marx compares man and animal in respect of the satisfaction of needs. What distinguishes the former from the latter is that man, as a species being, adopts the species (his own and that of other things) as the object of his activity, both practical and theoretical. While an animal's needs and means of satisfying them are strictly fixed and limited, man is capable of extending both indefinitely. He adapts the whole of nature to his needs in practice and he seeks to comprehend the whole of nature theoretically.

In creating an *objective world* by his practical activity, in *working-up* inorganic nature, man proves himself a conscious species being, i.e. as a being that treats the species as its own essential being, or that treats itself as a species being. Admittedly animals also produce...But an animal only produces what it immediately needs for itself or its young. It produces one-sidedly, whilst man produces universally. It produces only under the dominion of direct physical need, whilst man produces even when he is free from physical need and only truly produces in freedom therefrom. An animal produces only itself, whilst man reproduces the whole of nature...knows how to produce in accordance with the standard of every species, and knows how to apply everywhere the inherent standard of the object (*MER*, 76).

Although Marx does not make the point in this precise context it is clear that man's 'species being' is also the foundation of society, i.e. human cooperative relations. For Marx (as for Hegel) the human and the social are correlative terms.

[J]*ust as* society itself produces *man as man*, so is society *produced* by him. Activity and consumption, both in their content and their mode of existence, are *social*: *social* activity and *social* consumption; the *human* essence of nature first exists only for *social* man; for only here does nature exist for him as a *bond* with *man*...as the life-element of the human world; only here does nature exist as the foundation of his human existence...Thus *society* is the consummated oneness in substance of man and nature...the naturalism of man and the humanism of nature both brought to fulfilment (*MER*, 85).

Marx goes on to say that the social- or species-nature of man exists in man's individual as well as obviously social activity, in his theoretical as well as practical work.

When I am active *scientifically*, etc....then I am *social*, because I am active as a man. Not only is the material of my activity given to me as a social product (as is even the language in which the thinker is active): my *own* existence *is* social activity, and therefore that which I make of myself, I make of myself for society and with the consciousness of myself as a social being (*MER*, 86).

It is not always fully appreciated how close is Marx's viewpoint at this stage to that of Hegel. Marx's concept of 'species being' is substantially the same as the capacity (frequently stressed by Hegel) of human beings – or the power of the human mind – to rise above particular characteristics of things and grasp their common, universal property, the intellectual nature or concept (*Begriff*) of a class of things. In a few crucial paragraphs of the *Philosophy of Right*, belonging to the subsection 'The System of Needs' of the section on civil society, Hegel anticipates much of Marx's discussion of work as a conscious practical activity and the way in which it creates a social environment, which is social in a specifically human way. For example, in § 190 Hegel also compares man to animal in the matter of satisfying needs and points out that both man's needs and the means of satisfying them are far wider in scope and subject to essentially human and social processes such as work, cooperation, the division of labour, techniques of production, the multiplication of needs, concepts of a proper standard of living and ideas about shares of the social product ('general capital') to which men are entitled. Through this process man rises above his animal nature and becomes specifically human and social.

Needs and means, as things existent *realiter*, become something which has being for others by whose needs and work satisfaction for all alike is conditioned...This abstract character, universality, is the character of being recognized and is the moment which makes concrete, i.e. social, the isolated and abstract needs and their ways and means of satisfaction (§ 192).

Hegel goes on to say (in § 194) that

this social moment has in it the aspect of liberation, i.e. the strict natural necessity of need is obscured and man is concerned with his own opinion, indeed with an opinion which is universal, and with a necessity of his own making alone, instead of with an external necessity.

This is the specific mode in which work (and economic life generally) contributes to man's freedom according to Hegel, but liberation takes many other forms. Ethical life liberates man by giving him normative guidelines and habits of action instilled by education and thus enabling him to control his natural impulses (§ 149), while possession, property and other legal rights ('personality' in Hegel's terminology) enable man to assert himself against the natural world, and make use of it for his own ends with the approval and cooperation of others (§ 39).

Hegel and Marx, then, are in fundamental agreement on the liberating character of labour in the sense of it creating a social world, which expresses specifically human (Hegel would say 'spiritual') features of man's being. Nor do they disagree on the essentially social character of theoretical as opposed to practical work. Theoretical activity, which in the mature Hegelian system is subsumed under the category of 'absolute spirit' and *follows* the practical realm of 'objective spirit' in the *Encyclopaedia of the Philosophical Sciences* of 1817, is shown in the later lectures on the philosophy of history to have a definite social and historical context. It is characterized there as the outcome of the striving of men's minds to make sense of human experience, to relate different parts of this experience to each other, and to bring order and coherence into the whole. The language in which theoretical thoughts are expressed, as well as the conceptual apparatus, of, say, religion, science, and philosophy, are products of social, cooperative activity and generally reflect the historical characteristics of the society which gave rise to them.

The issue on which Marx and Hegel do differ, but which becomes abundantly clear only in *The German Ideology* (1845–6), is what we may call the centrality of the economic aspect of society. Family and political relations, and the activities which give rise to them or which they determine, are social relations just as much as the economic ones. Marx treats them as aspects of economic relations, determined by and subordinated to the central productive activity in society, which is work. Hegel treats them as equally (indeed in some societies and cultures as more) important components of a comprehensive social totality. From the standpoint which Hegel adopts in his writings all aspects of men's social life, practical as well as theoretical, are modes of interaction between spirit and nature, and they all make a contribution to man's development towards freedom, i.e. self-consciousness and self-determination. Instead of giving economic relations and activities a special status Hegel views them as something which is subordinate to and determined by social reality as a whole. Economic life exists in a wider cultural context of ethical, religious, legal and political life, a context which is itself under the influence of history, tradition and nationality.[9] The abstract human or cosmopolitan aspects of society ('the system of needs'), which Hegel acknowledges in §§ 190 and 209 of the *Philosophy of Right*, are simply historical tendencies of the modern age which, however strong they may be in a particular time or place, in no way determine all the other features of social reality.

For Marx, however, the economy as a context of man's primary interaction with nature, is a paradigm of all social life, all human activity. 'Religion, family, state, law, morality, science, etc., are only *particular* modes of production, and fall under its general laws' (*MER*, 85). Together with private property, all those other objective patterns of human relations and forms of consciousness corresponding to them are for Marx forms of 'estranged labour'. They are relegated to the category of secondary social and historical reality since they are only indirectly concerned with the satisfaction of human needs and labour. The only social reality which Marx from then on recognizes as not being subject to any mystification, false consciousness or 'ideological' distortion is the sum total of those productive relations which directly harness material forces to human needs and which he identifies with civil society. Hence not society as a whole, in all its aspects, but the economic aspect of society or civil society becomes the central focus of Marx's social theory.

The German Ideology provides a scientific underpinning of this view of society by means of the so-called materialist conception of history. Marx and Engels argue that the clue to the understanding of history is to be found in the 'material' basis of society — the way in which natural human powers are developed and natural resources exploited to satisfy human needs by the production and exchange of commodities. History can be divided into epochs according to the methods of production and forms of the division of labour predominant in society at that time. These are the basic historical factors. All other aspects of society in an epoch must be explained in terms of the economic base and the social structure directly resting upon it. Developments within the political and legal superstructure or in the still less practical realms of philosophy, science, religion and art — the sphere of 'ideology' as Marx and Engels now call it — are secondary and derivative historical factors and can never provide a valid *ground* of historical explanation. Since economic relations are the foundation of civil society, it follows that all true history is the history of civil society.

The form of intercourse determined by the existing forces at all previous historical stages, and in turn determining these, is *civil society*... we see how this civil society is the true source and theatre of history, and how absurd is the conception of history held hitherto, which neglects the real relationships and confines itself to high-sounding dramas of princes and states (*MER*, 163).

And again, a little later in *The German Ideology*:

This conception of history [which we advocate] depends on our ability to expound the real processes of production, starting out from the material production of life itself, and to comprehend the forms of intercourse connected with this and created by this mode of production (i.e. civil society in its various stages), as the basis of all history; and to show it in its action as State, to explain all the different theoretical products and forms of consciousness, religion, philosophy, ethics, etc., etc., etc., and trace their origins and growth from that basis (*MER*, 164).

The more Marx identified himself with the Hegelian conception of civil society, the more concerned he was to deny the validity of Hegel's distinction between it and the state as a political community, and above all to deny that the latter had some kind of ontological and historical primacy. But it is obvious that he transformed the concept of civil society as well. He confined it very much to what Hegel calls the 'system of needs' (production, exchange, division of labour and class structure), which is for Hegel only one of the 'moments' or essential elements of civil society (beside the judicial system, 'police' and corporation). In this narrowed sense civil society for Marx became not merely an aspect of the modern state that emerged in the eighteenth century and was doomed to extinction after the proletarian revolution. As the sum total of productive relations, the economic foundation of society, it was the foundation of all political and governmental institutions and thus ontologically and historically prior to the state. Marx made therefore a treble modification to the Hegelian conception. He narrowed down the meaning of civil society, he reversed its relation to the state, and he dehistoricized the idea. Throughout history men reveal their essential nature as members of society, i.e. as producers and exchangers. Their political consciousness and national characteristics are not essential features of their human nature. In all epochs of history, not just the bourgeois one, the notion of political community and national identity is an illusion and false consciousness. We have seen, however, that Marx was prepared to make an exception for ancient democracy where the consciousness of political unity did correspond to the facts of social life, at least for the freemen. He also acknowledged that, under feudalism, the distinctions between the social, civil and political were in practice and theory hard to draw.

There is no need to demonstrate further the tremendous impact Hegel's conception of civil society had on Marxian thought. Reinforced by the theories of the classical political economists it seemed to Marx and Engels to provide a secure foundation for an adequate explanation of all social reality. Moreover, with the powerful help of the Feuerbachian critique of Hegelian metaphysics, the conception of civil society could be turned against Hegel himself to invalidate his basic ideas, viz. the primacy of political and cultural over economic and material factors in world history, and the prior and superior character of the state, i.e. politically organized national community, vis-à-vis civil society. Such theoretical development was in line with Marx's and Engel's general strategy of searching for what they considered to be the rational kernel and prising it out of the mystical shell of the Hegelian system.

But the anchoring of Marxian social theory in the truncated Hegelian conception of civil society had certain far-reaching and far from fortunate consequences for marxism. The first and (from the standpoint of this essay) the foremost consequence, was the inability of Marx and Engels (and most subsequent marxists) to give due theoretical significance to the national factor in history since it was left outside the conceptual framework. Hegel had a peculiar conception of nationhood, which was far from perfect and reflected more the eighteenth-century ideas of Montesquieu and Rousseau than the nineteenth-century ideas of the German Romantics and the Historical School. It was too wide because in the term 'nation' (in German *Volk*) he included such diverse social groupings and historical phenomena as the citizens of ancient Greek city states, the dominant and the subordinate peoples of ancient despotic monarchies or empires, the *nationes* of medieval European kingdoms, the often very heterogeneous populations of seventeenth, eighteenth- and early nineteenth-century dynastic monarchies, and the homogeneous ethnic populations of modern nation-states such as France. On the other hand Hegel's conception of nationality may be thought to have been too narrow because it made an essentially political factor – sovereignty or independence – the central feature of nationhood. Ethnic or linguistic unity, heavily stressed by the German Romantics and political supporters of a greater Germany, meant little to the mature Hegel, who believed that viable national states could be constructed from segments of ethnic nations (e.g. Württemberg and Prussia). It was in Poland after Hegel's death, where Hegelian influence was high but the belief in national unity and self-determination equally strong, that a rather significant development of Hegel's theory of nationality took place.[10] Despite these constraints Hegel had a substantial theoretical basis for appreciating the significance and persistence of a whole range of socially and historically important phenomena.

The rejection of the conception of the state as a sovereign national community left Marx and Engels without such a theoretical basis or at least with a highly limited one. The conception of civil society is, as we have seen, grounded in a universalistic, cosmopolitan and rather abstract view of man and society; its basic categories, especially its narrow version as 'the system of needs', such as need, labour, relations of production, classes and capital, may be discussed without reference to national factors. They certainly presuppose the concept of some kind of state power in the sense of a coercive apparatus for the maintenance of law, order and independence, but not the idea that state power is generally a product of a historically formed nation and that it often serves as an instrument for the protection of national values or of national self-assertion.

Certain additional conceptual and empirical factors contributed to the depreciation of nationalism as a social and historical phenomenon. Marx accepted Hegel's distinction beween the particular and universal features of human nature and the belief that both must be given full scope for development. For Hegel civil society and the political community of the nation-state are the respective socio-historical contexts in which this development takes place in the modern world. For Marx and Engels civil society provides the arena of individual development only in the pathological form of general competition, egoism and privatization. The scope for the development of *genuinely social*, communal features of human nature they see partly in the class consciousness and solidarity of the proletariat, but mainly in the classless, stateless and nationless community of free cooperative producers of the future. They often stress the immense advantages of such a world-wide community (the progress towards which in *The Communist Manifesto*, they linked to the spread of capitalism in the world): unrestricted flow of goods and ideas, a rich culture composed of innumerable strands, the absence of alienating and restricting political and local allegiances and so on. What they ignore is the question whether such a vast world society could ever be perceived by anyone as a community, whether it could possibly become a real, meaningful focus of loyalty and unity for a vast multitude of individuals. With all their imperfections and disadvantages this is what national states still manage to do. And even if one were to admit the possibility of a world without governments and states, would not national communities based on historical traditions, ethnic customs or common culture and language not necessarily crystallize within communist society and create severe practical problems?

Marx and Engels were of course fully aware of the strength of national sentiments and nationalist theories in contemporary European society, despite their dismissal of them as 'false consciousness' or 'ideology'. A great deal of their journalistic writing was concerned with the subject, and their preoccupation with Irish and Polish nationalism was particularly striking.[11] But it seems to me that their interest in nationalism was essentially practical and not theoretical. They viewed it as a political force to be taken into account in analyzing the strength of class forces and in charting the revolutionary strategy of the proletariat in different countries, not as a phenomenon to be explained systematically in terms of definite economic and social conditions, still less of course in terms of cultural, historical and traditional factors having their own logic of development. They had no explanation, for instance, of *why* Polish patriotism in the nineteenth century was so intense and manifested itself in frequent uprisings against foreign powers, although they noted and praised it often in their writings.

In countries which were already independent states and 'mature' civil societies (such as Britain and France) Marx and Engels advocated that the proletariat ought to reject all organic conceptions of the national state or political community, and ought to claim to be identical with the 'people' as a whole. Nationalism could not be allowed to get in the way of the class struggle with the bourgeoisie. However, in nations which were not independent and which formed societies without a mature proletariat (such as Ireland and Poland) they accepted the value of class cooperation and the primacy of national over class struggle. Freedom from subjection to a foreign power, in their view, was generally a pre-condition of rapid economic and social development and hence of the ultimate emancipation of the proletariat. Hence political independence and national self-consciousness had purely instrumental value for Marx and Engels and lacked any instrinsic human, cultural or ethical significance.

We may conclude, then, that the failure of marxism to acquire a coherent and developed theory of nationalism, either of an empirical or a normative kind, is unquestionable. An examination of the heritage of the Hegelian conception of civil society in the thought of the founders of marxism throws (in my view) new light on, and helps to explain the reasons for, the failure.

NOTES

Introduction

1 See Antonio Gramsci, *Selections from Prison Notebooks* (London, 1971), ch. 2, sec. 3. For an assessment of Gramsci's concept of civil society see J. V. Femia, *Gramsci's Political Thought: Hegemony, Consciousness and the Revolutionary Process* (Oxford, 1981), *passim*.

2 M. Riedel, *Studien zu Hegels Rechtsphilosophie* (Frankfurt am Main, 1969), p. 156. The essay referred to in the text was first published in *Archiv für Rechts- und Sozialphilosophie*, vol. XLVIII (1972) under the title 'Der Begriff der "Bürgerlichen Gesellschaft" und das Problem seines geschichtlichen Ursprungs' ('The concept of "civil society" and the problem of its historical origin').

3 *Hegel's Political Writings*, trans. by T. M. Knox with an introductory essay by Z. A. Pelczynski (Oxford, 1964), p. 202.

4 See [§ 1. Concept of the state] in 'The German Constitution', *Hegel's Political Writings*, pp. 153–64 and *passim* afterwards.

5 The earliest attempt at an ethical theory of the state was the manuscript to which Hegel's editors afterwards gave the title 'System der Sittlichkeit'. Other attempts, equally experimental and very obscure, are in the Jena philosophy of spirit lectures of 1803–4 and 1805–6. See G. W. F. Hegel, *System of Ethical Life and Philosophy of Spirit*, trans. H. S. Harris and T. M. Knox (Albany, N.Y., 1979). Perhaps the clearest of these early attempts can be found in the last part of Hegel's article *Natural Law*, trans. T. M. Knox (Philadelphia, 1975).

6 See her essay 'Hegel's "Phenomenology": an elegy for Helas' in Z. A. Pelczynski (ed.), *Hegel's Political Philosophy* (Cambridge, 1971). The essay was subsequently expanded into a book: J. N. Shklar, *Freedom and Independence: A Study of the Political Ideas of Hegel's 'Phenomenology of Mind'* (Cambridge, 1976).

7 See C. Taylor, *Hegel* (Cambridge, 1975), ch. 15 and C. Taylor, *Hegel and Modern Society* (Cambridge, 1979), ch. 2, sec. 5.

8 See G. W. F. Hegel, *Vorlesungen über Rechtsphilosophie 1818–1831*, ed. K.-H. Ilting (Stuttgart–Bad Cannstatt, 1973), vol. I, pp. 189, 193.

9 See 'The Hegelian conception of the state' by Z. A. Pelczynski in Pelczynski (ed.), *Hegel's Political Philosophy*, esp. pp. 13, 14.

10 In R. Plant, *Hegel* (2nd ed., Oxford, 1983) and C. Taylor, *Hegel* (Cambridge, 1975).

11 R. Berki in his *On Political Realism* (London, 1981) argues that in political terms Hegel's general approach should be characterized as realism rather than idealism.

From self-consciousness to community

1 Piotr Hoffman, 'Hegel, Marx and the Other', *Philosophical Forum* (Spring/ Summer, 1976), pp. 220–1.

2 H.-G. Gadamer, 'Hegel's Dialectic of Self-Consciousness', in his *Hegel's Dialectic* (London, 1976), p. 59. *PS* in brackets in text indicates a page reference to Hegel's *Phenomenology of Spirit*, trans. A. V. Miller (Oxford, 1977).

3 A. Kojève in his *Introduction to the Reading of Hegel*, translated by James Nichols Jr., (London, 1969), while rightly emphasizing the place that the 'risk of life' has in Hegel's text, fails to appreciate the shift from·physical death to spiritual forms of death as constitutive of the shift to social experience.

4 Rosen in his *G. W. F. Hegel* (London, 1974), pp. 160–1, attributes a reading of this kind to Kojève and offers a refutation analogous to my own. However, Rosen also overlooks this passage and therefore is forced to ground his reading of the transition to self-consciousness on Hegel's Logic (ontology), which I shall show is altogether unnecessary.

5 'In part' because *an sich* and *für sich* do not possess the same meaning in all contexts of use. Each theoretical couplet they generate — unconscious/conscious; potential/actual; independent/dependent, etc. — requires separate justification. Despite this fact, Hegel's use of these terms is not arbitrary, and further, I am convinced that philosophical practice would be substantially, indeed, irreparably, impoverished without them. But that is an argument for another occasion.

6 'Utterer's meaning and intentions', *Philosophical Review* (April 1969), p. 151.

7 D. Dennett, 'Conditions of Personhood', in A. Rorty (ed.), *The Identities of Persons* (London, 1976), p. 189. It was Dennett's suggestive paper which first prompted me to see the relevance of contemporary work on the philosophy of mind to Hegel's account of self-consciousness.

8 Ibid., pp. 188–9.

9 (3) will later be shown to be of equal importance to (1) and (2).

10 Kojève, op.cit. p. 48. Kojève continues, showing how consciousness presupposes self-consciousness, thus: 'Now to be able to transform the natural given in relation to a *non*-natural idea is to possess a technique. And the idea that engenders a technique is a scientific idea, a scientific concept. Finally, to possess scientific concepts is to be endowed with Understanding, *Verstand*, the faculty of abstract notions.'

11 Hoffman, op.cit., p. 221.

12 Ibid., pp. 220–2.

13 More properly: Kant, in his distinction between Wille and Willkür, was fumbling after the freedom of action/freedom of will distinction; while Descartes identified freedom of action with freedom of will. Nevertheless, both thinkers proposed a *cogito* and an analogous but separate account of freedom.

I have tried to elucidate the connection between the *cogito* and freedom in Descartes in my *The Philosophy of the Novel: Lukács, Marxism and the Dialectics of Form* (forthcoming), ch. 5.

14 Hoffman, op.cit., correctly cites this as Hegel's problem situation (pp. 212–3), and rightly identifies Hegel's critique of the given with his critique of the thing-in-itself. However, he fails to make his starting point cohere with his positive theses.

15 The place and nature of 'experience' in the *Phenomenology* is elucidated by Heidegger in his *Hegel's Concept of Experience* (New York, 1970).

16 This argument is a compilation and synthesis of suggestion by Kojève, op.cit., pp. 3–5; and Q. Lauer, *A Reading of Hegel's 'Phenomenology of Spirit'* (New York, 1976), p. 94.

17 On this, see Jean Hyppolite's 'Hegel's Phenomenology and Psychoanalysis' in W. Steinkraus (ed.), *New Studies in the Philosophy of Hegel* (New York, 1971).

18 This formulation is David Lachterman's in D. P. Verene (ed.), *Hegel's Social and Political Thought* (Brighton, 1980), p. 32.

19 Ibid.

20 Ibid., p. 31.

21 See, especially, her *The Human Condition* (New York, 1959), ch. V, passim.

22 Hannah Arendt, 'What is Freedom?', in her *Between Past and Future* (London, 1961), p. 156.

23 Kojève, op.cit., p. 80.

24 Kojève himself sometimes claims, with Hegel he notes, that universal recognition was only present in germ. For a good discussion see P. Riley, 'Introduction to the Reading of Alexandre Kojève', in M. Freeman and D. Robertson (eds.), *The Frontiers of Political Theory* (Brighton, 1980). esp., pp. 241–2.

25 For an illuminating discussion of this issue see David Wiggins' 'Deliberation and Practical Reason', in Amélie O. Rorty (ed.), *Essays on Aristotle's Ethics* (London, 1980). See, also, John M. Cooper, *Reason and Human Good in Aristotle* (London, 1975), ch. 1.

26 For the present context of this problem see W. E. Connolly, 'A Note on Freedom Under Socialism', *Political Theory*, vol. 5, pp. 461–72.

27 Criticisms of Arendt's attempt sharply to distinguish politics from society are common. See, for example, Jurgen Habermas' 'Hannah Arendt's Communications Concept of Power', *Social Research* 44 (1977), pp. 3–24.

28 This point Hegel developed at length in the introduction to his lectures on the philosophy of history. See G. W. F. Hegel, *Lectures on the Philosophy of World History: Introduction*, trans. H. B. Nisbet, with an introduction by D. Forbes (Cambridge, 1975).

29 That Kant is a philosopher of practical reason is a familiar interpretation of his thought. Richard Kennington, in his 'The "Teaching of Nature" in Descartes' Soul Doctrine', *Review of Metaphysics* (xxvi, 1), has recently attempted to mount a similar kind of account of Descartes. 'Cartesian doubt is a means to indubitable foundations of the edifice of science, and not to a theoretical metaphysics of substance...Doubt is therefore a means to the ultimate science of "the tree of philosophy", "the perfect moral science" or the "fruits" thereof,

practice itself. Doubt partakes of the practical character of natural reason... Prudence, or practical judgment, governs, because the truth or falsity of sensation is determined for the sake of the practical end' (p. 101). Of course Hegel is not a philosopher of 'practical reason', but of praxis. Practical reason is the twin of theoretical reason when reason is conceived dualistically. Praxis, according to the Hegelian account, is the ontologically appropriate characterization of self-consciousness. Theoretical self-consciousness arises in response to the discovery of the 'unchanging' – nature as a complex of unalterable laws. This form of self-consciousness demoted into either simple means/end rationality or abstract autonomy (Kant and German Idealism). All this, however, is a topic for another essay.

Hegel, Plato and Greek 'Sittlichkeit'

1 Hegel distinguishes *Sittlichkeit* from *Moralität*. I have translated it as 'ethical life', and the corresponding adjective, *sittlich*, as 'ethical'. It is closely associated, for Hegel, with *Sitten*, customs.

2 See e.g. *Vorlesungen über die Ästhetik*, eds. E. Moldenhauer and K. M. Michel (Frankfurt am Main, 1970), vol. ii, pp. 13ff. Hegel's *Aesthetics: Lectures on Fine Art*, tr. T. M. Knox (Oxford, 1975), vol. i, pp. 427ff.

3 Hegel was a master of the sweeping generalization and his remarks about Greek society are often open to question. I have not in general explicitly questioned them, except where my argument requires it.

4 Cf. *Phänomenologie des Geistes*, ed. J. Hoffmeister (Hamburg, 1952), p. 310; *Hegel's Phenomenology of Spirit*, tr. A. V. Miller (Oxford, 1977), §436.

5 In Sophocles' *Antigone*. Cf. *PG(H)* pp. 313ff; *PS*, §§438ff.

6 *PG*, p. 497; *PS*, §712, distinguishes between the good and the beautiful, for which Socrates searched in his own thought, and petty practical details, which he left to his daemon or divine sign. For the daemon, see Plato, *Apology*, 31C ff.

7 Our other main source of information is Xenophon's *Memorabilia, Apology* and *Symposium*.

8 *Rep.* = Plato's *Republic*.

9 In 'Hegel's *Sittlichkeit*', *Proc. Arist. Soc.*, xxxvi, 1935–6, pp. 223–36, E. F. Carritt argued that Hegel's notion of *Sittlichkeit* involves a confusion between the analysis and definition of morality in general (moral philosophy) and a picture of the state of affairs which in many or all circumstances one should try to bring about or maintain (political propaganda). He regards Plato's account of justice in a man as a definition of morality, but his account of justice in the state as political propaganda. This is tempting, but it has little warrant in Plato, for whom both accounts are on a par.

10 *Vorlesungen über die Geschichte der Philosophie*, eds. E. Moldenhauer and K. M. Michel (Frankfurt am Main, 1971), vol. ii, pp. 106f; *History of Philosophy*, tr. E. S. Haldane and F. H. Simson (London, 1894), vol. ii, pp. 91f. (In subsequent references to them, these titles will be abbreviated to *GP* and *HP* respectively.)

11 Hegel translates Plato's word *polis* as *Staat*. Polis means city or city-state rather

than state, but no single English word conveys its full flavour. I have followed Hegel in speaking of the state, since, as far as I can see, no important point in the argument depends on it.

12 See Hegel's criticism of Kantian *Moralität* in e.g. *PhR* §§ 135ff.

13 See e.g. the remarks about the state of nature in *GP*, II, 107f; *HP*, II, 92f.

14 E.g. *GP*, II, 107: 'Das Recht ist das geistige Insich – und Beisichsein, das Dasein haben will, tätig ist, – Freiheit, die sich Dasein gibt; die Sache is mein, d.h. ich setze meine Freiheit in diese äusserliche Sache.' Haldane, *HP*, II, 92, interprets this as a reference to property. This may be right, but it is hard to see the relevance of property here, especially in the light of *GP*, II, 119, *HP*, II, 104, where Hegel stresses that for Plato justice is not concerned exclusively with property. Hegel is perhaps allowing his own views to intrude into his account of Plato.

15 Cf. note 12 above.

16 On this, see Hegel's article, 'Über die wissenschaftlichen Behandlungsarten des Naturrechts', in *Kritisches Journal der Philosophie*, II, 2 (Tübingen, 1803); reprinted in *Jenaer Schriften, 1801–1807*, eds. E. Moldenhauer and K. M. Michel (Frankfurt am Main, 1970), pp. 434ff; *Natural Law*, trs. T. M. Knox (Philadelphia, 1975). The third section of this article deals interestingly, but obscurely, with Plato's views on the matter.

17 Hegel exaggerates Plato's organicism. Plato tends to compare his state not to a living organism – except when he is stressing the analogy between the state and the soul of a man – but rather to a work of art: e.g. *Rep.* 420B ff. The precise significance of this comparison is controversial. For accounts of organicism, see Kant, *Kritik der Urteilskraft*, esp. part II, 'Kritik der teleologischen Urteilskraft'; E. Nagel, 'Wholes, Sums, and Organic Unities', in *Parts and Wholes*, ed. D. Lerner (New York, 1963); and H. J. McCloskey, 'The State as an Organism, as a Person, and as an End in Itself', in *The Philosophical Review*, LXXII (1963). There is some looseness of fit here with Hegel's logic. When speaking of the relation between the Greek state and its individual members, Hegel tends to appeal to the category of substance. The notion of an organism, which is applied to the relation between the social whole and the three classes, as well as individuals, is generally associated with the concept, rather than substance: e.g. *Wissenschaft der Logik*, eds. E. Moldenhauer and K. M. Michel (Frankfurt am Main, 1969), vol. II, p. 257; *Hegel's Science of Logic*, tr. A. V. Miller (London, 1969), p. 586.

18 These considerations complicate Carritt's contrast between moral or political advocacy and defining the nature of morality. Hegel would argue that this contrast arises only within the moral viewpoint. Within a purely ethical community neither advocacy nor definition would have a place. In particular, an ethical man cannot advocate the ethical. But this still leaves Plato's own position unclear. Plato himself blurs the distinction between description and prescription; he introduces his account of the just state as an account of what any state would have to be like: *Rep.*, 369B ff.

19 Hegel contrasts subjective freedom with objective freedom, because he does not believe that men who unquestioningly follow the rules of the practices in which

they engage are necessarily unfree. The plausibility of this is enhanced if we consider, for example, chess-players, mathematicians or musicians who do not question the rules which they follow.

20 Plato would have seen this distinction. Cf. *Rep.*, 339B ff. Hegel does not normally conflate making up one's own mind ('subjectivity') and acting self-interestedly ('particularity'). In *PR*, for example, they are treated quite separately, and in the *Philosophy of History* they are regarded as connected, but distinct: *Vorlesungen über die Philosophie der Geschichte*, eds. E. Moldenhauer and K. M. Michel (Frankfurt am Main, 1970), pp. 326ff; *Philosophy of History*, tr. J. Sibree (New York, 1956), pp. 267ff.

21 Cf. note 17 above.

22 We might expect Hegel to regard the warriors as the particular (*besonderes*) element and as concerned with the particular, but the arbitrariness of doing so seems to have restrained him. In any case, physical needs are elsewhere regarded as particular, e.g. *GP*, II, 108; *HP*, II, 93 (though Haldane misleadingly renders '*Besonderes*' as 'the individual element'). Cf. Hegel, *Enzyklopädie*, §§ 163 and 164 for this recurrent triad.

23 Cf. *PR*, §§ 41ff.

24 'Darin, dass ich Person bin, liegt ja vielmehr meine Fähigkeit zum Eigentum.' Cf. *HP*, II, 111, where the translation is, however, too free to be of service.

25 E.g. *PG*, pp. 313ff.; *PS*, §§ 438ff.

26 *PG*, pp. 330ff.; *PS*, §§ 464ff.

27 *PG*, pp. 317f.; *PS*, § 445.

28 A. C. MacIntyre, 'A Mistake about Causality in Social Science', in *Philosophy, Politics, and Society*, II, eds. P. Laslett and W. G. Runciman (Oxford, 1962), pp. 48–70, argues that 'in modern industrial society rational discourse is ineliminable', for the reason that its eliminators would have themselves to be rational. 'Rational discourse' presumably includes the ability to make up your own mind, without blindly following rules and conventions. But this consideration would apply as much to Plato's state and time as to Hegel's.

29 E.g. *PG*, *Einleitung*.

Political community and individual freedom in Hegel's philosophy of state

1 See Z. A. Pelczynski, 'The Hegelian conception of the state' in Z. A. Pelczynski (ed.), *Hegel's Political Philosophy: Problems and Perspectives* (Cambridge, 1971), pp. 13, 14.

2 G. W. F. Hegel, *Lectures on the Philosophy of World History: Introduction: Reason in History*, trans. by H. B. Nisbet with an Introduction by Duncan Forbes (Cambridge, 1975). Quotations from or references to this work in the text of the essay are abbreviated as '*LPhWH*'; the figures refer to page numbers. Elsewhere the work will be referred to as *Reason in History*.

3 See, e.g., references to Montesquieu in G. W. F. Hegel, *Natural Law* (Philadelphia, Pa., 1975), p. 128, in *Hegel's Philosophy of Right*, § 3 and *Reason in History*, pp. 101–2.

4 Charles Taylor in *Hegel and Modern Society* (Cambridge, 1979) perceptively discusses the relation between community and culture and sums it up as follows: 'men are expressive beings by virtue of belonging to a culture, and a culture is sustained, nourished and handed down in a community' (p. 2).

5 Hegel clearly recognizes the importance of historical experiences, traditions and myths in creating national identity. 'If he is asked, any Englishman will say of himself and his fellow citizens that it is they who rule the East Indies and the oceans of the world, who dominate world trade, who have a parliament and trial by jury, etc. It is deeds such as these which give the nation its sense of identity' (*LPhWH*, 103).

6 G. W. F. Hegel, *Lectures on the History of Philosophy*, trans. by E. S. Haldane and F. H. Simson, 3 vols. (London, 1892–6). References to this edition in the text are abbreviated as *LHPH*.

7 Cp. the eloquent description of the ancient Greeks' and Romans' attitude to their country in G. W. F. Hegel, *Early Theological Writings*, trans. T. M. Knox (Chicago, 1948), reprinted as paperback by the University of Pennsylvania Press (Philadelphia, 1971), pp. 154, 155.

8 In the Haldane–Simson translation of Hegel's *Lectures on the History of Philosophy*, vol. III, Hegel gives four and a half pages to Hobbes – more than to any other modern political thinker. He also discusses him in the *Natural Law* essay.

9 *The Social Contract*, bk 1, ch. 7 (G. D. H. Cole's translation, Everyman's Library edition, London 1913, p. 12).

10 Cf. G. W. F. Hegel, *The Phenomenology of Spirit*, trans. A. V. Miller (Oxford, 1977), (BB), VI, A, C, 'Legal status'; *The Philosophy of History*, trans. J. Sibree (New York, 1956), pt. III, sec. III ch. I, 'Rome under the Emperors'; and the *Philosophy of Right*, §357.

11 They are discussed in detail in the essays by S. Benhabib and A. Ryan in this volume. See also P. Stillman 'Property, freedom, and individuality in Hegel's and Marx's Political Thought' in *Property*, NOMOS, XXII, 1980.

12 For a full and illuminating discussion of 'ethical substance' see C. Taylor, *Hegel* (Cambridge, 1975), ch. 14.

13 Of course, Hegel even more strongly emphasizes hereditary monarchy as a necessary feature of the modern state, and he is much more explicit about the powers of the crown in the constitution. His main argument is that a monarch embodies 'the "personality" of the state' in the only adequate way (*PhR*, §279) and that he actualizes the self-consciousness and self-determination of the political community by willing laws or consenting to them (§279, last paragraph of the Remark). The argument sounds very implausible today, when the right to universal political participation in a meaningful form is generally accepted and counts as an essential element of political freedom.

14 Hegel excludes women from participation in public affairs, arguing that their proper role in ethical life is played in the family. It is unclear from his remarks whether they are even full members of civil society in his view (cf., e.g., *PhR*, §166 and Addition).

15 *Hegel's Philosophy of Mind*, trans. W. Wallace (Oxford, 1971) p. 272.

16 Valuable discussions of Hegel's concept of freedom (albeit with rather less

attention to social and institutional context) can be found in the following essays:
G. H. R. Parkinson, 'Hegel's concept of freedom' in *Royal Institute of Philosophy Lectures*, v (1970–1); J. Plamenatz, 'History as the realization of freedom' and M. Riedel, 'Nature and freedom in Hegel's *Philosophy of Right*' in Z. A. Pelczynski (ed.), *Hegel's Political Philosophy* (Cambridge, 1971); R. L. Schacht, 'Hegel on freedom' in A. MacIntyre (ed.), *Hegel: A Collection of Critical Essays* (Garden City, N.Y., 1972).

My essay has benefitted from the critical comments of Richard Dien Winfield, for which I wish to thank him warmly.

Hegel's rational idealism: family and state as ethical communities

1 *PhR*, §75. All passages from Hegel's *Philosophy of Right* will be identified in this manner. I have followed the corrected Knox translation (Oxford, 1945) with minor changes.

2 See ch. 4 of Hegel's *Phenomenology of Spirit*. For a critique of abstract recognition see the section entitled 'Der Rechtszustand' in ch. 6.

3 *Mere Christianity*, bk. 3, ch. 6.

4 Cf. Hegel, *Die Vernunft in der Geschichte*, ed. by J. Hoffmeister (Hamburg, 1955), pp. 111–12.

5 See Hegel's early polemic against the notion of political authority as a kind of personal property, especially in *The German Constitution*. Cf. *Hegel's Political Writings*, trans. T. M. Knox, with an introd. by Z. A. Pelczynski (Oxford, 1964), pp. 149–51.

6 Rousseau makes a definite break with Hobbes and Locke on this point, but since he retains the social–contract framework Hegel finds the break to be incomplete and remains ambivalent towards his thought. See *PhR*, §258. *Editor's Note*: The challenge of Rousseau's political thought to Hegel is discussed in Z. A. Pelczynski's first essay.

7 See especially *PhR*, §§209, 217–18 and 229.

8 *PhR*, §186. Hegel's reference here to necessity rather than freedom also suggests an element of compulsion, which Knox inserts into his translation. It is, of course, no uniquely Hegelian discovery that the market and those who manipulate it, whether in public or private capacities, often appear to participating individuals as external compulsion. Calling the system free enterprise cannot hide this fact except from those who do not wish to see it.

9 *PhR*, §§236, 239 and 241. On the problem of poverty see §§185, 185A, 195 and 245, along with the excellent discussion in S. Avineri, *Hegel's Theory of the Modern State* (Cambridge, 1972).

10 For more detailed examination of this theme see G. Heiman, 'The Sources and Significance of Hegel's Corporate Doctrine', in Z. A. Pelczynski (ed.), *Hegel's Political Philosophy: Problems and Perspectives* (Cambridge, 1971), and the essay by A. S. Walton in the present volume. Jacques Ellul's discussion of the atomization of society resulting from the disappearance of such natural social groups as *family* and *guild* is especially interesting in relation to Hegel's views

of the corporation. See *The Technological Society*, trans. by John Wilkinson with an introd. by Robert K. Merton (London, 1965), pp. 49ff.

11 Hegel links the notion of need with the Understanding by calling this state the *Not-und Verstandesstaat*. Cf. *PhR*, §§187 and 189 on the Understanding.

12 Cf. *PhR*, §199 and n. 8 above.

13 On Hegel's concept of freedom as self-determination see the essays by Plamenatz and Riedel in the Pelczynski volume cited in n. 10 and also my own essay, 'Hegel's Theory of the Concept' in Schmitz and Steinkraus (eds.), *Art and Logic in Hegel's Philosophy* (Atlantic Heights, N.J., 1980). The latter focuses on the conceptual analysis of freedom in §§5 to 7 of the *Philosophy of Right*.

14 Charles Taylor, *Hegel* (Cambridge, 1975), p. 376. On the notion of *Sittlichkeit* see all of ch. 14 of Taylor's book, entitled 'Ethical Substance' or the slightly briefer discussion under the same title in sec. 3 of ch. 2 of his *Hegel and Modern Society* (Cambridge, 1979). Also see sections 5C and 6A of my own *History and Truth in Hegel's Phenomenology* (Atlantic Heights, N.J., 1979).

15 On the transcendence of the natural see *PhR*, §§146 and 151.

16 Cf. *PhR*, §163A on the difference between marriage and concubinage.

17 Since 'natural' is contrasted with 'spiritual' rather than with 'unnatural' Hegel uses the term not only to refer to biological selfhood but to pre-ethical selfhood in the sense of pre-social(ized) selfhood. This is Rousseau's state of *nature*.

18 Compare *PhR*, §145 with §§162–3. This is the metaphor which underlies Hegel's talk about ethical substance and substantial ties.

19 On the link between universality and substantiality see the passages from *PhR*, §§258 and 260 cited below. English loses etymological linkages which are visible and audible in German between universality (*Allgemeinheit*), community (*Gemeinschaft*) and congregation (*Gemeinde*). Since Hegel takes these linkages very seriously, true universality never signifies for him abstract similarity but always concrete participation in some actual totality.

20 It is quite clear that Hegel here uses 'person' in its legal sense.

21 *PhR*, §§257 and 267–9.

22 In the so-called Frankfurt 'System Fragment' of 1800 Hegel formulates the unity of identity and difference as '*die Verbindung der Verbindung und der Nichtverbindung*'. Cf. *Werke* I, 422 (Suhrkamp, 1971). In the *Differenzschrift* it is '*die Identität der Identität und der Nichtidentität*. Cf. *Gesammelte Werke* IV, 64, (Hamburg, 1968).

23 Compare *PhR*, §268 with the discussion of love in sec. 5B of Westphal, *History and Truth*.

24 *PhR*, §§267, 273 and 276. For a helpful discussion of what Hegel means by 'the political state' see Pelczynski, 'The Hegelian Conception of the State', in the volume cited in n. 10 above.

25 *Lectures on the Philosophy of World History: Introduction*, trans. by H. B. Nisbet with an introd. by D. Forbes (Cambridge, 1975), p. 96.

26 *The Social Contract*, bk. 1, ch. 8.

27 The nationalism of Hegel's view of the state refuses to become the internationalism which his own logic calls for. International relations remain for him essentially contractual.

28 Thus government management of the economy as well as private economic activity is to be included in the transformation described as the sacramentalism of economic life in the remainder of this paragraph.

29 Autonomous economic life in this context means not the freedom of private interests from government regulation, but the primacy of economic goals in private and public life.

30 *PhR*, §270. In his early writings Hegel was especially sensitive to the conflict between the private pursuit of wealth and the health of what he understands by the state. See *Werke* I, 205–7, 213–14, 333–5, and 516–17 and *Gesammelte Werke*, IV, 456–8. For English translations see 'On Christianity' in *Early Theological Writings*, trans. by T. M. Knox and R. Kroner (New York, (1961), pp. 155–7, 164–5, 221–2, *Hegel's Political Writings*, pp. 189–90, and *Natural Law*, trans. by T. M. Knox (Philadelphia, 1975) pp. 100–2.

31 *PhR*, §§185, 190–5, 256.

32 See ch. 3 of John V. Taylor, *Enough is Enough* (Augsburg, Mn., 1977).

Hegel's concept of the state and Marx's early critique

1 It is, as is well known, of fundamental importance for the marxism of G. della Volpe (cf. G. Giannantoni, *Il marxismo di Galvano della Volpe*, Rome, 1976, 47ff.) and his school (cf., for instance, L. Colletti, *Il marxismo e Hegel*, (Bari, 1973), pp. 24ff and 87ff.)

2 Cf. on this point my investigation *Hegel diverso* (Bari, 1977), p. 224ff.

3 Cf. my edition: G. W. F. Hegel, *Vorlesungen über Rechtsphilosophie 1818–1831* (Stuttgart–Bad Cannstatt, 1973), vol. I, pp. 217–351.

4 §114, *PhR* 1818–19. The surviving text is not quite perfect. My suggested emendations in brackets.

5 Cf. §113, *PhR* 1818–19: 'The several branches of civil society must...be embodied in corporations, whose conflicting interests, as well as their general interconnections, in turn require overall supervision'.

6 '*Ideell*' is Hegel's term for all finite things the apparent independence of which is absorbed into the unity of a greater whole, and finally into the unity of an infinite whole. Cf. *Logic*, I, 1, 2: 'Infinity'.

7 *Theologische Jugendschriften*, edited by H. Nohl (Tübingen, 1907), p. 366.

8 Ibid. p. 222 (Hegel, 'On Christianity,' *Early Theological Writings* trans. T. M. Knox and Richard Kroner, New York, 1961, p. 154). See also p. 70: 'The free republican who, in the spirit of his people, expended his energies, his life, for his country and did it out of duty, did not esteem his efforts so highly as to demand payment or indemnity. He had worked for his Idea, his duty'.

9 Cf. *Jenenser Realphilosophie* I (*1803–1804*) (Leipzig, 1932), p. 233: 'Inasmuch as this communal work is the work of them all as consciousness, they externalize themselves in it; but this external is their own doing; it is only what they have made it; they have ceased to be active in it; and in this externality of themselves, in their existence as annulled agents, as mediator, they see themselves as *one* people, and this their work is thus their own mind itself'.

10 Cf. *Jenenser Realphilosophie* II (*1805–1806*) (Leipzig, 1931), p. 251; *Phänomenologie*

des Geistes, VI, A, c: 'Der Rechtzustand'; *PhR* 1820, §124R, §138R, §185R, §260 and §279R.

11 'It contains freedom in its reality and (has) its true strength only in so far as these spheres (family, private rights and private welfare) and their particular interests are independently developed within it, (and individuals) have *duties* towards it only in so far as these are at the same time their own *rights* acknowledged by the state'. (Text slightly emended; cf. §261 at *PhR*, 1820).

12 In the *Philosophy of Right* published in 1820 it is struck out *in toto* and replaced by §§265–7.

13 Here, as at many other points in his lecture of 1818–19, Hegel is attacking his old opponent, Fries, and the latter's supporters in the student fraternities. §118 shows that his polemic against Fries is novel in its sharpness, but not in its contents.

14 Hegel thus distances himself from contemporary constitutionalism. The Prussian King, Friedrich Wilhelm III, had of course solemnly promised, in 1815, to give his country a constitution, but had not kept that promise.

15 With this expression Hegel refers to his theory of the division of powers (cf. *PhR*, 1818–19, §121).

16 §119R, Cf. Hegel's discussion of the 'ethical tragedy' which the absolute constantly enacts with itself in his *Naturrechtsaufsatz* (1802): The 'political nullity' in which the members of this estate are private people has its 'compensation in the fruits of peace and trade and in the complete security of enjoyment of these'. For the young Hegel, the reconciliation lies in 'the recognition of necessity and in the right which ethical life cedes to its inorganic nature and to the subterranean powers by relinquishing and sacrificing a part of itself to them.' *Schriften zur Politik und Rechtsphilosophie*, ed. by G. Lasson (Hamburg, 1967), p. 383 f.; *Natural Law*, trans. by T. M. Knox (Philadelphia, 1975), pp. 103, 104. Hegel's ideas on sacrifice and reconciliation at this point are a re-interpretation of Euripide's *Eumenides*.

17 In the section on 'Public Law' in *The Metaphysics of Morals*, §45, Kant had stated that the relationship of the three state powers was like 'the three propositions in a practical syllogism: the law of the sovereign Will is like the major premise; the command to act according to the law is like the minor premise that is the principle of subsumption under the Will; and the adjudication (the sentence) that establishes what the actual Law of the land in the case under consideration is, is like the conclusion'. See Kant, *The Metaphysical Elements of Justice*, trans. with an introduction by John Ladd (Indianapolis/New York, 1965), p. 78.

18 We can see that this really is Hegel's opinion from his explanatory notes to §122: 'Princely power consists of the empty final decision; there is as yet no question of objective decisions based on reasons.' This is the business of the government. Cf. §124R 'The regent puts his name to it.' 'It is often not important *which* decision is made, only that *some* decision should be made.' (cf. Ilting, *Hegel diverso*, Bari, 1977, p. 35ff.).

19 Cf. H. O. Meisner, *Die Lehre vom monarchischen Prinzip im Zeitalter der Restauration und des Deutschen Bundes* (Breslau, 1913).

20 'Every people has its history, and realises its spirit (§121R).

21 Cf. §152: '...(he recognizes) as the end which moves him to act the universal which is itself unmoved'.

22 Cf. §270R: 'The state is the divine will, in the sense that it is spirit present [on earth] unfolding itself to be the actual shape and organisation of a world.'

23 In his essay on the Estates of Wurtemberg Hegel had, even in 1817, spoken of the 'idea hitherto accepted without thought or reason' 'that governments and princes were based on divine authority' (*Werke*, VI, p. 393).

24 The word 'only', which is indispensible for the sense, is missing here, although it was there in the corresponding passage of the lectures of 1818–19 (§117).

25 Since fulfilment of his duties as a subject does not directly guarantee the citizen protection of his rights, the sense of this expression must be: that in the *authoritarian* state the citizen is only granted rights *on the basis of* the fulfilment of his duties as a subject.

26 This tallies with his procedure in preparing the second and third impressions during the revision of the *Encyclopedia* (1827 and 1830); cf. my edition, Hegel *Rechtsphilosophie*, IV, 755–903.

27 No connection between social institutions and the state has been worked out in 1818–19; §119f. ('the spirit of the state in its finiteness') and §121 ('the universal') are set against each other.

28 This was stated more clearly at a different point in 1818–19: see above, n. 5.

29 The manuscript has 'Fassung', clearly a mishearing for 'Verfassung'.

30 See above, n. 17.

31 The first four pages of the manuscript (one sheet) have not survived. Marx obviously took the last paragraph of the section, 'Civil Society' (§256), as his starting point; for his table of contents begins with the title, 'On Hegel's Transition and Explanation'. The four lost manuscript pages must therefore have dealt with §§256–60. Cf. *MEGA*, I, i, Introduction lxxi, p. 553, footnote.

32 Quotations (page and line) from *MEGA*, I, i. Textual corrections from the editions *Marx Engels Werke* (Berlin, 1958) and *Karl Marx, Frühschriften*, ed. H.-J. Leiber and P. Furth (Stuttgart, 1962) are taken into account. (English translations are taken from *Karl Marx: Critique of Hegel's 'Philosophy of Right'*, ed. Joseph O'Malley (Cambridge, 1970).

33 A comment of Hegel's on the relevant passage (§117) of his lecture of 1818–19 makes this quite clear: For those who remain in particularity, the universal appears as an external necessity.

34 In social institutions, according to Hegel's account (§266) the mind (or 'spirit') of the state is still in a condition of 'necessity'; and thus forms 'a realm of appearance'. However the mind of the state also exists 'as the ideality' of this appearance, inasmuch as 'the heart' of these institutions becomes 'objective and actual to itself'. This 'necessity' thereby becomes a 'shape of freedom' for itself.

   The necessity of the transition from the social to the political plane, which in this text is more often implicit than explicit, is based on the idea that, in the discussions and decisions on the level of social institutions, one is still dealing with limited interests and aims. On a higher, i.e. political, level a coordination of interests must therefore be sought; and the stability of the whole must be secured. On the political level, social interests turn out to be one-sided (or 'ideal'; see above, note 6). The transition to this level is therefore necessary, because individuals and groups in society pursue only their own respective interests, and because coordination of interests and securing of stability are indispensible for a just and durable ordering of communal life.

When, on the other hand, Marx comments that 'the pure ideality of an actual sphere, however, could exist only as knowledge (*Wissenschaft*)' (410. 22–24), he has clearly completely failed to understand this idea of Hegel's.

35 This is especially clear in the following objection: § 268 contains a nice exposition concerning political sentiment, or patriotism, which has nothing to do with the logical development except that Hegel defines it as 'simply a product of the institutions subsisting in the *state* since rationality is actually present in the state', while on the other hand these institutions are equally an objectification of the political sentiment'.

What Marx here advances as a critical objection had already been said by Hegel himself in his philosophy-of-right lecture course of 1824–5, by way of amplification of his idea: 'Patriotism is the result of the institutions of the state, but this sentiment is just as much a cause; for through it and from it the state receives its confirmation and preservation.'

36 The activity of the government is not limited to the execution of prescribed laws, though the expression 'executive' does indeed seem to imply this. Neither judicial decisions (Kant) nor the political decisions of a monarch (Hegel) can be understood as a deduction from laws and government instructions.

37 Marx thus faithfully maintained the principle formulated by Feuerbach at the beginning of his *Preliminary Theses Towards the Reform of Philosophy* (1843): 'We need only turn predicate into subject, and make the resulting subject into object and principle, i.e. turn speculative philosophy on its head and we have the pure, clear, undisguised truth'.

38 According to Hegel, the end of the state is by no means confined to this, since the destiny of individuals is, of course, 'to lead a universal life'. But it is significant that Hegel makes no further mention of this at the end of his account, after he has restricted the political rights of citizens to participation in self-government in social institutions (§ 264).

39 Cf. on this point, Ilting, *Hegel diverso*, pp. 200ff.

40 Ibid. pp. 211ff.

41 In his dissertation, Marx construes the recent history of philosophy in the manner of Hegel as an immanent development process of the world mind; cf. ibid., pp. 131–3, 143, 64f.

42 Cf. Colletti, *Il marxismo e Hegel*, 94ff.

43 Cf. J. Habermas, *Hegel, Politische Schriften* (Frankfurt, 1966).

44 Cf. J. d'Hondt, *Hegel en son temps (Berlin 1818–1831)* (Paris, 1968); Ilting, *Hegel diverso*; D. Suhr, *Bewusstseinsverfassung und Gesellschaftsverfassung: über Hegel und Marx zu einer dialektischen Verfassungstheorie* (Berlin, 1975).

45 The world spirit 'goes ever on and on, because spirit is progress alone. Spirit often seems to have forgotten and lost itself, but inwardly opposed to itself, it is inwardly working ever forward (as when Hamlet says of the ghost of his father, 'Well said, old mole! canst work i' the ground so fast?'), until grown strong

in itself it bursts asunder the crust of earth which divided it from the sun, its Notion, so that the earth crumbles away. At such a time, when the encircling crust, like a soulless decaying tenement, crumbles away, and spirit displays itself arrayed in a new youth, the seven league boots are at length adopted.' *Vorlesungen über die Geschichte der Philosophie* in *Werke*, xix, 685; (*Hegel's Lectures on the History of Philosophy*, ed. & trans. by E. S. Haldane & Frances H. Simson, London, 1968, vol. iii, pp. 546–7). 'We have to give ear to its urgency – when the mole that is within forces its way on – and we have to make it a reality.' (ibid. *Werke*, xix, 691; Haldane & Simson translation p. 533). This conception of his philosophical task can be found even in a letter of Hegel's of 28/10/1808: 'Theoretical work, I am daily more firmly persuaded, achieves more than practical work: if only the realm of ideas is revolutionised, reality cannot resist.'

46 It may suffice here to refer to the verdict of G. della Volpe, *Umanesimo positivo e emancipazione marxista* (Milano, 1963), p. 9.

47 N. Bobbio, *Esiste una dottrina marxista dello Stato?* and *Quali alternative alla democrazia rappresentativa?* in *Mondoperaio*, 1975, no. 8 and no. 10. Cf. the discussion by D. Zolo, *Stato socialista e libertà borghese: una discussione sui fondamenti della teoria politica marxista* (Bari, 1976).

48 Marx, *Towards a Critique of Hegel's Philosophy of Rights*, in *MEGA*, i, i. pp. 613–41f.

Towards a new systematic reading of Hegel's philosophy of right

1 N. Luhmann, *Soziologische Aufklärung* (Opladen, 1971) p. 138. (The phrase refers to political society.) For a critique of Luhmann from the position of categorical social philosophy, see K. Hartmann, 'Systemtheoretische Soziologie und kategoriale Sozialphilosophie', *Philosophische Perspektiven* vol. 5 (1973), pp. 130–61, and K. Hartmann, 'Gesellschaft und Staat – Eine Konfrontation von systemtheoretischer Soziologie und kategorialer Sozialphilosophie', in 'Ist systematische Philosophie möglich?' Stuttgarter Hegel-Kongress 1975, *Hegel-Studien Beiheft* 15 (Bonn, 1977).

2 Cf. *Philosophy of Right*, Knox translation, §262 and Addition; cf. also §§260, 261, 265 and Additions.

3 We are thinking here of what Hegel means by *Vorstellung*. Cf. *Encyclopaedia* (1830), §20. (Vorstellung is sometimes translated as 'representation').

4 J. S. Mill, *Representative Government*, ch. 5. Mill is discussing the relationship between legislature and executive. Modern sociology dealing with problems of social organization, such as Luhmann's, also has important contributions to make in this field.

5 Hegel is sometimes guilty of obfuscation in only referring to the political state, once he has reached it, and in viewing the opposition state/political state as a consequence of a constitution involving representative government. See *Philosophy of History*, tr. J. Sibree (New York, 1956), p. 48. The problem is not without theoretical interest. Hegel wants to say a number of things. The politically constituted individuals encounter each other via the differentiated structure of the political state; the political state is categorically identical with them. On the other hand, the political state is the Idea of the state developed

to its differences (*PhR*, §269); thus the political state appears as a truer form of state, the sublation of the indeterminacy of the state at large. Two problems emerge, viz., that the dialectical movement of the *Philosophy of Right* is geared to a particular goal, with the implication of a dangerous overemphasis of the political state; and that sociological arguments to back up the political state as an organized group, as a *viable* political agent, cannot be accommodated within the theory.

6 Cf. *PhR*, §§272, 287. In the *Propaedeutic*, First Course, the judiciary is still a power of its own, together with the police. In what follows, we cannot go into the details of Hegel's theory of powers. To do this would involve us in a discussion of their mediation in terms of a logic of concept, the deeper reason for Hegel's rejection of the separation of powers, and clearly a point that would take us too far afield.

7 This has been pointed out by N. von Thaden. See K.-H. Ilting's edition of G. W. F. Hegel, *Vorlesungen über Rechtsphilosophie 1818–1831* (Stuttgart–Bad Canstatt, 1973), Vol. 1, p. 107.

8 K. Marx, *Kritik des Hegelschen Staatsrechts*, Cotta-Studienausgabe (Stuttgart, 1960) vol. 1, pp. 291ff.

9 In his essay 'The Structure of Hegel's Philosophy of Right"' (in *Hegel's Political Philosophy: Problems and Perspectives*, ed. by Z. A. Pelczynski (Cambridge, 1971), K.-H. Ilting talks about an 'unintelligible exception to the "dialectical order" of presenting [Hegel's] theories', p. 106. On this point, cf. K. Hartmann, *Die Marxsche Theorie* (Berlin, 1970), p. 103. Ilting thinks that the reasons for Hegel's avoidance of sovereignty of the people, which comes with his reversal of the dialectical order, are empirical ones, reasons which Hegel has claimed many times to be unworthy of philosophy (to wit, that the state would depend on the whims and fancies of individuals, making stable and rational government impossible). We believe that the problem lies deeper than that; it is a problem that has to do with the categorical distinction between individual, society and state.

10 *Encyclopaedia* (1830), §544.

11 Contrast *PhR*, §301R. Hegel objects to 'all' as opposed to 'many', arguing that what is meant is something 'quite indeterminate' and not the quite determinate 'all'. The many, he claims, are in any case not 'all' in the determinate sense since children and women, amongst others, are excluded. The objection is not a serious one; the indeterminacy of what 'all' should mean can be admitted; in fact, it calls for criteria regulating participation in the legislature.

12 Aristotle still sees this in a naive way, failing to distinguish society and state, when he thinks that a mixture of practical people and clever intellectuals in the management of the city state would do the trick. Cf. *Politics* 1282a14ff.

13 'Zur Kritik des gegenwärtigen Staats – und Völkerrechts', *Hallische Jahrbücher* 1840, no. 154, column 1228. Cf. the Griesheim lecture notes from 1824–5 in Ilting's edition of *Vorlesungen über Rechtsphilosophie*, vol. 4, pp. 52 and 670–6.

14 K.-H. Ilting, op.cit., vol. 1, pp. 81ff.

15 Ruge, *Hallische Jahrbücher*, 1840, no. 154, col. 1225. For Ruge's notion of a historical correction, see *Deutsche Jahrbücher*, 1842, cols. 755–68.

16 It is debatable whether Hegel did not, after all, view representation (*PhR*, §301)

as the way the state achieves self-reflection, despite his statement to the contrary in the *Philosophy of History* (cf. note 5 above).

17 M. Kriele, *Einführung in die Staatslehre* (Hamburg, 1975) pp. 113ff. and 224ff. One might read Hegel's rejection of a separation of powers in favour of a system of mediation between them as a denial of any sovereignty in the constitutional state, as maintained by Kriele. To accommodate this suggestion, one would have to go beyond the political state of Hegel's theory and embrace the state as including the politically constituted many who, deprived of any sovereignty of their own, will enjoy jurisdictions and rights within the constitutional state.

18 See Pius XI, *Quadragesimo anno*, in *Acta Apostolicae Sedis* 1931, vol. 23, pp. 203ff.; W. von Humboldt, *Ideen zu einem Versuch, die Grenzen des Staats zu bestimmen*; J. S. Mill, *On Liberty*, ch. 3. On our understanding of subsidiarity, non-central or non-state agents or agencies should be considered subsidiary to the state rather than things being the other way round, with the state serving as an agency subsidiary to the individual or to society (an ambiguity apparent in Catholic social theory). Our concept of subsidiarity may be understood as a reflexive concept in terms of which we proceed from the whole and consider its elements in relation to it. Despite reservations, we are close to the notion of subsidiarity developed by E. Forsthoff in his *Allgemeines Verwaltungsrecht*, 10th edition (Munich, 1973).

19 Cf. *Philosophy of History*, trans. J. Sibree (New York, 1956), p. 454.

20 Hegel only says that the 'individuals of the mass' are 'actual both as private and substantial [political] persons'; 'hence they attain satisfaction in part on the former [private] level, in an immediate manner, in part, however, on the latter [universal] level: in one way, they may find their essential self-consciousness in institutions which are the *universal* implicit in their particular interests, in another an institution such as the corporation supplies them with an occupation and an activity directed on a universal end' *PhR*, §264, Knox translation as adapted by the author. From this it is clear that subsidiarity is not thematized. Hegel is merely discussing how the individual can find satisfaction in the various spheres.

21 One might mention Lorenz von Stein in this regard. On his scheme, there is a tension between society and state which could be transformed by social reforms instituted by the state, such as measures conducive to prosperity (acquisition of capital on the part of workers), into a state of affairs where free personalities affirm the state. Cf., e.g. 'Der Begriff der Gesellschaft und die Gesetze ihrer Bewegung', reprint of the 1850 text in Lorenz von Stein, *Gesellschaft-Staat-Recht*, ed. by E. Forsthoff (Frankfurt, 1972), pp. 108–13.

22 An instrumental interpretation of the state, such as Forsthoff's popular thesis about the state as a *providing agency* (*Instanz der Daseinsvorsorge*) is comparatively remote from Hegel in as much as on such a reading the state would not figure as an object of affirmation except *qua* means for particular, if intersubjective, ends. Cf. Hegel's *Philosophy of Right*, Introduction.

23 We are thinking of J. Habermas' *Legitimationsprobleme im Spätkapitalismus* (Frankfurt, 1973).

Propaganda and analysis: the background to Hegel's article on the English Reform Bill

1 T. M. Knox and Z. A. Pelczynski (eds), *Hegel's Political Writings* (Oxford, 1964), p. 295, subsequently cited as (*PW*, 295). For a fuller statement of his views on the European background, see *Philosophy of History*, tr. J. Sibree, (Dover Publications, 1956), pp. 438–57; H. Schneider, 'Notizen Hegels zur Julirevolution' in *Hegel-Studien*, 11 (1976), 85–87.

2 K. Rosenkranz, *Hegels Leben* (Berlin, 1844), p. 419; F. Rosenzweig, *Hegel und der Staat* (Munich and Berlin, 1920), vol. 2, p. 230.

3 E. R. Huber, *Deutsche Verfassungsgeschichte* (Stuttgart, 1957), vol. 1, pp. 95–313.

4 Friedrich von Gentz (1764–1832) translated Burke into German (1794). In his *Neue deutsche Monatsschrift* (1795–1800) and *Historisches Journal* (1799–1801), he published numerous articles pointing out the merits of British institutions. His work was part of a general anti-French propaganda campaign; see C. S. B. Buckland, *Friedrich von Gentz* (London, 1933).

5 See his 'Sur le rétablissement de la dignité Impériale en Allemagne' (17 February 1815), in G. H. Pertz, *Das Leben des Ministers Frh. v. Stein*, 6 vols. (Berlin, 1849–55), IV, 329. Cf. H. Tiedemann, *Der deutsche Kaisergedanke vor und nach dem Wiener Kongress* (Breslau, 1932). Hegel had advocated something similar in 'The German Constitution' (1799–1802); see *PW*, 238–42.

6 See B. G. Niebuhr's (1776–1831) foreword to F. L. W. P. Vincke's (1774–1844) *Darstellung der inneren Verwaltung Grossbritanniens* (Berlin, 1815). One of the most quoted English tags in the Prussian political writings of the post-war period was Pope's: 'For forms of government let fools contest; Whate'er is best administered is best'. Cf. T. Wilhelm, *Die englische Verfassung und der vormärzliche Liberalismus* (Stuttgart, 1928).

7 'Über den Unterschied zwischen den landständischen und Repräsentative-Verfassungen', see J. L. Klueber, *Wichtige Urkunden für den Rechtszustand der deutschen Nation*, ed. C. Welcker (Mannheim, 1844), p. 213.

8 W. von Humboldt (1767–1835), C. F. von Beyme (1765–1838), H. von Boyen (1771–1848). For Humboldt's 'Über Preussens ständische Verfassung' (4 February 1819), see his *Gesammelte Schriften*, 17 vols. (Berlin, 1903–36), XIII, 225. Cf. P. Haake, *Der preussische Verfassungskampf* (Munich and Berlin, 1921); W. M. Simon *The Failure of the Prussian Reform Movement* (Ithaca and New York, 1955).

9 P. Clauswitz, *Die Städteordnung von 1808 und die Stadt Berlin* (Berlin, 1908), p. 180; *Morning Chronicle*, 15 September 1830, leader. Cf. W. Conze, *Staat und Gesellschaft im deutschen Vormärz* (Stuttgart, 1970), p. 101. The riots caused by social distress in Aachen, Cologne, Elberfeld, Berlin and Breslau did not become political.

10 R. F. Leslie, *Polish Politics and the Revolution of November 1830* (Westport, Conn., 1969), p. 223; *Morning Chronicle*, 7 September, 1 October, 10 November 1830.

11 In 1835 there were 329 of these local authorities. Cf. L. von Zedlitz-Neukirch, *Der Preussische Staat in allen seinen Beziehungen* (Berlin, 1835), I, 233. On the protracted negotiations which on 17 March 1831 eventually gave rise to the order

in cabinet outlining the reform of the municipalities, see H. Schneider, *Der Preussische Staatsrat* (Munich, 1952), p. 161.

12 'Allgemeine Gesetze wegen Anordnung der Provinzialstände' in *Gesetzesammlung für die Königlich Preussichen Staaten* (Berlin, 1823), no. 810. Cf. Huber, *Deutsche Verfassungsgeschichte*, I, 170.

13 See Schneider, *Der Preussische Staatsrat*.

14 R. Koselleck, *Preussen zwischen Reform und Revolution* (Stuttgart, 1975), p. 422.

15 C. T. Perthes, *Friedrich Perthes' Leben*, 3 vols. (Gotha, 1872), III, 331–52.

16 L. Ranke, *Historisch-Politische Zeitschrift*, 2 vols. (Hamburg and Berlin, 1832–6).

17 K. F. Eichhorn (1781–1854), F. C. von Savigny (1779–1861); cf. J. F. von Schulte, *Karl Friedrich Eichhorn* (Stuttgart, 1884), p. 177.

18 *Berliner Schriften 1818–1831*, ed. J. Hoffmeister (Hamburg, 1956), pp. 732, 738, 784. The earliest of these excerpts dates from June 1819, the latest from September 1831.

19 H. Schneider, 'Dokumente zu Hegels politischem Denken 1830/31' in *Hegel-Studien*, 11 (1976), 81–4. Beyme wrote on 16 May 1831, and Hegel replied on 21 May.

20 Of these thirty, all but seven were for reform. Of the fifty-four provincial papers surveyed, twenty were for reform, twenty-two tended to support it, five tended to oppose it and seven were against it.

21 19 September 1830. The peculiarities of this reporting were noticed abroad. On 23 August 1830, for example, the *Morning Chronicle* forecast, from the turn events had taken in France, that the *Allgemeine Preussische Staats-Zeitung* would 'be much more circumspect than formerly in speaking of the French liberals'. On 15 January 1831 the same paper observed: 'We may allow everything that has been mentioned in the Prussian State Gazette, respecting the beneficial institutions in the kingdom of Poland introduced by the Russian Government, and yet find the discontent of the Polish Chiefs, and of the Nobility, very easy to be accounted for. They, not the industrious citizens, the merchants or the manufacturers, who were powerfully supported by the government, thought they had reasons to be discontented.'

22 Spencer Perceval's speech of 9 March was reported on 17 March, Macaulay's of 2 March on 12 March, Sheil's of 21 March on 31 March. O'Connell's, delivered on 8 March, was appraised on 17 March.

23 Written in London on 18 March, published 26 March 1831, p. 706.

24 In the morning issue of 26 April, (*PW*, 295–304); in the evening issue (*PW*, 304–12); on 29 April (*PW*, 312–31).

25 The correspondence is to be found in *Berliner Schriften*, pp. 785–6. No copy of the printed version of the last part of the article has yet come to light, and it is not absolutely certain that it was published by order of the king. The main evidence is a letter from Hegel's wife to Niethammer, dated 2 December 1831.

26 Hegel probably began work on his article when the last reports of the Parliamentary debates appeared in the *Gazette* on 7 April, and seems still to have been writing it when the first parts were published on 26 April. Since we have the manuscript, we know, for example, that he inserted the reference to bribery at Liverpool (*PW*, 316) in the proofs. The *Gazette* did not report the matter until

2 May, but the English papers of 22 April, which carried news of it, arrived in Berlin on 28 April, the day before this section of the article was published. The observation concerning Henry Hunt in section four (*PW*, 324), which is part of the main manuscript text, is almost certainly based upon the English papers which arrived in Berlin on 25 April; see *Morning Chronicle*, 19 April: 'In the early part of the evening Mr *Hunt* cut rather an awkward figure, in consequence of the disclaimers from all quarters of his representation of the sentiments of the people.'

27 *Encyclopaedia*, §§236–44.

28 *Philosophy of Right*, tr. T. M. Knox (Oxford, 1962), p. 10.

29 *PW*, 239; K. Düsing, *Das Problem der Subjektivität in Hegels Logik* (Bonn, 1976). F. Nicolin, 'Hegel über konstitutionelle Monarchie' in *Hegel-Studien*, 10 (1975) 79–86, questions the issue raised by K.-H. Ilting in his *G. W. F. Hegel: Vorlesungen über Rechtsphilosophie 1818–1831*, 4 vols. (Stuttgart–Bad Cannstatt, 1973–4), I, 25–126, with regard to Hegel's conception of monarchy. *Editor's note* – K.-H. Ilting's view that Hegel altered his considered view of monarchy under the pressure of political circumstances is restated in his first essay in this volume.

30 *PW*, 313. On the critique of logical atomism, see *Encyclopaedia*, §98, and *PW*, 263. The history of Hegel's early ideas on this constitutional issue has been well surveyed and analysed by R. K. Hočevar, *Stände und Repräsentation beim jungen Hegel* (Munich, 1968).

31 *Rechtsphilosophie*, ed. Ilting, I, 314; III, 610; IV, 508, 520, 597 (economics); I, 209; II, 683; III, 599, 613, 704; IV, 494, 611 (class conflict); II, 101, 351; III, 304, 665; IV, 294, 535, 557, 561, 562, 564, 577 (legal system); II, 99, 699; III, 749, 794, 814, 815; IV, 252, 582, 677, 686, 707, 719, 738 (constitution); II, 219; III, 825; IV, 193, 649, 668, 728 (institutions). Hegel concluded his last main series of lectures on political philosophy in the spring of 1825.

32 *Rechtsphilosophie*, ed. Ilting, IV. 707. Cf. *PW*, 324–6.

33 *Quarterly Review*, XVI, 511–52, January 1817. The surviving note concerns Titus Oates (p. 523).

34 *Quarterly Review*, XIX, 79–118, April 1818. Hegel notes down the instances of the unreasonable formality of English legal procedures given on p. 116. For further evidence that he read the *Quarterly*, see his *Philosophy of Subjective Spirit* (tr. M. J. Petry, 3 vols. Dordrecht, 1978), I, p. cix, and *History of Philosophy* (tr. E. S. Haldane and F. H. Simson, 3 vols., London and New York, 1963), III, 186.

35 *Edinburgh Review*, XXIX, 217–37, November 1817. The article was certainly in Hegel's mind when he criticized the 'positivity' of the English legal system (*PW*, 299), and could have influenced his treatment of codification in *PhR*, §216.

36 M. J. Petry, 'Hegel and the Morning Chronicle', *Hegel-Studien*, 11 (1976), 11–80, which includes the texts of all Hegel's excerpts.

37 Largely on account of the income from its advertisements. See Ivon Asquith, 'Advertising and the press in the late eighteenth and early nineteenth centuries: James Perry and the *Morning Chronicle* 1790–1821', *The Historical Journal*, 4 (1975), 703–25.

38 Austin Mitchell, *The Whigs in Opposition 1815–1830* (Oxford, 1967), p. 44.

39 John Stuart Mill, *Autobiography*, ed. J. Stillinger (Oxford, 1971), ch. IV, p. 55.

40 *London Review*, January 1836, no. 4, pp. 302–5. Cf. Mill's *Government* (London, 1821), p. 8, the reprint of the article published in the supplement to the *Encyclopedia Britannica*; E. Halévy, *The Growth of Philosophic Radicalism*, tr. M. Morris, (London, 1972), pp. 418–21.

41 G. Wallas, *The Life of Francis Place* (London, 1925), p. 274; cf. E. Halévy, *Thomas Hodgskin* (Paris, 1903). Hodgskin's *Labour Defended against the Claims of Capital* (London, 1825; 3rd ed. New York, 1936), which is often referred to approvingly by Marx, was advertised in the *Chronicle*, and seems to have attracted Hegel's attention: *Hegel-Studien*, 11 (1976), 34.

42 Alexander Bain, *James Mill* (London, 1882), pp. 363–7.

43 Joseph Hamburger, *James Mill and the Art of Revolution* (New Haven, Conn., and London, 1963).

44 C. B. Cone, *The English Jacobins* (New York, 1968), pp. 162–4. For an excellent survey of the more general historical background, see John Cannon, *Parliamentary Reform 1640–1832* (Cambridge, 1973).

45 Cf. 8 January 1831: 'But great care is necessary that the zeal for enforcing the law be accompanied by sound discretion, and that the punishments be not more severe, than in the opinion of the society on which they are intended to operate as an example, they ought to be. If severity be such as to enlist the feelings of the people on the side of the guilty, then the object sought to be obtained by the punishment – the protection of property – is weakened, instead of being strengthened.' Cf. E. J. Hobsbawm and G. Rudé, *Captain Swing* (London, 1969).

46 See, for example, 9 November 1830. The king and his ministers cancelled their appointment at the Guildhall for fear that Wellington might be attacked by the mob. Cf. Wellington's *Despatches*, 8 vols. (London, 1867–80), VII, 353.

47 Leaders, 5, 8 and 11 February 1831. Cf. *PW*, 303–7; Petry, 'Hegel and the Morning Chronicle', extracts 8, 13, 16, 17, 18, 22, 27, 29, 42, 51.

48 18 November 1830, leader, written on the day on which the new ministry was formed.

49 14 January 1831, leader. Like Marx, Hodgskin claimed that a society which allowed capitalists to exploit labour-power and accumulate surplus-value gave rise to two basic classes, that of the workers and that of the 'leviathans who are so anxious to retain their power over us' (*Labour Defended*, p. 39). It is interesting to find Coleridge questioning the ontological foundations of this logic once the Reform committee's proposals had been announced: *Table Talk*, 20 March 1831, 'Government is not founded on property, taken merely as such, in the abstract; it is founded on *unequal* property; the inequality is an essential term in the position. The phrases – higher, middle, and lower classes, with reference to this point of representation – are delusive; no such divisions as classes actually exist in society. There is an indissoluble blending and interfusion of persons from top to bottom; and no man can trace a line of separation through them, except such a confessedly unmeaning and unjustifiable line of empiricism as 10 1.' W. R. Beyer, 'Der Stellenwert der französischen Juli-Revolution von 1830 im Denken Hegels', *Deutsche Zeitschrift für Philosophie*, 5 (1971), 628–43, has emphasized the importance of class difference in Hegel's conception of the situation in Britain.

50 Henry Earl Grey, *The Correspondence of the late Earl Grey with King William IV'*, 2 vols. (London, 1867), I, 94–104.

51 Hobsbawm and Rudé, *Captain Swing*, p. 257.

52 7 April 1831. Wallas, *Life of Francis Place*, p. 245.

53 2 March 1831. *Hansard's Parliamentary Debates*, 3rd series, vol. II, cols. 1190–1217.

54 D. J. Rowe, 'Class and Political Radicalism in London, 1831–2', *Historical Journal*, XIII (1970), 31–46.

55 G. A. Williams, 'The Insurrection at Merthyr Tydfil in 1831', *Transactions of the Honourable Society of Cymrodorion* (1965), p. 227. Cf. *Morning Chronicle*, 14 June 1831: 'On the Saturday red flags were used, and such was the ferocious feeling of the mob, that at Hirwain a large basin of calf's blood was obtained, and a flag actually washed in it, and borne to Merthyr by a flag-bearer, with his hands imbued and covered with blood.' Cf. also D. J. V. Jones, 'The Merthyr Riots of 1831', *Welsh History Review*, 3 (1966), 173–205.

56 F. O. Darvall, *Popular Disturbances and Public Order in Regency England* (Oxford, 1969).

57 *The Correspondence of Princess Lieven and Earl Grey*, ed. G. Le Strange, 3 vols. (London, 1890), II, 189.

58 Cannon, *Parliamentary Reform*, p. 250.

59 Grey, *Correspondence*, I, 65, 94–104.

60 As the result of it, the total electorate the Tories could claim to represent was only 50,000. Simply the four Whig members for Yorkshire could claim to represent twice that number of voters.

61 Bentham's works were not well known in Germany at that time. When L. F. W. Meynier published his translation of the *Essay on Political Tactics* (London, 1791) at Erlangen in 1817, he thought that the author of the book was dead. *The Introduction to the Principles of Morals and Legislation* (London, 1789) was translated by F. E. Beneke (2 vols. Berlin, 1830), one of the numerous enemies Hegel made while teaching at Berlin, but neither work seems to have attracted much attention. It is possible, but by no means certain, that the 'greatest happiness' principle had some influence upon Hegel's *Encyclopaedia*, §§ 469–80.

Obligation, contract and exchange: on the significance of Hegel's abstract right

1 C. B. Macpherson, *The Political Theory of Possessive Individualism* (Oxford, 1962).

2 H. Ritter, 'Person und Eigentum: zu Hegels "Grundlinien der Philosophie des Rechts"' in *Materialien zu Hegels Rechtsphilosophie*, ed. M. Riedel (Frankfurt am Main, 1974), pp. 152–76; K.-H. Ilting, 'The Structure of Hegel's "Philosophy of Right"', in *Hegel's Political Philosophy*, ed. Z. A. Pelczynski (Cambridge, 1971), pp. 90–106; Manfred Riedel, 'Nature and Freedom in Hegel's "Philosophy of Right"', ibid, pp. 136–50; Norberto Bobbio, 'Hegel und die Naturrechtslehre', in *Materialien zu Hegels Rechtsphilosophie*, ed. M. Riedel (Frankfurt am Main, 1975), vol. 2, pp. 18–109.

3 Max Weber, *The Theory of Social and Economic Organization*, ed. Talcott Parsons (New York, 1964), pp. 324ff.

4 Paul Chamley, 'Les origines de la pensée économique de Hegel', *Hegel-Studien*, 3 (1965); P. Chamley, *Economie politique et philosophie chez Steuart et Hegel* (Paris, 1963); George Lukács, *The Young Hegel*, trans. R. Livingston (London, 1975); R. Plant, 'Hegel and Political Economy', *New Left Review*, 103–4 (1977).

5 G. W. F. Hegel, *Natural Law*, trans. T. M. Knox (Philadelphia, 1975), p. 104. Where Knox's translation differs from the original I have used 'Über die wissenschaftlichen Behandlungsarten des Naturrechts, seine Stelle in der praktischen Philosophie und sein Verhältnis zu den positiven Rechtswissenschaften' in G. W. F. Hegel, *Jenaer Schriften (1801–1807)* (Frankfurt am Main, 1970); here, pp. 469ff.; cf. also Lukács, *The Young Hegel*, p. 375.

6 G. W. F. Hegel, *Jenaer Realphilosophie*, ed. J. Hoffmeister (Hamburg, 1967), pp. 217ff. (my translation). Cf. the analysis there with that of Marx's in order to appreciate the latter's indebtedness to Hegel as regards the structure of modern exchange relations; K. Marx, *Grundrisse*, trans. M. Nicolaus (New York, 1973), pp. 240ff.; *Capital*, trans. S. Moore and E. Aveling (New York, 1973), vol. 1, pp. 84ff.

7 Karl Polanyi, 'The Economy as Instituted Process', in *Trade and Markets in Early Empires*, eds. K. Polanyi, C. M. Arensberg and H. W. Pearson (Glencoe, Ill., 1957), pp. 254ff.

8 On premodern exchange relations, cf. ibid., pp. 64–97; 243–70; Weber, *The Theory of Social and Economic Organization*, pp. 168ff.; Marx, *Grundrisse*, pp. 459–515.

9 *Les structures élémentaires de la parenté* (Paris, 1967), p. 63.

10 Sir Henry Maine, *Ancient Law* (1861).

11 On contract and obligation, cf. H. L. A. Hart, 'Are There any Natural Rights?', in *Political Philosophy*, ed. A. Quinton (New York, 1973), pp. 55ff.

12 Hegel's ambivalence towards the French Revolution has been analyzed by J. Habermas, 'Hegel's Critique of the French Revolution' in *Theory and Practice*, trans. J. Viertel (Boston, 1973), p. 123. Hegel's rejection of the political thrust of contractarian argument raises a set of issues that cannot be adequately dealt with within the scope of this essay. I would define them as the normative and institutional aspects of 'sovereignty'. The question of the 'rule of law' discussed in this essay can be analytically distinguished from issues pertaining to sovereignty in previous contract theories and in Hegel's *Philosophy of Right*. Whereas the 'rule of law' defines the public procedural format within which the union of individuals constituting a social entity can be conceptualized, sovereignty defines the political identity, or the governmental form, to be assumed by such a social unity. At this point the metaphor of the 'contract' breaks down. While Hobbes writes of 'authorization' (*Leviathan*, introd. C. B. Macpherson, p. 217), Locke describes a 'fiduciary trust of government' (*Two Treatises of Civil Government*, ed. Peter Laslett, Cambridge, 1970, ch. 13), Rousseau postulates the metaphor of the 'general will' (*Du contrat social*, Paris, 1962, pp. 249ff.) and Kant resorts to the vision of the 'republican constitution' (*Metaphysical Elements of Justice*, trans. J. Ladd, New York, 1965, p. 112). On the distinction between the 'rule of law' and 'sovereignty', cf. Franz Neumann, 'The Governance of the Rule of Law' (Unpublished Diss. Ms., London School of Economics and Political

Science, 1936). I would like to thank Dr Alfons Söllner of the University of Berlin for having brought this manuscript to my attention.

13 Also G. W. F. Hegel, *Vorlesungen über Rechtsphilosophie 1818–1831*, ed. K.-H. Ilting (Stuttgart, 1974), vol. 4, pp. 251–4.

14 G. W. F. Hegel, 'The Constitution of Germany' in *Hegel's Political Writings*, trans. T. M. Knox, with an introductory essay by Z. A. Pelczynski (Oxford, 1964), p. 181.

15 Cf. Weber on 'patrimonial authority', *The Theory of Social and Economic Organization*, pp. 348ff.; Marc Bloch, *Feudal Society*, trans. L. A. Manyon (Chicago, 1961); Otto Gierke, *Political Theories of the Middle Ages*, trans. F. Maitland (Cambridge, 1936).

16 Prior to Fichte's *Grundlage des Naturrechts* and Kant's *Metaphysik der Sitten* the metaphors of the 'state of nature' and of the 'social contract' enjoyed an ambivalent status between fact and fiction, historical reality and analytical postulate. Hegel regards this as being the consequence of an essential ambiguity in the concept of 'nature' itself: 'The expression "nature" has this duality of meaning, that the nature of man is his spirituality, his rationality; his natural state, however, is that other state in which man acts according to his inclinations, instincts, etc. The rational is becoming master of the immediately natural', G. W. F. Hegel, *Vorlesungen über die Geschichte der Philosophie*, vol. 3 (Frankfurt am Main, 1971), p. 228; *Hegel's Philosophy of Mind*, trans. W. Wallace and A. V. Miller (Oxford, 1971), §431, 'Zusatz'; *Philosophy of Right*, §187. Although Hobbes, Locke and Rousseau reject the old Aristotelian sense of nature as an intelligible order whose teleological functioning reveals a normatively binding structure, they are not quite consistent about the concept. 'Nature', in their moral theories, is understood at times as that which man cannot avoid doing given his anthropological constitution while at others it shifts its meaning to that to which man has a moral and rational entitlement. This ambiguity is resolved only with the distinction, first introduced by Kant, between autonomous and heteronomous moral theories. Hegel accepts this Kantian meta-ethical turn in the argument which eliminates the normative ambiguity surrounding the concept of nature. I have dealt with this question at length in *Natural Right and Hegel: An Essay in Modern Political Philosophy* (Yale University Ph.D. Dissertation, 1977).

17 I. Kant, *The Metaphysical Elements of Justice*, pp. 76ff.; I. Kant, *On the Old Saw: That may be Right in Theory, but it won't Work in Practice*, trans. E. B. Ashton (Philadelphia, 1974), pp. 67ff.

18 On equality, cf. Hobbes, *Leviathan*, pp. 183ff.; Locke, *Second Treatise*, p. 289; Rousseau, *Du contrat social*, pp. 239ff., and 'De l'inégalité parmi les hommes' in *Du contrat social*, pp. 25ff.; Kant, *Metaphysical Elements of Justice*, p. 79, 93; J. G. Fichte, *Grundlage des Naturrechts nach Prinzipien der Wissenschaftslehre*, ed. I. H. Fichte (Berlin, 1971), pp. 85–92.

19 On the 'generality' and 'publicity' of laws, cf. Hobbes, *Leviathan*, pp. 311ff.; Locke, *Treatise*, pp. 371ff.; Kant, *Metaphysical Elements of Justice*, pp. 112ff.; Rousseau, *Du contrat social*, pp. 257–60; Fichte, *Grundlage*, pp. 103–10.

20 To include relations between husband and wife, father and child, master and servant under the concept of the 'state of nature', as Locke and Kant do, means

to exclude domestic or household relations from the jurisdiction of civil government. These social relations still continue to bind the individual on the basis of tradition and patriarchy. Kant retains some of the older juridical categories concerning the rights of the lord and the household, and writes of *jus realiter personalia* – the rights that the male head of household has over his wife, children, and servants (*Elements of Justice*, pp. 71ff.). Hegel's critique again reveals the extent to which he has 'rationalized' the contractarian tradition by eliminating the vestiges of patriarchy in the family (*PhR*, §40). Relations of authority and obligation in the household are reestablished by Hegel on psychological and anthropological grounds (*PhR*, §165; Addition to §116).

21 Cf. F. L. Neumann, 'The Governance of the Rule of Law', pp. 14–41.

22 For modern and premodern legal systems, cf. Roberto Unger, *Law in Modern Society* (New York, 1976), pp. 134–92, and the excellent discussion of law in Hegel, M. B. Foster, *The Political Philosophies of Plato and Hegel* (New York, 1965), pp. 110ff.

23 *PhR*, §270 on the right of subjectivity, and §§182 and 189 on the right of particularity.

24 'Rationality, taken generally and in the abstract, consists in the thorough-going unity of the universal and the single. Rationality, concrete in the state, consists (a) so far as its content is concerned, in the unity of objective freedom...and subjective freedom; and...(b) so far as its *form is concerned, in self-determining action on laws and principles which are thoughts and so universal*' (*PhR*, §258) (Emphasis mine).

25 *Phenomenology of Mind*, trans. J. B. Baillie (New York, 1967), pp. 665–79; *Phenomenology of Spirit*, trans. A. V. Miller (Oxford, 1977), pp. 399–409.

26 '...the concept of right, so far as its coming to be is concerned, falls outside the science of right; it is taken up here as given and its deduction is presupposed (*PhR*, §4). Unlike Knox, I do not take this deduction to be given in the *Encyclopaedia of the Philosophical Sciences* alone (Translator's Notes, p. 305). While in *PhR*, §4 Hegel himself argues that the 'proof that the will is free' has been established in the *Encyclopaedia*, the concept of 'right' discussed in the *Philosophy of Right* is historically and institutionally specific. To establish that freedom of the will is possible for humans, Hegel naturally proceeds from the premises of a philosophy of nature and of mind. But while 'mind, in general, is the basis of right' (§4), this does not imply that the specific historical forms assumed by 'right' are irrelevant in our defining this concept. Hence I consider my discussion of the *Phenomenology* to illuminate the historical genesis of the modern structure of right to be systematically justified.

27 J. Habermas, 'Labor and Interaction: Remarks on Hegel's *Jena Philosophy of Mind*', in *Theory and Practice*, pp. 144ff.

28 Hobbes, *Leviathan*, pp. 129–30.

29 *Phenomenology of Mind* (Baillie), p. 226; *Phenomenology of Spirit* (Miller), p. 110.

30 Ibid. (Baillie), p. 229; (Miller), p. 111.

31 Cf. the various formulas of the 'moral law', I. Kant, *Groundwork to the Metaphysics of Morals*, trans. H. J. Paton (New York, 1964), pp. 96ff.; 105ff.

32 Georg Simmel, *Kant* (München, 1921), p. 254.

33 I. Kant, *The Critique of Pure Reason*, trans. N. K. Smith (New York, 1965), B 135; Dieter Heinrich, 'Fichtes ursprüngliche Einsicht', D. Heinrich and H. Wagner (eds), in *Subjektivität und Metaphysik* (Frankfurt am Main, 1966).
34 *Hegel's Philosophy of Mind*, §490, p. 244.
35 *Natural Law*, p. 63; *Naturrecht*, p. 455 (translation is modified).
36 *Natural Law*, p. 113; *Naturrecht*, p. 505 (translation is modified). Knox curiously renders 'das Volk ist eher der Natur nach als der Einzelne' as 'The state comes by nature before the individual.' In the natural law Essays Hegel consciously juxtaposes Plato's and Aristotle's ideas on ethics to the 'naturalistic' conceptions of Hobbes and 'rationalistic' conceptions of Kant, which he finds profoundly inadequate.
37 Macpherson, *Political Theory of Possessive Individualism*, pp. 263ff.
38 Locke, *Second Treatise*, sec. 26; cf. Hannah Arendt's illuminating discussion in *The Human Condition* (Chicago, 1973), pp. 111ff.
39 Ibid., p. 306; cf. Gunnar Myrdal, *The Political Element in the Development of Economic Theory* (Cambridge, Mass., 1954), pp. 37–42; 60ff.
40 *Jenaer Realphilosophie*, pp. 205–6.
41 *Hegel's Philosophy in Mind*, §491.
42 Cf. Hegel's discussion of 'Revealed Religion', *Phenomenology of Mind* (Baillie), pp. 750–85; *Phenomenology of Spirit* (Miller), pp. 453–78.
43 Hegel, *Natural Law*, pp. 94ff.
44 Charles Taylor, *Hegel* (Cambridge, 1975), pp. 537ff.
45 Max Horkheimer, 'Traditional and Critical Theory', in *Critical Theory*, trans. M. J. O'Connel (New York, 1972); Karl Korsch, *Marxism and Philosophy*, trans. F. Halliday (New York, 1970); J.-P. Sartre, *Critique de la raison dialectique* (Paris, 1955); Maurice Merleau-Ponty, *Les aventures de la dialectique* (Paris, 1955).
46 Habermas, 'Labor and Interaction', in *Theory and Practice*, p. 16.
47 Karl Marx, *Critique of Hegel's Philosophy of Right*, trans. A. Jolin and J. O'Malley (Cambridge, 1970), pp. 63ff.; L. Krieger, *The German Idea of Freedom* (Chicago, 1957), pp. 86ff.
48 Cf. A. S. Walton's essay, 'Economy, utility and community', in this volume.
49 Cf. Raymond Plant's essay, 'Hegel on identity and legitimation', in this volume.
50 J. Habermas, *Legitimation Crisis*, trans. T. M. McCarthy (Boston, 1973), part II.

Hegel on work, ownership and citizenship

1 Charles Reich, 'The New Property' in C. B. Macpherson (ed.), *Property* (Oxford, 1979), pp. 179–98.
2 M. Djilas, *The New Class* (New York, 1957).
3 L. Trotsky, *The Revolution Betrayed* (New York, 1973), pp. 248–50.
4 A. Giddens, *The Class Structure of the Advanced Societies* (London, 1973), ch. 13.
5 Giddens, *The Class Structure* and R. Dahrendorf, *Class and Class-Conflict in Industrial Society* (London, 1959).
6 J. Locke, *Two Treatises on Government* (Cambridge, 1960), Bk. II, ch. V.
7 J.-J. Rousseau, *The Social Contract and Discourses* (Everyman edition, 1973), p. 83.
8 H. Reiss (ed.), *Kant's Political Writings* (Cambridge, 1970), pp. 41–53.

9 J. Mill, *Essay on Government* (Indianapolis, Ind., 1955), pp. 52–4.
10 Ibid., pp. 89–91.
11 D. Hume, 'Idea of a Perfect Commonwealth' in *Essays* (Oxford, 1963), pp. 499–515.
12 Charles Taylor, *Hegel* (Cambridge, 1975), pp. 456ff.
13 L. Easton & K. Guddat, *Writings of the Young Marx* (New York, 1967), p. 320.
14 A. Kojève, *Introduction to Reading Hegel*, trans. Allan Bloom (New York, 1969).
15 R. Dworkin, 'Liberalism' in B. Williams and S. Hampshire (eds.), *Public and Private Morality* (Cambridge, 1979).
16 Locke, *Two Treatises*, pp. 305–6.
17 R. Nozick, *Anarchy, State and Utopia* (Oxford, 1975), pp. 174–82.
18 Locke, *Two Treatises*, p. 311 and footnote.
19 A. Honoré, 'Ownership' in A. G. Guest (ed.), *Oxford Essays in Jurisprudence* (Oxford, 1961), pp. 107–47.
20 H. Arendt, *The Human Condition* (Chicago, 1953), pp. 136–7.
21 K. Marx, *Critique of Hegel's 'Philosophy of Right'* (Cambridge, 1970), p. 106.

Subjectivity and civil society

1 This essay is a modified version of a study which first appeared in French under the title 'Remarques sur le rapport entre subjectivité et société civile' in *Dialogue*, IX (1970), no. 2.
2 'Concept' is used here in the technical Hegelian sense. Cf. Hegel's *Philosophy of Right*, tr. T. M. Knox, (hereafter cited as *PhR*), pp. viii. ix.
3 *Sämtliche Werke*, ed. H. Glockner (Stuttgart, 1927), I, 509; *Natutral Law*, trans. T. M. Knox (Philadelphia, 1975).
4 M. Riedel, 'Der Begriff der "Bürgerlichen Gesellschaft" und das Problem seines geschichtlichen Ursprungs' in *Archiv für Rechts-und-Sozialphilosophie*, XLCIII (1962), 539ff.; reprinted in M. Riedel, *Studien zu Hegels Rechtsphilosophie* (Frankfurt am Main, 1969).
5 See A. Gehlen, 'Über die Geburt der Freiheit aus der Entfremdung' in *Studien zur Anthropologie und Soziologie* (Neuwied, 1963), p. 232ff.
6 *Hegels Theologische Jugendschriften*, ed. H. Nohl (Tübingen, 1907), p. 219ff.; English translation by T. M. Knox, G. W. F. Hegel, *Early Theological Writings* (Chicago, 1948), pp. 151ff. See J. Habermas, 'Hegel Kritik der französischen Revolution' in *Theorie und Praxis* (Neuwied, 1963), p. 89.
7 Habermas, *Theorie und Praxis*, p. 89ff.
8 *Über die wissenschaftlichen Behandlungsarten des Naturrechts*, Glockner, *op. cit.*, vol. I, p. 497ff., p. 510ff.; 'System der Sittlichkeit', in *Schriften zur Politik und Rechtsphilosophie*, ed. G. Lasson (Leipzig, 1913), p. 470ff.; English translation by H. S. Harris and T. M. Knox, cf. G. W. F. Hegel, *System of Ethical Life (1802/3) and First Philosophy of Spirit* (Albany, 1979).
9 Lasson *op. cit.*, p. 446ff.
10 See M. Riedel, 'Tradition und Revolution in Hegels "Philosophie des Rechts"' in *Zeitschrift für philosophe Forschung*, 16 (1962), 196–218.
11 *Jenenser Realphilosophie* II, ed. J. Hoffmeister (Leipzig, 1931), pp. 213, 221. See

also J. Ritter, 'Person und Eigentum: Zu Hegels "Grundlinien der Philosophie des Rechts"', §§ 34–81' in *Marxismusstudien* IV (1962), 196–218.

12 *Jenenser Realphilosophie* II, p. 206.

13 *Phänomenologie des Geistes*, ed. J. Hoffmeister (Hamburg, 1952), p. 20, afterwards cited as *PG*. *Phenomenology of Mind*, tr. J. B. Baillie, 2nd edition (London, 1931), p. 80, cited as *PM*.

14 *Differenz des Fichte'schen und Schelling'schen Systems der Philosophie* (Hamburg, 1962), p. 12.

15 *PG*, p. 418ff.; *PM*, p. 605ff.

16 *Differenz*, p. 217. See also J. Ritter, *Hegel und die Französische Revolution* (Frankfurt, 1965).

17 *Differenz*, pp. 12–13; Ritter, *Hegel und die Französische Revolution*, p. 40ff.

18 J. Habermas, 'Nachwort' to *Hegels Politische Schriften* (Suhrkamp edition, Frankfurt am Main, 1966) pp. 343–70.

19 See Habermas, *Theorie und Praxis*, p. 89.

20 See J. Habermas, *Strukturwandel der Öffentlichkeit* (Neuwied, 1962), p. 117.

21 Hegel, *Wissenschaft der Logik*, ed. G. Lasson (Hamburg, 1963), p. 482.

22 See Karl Marx, 'Critique of Hegel's *Philosophy of Right*', in *Marx-Engels Werke* (Berlin, 1964), I, 273–85; English translation by J. O'Malley (Cambridge University Press, 1970). See also Habermas, 'Nachwort', *Hegels Politische Schriften*, p. 368.

23 These ideas are developed in the following works: M. Horkheimer, 'Traditionelle und Krittische Theorie' in *Kritische Theorie der Gesellschaft* (Frankfurt, 1968), p. 137ff.; M. Horkheimer and Th. W. Adorno, *Dialektik der Aufklärung* (Amsterdam, 1947); Th. W. Adorno. *Negative Dialektik* (Suhrkamp, 1966); J. Habermas, *Theorie und Praxis* (Neuwied, 1963); H. Marcuse, *Der Eindimensionale Mensch* (Neuwied, 1967). The following English translations exist: M. Horkheimer and Th. W. Adorno, *Dialectic of Enlightenment*, tr. J. R. Cumming (London, 1973); Th. W. Adorno, *Negative Dialectics*, tr. E. B. Ashton (London, 1973); J. Habermas, *Theory and Practice*, tr. J. Viertel (London, 1974); H. Marcuse's *One Dimensional Man* originally appeared in English.

24 See especially A. Gehlen, *Die Seele im technischen Zeitalter* (Hamburg, 1957); *Urmensch und Spätkultur* (Frankfurt am Main, 1964).

25 *Differenz*, pp. 12–21; *PG*, p. 29ff.

26 Habermas, 'Dogmatismus, Vernunft und Entscheidung' in *Theorie und Praxis*, pp. 231–60.

27 See J. Habermas, *Erkenntnis und Interesse* (Frankfurt am Main, 1968); English translation by J. J. Shapiro, *Knowledge and Human Interests* (London, 1972). See also G. Kortian, *Metacritique: The Philosophical Argument of J. Habermas* (Cambridge, 1980).

The dialectic of civil society

1 *Marx-Engels Werke*, I, 205; Joseph O'Malley (ed.), *Critique of Hegel's Philosophy of Right by Karl Marx* (Cambridge, 1970), p. 7.

2 *MEW*, I, 206; O'Malley's translation, p. 8.

3 A lecture by Iring Fetscher on the contemporary relevance of Hegel's political philosophy, and the ensuing discussion in R. Heede and J. Ritter (eds.), *Hegel-Bilanz: Zur Aktualität und Inaktualität der Philosophie Hegels*, (Frankfurt am Main, 1973, pp. 193–230) may be cited as an example.

4 *PhR*, Preface, 73, 14; Knox, p. 12. Unless otherwise stated, source references (page and line) refer to the second volume of my four volume edition: G. W. F. Hegel, *Vorlesungen über Rechtsphilosophie 1818–1831* (Stuttgart–Bad Cannstatt, 1973–4). All quotations from Hegel are taken from T. M. Knox's translation, *Hegel's Philosophy of Right* (Oxford, 1962), referred to in the main text as 'Knox'.

5 Cf. *PhR*, Preface (58, 8–10; 59, 6–10; 74, 24–26) and §§2 (82, 2–5) and 31 (174, 8–10; 176, 1–12).

6 Excellent comments on Hegel's dialectical interpretation of civil society can be found in the essays by Francesco Valentini, 'Aspetti della "Società Civile" hegeliana', in *Giornale Critico della Filosofia Italiana*, 1968, pp. 92–112 and by Giuliano Marini, 'Aspetti sistematici della Società civile hegeliana', in *Filosofia*, xxviii, pp. 19–40; see also his *Libertà soggettiva e libertà oggettiva nella Filosofia del diritto hegeliana* (Naples, 1978).

7 Cf. *PhR*, Preface (58, 26ff.); §§2R (88, 14f.), 7R (126, 10ff.), 31 (1974, 8ff.) and 141R (538, 2f.).

8 Hegel is here doubtlessly orientating himself on the theory which bases the origin of the village community in the family, to be found in Aristotle's *Politics* (A, 2; 1252b, 15f.).

9 Hegel explains the connection in more detail in the remarks to §§124 and 185. He says there that the 'principle of the self-subsistent inherently infinite personality...dawned in an inward form in the Christian religion and in an external form...in the Roman world' (636, 3–7).

10 Hegel draws attention to this connection in *PhR*, §161.

11 Cf. Marx, *MEW*, I, 213; Hegel 'does not develop his thought out of what is objective, but what is objective in accordance with a ready-made thought which has its origin in the abstract sphere of logic' (O'Malley's translation, p. 14). *MEW*, I, 216: 'Logic is not used to prove the nature of the state, but the state is used to prove the logic' (O'Malley's translation, p. 18).

12 In *PhR*, §4, Hegel explains that the freedom of the will is the 'point of origin' for his development of the Idea of right; he expounds the system of right as 'the realm of freedom made actual'. This conception determines the dialectical structure and the course of his exposition throughout the *Philosophy of Right*.

13 Cf. *Logic*, III, 3, 2 (*Werke*, v, 263, 16f.): 'The elevation of the concept over life is that its reality is the concept-form released into universality.'

14 In *PhR*, §2, Hegel says expressly that the 'self-movement of the Idea' means nothing other than the philosophical reconstruction of the development of an

Idea: the philosophy of right's 'task is to develop the Idea – the Idea being the rational factor in any object of study – out of the concept, or, what is the same thing, to look on at the proper immanent development of the thing itself'. In § 31R Hegel says, rather more precisely, that 'thinking, as something subjective', merely observes the development of the Idea. According to Hegel, then, we must distinguish between philosophical reconstruction, which develops the reason of an object, and subjective thinking, which observes this development 'without for its part adding to it any ingredient of its own' (176, 8f.). As a philosophical method, dialectic is, then, that reconstruction of an object of knowledge which merely lays bare whatever implicit assumptions it contains. Inasmuch as this method also determines the presentation of a philosophical work, dialectic is also a mode of presentation. H. Fr. Fulda ('Hegels Dialektik als Begriffsbewegung und Darstellungsweise', in R. P. Hortsmann (ed.), *Seminar: Dialektik in der Philosophie Hegels* (Frankfurt am Main, 1978), pp. 124–74) uses the expression 'mode of presentation' in the sense of 'a linguistic form which takes on a certain philosophical programme in its execution' (p. 128). For this reason 'movement of concept' and 'mode of presentation' diverge rather more strongly in his analysis.

15 The 'philosophical Idea', thus defined, corresponds to what, in the *Logic*, is, as 'absolute Idea', the result of the movement of knowledge.

16 I have described this beginning of a rational theory of right in my essay, 'Wahrheit und Verbindlichkeit' in Kuno Lorenz (ed.), *Konstruktionen versus Positionen* (Berlin and New York, 1979), II, 115–45.

17 This is an Aristotelian expression. Cf. Arist. *Met.* A, 8; 989a15f.: 'That which is later in generation is prior in nature (φύσει)'. Similarly θ, 8; 1050a4f.: Actuality (ἐνέργεια) is prior in substantiality (οὐσία) 'because things that are posterior in becoming are prior in form (εἶδος) and in substantiality (οὐσία)'. Thus Aristotle distinguishes what is prior in knowledge 'for us' (πρὸς ἡμᾶς πρότερον) and what is prior in nature (φύσει) or 'in itself' (ἀπλῶς). Cf. *Post. Anal.* A, 2; 71b33: what is 'for us' posterior is 'in itself' prior. (Cf. *Phys.* A, 1; 184a16–21: The road to knowledge begins with what is more familiar 'to us' and leads to what is more familiar 'by nature'.) Hegel took over these conceptions from Aristotle; but, departing from Aristotle, he distinguishes terminologically between what is known 'in itself' or 'to us' as observers and what is 'established for it' (viz. consciousness on the way to its knowledge). I have dealt in detail with this connection between the Aristotelian theory of knowledge and Hegel's dialectic in my sketch, 'Zur Dialektik in der Rechtsphilosophie' (in *Hegel-Jahrbuch 1975*, ed. W. R. Beyer, Cologne, 1976, pp. 38–45).

18 Cf. my essay, 'Rechtsphilosophie als Phänomenologie des Bewusstseins der Freiheit', in Dieter Heinrich and Rolf-Peter Horstmann (eds), *Hegels Philosophie des Rechts: die Theorie der Rechtsformen und ihre Logik* (Stuttgart, 1982).

19 Hegel states explicitly that the problem of pauperism is connected with the protection of private property in early capitalist society: 'dependence and want increase *ad infinitum*, and the material to meet these is permanently barred to the needy man because it consists of external objects with the special character of

being property, the embodiment of the free will of others' (*PhR*, §195). Cf. *PhR*, §189.

20 Cf. Kant, *Metaphysics of Morals*, 'Theory of Right', §15.

21 Not until *PhR*, §299 is it stated that 'laws dealing with all sorts of private rights' are part of the competence of the law-giving authority. In §261R Hegel emphasises that 'laws concerning the rights of persons' depend on the 'specific character' of a state.

22 This dual aspect of a movement of the particular to the universal in Hegel's account of civil society, the development of the universal in its institutions and the raising of individuals to universality has been very well described by Giuliano Marini, *Libertà*, p. 50ff.

23 The 'formal' freedom and universality of the *bourgeois* which Hegel is discussing here is to be distinguished from the 'substantial freedom' of the *citoyen* (*PhR*, §257).

24 According to this view, then, the state is 'the actuality of the ethical Idea' (*PhR*, §257).

25 Cf. *PhR*, §185R (636, 3–7): 'The principle of the self-subsistent inherently infinite personality of the individual..., linked with abstract universality', 'dawned...in the Roman world.'

26 A bit later, (ibid., 21f) Hegel explains: 'it is the Idea of the state itself which disrupts itself into these two moments' (viz. family and civil society). This formulation is presumably based on an oversight: the state is indeed the basis of family and civil society, but precisely for this reason it is not absorbed into them.

27 Cf. Kant, *Grundlegung zur Metaphysik der Sitten*, Akademie-Ausgabe, IV, 408; Kant, *Critique of Practical Reason and other Writings in Moral Philosophy*, trans. & ed. L. W. Beck (Chicago, 1949), p. 68.

28 Cf. Kant, *Kritik der praktischen Vernunft*, Akademie-Ausgabe, V, 46; Beck's translation, p. 156.

Hegel on identity and legitimation

1 J. Habermas, *Legitimation Crisis* (London, 1976).

2 J. O'Connor, *The Fiscal Crisis of the State* (New York, 1973).

3 W. D. Narr and C. Offe, *Wohlfahrtsstaat und Massenloyalität* (Cologne, 1973).

4 C. Offe, *Struktureprobleme des kapitalistischen Staates* (Frankfurt am Main, 1972).

5 M. Best and W. E. Connolly, *The Politicised Economy* (Lexington, Mass., 1976).

6 F. A. Hayek, *The Constitution of Liberty* (London, 1957).

7 F. A. Hayek, *The Mirage of Social Justice* (London, 1976).

8 J. Habermas, 'On Social Identity', in *Telos*, vol. 19 (1974), pp. 97–8.

9 G. W. F. Hegel, *Natural Law*, trans. T. M. Knox with an introduction by H. B. Acton (1975), particularly pp. 94–5.

10 For a detailed discussion of *The Philosophy of Right* see my 'Hegel and Political Economy', *New Left Review*, nos. 103 and 104, 1977.

11 F. Hirsch, *The Social Limits to Growth* (London, 1976).

12 National-Ausgabe (Vienna, 1962), vol. 20, p. 322.

13 G. W. F. Hegel, *Jenenser Realphilosophie*, I, ed. J. Hoffmeister (Leipzig, 1932), p. 289.

14 *Jenenser Realphilosophie*, I, op. cit. p. 239.

15 G. W. F. Hegel, *Jenenser Realphilosophie*, II, ed. J. Hoffmeister (Leipzig, 1931), pp. 232–3.

16 K. Rosenkranz, *Hegels Leben* (Berlin, 1944), p. 86.

17 J. Ritter, *Hegel und die Französische Revolution* (Cologne, 1957).

18 G. W. F. Hegel, *Theologische Jugendschriften*, ed. H. Nohl (Tübingen, 1907), p. 223.

19 G. Heiman, 'The Sources and Significance of Hegel's Corporate Doctrine', in *Hegel's Political Philosophy*, ed. Z. A. Pelczynski (Cambridge, 1971).

20 G. W. F. Hegel, *Schriften zur Politik und Rechtsphilosophie*, ed. G. Lasson (Leipzig, 1932), p. 492.

21 *Phenomenology of Mind*, trans. J. Baillie (London, 1910), p. 377.

22 *Schriften zur Politik und Rechtsphilosophie*, p. 420.

23 *Jenenser Realphilosophie*, I, p. 221.

24 G. A. Kelly, 'Hegel's America', in *Philosophy and Public Affairs*, II, 236.

25 Ibid.

26 J. M. Buchanan and G. Tulloch, *The Calculus of Consent*, 2nd ed. (Ann Arbor, Mich., 1965).

27 S. Avineri, 'The Dialectics of Civil Society in Hegel's Thought' in *Hegel-Jahrbuch* 1975 (Cologne, 1976), p. 78.

Economy, utility and community in Hegel's theory of civil society

1 Raymond Plant argues that for Hegel the individual is involved in a complex of economic interdependencies which he scarcely understands and that rational control over the external world is achieved through the agency of the state; *Hegel* (2nd ed., Oxford, Blackwell, 1973), p. 111. I shall not attempt to deny that for Hegel the role of the state is critical, but will suggest that it is not *only* external control of civil society by the state which harnesses economic activity as constitutive of the development of self-consciousness; I shall suggest that Hegel advocates fundamental changes in the consciousness and organisation of civil society itself.

2 In his article 'Nature and Freedom in Hegel's Philosophy of Right' in *Hegel's Political Philosophy: Problems and Perspectives*, ed. Z. A. Pelczynski (Cambridge, 1971), Manfred Riedel has suggested that Hegel does not solve the problems of the relationship between nature and freedom at the level of civil society and the state. Civil society remains a sphere of experience characterised only by the necessity of needs. I shall suggest that Hegel's theory of civil society, while not unproblematic, does exhibit strenuous efforts on Hegel's part to integrate economic activity and the pursuit of individual interests into a theory of rational self-consciousness.

3 S. Avineri, *Hegel's Theory of the Modern State* (Cambridge, 1972), p. 154. R. Plant, 'Hegel and Political Economy', *New Left Review*, no. 103, May–June 1977, and no. 104, July–August 1977.

4 The Griesheim notes are contained in the fourth volume of the Ilting edition of Hegel's *Philosophy of Right*. K.-H. Ilting (ed.) *Vorlesungen über Rechtsphilosophie 1818–1831* (Stuttgart–Bad Cannstatt, 1973–4) (henceforth referred to as Ilting 4).

5 The empiricist searches for irreducible foundations of knowledge in the form of empirical data. See A. Quinton, 'The Foundations of Knowledge' in *British Analytical Philosophy*, ed. R. Williams and A. Montefiore (London, 1966). In *Reasons for Actions* (Oxford, 1971), p. 24, Richard Norman associates this notion with the idea of psychological states in utilitarianism.

6 The assumptions underlying utilitarian economic theory, in the form of neoclassical economics, are criticised at length by M. Hollis and E. Nell, *Rational Economic Man* (Cambridge, 1975).

7 Adam Smith did not regard economic progress and government action as entirely mutually exclusive. He recognised that a legal framework was essential to the effective functioning of the market. See J. M. Buchanan, 'Public Goods and Natural Liberty' in *The Market and the State: Essays in Honour of Adam Smith*, ed. T. Wilson and A. Skinner (Oxford, 1976), pp. 272–3.

8 K. Marx, *Critique of Hegel's 'Philosophy of Right'*, ed. J. O'Malley (Cambridge, 1972).

9 See *Encyclopaedia*, §131. C. Taylor, *Hegel* (Cambridge, 1975), pp. 273–6.

10 *Phänomenologie des Geistes*, ed. J. Hoffmeister (Hamburg, 1952), p. 288.

11 Cf. 'Rationality, taken generally and in the abstract, consists in the thoroughgoing unity of the universal and the single', *PhR*, §258.

12 This is the force of Hegel's claim that civil society must not be confused with the state. See *PhR*, §258.

13 R. Plant, *Hegel*, p. 16.

14 Unlike, for example, Durkheim, Hegel does not speak of the community as both the source and end of morality. On this theme in Durkheim see R. Norman, *Reasons for Actions*, p. 115.

15 This interpretation of Hegel's theory of community and of the relationship between the community and the individual resembles in some respects Oakeshott's concept of a 'practice' as it is developed in the second chapter of *On Human Conduct* (Oxford, 1975).

16 While criticising laissez-faire Hegel does not wish to argue that individuals should not be free to make a significant range of economic decisions. His solution to the problems of civil society does not as we shall see, lie only in greater state intervention but in a re-orientation of consciousness within civil society and a restructuring of economic relationships.

17 S. Avineri, *Hegel's Theory of the Modern State*, p. 149; R. Plant, 'Hegel and Political Economy', *New Left Review*, No. 104, p. 112.

18 *Hegel's Political Writings*, p. 324.

19 Ibid.

20 S. Avineri, *Hegel's Theory of the Modern State*, p. 154.

21 Some aspects of Hegel's attitude towards political economy and economic activity are usefully discussed in R. Plant, 'Hegel and Political Economy'. See especially *New Left Review* No. 103, pp. 88–92.

22 R. Plant, 'Hegel and Political Economy', *New Left Review* No. 103, pp. 91–2.

23 Ilting 3, p. 599 (from the Hotho lecture notes). The reference to England is
   significant. What I am suggesting here is that Hegel's depiction of the system
   of needs should be taken as a critique of classical political economy in general
   and England in particular. This critique provides the framework of the
   development of his own model of rational economy and society.

24 Hegel speaks of the degradation arising from the division of labour which grossly
   simplifies the productive process thereby making work routine and monotonous.
   Ilting 3, p. 611.

25 On the subject of corporations in Hegel see G. Heiman's essay in Pelczynski (ed.),
   Hegel's Political Philosophy.

26 S. Avineri, *Hegel's Theory of the Modern State*, p. 154; R. Plant, 'Hegel and
   Political Economy', *New Left Review*, no. 104, p. 113.

Nation, civil society, state

1 Georges Haupt et al. (eds), (Paris, 1974), p. 371.

2 Reprinted as 'Nationalism: past neglect and present power' in Isaiah Berlin,
  Against the Current: Essays in the History of Ideas (London, 1979).

3 *The Marx-Engels Reader*, ed. by Robert C. Tucker, 2nd ed. (New York, 1978),
  p. 4. Subsequent quotations from this work will be abbreviated as 'MER, 4'.
  4'.

4 See especially pp. 101–2 of G. W. F. Hegel, *Lectures on the Philosophy of World
  History: Introduction*, tr. by H. B. Nisbet (Cambridge, 1975).

5 See especially [§ 1. Concept of the State] of 'The German Constitution in *Hegel's
  Political Writings*, tr. by T. M. Knox (Oxford, 1964), pp. 153–64.

6 See A. Walicki, *Philosophy and Romantic Nationalism: the Case of Poland* (Oxford,
  1982), pp. 375–81.

7 See, e.g., G. W. F. Hegel, *Early Theological Writings*, tr. by T. M. Knox
  (Philadelphia, University of Prnnsylvania Press, 1971), pp. 154–5.

8 See *Hegel's Political Writings*, p. 160, 202–6.

9 See *Lectures on the Philosophy of World History*, pp. 96–7, 101, 102–3.

10 See Walicki, *Philosophy and Romantic Nationalism*, pt. II.

11 Walicki, *Philosophy and Romantic Nationalism*, pt. IV. As a proof of Marx's and
   Engels's interest in the cause of Polish independence see the two-volume edition
   Marks i Engels o Polsce [*Marx and Engels on Poland*], ed. by H. Michnik (Warsaw,
   1960), vol. I, pp. xcv, 444; vol. II, pp. 495. See also Karl Marx, *Beiträge zur
   Geschichte der Polnischen Frage: Manuskripte aus den Jahren 1863–1864* in parallel
   German–Polish version, eds. H. Michnik and S. Bergman (Warsaw, 1971), pp.
   lix, 1030. On Ireland see *Marx, Engels, Ireland and the Irish Question* (London,
   1978), p. 665.

SELECT BIBLIOGRAPHY

A. Works by Hegel

(English translations are given wherever possible)

Aesthetics: Lectures on Fine Art, tr. T. M. Knox, 2 vols. (Oxford, 1975).

The Difference between Fichte's and Schelling's System of Philosophy, tr. H. S. Harris and W. Cerf (Albany, 1977).

Early Theological Writings, tr. T. M. Knox and R. Kroner (Chicago, 1948; paperback edition, Philadelphia, 1971).

Hegel and the Human Spirit: A Translation of the Jena Lectures on the Philosophy of Spirit (1805–6) with Commentary, tr. L. Rauch (Detroit, 1983).

Hegel's Philosophy of Mind, tr. W. Wallace and A. V. Miller (Oxford, 1971).

Hegel's Philosophy of Right, tr. T. M. Knox (Oxford, 1942).

Hegel's Philosophy of Subjective Spirit, tr. M. J. Petry, 3 vols. (Dordrecht, 1978).

Hegel's Political Writings, tr. T. M. Knox (Oxford, 1964).

Hegel's Science of Logic, tr. A. V. Miller (London, 1969).

Hegel's System of Ethical Life and First Philosophy of Spirit, tr. H. S. Harris and T. M. Knox (Albany, 1979).

Jenaer Schriften, 1801–1807, eds. E. Moldenhauer and K. M. Michel (Frankfurt am Main, 1970).

Lectures on the History of Philosophy, tr. E. S. Haldane and F. Simson, 3 vols. (London, 1892–6).

Lectures on the Philosophy of History, tr. J. Sibree (New York, 1956).

Lectures on the Philosophy of World History. Introduction: Reason in History, tr. H. B. Nisbet (Cambridge, 1975).

The Logic of Hegel, tr. W. Wallace (Oxford, 1892).

Natural Law, tr. T. M. Knox (Philadelphia, 1975).

The Phenomenology of Mind, tr. J. B. Baillie, 2nd ed. (London, 1931).

The Phenomenology of Spirit, tr. A. V. Miller (Oxford, 1977).

Die Philosophie des Rechts: Die Mitschriften Wannenman (Heidelberg, 1817/18) und Homeyer (Berlin 1818/19), ed. K.-H. Ilting (Stuttgart, 1983).

Philosophie des Rechts: Die Vorlesung von 1819–20 in einer Nachschrift, ed. D. Henrich (Frankfurt am Main, 1983).

Vorlesungen über Naturrecht und Staatswissenschaft (1817–18), Nachschrift P. Wannenmann, eds. C. Becker *et al.* (Hamburg, 1983).

Vorlesungen über Rechtsphilosophie, 1818–1831, ed. K.-H. Ilting, 4 vols. (Stuttgart–Bad Cannstatt, 1973–4).

B. Secondary works and articles

Avineri, S. *Hegel's Theory of the Modern State* (Cambridge, 1972).

Baczko, B. 'Le problème du lien social chez Hegel et Rousseau', *Studia Filozoficzne*, Numer Obcojęzyczny 1 (Foreign Languages Issue no. 1), 1962.

Benhabib, S. 'The Logic of Civil Society: A Re-consideration of Hegel and Marx' in *Philosophy and Social Theory*, Summer, 1982.

Berki, R. *On Political Realism* (London, 1981).

Berry, C. J. *Hume, Hegel and Human Nature* (The Hague, 1982).

Beyer, W. R. 'Der Stellenwert der französischen Juli-Revolution von 1830 im Denken Hegels' in *Deutsche Zeitschrift für Philosophie*, vol. 5, 1971.

Bobbio, N. *Studi hegeliani* (Turin, 1981).

Bobbio, N. and Bovero, M. *Società e stato nella filosofia politica moderna: modello giusnaturalistico e modello hegelo-marxiano* (Milano, 1979).

Bodei, R. *Hegel e Weber: egemonia e legittimazione* (Bari, 1977).

Carritt, E. F. 'Hegel's Sittlichkeit' in *Proceedings of the Aristotelean Society*, XXXVI, 1935–6.

Cesa, C. *Hegel filosofo politico* (Naples, 1976).

Cesa, C. (ed.) *Il pensiero politico di Hegel: guida storica e critica* (Bari, 1979).

Chamley, P. *Économie politique et philosophie chez Steuart et Hegel* (Paris, 1963).
'Les Origines de la pensée économique de Hegel' in *Hegel-Studien*, 3, 1965.

Colletti, L. *Marxism and Hegel*, tr. L. Garner (London, 1973).

Cullen, B. *Hegel's Social and Political Thought* (Dublin, 1979).

D'Hondt, J. *Hegel en son temps: (Berlin, 1818–1831)* (Paris, 1968).

D'Hondt, J. (ed.) *Hegel et le Siècle des Lumières* (Paris, 1974).

Findlay, J. N. *Hegel: A Re-examination* (London, 1958).

Fleischmann, E. *La philosophie politique de Hegel* (Paris, 1964).

Foster, M. B. *The Political Philosophies of Plato and Hegel* (Oxford, 1935; reprinted New York, 1965).

Gadamer, H.-G. *Hegel's Dialectic: Five Hermeneutical Studies*, tr. P. Christopher Smith (London, 1976).

Gray, J. G. *Hegel's Hellenic Ideal* (New York, 1941); reprinted as *Hegel and Greek Thought* (New York, 1968).

Grégoire, F. *Études hégéliennes* (Louvain, 1958).

Habermas, J. *Theory and Practice*, tr. J. Viertel (Boston, 1973).

Harris, H. S. *Hegel's Development: Toward the Sunlight 1770–1801* (Oxford, 1972).
Hegel's Development: Night Thoughts (Jena, 1801–06) (Oxford, 1983).

Heede, R. and Ritter, J. (eds.) *Hegel-Bilanz: Zur Aktualität und Inaktualität der Philosophie Hegels* (Frankfurt am Main, 1973).

Heidegger, M. *Hegel's Concept of Experience* (New York, 1970).

Hočevar, R. *Hegel und der preussischer Staat* (Munich, 1973).
   Stände und Repräsentation beim jungen Hegel (Munich, 1968).
Horstmann, R. P. (ed.) *Seminar: Dialektik in der Philosophie Hegels* (Frankfurt am Main, 1978).
Hyppolite, J. *Genesis and Structure of Hegel's 'Phenomenology of Spirit'*, tr. S. Cherniak and J. Heckman (Evanston, 1974).
   Studies on Marx and Hegel, ed. and tr. J. O'Neill (London, 1969).
Ilting, K.-H. *Hegel diverso* (Bari, 1977).
Inwood, M. J. *Hegel* (London, 1983).
Jaeschke, W. 'Hegel's Last Year in Berlin' in *Bulletin of the Hegel Society of Great Britain*, no. 4, Autumn/Winter 1981.
Kainz, H. P. *Hegel's Philosophy of Right with Marx's Commentary: A Handbook for Students* (The Hague, 1974).
Kaufmann, W. *Hegel: Reinterpretation, Texts and Commentary* (London, 1966).
Kaufmann, W. (ed.) *Hegel's Political Philosophy* (New York, 1970).
Kelly, G. A. *Hegel's Retreat from Eleusis: Studies in Political Thought* (Princeton, 1978).
Kojève, A. *Introduction to the Reading of Hegel: Lectures on the 'Phenomenology of Spirit'*, ed. A. Bloom; tr. J. H. Nichols (New York, 1969).
Lauer, Q. *A Reading of Hegel's 'Phenomenology of Spirit'* (New York, 1976).
Lugarini, L., Riedel, M. and Bodei, R. *Filosofia e società in Hegel* (Trento, 1977).
Lukács, G. *The Young Hegel: Studies in the Relations between Dialectics and Economics*, tr. R. Livingstone (London, 1975).
MacIntyre, A. (ed.) *Hegel: A Collection of Critical Essays* (Garden City, N.Y., 1972).
Marcuse, H. *Reason and Revolution: Hegel and the Rise of Social Theory* (London, 1941; 2nd ed. 1955).
Marini, G. 'Aspetti sistematici della Società civile hegeliana' in *Filosofia*, XXVIII.
   Libertà soggettiva et libertà oggettiva nella 'Filosofia del diritto' hegeliana (Naples, 1978).
Marx, K. *Critique of Hegel's Philosophy of Right*, ed. J. O'Malley (Cambridge, 1970).
Mure, G. R. G. *An Introduction to Hegel* (Oxford, 1940).
   'The Organic State' in *Philosophy*, 1949.
   The Philosophy of Hegel (Oxford, 1965).
Nicolin, F. 'Hegel über Konstitutionelle Monarchie' in *Hegel-Studien*, 10, 1975.
Norman, R. *Hegel's Phenomenology: A Philosophical Introduction* (Brighton, 1976).
O'Brien, G. D. *Hegel on Reason and History: A Contemporary Interpretation* (Chicago, 1975).
Ottmann, H. *Individuum und Gemeinschaft bei Hegel* (Berlin, 1977).
Pelczynski, Z. A. (ed.) *Hegel's Political Philosophy: Problems and Perspectives* (Cambridge, 1971).
   'Hegel's Relevance Today: Culture, Community and Political Power in the *Philosophy of Right* (1821)' in *Europa*, vol. 2, no. 2, Spring 1979.
Peperzak, A. T. *Le jeune Hegel et la vision morale du monde* (La Haye, 1961; 2nd ed. 1969).
Petry, M. J. 'Hegel and the Morning Chronicle' in *Hegel-Studien*, 11, 1976.
Plamenatz, J. *Man and Society*, vol. 2 (London, 1963).
Plant, R. *Hegel: An Introduction* (2nd ed., Oxford, 1983).
   'Hegel and Political Economy' in *New Left Review*, nos. 103–4, 1977.
Pöggeler, O. (ed.) *Hegel: Einführung in seine Philosophie* (Freiburg/Munich, 1977).

Quelquejeu, B. *La volonté dans la philosophie de Hegel* (Paris, 1972).

Reyburn, H. A. *The Ethical Theory of Hegel* (Oxford, 1921).

Riedel, M. *Bürgerliche Gesellschaft und Staat bei Hegel* (Neuwied, 1970).

(ed.) *Materialien zu Hegels Rechtsphilosophie*, 2 vols. (Frankfurt am Main, 1975).

Between Tradition and Revolution. The Hegelian Transformation of Political Philosophy (Cambridge, 1984).

System und Geschichte: Studien zum historischen Standort von Hegels Philosophie (Frankfurt am Main, 1973).

Ritter, J. *Hegel: Essays on the Philosophy of Right and the French Revolution* (Cambridge, Mass., 1982).

Metaphysik und Politik: Studien zu Aristoteles und Hegel (Frankfurt am Main, 1969).

'Person und Eigentum: Zu Hegels "Grundlinien der Philosophie des Rechts"' in *Marxismusstudien*, IV, 1962.

Robinson, J. *Duty and Hypocrisy in Hegel's 'Phenomenology of Mind': An Essay in the Real and the Ideal* (Toronto and Buffalo, 1977).

Rose, G. R. *Hegel contra Sociology* (London, 1981).

Rosen, M. *Hegel's Dialectic and Its Criticism* (Cambridge, 1982).

Rosen, S. *G. W. F. Hegel: An Introduction to the Science of Wisdom* (New Haven, 1974).

Rosenkranz, K. *Hegels Leben* (Berlin, 1844).

Rosenzweig, F. *Hegel und der Staat*, 2 vols. (Munich and Berlin, 1920).

Rotenstreich, N. *From Substance to Subject: Studies in Hegel* (The Hague, 1974).

Schneider, H. 'Dokumente zu Hegels politischem Denken 1830–31' in *Hegel-Studien*, 11, 1976.

'Notizen Hegels zur Julirevolution' in *Hegel-Studien*, 11, 1976.

Seade, E. D. de, 'State and history in Hegel's concept of people' in *Journal of the History of Ideas*, 40, 1979.

Shklar, J. N. *Freedom and Independence: A Study of the Political Ideas of Hegel's 'Phenomenology of Mind'* (Cambridge, 1976).

Singer, P. *Hegel* (Oxford, 1983).

Soll, I. *An Introduction to Hegel's Metaphysics* (Chicago, 1969).

Steinkraus, W. E. (ed.) *New Studies in the Philosophy of Hegel* (New York, 1971).

Steinkraus, W. E. and Schmitz, K. L. (eds.) *Art and Logic in Hegel's Philosophy* (Atlantic Heights, N.J. and Brighton, 1980).

Stepelevich, L. S. and Lamb, D. (eds.) *Hegel's Philosophy of Action* (Brighton, 1983).

Stillman, P. 'Hegel's critique of liberal theories of right' in *American Political Science Review*, 68, 1974.

'Property, freedom and individuality in Hegel's and Marx's political thought' in *Property, NOMOS*, XXII, 1980.

Suhr, D. *Bewusstseinsverfassung und Gesellschaftsverfassung: Über Hegel und Marx zu einer dialektischen Verfassungstheorie* (Berlin, 1975).

Taylor, C. *Hegel* (Cambridge, 1975).

Hegel and Modern Society (Cambridge, 1979).

Toews, J. E. *Hegelianism: The Path Toward Dialectical Humanism, 1805–1841* (Cambridge, 1980).

Tronti, M. *Hegel politico* (Rome, 1975).

Valentini, F. 'Aspetti della "Società Civile" hegeliana' in *Giornale critico della filosofia italiana*, 1968.

Verene, D. P. (ed.) *Hegel's Social and Political Thought: the Philosophy of Objective Spirit* (Atlantic Heights, N.J. and Brighton, 1980).

Walsh, W. H. *Hegelian Ethics* (London, 1969).

Weil, E. *Hegel et l'état* (Paris, 1950).

Westphal, M. *History and Truth in Hegel's 'Phenomenology'* (Atlantic Heights, N.J. and Brighton, 1979).

(ed.) *Speculation and Method in Hegel's 'Phenomenology'* (Atlantic Heights, N.J. and Brighton, 1982).

INDEX

Numbers in **bold** *type refer to essays in the book dealing with the subject listed.*